Thomas Kenny

The Life and Genius of Shakespeare

Thomas Kenny

The Life and Genius of Shakespeare

ISBN/EAN: 9783337060671

Printed in Europe, USA, Canada, Australia, Japan

Cover: Foto ©Thomas Meinert / pixelio.de

More available books at **www.hansebooks.com**

THE LIFE AND GENIUS

OF

SHAKESPEARE.

BY

THOMAS KENNY.

"A BREATH THOU ART,
SERVILE TO ALL THE SKYEY INFLUENCES."
"*Measure for Measure*," Act III. Scene I.

LONDON:
LONGMAN, GREEN, LONGMAN, ROBERTS, AND GREEN,
PATERNOSTER ROW.

1864.

CONTENTS.

	PAGE
PREFACE.	
INTRODUCTION ...	1
SHAKESPEARE'S LIFE ...	14
SHAKESPEARE'S CHARACTER ...	67
THE GENIUS OF SHAKESPEARE ...	99
THE IMAGINATION AND EXPRESSION OF SHAKESPEARE ...	116
THE DEFECTS OF SHAKESPEARE'S DRAMAS ...	132
THE TRAGEDY AND COMEDY OF SHAKESPEARE ...	142
THE MEN AND WOMEN OF SHAKESPEARE ...	151
THE PLAYS OF SHAKESPEARE ...	158
THE TWO GENTLEMEN OF VERONA ...	163
THE COMEDY OF ERRORS ...	166
LOVE'S LABOUR'S LOST ...	168
MUCH ADO ABOUT NOTHING ...	170
A MIDSUMMER NIGHT'S DREAM ...	174
THE MERCHANT OF VENICE ...	181
AS YOU LIKE IT ...	184
THE MERRY WIVES OF WINDSOR ...	188
TWELFTH NIGHT; OR, WHAT YOU WILL ...	197
ALL'S WELL THAT ENDS WELL ...	202
CYMBELINE ...	208
THE TEMPEST ...	214
KING HENRY IV.—PART I. ...	224
KING HENRY IV.—PART II. ...	233

CONTENTS.

		PAGE
King Henry V.	237
King Henry VI.—Part I.	245
King Henry VI.—Parts II. and III.	277
Hamlet	367
Macbeth	385
Appendix—Note 1. The Spelling of Shakespeare's Name	403
Note 2. New Place	404
Note 3. Aubrey's Account of Shakespeare	406
Note 4. Dówdall's Account of Shakespeare	407
Note 5. Davies' Account of Shakespeare	408
Note 6. Ward's Account of Shakespeare	409
Note 7. Shakespeare and Ben Jonson	410

PREFACE.

WE believe that we need make no apology for the publication of this volume. We cannot, indeed, help fearing that Shakespearian criticism, in some, at least, of its forms, has already become an overgrown excrescence. But the very rapidity with which works succeed one another in illustration of the personal and literary history of the poet, shows that the curiosity which it excites is still unexhausted. The last word has evidently not yet been told upon this subject; and any new attempt to solve the riddle—as far as it admits of solution—of Shakespeare's life and genius, will still, no doubt, be judged upon its own merits.

We do not know whether we have been able to make any really useful addition to the already unmanageable stores of this branch of our national literature; and that is a matter on which we have no desire to indulge in any idle conjectures. But there are some points connected with the mode in which we have executed the task we have undertaken, on which we wish at once to offer a few words of explanation.

We have, first of all, to state that we make no pretension to any profound scholarship of any kind. We have made no striking discovery in the by-ways of Elizabethan literature. We do not believe that any such discovery is now possible. All the facts which can be ascertained in relation to the life and the labours of Shakespeare have already, in one shape or another, been laid before the world. We merely use the materials accumulated by our predecessors, arranging them in our own way, and drawing from them our own conclusions.

We are aware that we have dwelt on some portions of our task with an exceptional minuteness. We have only attempted, however, to follow what we thought the reasonable rule of selecting, for special study, those topics which seemed to afford us the most favourable opportunities of throwing a new light of any kind upon the growth or the characteristics of the poet's genius.

The discoveries of the Shakespearian antiquaries are for the most part singularly disconnected. Whenever a number of those scraps of evidence, extending over a series of years, relate to one and the same subject, we have not thought it necessary to state them in their strict chronological order. We have preferred grouping them under some distinctive epoch; and we have thus, perhaps, been enabled to give a meaning and a consistency to details which would otherwise only serve to weary and to bewilder the minds of our readers.

Every historian or critic of Shakespeare will have to choose his side in a variety of petty controversies. There is one of those perplexities which we have had to meet at the very outset of our labours. We have given the poet's name as "SHAKESPEARE;" and for reasons which appear to us to be quite sufficient. It is the printed form under which he was longest known in our literature. It now again receives the almost unanimous sanction of our foremost Shakespearian scholars; and, in a matter which is of such very small intrinsical importance, we should be prepared, under any circumstances, to yield to this law of usage.*

We have had another selection to make in the printing of all our earlier quotations. The great majority of the modern critics adopt in those passages the original spelling. But we see no reason whatever for presenting the writings of Shakespeare's contemporaries in an obsolete and uninviting form, which we do not give to the writings of Shakespeare himself. We have not, however, thought it necessary to adhere with rigorous exactitude to our general rule upon this subject; and we have retained the old spelling in any cases in which it seemed to us to be specially characteristic or appropriate.

We may save many of our readers from a trifling perplexity by stating that in the sixteenth and seventeenth centuries the year was supposed to begin, not on the 1st of January, but on the 25th of March. In any case in which this mode of reckoning occurs, we shall follow what is now the common

---

* We give in Appendix, Note 1, some observations on the spelling of Shakespeare's name.

practice of adding the figure which would be employed at the present day; and, whenever we do not make that addition, we must be understood to adopt the modern computation of time. We shall thus, for instance, hold ourselves at liberty to state that Queen Elizabeth died either on the 24th of March, 1602-3, or on the 24th of March, 1603, without any explanation.

We have exercised the most complete freedom in judging the genius and the writings of Shakespeare. It is probable that in doing so we shall sometimes offend the taste, or the prejudices, of a portion, at least, of our readers. Among a large class in this country, the admiration of the great poet seems to have assumed the form of an unqualified and unquestioning idolatry. We can perceive nothing to justify this feeble superstition. We believe that the spirit of free inquiry will not be found hostile to the fame of Shakespeare; and we are sure that it is only by following its impulse we shall be able, upon this or upon any other subject, to discover that truth which can alone be the ultimate object of all legitimate veneration.

… THE

LIFE AND GENIUS OF SHAKESPEARE.

INTRODUCTION.

"The best in this kind are but shadows; and the worst are no worse, if imagination amend them."—
A MIDSUMMER NIGHT'S DREAM, *Act V., Scene I.*

THE genius of Shakespeare is the most wonderful phenomenon in the annals of literature. In airy vitality, in abounding fulness, in sweetness, and in strength, in the depth and the truth of its insight, it stands without a parallel throughout the world of creative imagination. This vast faculty must, under any circumstances, have presented a subject of curious contemplation, and the perplexity which it is naturally calculated to awaken is singularly complicated by all the conditions under which it was developed. The life of the great poet passed away all but utterly unheeded in the midst of a most active and intelligent society; his works were given to the world almost wholly accidentally, and with the most unthinking carelessness; and the result is that, in nearly every topic connected with his name, the eager curiosity of modern ages has found a subject of more or less doubt and controversy.

We are all probably now disposed to form an exaggerated conception of the position which the poet held among his contemporaries, and we are thus unprepared to accept the limitations which must almost necessarily have accompanied any revelations that could have reached us of his history and his character. But, in addition to this inevitable source of perplexity and disappointment, a series of petty fatalities seem to have conspired to remove him as far as possible beyond the

B

reach of our direct and definite knowledge. At various points we think we are about to touch him, and then some strange object intervenes, and, like a darkness flitting through the air, casts his image into remote and indistinct shadow. The impersonality of his dramatic genius seems to follow him in his life. Now, we come across his name in the writings of some contemporary, and, naturally expect that its introduction will lead to some notice of his character; but the account is withheld, as if it could only refer to some topic which was already universally known, or in which no human being could feel the most passing interest. At another moment, we meet with a direct statement which, at first sight, seems likely to explain some incident in his career, or some passage in his writings; but, on inquiry, we perceive that it relates to some doubtful or unknown personage, or else that it is couched in language so obscure that it can convey no certain information of any kind; and thus it not unfrequently happens that the very light we hoped had arisen for our guidance hardly serves any other purpose than to disclose to us some new problem as perplexing perhaps, in its way, as any for which we had previously, in vain, endeavoured to find a solution.

It certainly is not from a want of biographers or of critics that any mystery still hangs over Shakespeare's memory. No other writer, perhaps, that ever lived has been the object of half so much minute, and patient, and varied research. The very multiplicity, combined with the incompleteness of the details which the antiquaries have discovered, has in no small degree contributed to complicate and to darken the very elements upon which any judgment we may form of him must be founded. Englishmen, however, owed it to the fame of their wonderful poet that they should endeavour to shed every accessible light on his life and his labours; and we have all some reason to feel grateful to the men who have, with such immense toil, and with such proportionately small results, devoted themselves to this undertaking.

Our knowledge of Shakespeare's history is derived from a

variety of sources, every one of which, however, is more or less casual, scanty, and unsatisfactory. We meet with some brief, but still instructive, notices of him in contemporary writers. We also find a few paragraphs in which his name is introduced scattered over the literary remains of the two or three succeeding generations; but the statements which they contain are usually of no great importance in themselves, and are hardly ever supported by any perfectly reliable evidence. Rowe prefixed to his edition of Shakespeare's works, in the year 1709, an account of the poet's life—the first account of it ever attempted—which was drawn principally, as he himself tells us, from traditions collected by Betterton, the actor, towards the commencement of the last century, or the close of the century which preceded. We are inclined to attach to the statements of Rowe considerable credit. They are made with remarkable moderation; and they have, as far as was possible under the circumstances, been substantially confirmed by the subsequent discovery of unquestionable collateral testimony. They may be regarded as almost the last link in that slight chain of oral tradition which enables us to ascend to the personality of William Shakespeare; and all later writers have had to look almost exclusively to the incidental notices in old documents for any fresh illustration of the poet's history. The public records at Stratford-upon-Avon, and a few papers of a similar description in London and elsewhere, here form the principal source of our knowledge; and it is somewhat singular to observe how much we have been able to learn through these cold, formal, but most impartial and most truthful witnesses. This was a narrow but a safe field for the industry of the antiquaries, and in it their labours have met with as large a reward as we could reasonably have expected. The most successful of them all in past times was the honest and indefatigable Malone. In our own day, Mr. Collier was for many years regarded as the great collector of those scraps of documentary evidence from which nearly all our direct Shakespearian information is derived; but, unfortunately, we have now reason to doubt the genuineness of all the most important of the different manuscripts which he professes to have discovered.*

Mr. Halliwell, we also think it right to acknowledge, has helped to give greater distinctness to our conceptions of the poet's history, by the ample extracts from old registers and other manuscripts which he has inserted in his " Life of William Shakespeare."

The very text of Shakespeare's writings has long been a fertile source of learned embarrassment and conjecture; and at this we cannot feel surprised, when we remember the circumstances which accompanied their publication. Of the thirty-seven plays which are now commonly held to form his dramatic works, we know that seventeen, at least, were printed in separate quarto volumes before the whole series was given to the world in a connected form. Sixteen of those detached publications were issued in his lifetime, but were issued, as far as we can learn, without his superintendence, and very probably even without his sanction. They seem to have been, in many instances, made up from the copies of players or of stage prompters, or from notes taken by frequenters of the theatres.† They are, as might be expected, printed with different degrees of correctness; but they all contain many evident errors of typography, or of transcription; and some of them differ so materially from the later and better texts that we find some difficulty in determining whether we ought to

---

* It has been Mr. Collier's singular fortune, after a life devoted to the study of Shakespeare, to find that the most conspicuous result of his labours is the creation of a new Shakespearian controversy. The authenticity of the papers he has produced from the "Ellesmere," or "Bridgewater House," collection, or from the State Paper Office, has, upon special examination, been denied by some of the most competent of all judges; and until he thinks proper to appeal in his own defence to some new tribunal, his alleged discoveries can prove nothing, and must be held to be practically worthless.

† That dramas were sometimes imperfectly taken down in the theatre, and afterwards published in a mutilated state, is decisively proved by the

regard them as mere corruptly printed copies, or as imperfect sketches, as they came from the author's own hand, of subsequently improved compositions.*

We subjoin a list of those early quartos, with the dates at which they were first issued:—

Hamlet	.. .. 1603†	The Merry Wives of Windsor	 1602
King Henry IV.: First Part	 1598	A Midsummer Night's Dream	 1600
King Henry IV.: Second Part	 1600	Much Ado about Nothing	1600
King Henry V.	 1600	Othello	 1622
King Richard II.	 1597	Pericles	 1609
King Richard III.	 1597	Romeo and Juliet	 1597
King Lear	 1608	Titus Andronicus	 1600
Love's Labours Lost	.. 1598	Troilus and Cressida	.. 1609
The Merchant of Venice	1600		

"Othello," it will be seen, is the only one of these seventeen works that was not printed previously to the poet's death, which took place in the year 1616.

We have another explanation to offer in reference to the above list. A play, resembling the "Second Part of King Henry VI.," was published in the year 1594, under the title of "The First Part of the Contention betwixt the two famous Houses of Yorke and Lancaster,"&c.; and a play resembling the

---

prologue to a play entitled, "If You Know not Me, You know Nobody;" by Thomas Heywood, 1623:

" ————————— 'Twas ill nurst,
And yet receiv'd as well perform'd at first;
Grac'd and frequented; for the cradle age
Did throng the seats, the boxes, and the stage,
So much, that some by stenography drew
The plot, put it in print, scarce one word true."

* We are here particularly referring to the earliest editions of "Hamlet," "King Henry V.," and the "Merry Wives of Windsor." The first issue of "Romeo and Juliet" is open, although in a less degree, to a similar suspicion.

† There was another and a greatly enlarged and improved edition of this play, published in 1604.

"Third Part of King Henry VI.," was published in the year 1595, under the title of "The True Tragedie of Richard Duke of Yorke," &c. We believe that these are but imperfect copies of Shakespeare's two undoubted dramas, and we shall hereafter endeavour to establish that position. But the majority of the modern commentators are of a different opinion; and we are unwilling to hazard, in this portion of our work, any statement which could involve us in any prolonged controversy.

At length, in the year 1623, seven years after the poet's death, the first complete edition of his dramatic works was given to the world by his fellow-actors, John Heminge and Henry Condell, in a folio volume, bearing the following title :—

"Mr. William Shakespeare's Comedies, Histories, & Tragedies. Published according to the True Originall copies. London. Printed by Isaac Jaggard and Ed. Blount. 1623."

"Pericles" is not inserted in this volume, which contains, therefore, only thirty-six plays.

This is the famous Shakespeare "Folio of 1623"—the first and necessarily the most important edition of the poet's dramatic works. It presents, however, on the very face of it, many great defects. The editors, in announcing that these "comedies," &c., were "published according to the true original copies," seem to have been indulging in a mere trading device. In all probability they had no such copies in their possession, and the manuscripts of Shakespeare had either been destroyed by the fire which consumed the Globe Theatre in the year 1613, or had become lost or defaced through human thoughtlessness, or the wear and tear of time. It is manifest, at all events, that several portions of this folio edition must have been copied from the preceding quarto volumes; and it is equally certain that this is one of the most carelessly and incorrectly printed books, of any considerable importance and pretension, that ever issued from the press. Its publication, however, forms one of the great episodes in the history of letters: and we cannot now forget that we directly owe to it many of the poet's greatest works, which, without it, might never have reached a distant age. In its pages the following twenty plays* were printed for the first time:—

All's Well that Ends Well.	King Henry VI.: Third Part.
Antony and Cleopatra.	King Henry VIII.
As You Like It.	Macbeth.
Comedy of Errors.	Measure for Measure.
Coriolanus.	The Taming of the Shrew.
Cymbeline.	The Tempest.
Julius Cæsar.	Timon of Athens.
King John.	Twelfth Night.
King Henry VI.: First Part.	The Two Gentlemen of Verona.
King Henry VI.: Second Part.	The Winter's Tale.

The second complete edition of Shakespeare's dramatic works appeared, in the shape of another folio volume, in the year 1632. It differs in no important respect from its predecessor. A third folio was published in the year 1664, containing, for the first time, not only "Pericles," but six other plays, which, although some of them were published in quarto volumes during the poet's lifetime, with his name, are now held by nearly all the critics of this country to be apocryphal.† A fourth folio, copying the third, followed in the year 1685. These four folio volumes, which did not probably amount altogether to more than 2,000 copies, were the only complete editions of the poet's dramas which were published during the whole, or nearly the whole, of the first one hundred years from the period at which he closed his literary labours.

Throughout the last century those great works obtained a

---

* We are still supposing that the "First Part of the Contention," &c., and the "True Tragedie of Richard Duke of Yorke," &c., were not mere imperfect versions of the Second Part and the Third Parts of "King Henry VI."

† In the title-page of this edition of 1664 we find it stated that to the volume are added "seven plays, never before printed in folio, viz.: 'Pericles, Prince of Tyre;' 'The London Prodigall;' 'The History of Thomas Ld. Cromwell;' 'Sir John Oldcastle, Lord Cobham;' 'The Puritan Widow;' 'A Yorkshire Tragedy;' 'The Tragedy of Locrine.'"

new popularity, and circulated, with an ever-increasing rapidity, in volumes, edited under the auspices of various men of letters, of whom the most celebrated were Rowe, Pope, Theobald, Sir Thomas Hanmer, Warburton, Dr. Johnson, Capell, Steevens, and Malone. The editions published in our own time are practically innumerable. We believe that the most popular, or the most important, among them are those of Mr. Knight, Mr. Collier, Messrs. Singer and Lloyd, Mr. Dyce, and Mr. Staunton.*

All the editors we have mentioned, whether of the last or of the present century, have contributed something to the correction or the elucidation of the poet's text. Their labours were sometimes conducted under strong feelings of personal rivalry. But this was precisely the kind of undertaking which was sure to be best promoted by the exercise of the ingenuity, or the research, of a multitude of independent minds. Any scholar, through some happy perception, or by a careful collation of the old copies, might be able to offer some useful suggestion for the removal of the errors in which nearly every one of those copies abounds. The vast amount of patient attention devoted to this subject has not, certainly, been expended in vain; and we feel persuaded that we have now, in any of the best known editions of our great dramatist, a reading sufficiently correct to satisfy all the requirements of a legitimate curiosity and a cultivated taste.

It is, however, manifest that no absolutely authoritative edition of Shakespeare's works can ever be produced. The details of the text must sometimes be selected not only from a

---

* We can hardly include in our list the edition brought out, in twelve folio volumes, by Mr. Halliwell, with all the magnificence of the finest and most costly type and paper. Only 150 copies of it were printed, and it is, of course, placed entirely beyond the reach of the general public. The "Cambridge Shakespeare," edited by Mr. W. G. Clark and Mr. W. A Wright, is now being passed through the press; it appears to be founded on a most careful collation of the early folios and quartos.

variety of old editions, but from a variety of conjectural emendations, which it will be impossible wholly to discard. There appears, in many cases, to be little room for a preference between one reading and another; and it is curious to observe how little our ultimate estimate of the poet's labours is affected by the petty diversities of phraseology on which his editors have often angrily disagreed.

It seems to be very generally supposed that Shakespeare displayed some extraordinary indifference to literary fame by neglecting to supervise the publication of his own dramas. But that opinion, taken literally, cannot be said to rest upon any sufficient foundation. We believe that Shakespeare, in this respect, only conformed to the almost universal practice of his age. The works of popular dramatists were then written solely that they might be acted, and never, apparently, with a view to their being read. They were sold to theatrical companies, whose interest it was to keep them unpublished as long as they continued to attract large audiences. The authors themselves seem to have readily acquiesced in this arrangement. They did not desire to attain notoriety by committing their works to the press, either because they conceived that a sort of discredit attached to any professional connection with the stage, or because they felt that a drama would lose its main effect by being deprived of the accompaniments of theatrical representation. When they did publish their works they appear to have published them for the purpose of anticipating the issue of mutilated and piratical copies, or for the purpose of doing justice to their own reputations, after such copies had actually been printed; and some of them appear to accept very unwillingly the task which was thus imposed upon them in their own defence. Marston, in printing his "Parasitaster; or, the Fawn," in the year 1606, states in an address or preface:—

If any shall wonder why I print a comedy, whose life rests much in the actor's voice, let such know that it cannot avoid publishing; let it, therefore, stand with good excuse that I have been my own setter out.

Again, the same writer, in publishing his "Malcontent," in 1604, tells his readers:—

Only one thing afflicts me: to think that scenes invented merely to be spoken, should be inforcively published to be read, and that the least hurt I can receive is to do myself the wrong. But since others otherwise would do me more, the least inconvenience is to be accepted."

Heywood, in the preface to his "Rape of Lucrece," published in 1630, writes in a similar strain:—

For though some have used a double sale of their labours, first to the stage and after to the press, for my own part I here proclaim myself ever faithful to the first, and never guilty of the last: yet since some of my plays have (unknown to me, and without any of my direction) accidentally come into the printer's hands, and, therefore, so corrupt and mangled (copied only by the ear), that I have been as unable to know them as ashamed to challenge them, &c.

Sir Thomas Bodley, who began to form the great collection of books which still bears his name, towards the close of the sixteenth century, calls plays "riffe raffes," and declares, "they shall never come into my library." It is a striking proof of the change of tastes and customs that some of the most costly volumes in the great Bodleian Library of the present day are the very works, as published in his own time, which its founder treated with such special contempt.

There is one division, at least, of Shakespearian literature through which runs a broad track of light. The dramas themselves form a subject of study which admits of no other controversies than those to which the diversities of our own tastes and capacities may give rise. Shakespeare's fame, however, even in England, has not been by any means of a uniform and steady growth. His genius was but partially recognised by his contemporaries; and among the two or three generations which followed, we find that the spread of the puritanical spirit, the agitations of the great Civil War, and finally, the ascendency of frivolous foreign tastes in the days of the Stuart Restoration, contributed to throw his name into dark or doubtful eclipse. For a period of one hundred years his works were not much read, and throughout a portion of that time, and even down to a much later date, several of his greatest dramas only held possession of the stage in the corrupted versions of feeble or irreverent hands. It was not until about the middle of the last century that the national admiration of our great poet, in any large sense of the words, began to arise. Our enthusiasm was soon stimulated by the teachings and the example of the critics and scholars of Germany. Lessing was, perhaps, the first man that formed and proclaimed what the most competent judges would now regard as an adequate conception of the profound truth and the astonishing range of Shakespeare's genius; and almost all the most eminent literary men of his country have since zealously continued the work which he began. A corresponding school of Shakespearian critics soon appeared in England; but we have never, as a nation, fully shared the intoxication of the German idolatry of our own great dramatist. The less demonstrative form of our admiration arises mainly, no doubt, from our generally more sober and more reserved temperament; but it is also, perhaps, in some measure to be traced to the specially practical and laborious nature of the task which we have had to perform. Shakespearian criticism among us fell almost exclusively into the hands of editors, commentators, and antiquaries. All the obscure literature of a whole age had to be explored for the purpose of fixing the poet's text, explaining his allusions, ascertaining the sources from which he derived his stories. The German mind, in its study of Shakespeare, had no such preliminary labour to encounter; and, freed from this restraining influence, it rushed with its accustomed enthusiasm into that region of boundless speculation to which it seemed to have been, from its very position, immediately invited.

The personality of Shakespeare forms undoubtedly the most perplexing subject to which the Shakespearian student can direct his contemplation. We have already made an ample admission of the incompleteness of the evidence which has reached us respecting the poet's history. But that evidence is so various that we believe it must light us to a fair general knowledge of his life and of his character, if we will only look at it in a clear and an unprejudiced spirit. In his own numerous writings we cannot fail to find manifestations not only of his genius, but of his tastes and his temper. The antiquarian discoveries, too, will afford us an important aid in our attempt to realise and define this wonderful personality. Those discoveries are, no doubt, strangely limited and disconnected; but they come to us from a great variety of quarters; and small as they are, when taken separately, if we should find, as we think we are sure to find, on a careful inquiry, that they all point to the same general conclusions, we may place even greater confidence in their accidental testimony than in more detailed revelations proceeding from fewer sources, and arranged upon some more preconcerted plan.

We are well aware, however, that it will still be easy to make light of the results in which the immense labour of the antiquaries has ended. Towards the close of the last century, Steevens summed up in this well-known sentence all the information with regard to Shakespeare which the world, as he believed, then possessed:—

> All that is known with any degree of certainty concerning Shakespeare is—that he was born at Stratford-upon-Avon—married and had children there—went to London, where he commenced actor, and wrote poems and plays—returned to Stratford, made his will, died, and was buried.

Mr. Hallam has pronounced what is substantially a similar judgment, in a tone of more philosophic earnestness:—

> All that insatiable curiosity and unwearied diligence have hitherto detected about Shakespeare serves rather to disappoint and perplex us than to furnish the slightest illustration of his character. It is not the register of his baptism, or the draft of his will, or the orthography of his name, that we seek. No letter of his writing, no record of his conversation, no character of him, drawn with any fulness by a contemporary, has been produced.

There is a considerable amount of truth in these statements; but they do not contain the whole truth. We have learned a number of minute details, which we are sure must have exercised no small influence over Shakespeare's way of life, or which serve directly to reveal to us his habitual state of thought and feeling. The very neglect of his contemporaries to tell his history is in itself instructive. From their silence we may fairly conclude that they, at least, believed there was little or nothing for them to record. Unquestionably we know much less of Shakespeare than we all desire to know. But we can learn much more of him than the world in general appears to imagine; and we must now remember that we have here no fresh testimony to expect. The facts have all most probably been told; the evidence is closed; and it only remains for us to make the most of our knowledge, or to resign ourselves to an ignorance which we can never hope to dispel.

SHAKESPEARE'S LIFE.

"The web of our life is of a mingled yarn, good and ill together."—
ALL'S WELL THAT ENDS WELL, *Act IV., Scene III.*

WILLIAM SHAKESPEARE was born in the year 1564, at Stratford-upon-Avon, in the county of Warwick. He was baptised on the 26th of April in that year;* but the precise day on which he first saw the light cannot be fixed with any certainty. According to a tradition, which we are unable to trace to any more remote authority than Oldys, the antiquary, who wrote about the middle of the last century, his death took place on the anniversary of his birth; and we know that he died on the 23rd of April, 1616.†

---

* Under this date we find the following entry in the baptismal registers at Stratford:—"Gulielmus filius Johannes Shakspere." The *Johannes* for *Johannis* is in the original. The Latin Muses do not seem to have watched over the poet's cradle.

† Oldys died in 1761, leaving behind him some manuscript collections for a biography of Shakespeare. It is impossible for us now to determine what is the precise amount of credit due to the tradition which he has preserved. It appears certain, at all events, that Shakespeare was not born upon a later day than the 23rd of April, 1564; for we find it stated, in the inscription on his monument, that he died in the fifty-third year of his age. We shall, perhaps, feel less anxious about the attainment of any absolute exactness upon this point if we remember that what was called the 23rd of April, both in the sixteenth and in the seventeenth centuries, would, under the reformed calendar which we now adopt, be reckoned as the 3rd of May. Many of our readers may not be aware that the 23rd of April was already memorable in our national life as St. George's Day—the festival of the patron saint of England.

His father, John Shakespeare, was very probably the son of Richard Shakespeare, of Snitterfield, a hamlet, three miles from Stratford; and his mother, whose maiden name was Mary Arden, was the youngest of seven daughters, the co-heiresses of Robert Arden, of Wilmecote, in the parish of Aston Cantlow.

The name of Shakespeare is found in various records of the county of Warwick throughout the fourteenth, fifteenth, and sixteenth centuries. It does not appear to have been borne by any person who rose to any marked social distinction. The family of Arden, on the other hand, had some claims to a place in the ranks of the English country gentry. The grandfather of Mary Arden is supposed by some of the poet's biographers, although upon very imperfect evidence, to have been groom of the chamber to Henry VII., and nephew of Sir John Arden, esquire of the body to that sovereign. There is no doubt that Robert Arden, her father, although in his will he is only styled "husbandman," possessed several hundred acres of landed property.

We first hear of the connection of any of the Shakespeares with the town of Stratford-upon-Avon on the 29th of April, 1552, when "Johannes Shakyspere," the father, we may take it for granted, of the poet, is stated, in a register written in Latin, to have been fined for having neglected to keep in the required state of cleanliness the ground near his house, in "Hendley Strete." We know nothing more of him until the 17th of June, 1556, when a proceeding was instituted in the Stratford Bailiff Court against John "Shacksper" for the recovery of a debt of £8. In the Latin record of this suit the word "glover," in English, is attached to his name. On the 2nd of October in the same year he became the purchaser of two copyhold houses in Stratford, one of which was situated in Greenhill Street, and the other in Henley Street. It seems very probable that his marriage with Mary Arden took place in the course of the year 1557. At the date of her father's will, which was executed on the 24th of November,

1556, and proved on the 17th of December in the same year, she was still unmarried; and we find, from the Stratford registers, that a child of John Shakespeare's was baptised on the 15th of September, 1558. She inherited the sum of £6 13s. 4d. in money, and a small estate, called Ashbies, or Asbies, consisting of fifty acres of arable land, and six acres of meadowing or pasturage; and she also appears to have possessed some other small property, or reversionary rights in land at Snitterfield.

In the year 1550 her father executed a deed, providing for the conveyance to three of his daughters of certain lands and premises in Snitterfield, of which Richard Shakespeare was then the tenant. If this Richard Shakespeare were the father of John Shakespeare, of Stratford, it would be easy to understand how the latter formed the acquaintance in which his marriage originated; and the suspicion thus created of the existence of such a relationship between them is strongly confirmed by those further facts which we learn from the records of the time—that John Shakespeare had a brother Henry, and that a Henry Shakespeare lived at Snitterfield.

The child born to John and Mary Shakespeare in 1558 was a daughter, called Joan, of whom we have no further record, but whom they must have soon lost, as another of their children received the same name in the year 1569. The next fruit of their union, as far as we can ascertain from the Stratford registers, was also a daughter, who was baptised under the name of Margaret, on the 2nd of December, 1562, and who was buried on the 30th of April, 1563.

Their third child was the future "poet of all time," William Shakespeare. He was not quite two months old when the plague broke out at Stratford, where it carried off, before the close of the year, 270 people, or about one-fifth of the whole population.

The Shakespeare family was increased by the births of five more children: Gilbert, who was baptised on the 13th of October, 1566, and who lived in Stratford and signed a deed there in the month of March, 1609-10, but of whom we have no later record; Joan, who was baptised on the 15th of April, 1569, who married William Hart, and who died in 1646; Anne, who was baptised on the 28th of September, 1571, and who was buried on the 4th of April, 1579; Richard, who was baptised on the 11th of March, 1573-4, and who was buried on the 4th of February, 1612-13; and Edmund, who was baptised on the 3rd of May, 1580, and who appears to have been an actor, and to have died in London, in December, 1607.

In these brief records we seem to catch a glimpse of the home companionships in which the sensibilities of the future poet expanded. "Here we find that two of his sisters were removed by death, probably before his birth. In two years and a half another son, Gilbert, came to be his playmate; and when he was five years old, that most precious gift to a loving boy was granted—a sister, who grew up with him. Then came another sister, who faded untimely. When he was ten years old he had another brother to lead by the hand into the green meadows; and when he was grown into youthful strength, a boy of sixteen, his youngest brother was born."*

It is not improbable that John Shakespeare was settled during all the early years of his married life in Henley Street, and in the house which tradition points out as his son's birth-place. We have no conclusive evidence upon this point; but we know that he lived in that street in the year 1552, and that he purchased a copyhold house there in the year 1556, and two freehold houses in the year 1575. It seems very likely that it was in one of the latter dwellings he resided, for they were both in the possession of his family after his death, while we hear no more of the property he acquired in 1556, which appears to have been in some way lost or alienated. In the year 1570 he held, at the high annual rent of £8, a farm called Ingon Meadow, consisting of fourteen acres.

Shakespeare was manifestly a growth of rural England.

---

* Mr. Knight's "William Shakspere: a Biography."

In her "green lap was Nature's darling laid." He was a descendant of the inhabitants of our tranquil valleys, our grassy slopes, and soft woodlands. His native town has most probably been, from its very origin, the small centre of a purely agricultural population. Its principal trade, even at this day, is in corn, malt, and cattle. Its population amounted in 1861 to 3,672 souls; and in the sixteenth century the number reached, as far as can be judged from the registered births and burials, about 1,400. Its principal monuments are a fine old cruciform church, and a bridge of fourteen arches, built in the reign of Henry VII., and spanning that Avon by whose "lucid"* waters the young Prodigy must often have lovingly wandered.

John Shakespeare seems to have been, at the period of his marriage and for many years afterwards, one of the most respectable inhabitants of Stratford. It is probable that he did not continue for any length of time to carry on the trade of a glover, but that he early devoted himself to agricultural pursuits, and to the various occupations which might enable him in a country town to turn his small landed property to the most profitable account. Rowe says that he was a "considerable dealer in wool," and Aubrey tells us that he was a "butcher;"† and it is quite possible that both those statements may be correct to this extent, that he sold different descriptions of produce raised upon his own land. In the year 1556 he brought an action against "Henry Fyld," for unjustly detaining from him a quantity of barley; and in the year 1564 he sold to the corporation some timber—"a pec tymbur." In this latter year he is credited with the highest sum, with one exception, contributed by any burgess, not an alderman, to the relief of the poor. In the year 1579 we find the word "yoman" attached to his name, and he is never designated as a glover, except upon that single occasion in the year 1556 to which we have already referred.

---

* " Where lucid Avon strayed."—GRAY.

† For Aubrey's account of Shakespeare see Appendix, Note 3.

Municipal distinctions soon accompanied the social respectability to which he attained. In the year 1557, or during the four or five succeeding years, he passed through the offices of an ale-taster,* a constable of the borough, an " affeeror,"† and a chamberlain. In the year 1565 he was elected an alderman; and from Michaelmas, 1568, to Michaelmas, 1569, he filled the office of high-bailiff, or head of the corporation. From the month of September, 1571, to the month of September, 1572, he acted as chief-alderman; and here closes the list of the local honours to which he attained.

We are now losing the light of that treacherous prosperity which played upon the poet's early home. John Shakespeare, we cannot help suspecting, must have been one of those men, not uncommon in any age, whose worldly means bear no adequate proportion to their taste for lavish expenditure, and their ambition to figure in a higher social position than that in which, through the chances of life, they had originally been placed. As far as we can see, the substance of his property consisted of the fifty-six acres of land called Ashbies, which he had acquired through his wife; and this small holding must have afforded but a very insufficient foundation for maintaining the dignity of a public office, and the cost of a correspondingly expensive domestic establishment. At all events, he was soon exposed to one of the most painful visitations of fortune; and the antiquaries are enabled to track his footsteps through the usual unsparing processes of the law, to debt, mortgages, and not improbably to flight or imprisonment.

The first apparent intimation of his embarrassments meets us at the commencement of the year 1578. At a hall of the corporation, held in the month of January of that year, a

---

* An officer commissioned to look after the assize of ale, bread, and corn.

† An officer whose duty it was to determine the amount of fines to be imposed for offences to which no express penalty was attached by statute.

resolution was passed, to the effect that each of the aldermen should pay 6s. 8d. for the maintenance or equipment of certain officers, with the exception of "Mr. Shaxpeare" and another member of the court, who were to be liable to a charge of only 3s. 4d. and 5s. respectively. In the month of November of the same year he was exempted from an order providing that each alderman should pay fourpence a week towards the relief of the poor; and in an account of sums levied on the inhabitants of Stratford in the month of March, 1579, for the purchase of armour and defensive weapons, his name is found among the defaulters. Again, the will of a baker, named Roger Sadler, which is dated the 14th of November, 1578, contains a list of his debtors, and in that list two people are mentioned as owing him £5 "for the debte of Mr. John Shaksper."

There are other and more decisive proofs of the straits to which he was ultimately reduced. In the spring of 1578 John and Mary Shakespeare mortgaged their property of Ashbies to her brother-in-law, Edmund Lambert, for the sum of £40. In the year 1579 we find them selling to Robert Webbe their share in a property at Snitterfield, for the small amount of £4; and in the following year they parted with her reversionary interest in the same property for another sum of £40.

We have evidence of another kind to show that John Shakespeare did not escape those personal penalties which usually attach to troubled fortunes. A writ of distraint was issued against him, and the return made to it, on the 19th of January, 1586, was that he had no goods on which distraint could be levied; and in the month of March, 1587, we are told of his producing a writ of *habeas corpus*—a sufficient proof, it is held, that he was at the time suffering imprisonment for debt. We meet his name again, in a curious document of the date of 25th September, 1592. On that day Sir Thomas Lucy, and other commissioners, who had been appointed to inquire and report respecting "such recusants as have been heretofore presented for not coming monthly to the church," signed a return, in which the names of various "recusants" are given, and among them those of "Mr. John Shackespere," and of eight others, with this comment:—"It is said that these last nine come not to church for fear of process for debt."

These accumulated embarrassments naturally ended in the cessation of John Shakespeare's connection with the corporation of Stratford. He first began to absent himself from their meetings at the commencement of the year 1577; and he only rarely attended them after that period. On the 31st of August, 1586, he was deprived of his alderman's gown, on the ground that—"He doth not come to the halls when they be warned, nor hath not done of long time."

We are aware that some of the poet's biographers have endeavoured to show that a portion of the details we have just cited may be accounted for upon the supposition that John Shakespeare did not permanently reside in Stratford, but removed occasionally to one or other of his small farms, and thus became exempt from the payment of the full amount of the borough charges. But this conjecture possesses no internal probability, and it is almost directly opposed to unquestionable documentary evidence, from which we learn that when he signed the deed for the sale of his wife's property, in the year 1579, he was known as "John Shackspere, of Stratford-upon-Avon;" and again, that he was summoned on a jury of the Stratford Court of Record in the year 1586, the year in which he was deprived of his alderman's gown. There are, however, some other circumstances which go to create a presumption that his position was never so absolutely desperate as the above entries, taken by themselves, would naturally lead us to infer. He seems never to have lost his freehold property in Henley Street, which afterwards descended to his son; and what is, perhaps, still more remarkable, he appears more than once as a litigant in the local court at the very time when we should have supposed that his means of obtaining the very necessaries of life must have been utterly exhausted. It is not unlikely, therefore, that a portion of the suspicious incidents in which he figures may have arisen from some peculiarity in his position, or from some special fractiousness in his own temper. But we still entertain no doubt of the meaning of some of the sacrifices to which he was compelled to submit. He obtains bread upon the security of others; he mortgages what was perhaps his most valuable property; he parts with the reversionary rights of his family; and it is impossible for us not to read in such incidents the outlines of one of the painful dramas of humble life.

How wide are the sympathies evoked by genius, and how long is the trail of its glory. How little these poor people could have dreamt in their lifetime of the restless curiosity which was to pursue their memories more than two centuries after the grave had enfolded their remains in its unbroken silence. There is still, however, a wide blank in our knowledge of John and Mary Shakespeare. He is only known to us by the partial brightness, or the dark shadow, which his name casts over old, passionless records. The mother of the poet must naturally form for us an object of still more eager interest. We should all be glad to know how far the intellect or the character of the young Phenomenon was likely to have been influenced by her fine sense or her loving tenderness; but in the utter obscurity in which she has disappeared, we feel that it would be vain for us to indulge this curiosity. Not a word, or a look, or a gesture of hers pierces the night of ages to light up for a moment her image.

We have no further facts of any moment to record with respect to this couple, except that John Shakespeare was buried in Stratford on the 8th of September, 1601, and that the remains of his wife were laid, as we may assume, by his side on the 9th of September, 1608. We may take it for granted that, with the help of their illustrious son, they were enabled to pass tranquilly the later evening of their days. Many readers will perhaps be surprised to learn that neither of them could write; but there is no room for any reasonable doubt upon this point. A number of documents are still extant which John Shakespeare signed with his mark; and in the only instance in which we meet with the signature of his wife, it is made in the same form. This was, however, no unusual circumstance among people of their position in the days of Queen Elizabeth. Out of nineteen aldermen and burgesses of Stratford who signed a deed in the year 1565, not less than thirteen—among whom were the bailiff, the chief alderman, and John Shakespeare—were unable to attach their names to it in their own handwriting.*

The vicissitudes of fortune in the obscure household at Stratford, which we have just enumerated, must have formed for the youthful William Shakespeare a painful, but very probably a most instructive, experience. No information, however, has reached us with respect to the mode in which the misfortunes of his family affected either his character or his worldly position. The amount of his learning is one of the many debatable topics in his history. Everybody believes that he must, at one time or another, have been at some kind of school; but, for all the details of his education, we are left by his contemporaries in our usual state of absolute, unqualified ignorance. It so happens, however, that upon collateral testimony we can point out, with considerable confidence, the establishment in which his first knowledge of books was acquired. There still exists in Stratford-upon-Avon a free grammar school, which was founded in the time of Henry VI., and which received from Edward VI. a charter of incorporation; and here, we may take it for granted, the son of Alderman Shakespeare was in due time placed, like other youths of his class. It was, as a matter of course, the best establishment of the kind to

---

* The various incidents in which "John Shakspere" figures in the Stratford registers were for some time a source of considerable perplexity to the antiquaries. They have, however, completely extricated themselves from the difficulty by ascertaining that, towards the close of the sixteenth century, there were two persons in the town who bore that name. One of them was a shoemaker, who lived in Bridge Street, and who does not appear to have been in any way related to the poet.

which he could have been sent. It seems likely, however, that his stay there was not very prolonged. The whole character of his acquirements leads us to the belief that his classical education, at all events, was never completed; and a uniform tradition points—and points very naturally—to the date of the commencement of his father's embarrassments—that is to say, to the year 1577, or the year 1578—as the period at which it was brought to a premature close. The precise spot in which the school was held in the days of this most "marvellous boy" cannot now be ascertained; but there is some slight evidence to show that it was either the chapel of the Guild, or some adjoining room. The masters of the school, from 1570 to 1578—that is to say, from Shakespeare's sixth to his fourteenth year—were Walter Roche, Thomas Hunt, and Thomas Jenkins.

Any detailed notice of the life of our great poet must be little more than a collection of small facts, sustaining large guesses and conjectures with more or less of apparent solidity. The period which elapsed between his withdrawal from school and his first settlement in London is one specially fertile in traditions and suppositions, and quite as specially unillumined by any definite and reliable evidence. Aubrey not only states that his father was by trade a butcher, but gives a graphic account of the mode in which he himself, in his youth, engaged in the same business; and this old gossip also informs us that "in his younger days he was a schoolmaster in the country." The first of these two stories receives some support from a statement made in the year 1693, to a person of the name of Dowdall, by the parish clerk of Stratford, who was then "above eighty years old." That statement is to the effect that Shakespeare was apprenticed to a butcher, but ran away from his master to London.* The other rumour, first mentioned by Aubrey, that the poet in his youth was a schoolmaster, has found favour with some writers; while others are

---

* See Dowdall's statement in Appendix, Note 4.

disposed to give credit to another supposition—that he was at one time employed as a lawyer's clerk. We can see no use in discussing the probabilities of these various traditions or conjectures. The most reasonable conclusion, perhaps, which we can draw from them is, that Shakespeare very probably had in his youth no very definite, or at least no very profitable and congenial, occupation; that his way of life was unsettled; and that in his necessities he turned readily to one or other of a number of employments, as they seemed to give him a chance of subsistence for the hour.

We now come to one event, at least, in his history, which is not wholly involved in doubt and obscurity. We derive all our knowledge of it from those brief, prosaic, but faithful records, which have already shed the only certain light that gleams for us over his early home. The marriage licence of William Shakespeare and Anne Hathaway was signed in the city of Worcester, on the 28th of November, 1582. The most remarkable provision in this document is that they were to be allowed to marry "with once asking the bans." We have no record of the marriage itself; but we can have no doubt that it took place with as little delay as possible, or early in the month of December of the same year; and under the date of the 26th of the month of May in the year 1583, or less than six months afterwards, we find the following entry in the baptismal registers of Stratford:—"Susanna, daughter to William Shakspere."

Anne Hathaway, we have reason to believe, was the daughter of Richard Hathaway, a farmer, residing at Shottery, a hamlet situated in the parish of Stratford-upon-Avon, and one mile distant from the town. Shakespeare at the time of his marriage was about eighteen years and eight months old, and his wife must have been in her twenty-sixth or twenty-seventh year. She died, according to the inscription on her tomb, on the 6th of August, 1623, at the age of sixty-seven; and she was, therefore, some seven or eight years older than her husband.

We have now related all the known circumstances of this union, and we think it is impossible to mistake the conclusions to which they naturally lead. Nothing, we believe, can be much clearer than the meaning of this licence obtained in a distant city; of the speedy birth of the first child of the contracting parties; of the disparity in their own years, and of the extreme youth of the husband—who must, besides, have been placed at the time in circumstances which rendered such an engagement upon his part peculiarly undesirable. The young poet's marriage, then, we may fairly conclude, was an imprudent one; and, from the fact that his wife seems never to have shared his home in London during all the busiest and most prosperous period of his career, we feel that we have also some reason to suspect that no fresh stream of confiding tenderness ever rose to efface the unwelcome memory of the error in which it originated.

Shakespeare had but two other children, a boy and a girl; they were twins, and they were baptised in Stratford Church, on the 2nd of February, 1584-5, under the respective names of Hammet and Judith. Both the poet's daughters survived him; his son died in the month of August, 1596.

The birth of his three children is the only fact in Shakespeare's history from the period of his marriage until we find him established, several years afterwards, as a player and as a writer for the stage in London, that we know with any kind of certainty and precision. A tradition meets us from more than one quarter, that he was engaged in a deer-stealing adventure, which brought him under the legal correction of Sir Thomas Lucy, of Charlecote, near Stratford; and this is generally supposed to have been the immediate cause of his removal from his native town to London. Our earliest authority for the story is the Rev. Richard Davies, rector of Sapperton, in Gloucestershire, who died in the year 1708, and who in some manuscript notes, which are now preserved in the library of Corpus Christi, Oxford, states not only that Shakespeare was guilty of this offence, but that he was " oft whipt" for it at the instance of Sir Thomas Lucy.* Rowe also relates the main incident in the tradition :—

He had, by a misfortune common enough to young fellows, fallen into ill company; and, amongst them, some that made a frequent practice of deer-stealing, engaged him more than once in robbing a park that belonged to Sir Thomas Lucy, of Charlecote, near Stratford. For this he was prosecuted by that gentleman, as he thought, somewhat too severely; and, in order to revenge that ill-usage, he made a ballad upon him. This, probably the first essay of his poetry, is said to have been so very bitter that it redoubled the prosecution against him to that degree that he was obliged to leave his business and family in Warwickshire for some time, and shelter himself in London.

Oldys not only confirms this story, but actually produces the first stanza of the ballad, which he says was handed down by a "very aged gentleman, living in the neighbourhood of Stratford, where he died about fifty years since." † Capell, whose personal truthfulness is unquestionable, writing before the year 1781, gives some further details with respect to the mode in which those verses were preserved. He states that—

Mr. Jones, who dwelt at Tarbick, in Worcestershire, a few miles from Stratford-upon-Avon, and died in the year 1703, aged upwards of ninety, remembered to have heard from several old people at Stratford, the story of Shakespeare's robbing Sir Thomas Lucy's park. * * * Jones put down in writing the first stanza of this ballad, which was

---

* The whole of Davies' statement in reference to Shakespeare will be found in Appendix, Note 5.

† This stanza, the supposed "first essay of Shakespeare's poetry," is as follows :—

> "A Parliament member, a justice of peace,
> At home a poor scarecrow, at London an ass;
> If lousy is Lucy, as some folk miscal it,
> Then Lucy is lousy, whatever befal it.
> He thinks himself great,
> Yet an ass in his state
> We allow by his ears but with asses to mate.
> If Lucy is lousy, as some folk miscal it,
> Sing lousy Lucy, whatever befal it."

Some additional stanzas were afterwards produced as the continuation of the ballad. They appear to have been the work of a person named Jordan, a native of Stratford.

all he remembered of it, and Mr. Thomas Wilkes (my grandfather) transmitted it to my father by memory, who also took it in writing, and his copy is this——

Capell then copies the lines almost identically as they are given by Oldys. This is respectable testimony in support of the tradition, but it comes too late to enable us to rely upon it with any certainty. It is of course quite possible that such an incident did occur in the life of the poet; but stories grow with time, and usually bear, after the lapse of ages, little or no resemblance to past realities. We are not, however, by any means prepared absolutely to reject the whole statement. Malone endeavoured to show that it must be unfounded, because Sir Thomas Lucy had at Charlecote no park coming within the terms of a statute passed some time previously for the protection of game. It has been contended, on the other hand, that, even if that were true, he might have kept deer within some enclosure, and he might have protected his property against trespassers. The most interesting aspect, perhaps, to us now of the whole story is its supposed connection with the satire, which seems very unmistakably to be directed against Sir Thomas Lucy, in the representation of the character of Justice Shallow; and, upon that subject we will here only state that we do not think it likely Shakespeare, in the maturity of his powers, and removed to an entirely new scene, would have bitterly remembered the history of one of his own youthful frolics.

It is quite certain, at all events, that considerations either of taste, or of prudence, or of necessity, induced Shakespeare in early manhood to seek a livelihood in the centre of English commercial and intellectual activity. But here again dark clouds intercept our prospect of this coming daybreak of his glory. We have no means whatever of fixing the date even of his arrival on this great scene of his labours. It probably took place some time about the year 1586; but it may have happened, for all that we know with any certainty, a few years earlier, or even—although this is more unlikely—a few years later than that period. There can be no doubt, however, that after having once reached London he soon became connected, in some capacity or another, with the stage. This was the profession to which the whole bent of his genius must have instinctively directed him; it is the only one we find any trace of his having ever embraced in the metropolis; and we are acquainted with circumstances which we can easily perceive may have influenced him in making this choice of a career, even before he had left his native town. Theatrical companies frequently visited Stratford in the days of his youth. We first hear of their acting, in the Corporation Hall, during his father's tenure of the office of bailiff, in the year 1569; and we know that Burbadge, and some other of their leading members, came, like himself, originally from Warwickshire.

Under those circumstances, we may take it for granted that immediately after his arrival in London he found employment in one or other of the theatres; but in attempting to discover what was the exact nature of that employment we encounter another of our many Shakespearian perplexities. The only positive statement upon the subject that has reached us is one which is supported by a singularly complicated, and, so far, a specially unsafe, chain of testimony. According to Rowe "he was received into the company at first in a very mean rank," and this announcement coincides with the information communicated to Dowdall by the parish-clerk of Stratford, in the year 1693, that "he was received into the play-house as a serviture." The precise nature of this "mean rank," or "service," is set forth in a tradition which, as it is alleged, had been transmitted from Sir William Davenant, first through Betterton, then through Rowe, then through Pope, then through Dr. Newton, and finally through Dr. Johnson. The purport of it is, that Shakespeare, on his arrival in London, gained a livelihood by taking care of the horses of the gentlemen who rode to the theatre; and it is added that he performed this service so much to the satisfaction of his employers that he soon had more business than he could personally discharge, and that he consequently hired assistants, who were known as "Shakespeare's boys." We have learned nothing further in reference to this story, and there could at this time be no use in our entering into any discussion for the purpose of deciding upon its truth, or even upon its probability.

Shakespeare could not now have remained long undistinguished. The precise gradations, however, in his rise to the prominent position which we know that he acquired by the labours of a few years among the dramatists and actors of his time are involved, like so many other details in his career, in almost complete obscurity. Mr. Collier has published from the "Ellesmere Papers" an alleged certificate addressed to the Privy Council, which would show that in the year 1589 the poet was already a sharer in the profits of the Blackfriars Theatre. But this document is involved in the general suspicion which attaches to the whole of Mr. Collier's discoveries in the same quarter; and we can place on it no kind of reliance. If its genuineness were established, it would lead us to the conclusion that Shakespeare's arrival in London must have been earlier, or that his professional success must have been more rapid than has hitherto been generally imagined.

It is not until the year 1592 that we obtain the first undisputed evidence of the growing fame of Shakespeare as an actor and as a dramatist; and that evidence itself, it must be confessed, is more valuable for the conclusions which it indirectly suggests than for the minuteness or the distinctness of its own revelations. On the 3rd of September in that year death brought to a close the reckless career of Robert Greene, the dramatist and pamphleteer, who seems to have spent the last few days of his life in the composition of a tract, entitled "A Groat's worth of Wit bought with a Million of Repentance," which was afterwards published by his friend, Henry Chettle. In this strange, fierce production Greene addresses, without directly naming them, three of his fellow-dramatists, who were, most probably, Marlowe, Lodge, and Peele, exhorting them to amend their lives, and to renounce the worthless or immoral occupation of writing for the stage. Marlowe he clearly charges, in the following words, with the profession of atheism :—

Wonder not (for with thee will I first begin), thou famous gracer of tragedians, that Greene, who hath said with thee, like the fool in his heart, 'There is no God,' should now give glory unto his greatness.

He afterwards refers to the two other writers, and he then proceeds in this curious passage :—

Base-minded men, all three of you, if by my misery you be not warned, for unto none of you, like me, sought those burs to cleave ; those puppets, I mean, that speak from our mouths, those antics garnished in our colours. Is it not strange that I, to whom they all have been beholden, is it not like that you, to whom they all have been beholden, shall, were you in that case that I am now, be both of them at once forsaken? Yes, trust them not, for there is an upstart crow beautified with our feathers, that with his *tiger's heart wrapt in a player's hide*, supposes he is as well able to bombast out a blank verse as the best of you, and being an absolute *Johannes Fac-totum*, is, in his own conceit, the only Shake-scene in a country.

This last sentence undoubtedly refers to Shakespeare, and evinces the soreness with which Greene witnessed the unexpected rise on the dramatic horizon of this new and surpassing luminary. The allusion to the "upstart crow beautified with our feathers" shows that, in the opinion of the writer, he himself and his three companions had contributed to the formation of the new dramatist. The individual against whom Greene's invective is directed is still more clearly indicated by the mention of the "only Shake-scene in a country," and by the introduction of the "tiger's heart wrapt in a player's hide," which is but a parody of the line,

"Oh, tiger's heart wrapt in a woman's hide,"

in Shakespeare's "Third Part of King Henry VI.," and in the corresponding drama of "The True Tragedie of Richard Duke of Yorke."

Chettle must have learned that both Marlowe and Shakespeare had taken offence at the reference made to them in the tract brought out under his auspices, and in his address

" to the gentlemen readers," prefixed to his " Kind Heart's Dream," which was published at the close of the same year (1592), he offers the following explanation of his connection with the publication of the work, as far as they were concerned : —

About three months since died Mr. Robert Greene, leaving many papers in sundry booksellers' hands; among other, his " Groat's worth of Wit," in which a letter written to divers play-makers is offensively by one or two of them taken. * * * With neither of them that take offence was I acquainted, and with one of them [Marlowe, no doubt] I care not if I never be : the other [Shakespeare], whom at that time I did not so much spare as since I wish I had, for that I have moderated the heat of living writers, and might have used my own discretion (especially in such a case), the author being dead. That I did not I am as sorry as if the original fault had been my fault, because myself have seen his demeanour no less civil than he excellent in the quality he professes. Besides, divers of worship have reported his uprightness of dealing, which argues his honesty, and his facetious grace in writing, that approves his art.

These extracts afford us a glimpse of what must have been one of the more or less annoying episodes in the life of the poet. They seem to indicate that at one time he, as well as some other person whose name is now unknown, cultivated in some special manner the acquaintance of Greene—" unto none of you, like me, sought those burs to cleave ; " that he kept more aloof from this dangerous and compromising companion in the later and more discreditable portion of his career; and that, at the last, with the worldly prudence which so strongly marks his whole history, he refused to afford some expected aid to the desperate and unprincipled spendthrift.

In 1593 we again meet Shakespeare, not as a mere fleeting shadow, but as an actual man, doing actual work. In that year he published his " Venus and Adonis," prefixing to it the following dedication addressed to Henry Wriothesley, Earl of Southampton, and written in the quaint and somewhat stiff and affected style common to all the personal compliments, and, indeed, more or less, to all the prose writing of that age :—

Right Honourable,—I know not how I shall offend in dedicating my unpolished lines to your Lordship, nor how the world will censure me for choosing so strong a prop to support so weak a burden: only, if your Honour seem but pleased, I account myself highly praised, and vow to take advantage of all idle hours till I have honoured you with some graver labour. But if the first heir of my invention prove deformed, I shall be sorry it had so noble a godfather, and never after ear* so barren a land, for fear it yield me still so bad a harvest. I leave it to your honourable survey, and your Honour to your heart's content; which I wish may always answer your own wish, and the world's hopeful expectation.—Your Honour's in all duty,

WILLIAM SHAKESPEARE.

In the course of the following year he produced his "Lucrece," which he dedicated to the same nobleman in a similar strain of formal, though still warmer, courtesy.

The love I dedicate to your Lordship is without end; whereof this pamphlet, without beginning, is but a superfluous moiety. The warrant I have of your honourable disposition, not the worth of my untutored lines, makes it assured of acceptance. What I have done is yours; what I have to do is yours; being part in all I have, devoted yours. Were my worth greater, my duty would show greater; meantime, as it is, it is bound to your Lordship, to whom I wish long life, still lengthened with all happiness.—Your Lordship's in all duty,

WILLIAM SHAKESPEARE.

Some of the commentators have concluded, from the poet's designation of the "Venus and Adonis" as the "first heir of his invention," that this work was his first composition, and even that it was, in all probability, written before his removal from Stratford to London. We believe that the words will not fairly bear any such interpretation, and that they merely indicate that this was the first book which he published. Both the poems won the immediate and the marked admiration of his contemporaries, and nearly all the writers of his time who allude to his literary labours class them among the most characteristic manifestations of his genius. The "Venus" passed through a fifth edition in the year 1602; and a fourth edition of the "Lucrece" was published in the year 1607.

Lord Southampton is entitled to the high honour of having been the warmest and the most generous of the early patrons

---

* Plough, or cultivate.

and friends of Shakespeare. Rowe tells us he had been "assured" that "a story was handed down by Sir William Davenant, who was probably very well acquainted with his [Shakespeare's] affairs," to the effect that "Lord Southampton at one time gave him a thousand pounds to enable him to go through a purchase that he had a mind to." It is not at all unlikely that there is some foundation for this story; but modern writers are disposed to think that the gift could not have reached so large a sum as £1,000, which would have been equivalent at that period to four or five times the same amount at the present day.*

The wonder with which we naturally contemplate the magnificence of Shakespeare's dramatic achievements is vastly increased by all the knowledge we obtain of the circumstances under which they were accomplished. The stage was in his time under the ban of a large portion of the nation, and to the profession of an actor a positive discredit was universally attached. It is true that both Queen Elizabeth and James I. patronised the drama to some extent; but they do not appear to have ever assisted at the performance of plays, except in their own palaces, or in other private residences. The public theatres were mean and incommodious

---

* The Globe Theatre was most probably built in the year 1594; and Mr. Collier conjectures that Lord Southampton "presented Shakespeare with £1,000, to enable him to make good the money he was to produce, as his proportion, for its completion." Lord Southampton was born on the 6th of October, 1573, and was, therefore, Shakespeare's junior by more than nine years. We find a remarkable proof of his love for the drama in the following passage in a letter addressed by Rowland Whyte to Sir Robert Sidney, on the 11th of October, 1599 :— " My Lord Southampton and Lord Rutland come not to the court: the one doth but very seldom : they pass away the time in London merely in going to plays every day." The Earl of Essex was at that time kept in confinement at the Lord Keeper's, in consequence of his having returned from Ireland without the permission of the queen, and it was, no doubt, that circumstance which induced his friend Southampton to absent himself from court.

buildings. They contained no movable painted scenery.* Throughout the reign of Elizabeth they were often open on the Sundays as well as on the other days of the week. There were no women in any of the companies, and the female characters were always personated by boys, who occasionally wore vizards. We need hardly stop to observe how strongly this latter circumstance is calculated to add to our astonishment at the enchantment which the poet has thrown over his Juliets, and his Rosalinds, and his Mirandas. The performances commenced at three o'clock in the afternoon; and, in all probability, the audiences were usually more noisy and unruly than any that we should now meet in the least fastidious of our London suburban places of dramatic entertainment. But those rude people were, no doubt, under the influence of one earnest and inspiring passion—an intense love of the amusement in which they boisterously engaged.

There were at the time two kinds of theatres, one called public, and the other private. The principal difference between them appears to have been that the former were partially open to the sky in the centre, while the private houses were entirely covered in. We have no means of ascertaining what was the company to which Shakespeare was attached, until the year 1593 or 1594, when he was one of what was called the Lord Chamberlain's servants, who usually performed at the Blackfriars Theatre. This building was raised in the year 1576, and stood near the site of the present Apothecaries' Hall.† The same company built the Globe Theatre, on the Bankside,

---

* " The air-blest castle, round whose wholesome crest
     The martlet, guest of summer, chose her nest,
     The forest-walks of Arden's fair domain,
     Where Jaques fed his solitary vein,—
     No pencil's aid as yet had dar'd supply,
     Seen only by the intellectual eye."
                                                CHARLES LAMB.

† Playhouse Yard, to the east of Apothecaries' Hall, still recalls the spot near which the theatre once stood.

near the south end of old London Bridge, in the year 1594.* They performed at the Globe in summer, and at the Blackfriars in winter, until the commencement of the seventeenth century, when the latter house appears to have for several years passed out of their hands. The Globe was the more spacious building, but it afforded no sufficient protection from the severity of the winter weather. It was burnt down on the 29th of June, 1613, in consequence of the thatch having taken fire from the wadding used in letting off a small piece of ordnance.

We can hardly state with certainty the precise year in which any one of the plays of Shakespeare was produced; but we know that many of them must have been composed previously to some definite and limited period; and this knowledge itself is often very valuable and interesting. The most important testimony that has descended to us in reference to the chronology of the Shakespearian drama is the following passage in a work by Francis Meres, published in the year 1598, and entitled "Palladis Tamia, Wit's Treasury; being the Second Part of Wit's Commonwealth:"—

As the soul of Euphorbus was thought to live in Pythagoras, so the sweet, witty soul of Ovid lives in mellifluous and honey-tongued Shakespeare; witness his "Venus and Adonis," his "Lucrece," his sugared Sonnets among his private friends, &c.

As Plautus and Seneca are accounted the best for comedy and tragedy among the Latins, so Shakespeare among the English is the most excellent in both kinds for the stage; for comedy, witness his "Gentlemen of Verona," his "Errors," his "Love's Labour's Lost," his "Love's Labour's Won," his "Midsummer Night's Dream," and his "Merchant of Venice;" for tragedy, his "Richard II.," "Richard III.," "Henry IV.," "King John," "Titus Andronicus," and his "Romeo and Juliet."

As Epius Stolo said that the Muses would speak with Plautus's tongue, if they would speak Latin, so I say that the Muses would speak with Shakespeare's fine-filed phrase, if they would speak English.

---

* We are only enabled to fix this date from the fact that Burbadge, as the representative of the company, signed a bond for the construction of this theatre on the 22nd of December, 1593.

The commentators in general are of opinion that the play mentioned in this passage as "Love's Labour's Won," is the one which has come down to us under the title of "All's Well that Ends Well." Here we have six comedies and six tragedies enumerated, and among them some which still hold a high place in Shakespeare's collected dramas. It is quite possible, too, that Meres may have forgotten to include in his list some works which he would otherwise have mentioned; and, indeed, the very words with which he introduces it shows that he did not himself pretend that it was to be absolutely a complete one.

We cannot escape from a suspicion that, in the midst of all these manifestations of matchless intellectual activity and power, an event which occurred about the period at which we have now arrived must have cast a dark and fixed shadow over the poet's heart and memory. On the 11th of August, 1596, his only son, Hammet, was buried in the parish church of Stratford. This is all we know, from the period of his baptism in 1585, of this heir to so great a name; and neither have we obtained the smallest record of the effect produced by this loss upon Shakespeare himself. But all the glimpses which we catch of his individuality lead us to think that he must have been peculiarly sensitive to an affliction such as this, falling upon a father—

." —— All whose joy is nothing else
But fair posterity."

Under the date of 1596 we have another of the disputed papers first published by Mr. Collier. It purports to be a petition addressed by the players of the Lord Chamberlain's company to the Privy Council, in which they pray that they may be allowed to repair and enlarge the Blackfriars Theatre. "William Shakespeare" is the fifth name in the list of petitioners. Mr. Collier has adduced strong evidence to show that this document was known at the State Paper Office before he commenced his researches in that quarter; but upon the formal decision of Sir Francis Palgrave, Sir Frederic Madden, and other judges of ancient handwriting, we feel bound to disbelieve its authenticity, whoever may have been its author.

Before the close of the sixteenth century we meet with many indications of the growing worldly prosperity of Shakespeare; and there is one incident which serves curiously to show that his acquisition of property was accompanied by a desire for a position of corresponding social respectability. In the year 1596 an application must have been made by John Shakespeare, the poet's father, who no doubt represented the poet himself, for a grant of arms, and two drafts of such a grant are preserved in the College of Arms. In those documents it is stated by William Dethick, Garter King of Arms, that he had been, by "credible report, informed" that the "parents and antecessors" of John Shakespeare, of Stratford-upon-Avon, "were, for their valiant and faithful service, advanced and rewarded by the most prudent prince, King Henry the Seventh, of famous memory, since which time they have continued at those parts in good reputation and credit; and that the said John having married Mary, daughter and one of the heirs of Arden, of Wilmecote, in the said county," &c. At the bottom of the second draft the following curious note is inserted :—

This John hath a pattern thereof under Clarencieux Cooke's hand in paper twenty years past.

A justice of peace, and was bailiff, officer, and chief of the town of Stratford-upon-Avon fifteen or sixteen years past.

That he hath lands and tenements of good wealth and substance, £500.

That he married a daughter and heir of Arden, a gent. of worship.

A complaint must have been made from some quarter that this application had no sufficient foundation, for we have, in the Heralds' College, a manuscript, which purports to be "the answer of Garter and Clarencieux Kings of Arms, to a libellous scrowl against certain arms supposed to be wrongfully given;" in which the writers state, under the head, "Shakespeare," that—"the person to whom it was granted hath borne magistracy, and was justice of peace, at Stratford-upon-Avon: he married the daughter and heir of Arden, and was able to maintain that estate."

The whole of this transaction is involved in considerable, and perhaps to a great extent intentional, obscurity; and it still seems doubtful whether any grant was actually made in the year 1596. In the year 1599 the application must have been renewed in a somewhat altered form. Under that date there exists a draft of another grant, by which John Shakespeare was further to be allowed to impale the ancient arms of Arden. In this document a statement was originally inserted to the effect that "John Shakespeare showed and produced his ancient coat of arms, heretofore assigned to him whilst he was Her Majesty's officer and bailiff of that town." But the words " showed and produced " were afterwards erased, and in this unsatisfactory manner the matter appears to have terminated.

It is manifest that the entries we have quoted contain a number of exaggerations, or even of positive misstatements. The "parents and antecessors" of John Shakespeare were not advanced and rewarded by Henry VII., but the maternal ancestors, or, more probably, some much more distant relatives of William Shakespeare, appear to have received some favours and distinctions from that sovereign. The pattern of arms given, as it is stated, under the hand of Clarencieux Cooke, who was then dead, is not found in his records, and we can place no faith in this allegation. John Shakespeare had been a justice of the peace, merely *ex officio*, and not by commission, as is here insinuated; in all probability he did not possess "lands and tenements of the value of £500;" and Robert Arden of Wilmecote was not a "gentleman of worship."

The crest or cognisance selected by the poet—for we suppose that he exercised some sort of selection in the matter—was a falcon with his wings displayed, standing on a wreath of his colours, supporting a spear; and the motto was the proud one to which the civilised world will now take no exception—*non sanz droict*.

No letter written by Shakespeare has come down to us, and there is only one now known to be extant of the many which he must have received. In the year 1598 Richard Quiney, an alderman of Stratford-upon-Avon, was in London, transacting some business of the corporation, and having been in want of money, he applied to his already prosperous and famous fellow-townsman for the loan of what was at that time the large sum of £30. The letter which contains this application is of no value in itself, but it possesses, in a very unusual degree, the indirect interest of memorable associations. Here it is, as it once met the strange eyes of William Shakespeare :—

Lovinge contreyman, I am bolde of yow, as of a ffrende, craveinge yowr helpe with xxx. *li.* uppon Mr. Bushells and my securytee, or Mr. Myttons with me. Mr. Rosswell is nott come to London as yeate, and I have especiall cawse. Yow shall ffrende me muche in helpeing me out of all the debettes I owe in London, I thanck God, and muche quiet my mynde, which wolde nott be indebeted. I am nowe towardes the Cowrte, in hope of answer for the dispatche of my buysenes. Yow shall nether loose croddytt nor monney by me, the Lorde wyllinge; and nowe butt perswade yowrselfe soe, as I hope, and yow shall nott need to feare butt with all heartie thanckefullnes I wyll holde my tyme, and content yowr ffreende, and yf we bargaine farther, yow shalbe the paie-master yowrselfe. My tyme biddes me hasten to an ende, and soe I committ thys [to] yowr care and hope of yowr helpe. I feare I shall nott be backe thys night ffrom the Cowrte. Haste. The Lorde be with yow and with us all, Amen! ffrom the Bell in Carter Lane, the 25. October, 1598.

Yowrs in all kyndenes,
RYC. QUYNEY.

The superscription on this letter is as follows :—

To my loveinge good ffrend and contreyman Mr. Wm. Shackespere deliver these.

The only notice we obtain of the poet's answer to this application is one of an indirect character, but it naturally leads us to the conclusion that he must have advanced the money.

We have no communication from Quiney himself upon the subject; but we find that one of the aldermen at Stratford, writing to him shortly afterwards, expresses his gratification at learning that " our countryman, Mr. William Shakespeare, procures us money."

Whatever may be our general dearth of Shakespearian information, ample evidence has reached us of the poet's large gains and of his careful and judicious economy. During the Easter term of 1597 he purchased of William Underhill, for £60 (equal to nearly £300 of our money), New Place, one of the best and largest residences in Stratford. It was built by Sir Hugh Clopton, in the reign of Henry VII., and throughout the earlier portion of the sixteenth century it was inhabited by members of the Clopton family, and was then known as "the great house." Shakespeare passed in it all the latter years of his life, and it was in it that he died. There can hardly be any doubt that his family removed to it immediately after the purchase, and it is not at all improbable that he himself, from the same period, paid to it frequent and lengthened visits.*

In the winter of 1597-8 Stratford suffered from a great scarcity of provisions. During the month of February an account was drawn up of the amount of corn and malt held by the various inhabitants; and in that document we find attached to the name of " Wm. Shackespere," in the list for the Chapel Street ward—the ward in which " New Place " was situated—the large quantity of " X quarters." An ample provision, certainly, against a famine; and it was to be found, too, in the home of a poet, and even of the very chief of poets.

Before the lapse of many years Shakespeare added to his mansion in his native town a more profitable description of property. In the month of May, 1602, he purchased for £320, from William and John Combe, 107 acres of arable

---

* We give an account of New Place in Appendix, Note 2.

land, situated in the parish of Old Stratford. In the month of September of the same year a house, in Dead Lane, Stratford, near "New Place," was surrendered to him by Walter Getley. And again, during the Michaelmas term of that year, he bought from Hercules Underhill, for the sum of £60, a property in the town of Stratford, which is described as consisting of one messuage, two barns, two gardens, and two orchards.

The largest of all his known purchases was made in 1605. In the month of July of that year he paid the sum of £440 for the unexpired term of a moiety of a lease, granted in 1544, for a period of ninety-two years, of the tithes of Stratford, Old Stratford, Bishopton, and Welcombe. The lease had still thirty-one years to run; and we know from the records of some law proceedings in which he afterwards became engaged, that the sum he derived from this investment was £60 a year.

His next and his last acquisition of property, as far as we can now learn, was made in 1613. On the 10th of March of that year, he bought from Henry Walker a house in the Blackfriars, London. The sum he was to give for it was £140. It appears that out of this amount he paid down only £80, and that on the following day he mortgaged the premises to the vendor for the remaining £60. At a subsequent period he paid off the whole of the purchase-money, and leased the house to John Robinson. There are, even at the present day, some interesting circumstances connected with the whole of this transaction. The counterpart of the original conveyance of the property, with Shakespeare's signature, is now in the possession of the Corporation of the City of London, who purchased it, in 1841, for £145. The mortgage deed was discovered in 1768; and after having been for some time in the possession of David Garrick, and having been lent to Steevens, it was supposed for many years to have been lost. It was again, however, recovered, and was sold by auction in 1858, when it was purchased for the trustees of the British Museum, for £315. To it is attached the only other indisputable signature of the poet at present known to be in existence, with the exception of the three inserted in his will.

The successful actor and dramatist was by no means wholly free throughout all this period from the small vexations which usually accompany busy worldly prosperity. In the year 1597, we find his father and mother engaged—no doubt at his instance—in a suit for the recovery of the property of Ashbies, which they had mortgaged to Edmund Lambert in the year 1578, for the sum of £40. It appears that the mortgage was to be considered a sale, unless the £40 were returned by the Michaelmas of the ensuing year. The Shakespeares tendered the amount of the debt within that period, but their creditor refused to accept it unless certain other sums which were also due to him were paid at the same time; and as this condition was not complied with, he continued to hold possession of the property. The object of the Shakespeares in instituting the proceedings of 1597 was to compel John Lambert, the son and heir of Edmund Lambert, to deliver up the land which he and his father had thus unjustly retained. We have no record of the termination of this suit, but it is naturally conjectured that it must have been brought to a close by the surrender of Ashbies to its original owners.

We have other remarkable proofs that our great poet knew well how to preserve the property he had so industriously acquired. In the year 1604, we find him bringing an action against Philip Rogers for the recovery of a sum of £1 15s. 10d. The declaration was filed in the Stratford Court of Record, and from it we find that at different times between the month of March and the month of May in that year, Shakespeare had sold to Rogers malt to the value of £1 19s. 10d., and that he had also, on the 25th of June, lent him 2s.; and, as Rogers had paid 6s. only out of this double debt, the action was instituted for the recovery of the remainder of the entire sum.

In the year 1608, Shakespeare was engaged in another small suit in the Stratford Court of Record. This was an action which he brought against John Addenbroke for the recovery of a debt. After a delay of some months, a verdict was given in his favour for £6, and £1 4s. costs. The defendant, however, was not to be found, and Shakespeare then proceeded against Thomas Horneby, who had become his bail.

From the draft of a bill to be filed before Lord Ellesmere, we learn that the poet was engaged in a law-suit, at a time not specified, but which was no doubt about the year 1612, arising out of the possession of the tithe property which he had purchased in the year 1605. The draft informs us that some of the lessees refused to contribute their proper share of a reserved rent which they were bound to pay under peril of forfeiture, and that an excessive charge was thus imposed upon Shakespeare and others. The result of the suit is not recorded, but it is from this draft we ascertain the fact that the poet's income from this property amounted to "threescore pounds."

These are no doubt very small details, but they are also very curious details in connection with such a name. They serve at all events to show us that a great poet, with eyes that "glanced from heaven to earth, from earth to heaven," could also keep a sharp look-out after his own little place "i' the sun." *

The composition of the grandest drama of all ages, with all its multitudinous life, seems to have pressed as lightly as the most familiar task-work on the energies of this extraordinary being. In the very noontide of his supreme dominion over the widest realms of creative imagination, he still found time and patience to attend to the duties of a laborious profession. William Shakespeare was an actor as well as a dramatist, presented himself in person before actual and living audiences, delivered with his own lips the words in which he had clothed his own fancies, "strutted and fretted his hour upon the stage." We can arrive at no definite and unquestionable conclusion with respect to the precise position which he

---

* *C'est-là ma place au soleil, disaient ces pauvres enfans.* PASCAL, "*Pensées.*"

occupied in his profession, but the general tendency of all the evidence which has reached us upon the subject leaves us little room to doubt that, in the representation of character upon the stage, he was distinguished by no extraordinary breadth or energy of action. A contemporary dramatist, Henry Chettle, states in a passage which we have already quoted,* that he was "excellent in the quality which he professed." But in a manifestly apologetic and complimentary publication, this eulogy implies no very transcendent merit. Aubrey states that "he did act exceedingly well." Wright, a dramatic historian or critic, tells us under the date of 1699, that he had "heard" Shakespeare was "a much better poet than player." And Rowe, writing in 1709, says that soon after joining his company he was distinguished, "if not as an extraordinary actor, yet as an excellent writer." This biographer then adds, "Though I have inquired, I could never meet with any further account of him this way than that the top of his performance was the Ghost in his own 'Hamlet.'" According to another vague tradition, he performed upon one occasion the part of Adam in his own "As You Like It."† We

---

* Page 32.

† This tradition is found for the first time in Oldys's manuscripts. The purport of Oldys's statement is, that a brother of Shakespeare's, who lived to a very advanced age—even until "after the restoration of Charles II."—used to relate that he remembered having seen "his brother Will," as he called him, personate the character of a very old man, in which "he appeared so weak and drooping, and unable to walk, that he was forced to be supported and carried by another person to a table, at which he was seated among some company who were eating, and one of whom sang a song." If there is any truth in this story, the brother in question was no doubt Gilbert, who was born in 1566, and of whose death we have no record. But as no mention is made of him in the poet's will, dated 1616, it does not seem likely that he was alive even at that time. Capell gives another version of the tradition. It is to the effect that a very old man at Stratford, of weak intellect, used to say that he remembered having once seen Shakespeare "brought on the stage upon another man's back," a statement which would identify the poet with Adam in Act ii., scene 7, of "As You Like It."

cannot perhaps attach any absolute credit to stories of this description, but we obtain indirectly the most conclusive proof that Shakespeare never acquired a reputation of the highest class by his acting. That distinction is exclusively assigned by his contemporaries to Edward Alleyn and Richard Burbadge in the more elevated impersonations of the drama, while Kemp appears to have been the great comic favourite of our theatrical audiences at the same epoch. Alleyn, who is still so well remembered as the founder of Dulwich College, was the leading actor of the company of which Henslowe seems to have been the principal manager or capitalist, or the Lord Admiral's servants, as they were at one time called. Burbadge was associated with Shakespeare as one of the servants of the Lord Chamberlain, and upon him devolved the singular distinction of having been the first representative of the principal characters in all the poet's greatest dramas.*

Ben Jonson gives the names of the principal actors in his plays, but his lists never state what was the particular part sustained by any individual performer. We thus learn that in 1598, Shakespeare represented one of the characters in Jonson's "Every Man in his Humour," and that in 1603 he played in the same writer's "Sejanus." This is the last record we have of his appearance on the stage, and it is probable that he soon afterwards renounced the profession of an actor.

Throughout the whole of this great productive era of the English drama, players were discountenanced by the gravest,

---

* From an "Elegy" on Burbadge, which seems to have been written immediately after his death, we learn that he was the original Hamlet, Romeo, Prince Henry, and Henry V., Richard III., Macbeth, Brutus, Coriolanus, Shylock, Lear, Pericles, and Othello. It was no doubt in reference to his personal appearance that the Queen in the last act of "Hamlet" gives us this very unpoetical image of her son:— "He's fat and scant o' breath." The "Elegy" on Burbadge is inserted by Mr. Collier in his "Memoirs of the Principal Actors in Shakespeare's Plays," one of the volumes printed for the Shakespeare Society.

and perhaps we might add, the most active and influential, portion of the nation; but they found some compensation for this discredit in the countenance extended to them by the Court, and still more in the enthusiastic support and favour of the great mass of the people. Elizabeth and James I. were both patrons of the drama, and they both seem to have possessed sufficient discernment to recognise in Shakespeare the foremost dramatic writer of his age. Ben Jonson, in his verses prefixed to the Shakespeare Folio of 1623, bears a sort of general testimony to the delight which these two sovereigns took in the productions of the poet's genius :—

> " Sweet Swan of Avon, what a sight it were
> To see thee in our waters yet appear,
> And make those flights upon the banks of Thames
> That so did take Eliza and our James ! "

Elizabeth died on the 24th of March, 1603 ; and, before the close of that year, Henry Chettle, in his "England's Mourning Garment," thus remonstrates with Shakespeare, whom he addresses under the name of Melicert, for neglecting to pay some poetical tribute to her memory :—

> " Nor doth the silver-tongued Melicert
> Drop from his honied muse one sable tear,
> To mourn her death that graced his desert,
> And to his lays open'd her royal ear.
> Shepherd, remember our Elizabeth,
> And sing her rape, done by that Tarquin, Death."

These lines, whatever may be their poetical merit, seem to show that Elizabeth evinced in some marked manner her appreciation of the great genius who gave so splendid an illustration to her reign.

James I. seems to have been a still more ardent lover of the drama than his immediate predecessor; and of all the contemporary writers for the stage, our great poet, it is manifest, received the largest share of his admiration and patronage. On the 17th of May, 1603, only ten days after his first arrival in London, a warrant was issued in his name, by which the Lord Chamberlain's company were taken into his own service, and under which they were thenceforward known as "the King's Players." In this document the first member of the company mentioned is "Lawrence Fletcher," and then follow "William Shakespeare, Richard Burbadge," and six others.

There can be no doubt that Fletcher was already known to King James, and that it was to that circumstance he owed this mark of royal favour. Towards the close of the year 1599 a company of English players had travelled to Edinburgh. Immediately after their arrival the king granted them his licence to perform within the burgh, and then, in opposition to the local ministers, supported them with considerable spirit in the exercise of their profession. They appear to have remained in Scotland until near the close of the year 1601, for we find, from a register of the town-council of Aberdeen, that they performed in that city in the month of October of that year. Fletcher was at their head, and it is clear that, after his return to London, he was a member of the company to which Shakespeare also belonged; but we have no evidence to show that it was not then he joined them for the first time. It has been thought that Shakespeare himself may have been one of the band of travellers, and that he may thus have been enabled to describe Macbeth's castle from actual observation. But the supposition is, in every way, one of a very improbable description. We do not know that he was at the time at all associated with Fletcher. He must, besides, have always made his profession as an actor subordinate to his labours as a dramatist; and the lengthened absence of Fletcher and his companions from England is almost alone sufficient to show that he could not have formed one of their number.

In a poem by John Davies, of Hereford, entitled "The Scourge of Folly," which seems to have been printed about the year 1611, we find the following perplexing lines:—

"To our English Terence, Mr. Will. Shakespeare.
"Some say, good Will, which I in sport do sing,
    Hadst thou not played some kingly parts in sport,
    Thou hadst been a companion for a king,
    And been a king among the meaner sort.
Some others rail; but rail as they think fit,
Thou hast no railing, but a reigning wit;
And honesty thou sow'st, which they do reap,
So to increase their stock, which they do keep."

These verses seem to point to some offence which Shakespeare was supposed to have given at Court by personating some royal character on the stage. We can hardly think it possible that, with his fine sense and his ready acknowledgment of the traditionary claims of rank and power, he would have committed himself to any theatrical representation which could have been personally disagreeable to a reigning monarch. But, at the same time, we cannot read, after Davies's verses, one of the small episodes in the history of that time without supposing that there may exist between them some connection, the particulars of which we are now unable to ascertain. The following passage in a letter from John Chamberlaine to Sir R. Winwood, dated December 18th, 1604, shows that the King's Players had recently excited the strong displeasure of the Court by producing a tragedy on the subject of the Gowry conspiracy:—

The tragedy of "Gowry," with all the action and actors, hath been twice represented by the King's Players, with exceeding concourse of all sorts of people. But whether the matter or manner be not well handled, or that it be thought unfit that princes should be played on the stage in their lifetime, I hear that some great councillors are much displeased with it, and so 'tis thought shall be forbidden.

We must leave coincidences of this kind in the poet's history in the obscurity in which we find them. The language of Chamberlaine does not necessarily imply that there was anything really offensive in the play which he mentions. It is true that Davies distinctly abstains from vouching for the accuracy of the rumour to which he refers; but he addresses Shakespeare as a familiar acquaintance, and he must have known all the passing details of his history. We have no means whatever of determining whether Shakespeare may not still have occasionally appeared as an actor in the year 1604. The only fact we know with respect to his connection with the stage at this period is that in the preceding year he performed one of the parts in Ben Jonson's "Sejanus."

According to one of the many doubtful Shakespearian traditions, James at one time wrote an "amicable letter" to our poet. In the advertisement to Lintot's edition of Shakespeare's poems, published in the year 1710, it is stated that this letter, "though now lost, remained long in the hands of Sir William Davenant, as a credible witness now living can testify;" and Oldys alleges that the Duke of Buckingham (Sheffield) told Lintot that he had seen it in the possession of Davenant.

In Mr. Cunningham's "Extracts from the Accounts of the Revels at Court," we find a number of entries which give us some small insight into the dramatic tastes of our first Stuart king; and from them we take one or two details:—On November 1st, 1604, "The Moor of Venice" was performed at the "Banqueting House, Whitehall;" on "the Sunday following," "the Merry Wives of Windsor;" on "Shrove Sunday," March 24th, 1605, the "Merchant of Venice," and this performance was repeated on the following "Shrove Tuesday," the same play having been "again commanded by the King's Majesty;" on November 1st, 1611, the "Tempest;" and on November 5th, 1611, the "Winter Night's Tale." On the 26th of November, 1607, "King Lear" was entered in the Stationers' Registers, as it had been "played before the King's Majesty, at Whitehall," on the 26th of December in the preceding year.

An important event in the family history of the poet took place in 1607. On the 5th of June in that year, his elder daughter, Susanna, was married to John Hall, a physician residing at Stratford, where he appears to have acquired a considerable professional reputation. Their only child, Elizabeth Hall, was baptised on the 21st of February, 1608.

Among Mr. Collier's "Ellesmere Papers," there is one which purports to be a "copia vera," or true copy of a letter signed "H. S." (Henry, Earl of Southampton), and supposed to be addressed to Lord Keeper Egerton, for the purpose of ensuring his good offices in favour of the company of King's Players, whose theatre at the Blackfriars the Corporation of London were then endeavouring to suppress. This communication bears no date; but it is naturally assigned to the year 1608, when, as we know from other sources, the City authorities were engaged in their contest with the players. The writer alludes in a very complimentary manner to Burbadge, and makes mention in still warmer language of Shakespeare, whom he calls "my especial friend." This document would now possess some interest, if we could rely on its authenticity; but the origin of the whole of those papers, as we have already had occasion more than once to observe, is involved in considerable suspicion; and this "copia vera" cannot be held to be entitled to any kind of credit.

From another of those very questionable documents, it would appear that the City of London Corporation must at this time have entered into some inquiries for the purpose of ascertaining whether it would be advisable that they should buy out the interest of the different proprietors of the Blackfriars Theatre; and a return is actually produced, in which the owners set forth the value of their respective shares in the property. Richard Burbadge stands the highest in this list. He "oweth the fee" which he values at £1,000, and four shares, which he estimates at £933 6s. 8d. The next largest shareholder is "W. Shakespeare," who "asked for the wardrobe and properties of the same playhouse 500li, and for his four shares the same as his fellows, Burbadge and Fletcher, viz.: 933li. 6s. 8d.;" making a total of £1,433 6s. 8d. The entire cost of the property to the "Lord Mayor and the citizens" is estimated "at the least 7,000li."

In the year 1599 there was published, under Shakespeare's name, a small volume of poems, under the title of "The Passionate Pilgrim." Two of those poems had already appeared, with some slight variations, in "Love's Labours Lost," the first edition of which was printed in 1598; and two more of them—namely, the sonnet, "If music and sweet poetry agree," &c., and the ode, "As it fell upon a day," &c., had been inserted by Richard Barnfield in a poetical collection of his, published in the same year, but were omitted from another edition of the same work issued in 1605. The natural inference from these facts is, that Barnfield had improperly claimed them in the first instance; and we think it extremely probable that Shakespeare was their real author. If we are not mistaken in this conclusion, the lines, "If music," &c., possess a peculiar interest, inasmuch as they contain the only compliment the great dramatist is known to have ever paid to a contemporary writer; and we should certainly feel no surprise at finding that it was the musical flow of Spenser's fancy that elicited from him this exceptional mark of admiration.

We now come to what is at once one of the great revelations, and one of the great perplexities, in the history of Shakespeare. In the year 1609 his 154 Sonnets were published by Thomas Thorpe, who prefixed to the work the following dedication :*—

TO . THE . ONLIE . BEGETTER . OF .
THESE . INSUING . SONNETS .
MR. W. H. ALL . HAPPINESSE .
AND . THAT . ETERNITIE .
PROMISED .
BY .
OUR . EVER - LIVING . POET .
WISHETH .
THE . WELL - WISHING .
ADVENTURER . IN .
SETTING .
FORTH .   T. T.

---

* We print it as it stands in the original, because an attempt has been made to found upon the collocation of the words an argument in support of a most singular interpretation which has recently been given to them.

We know that this "T. T." is Thomas Thorpe, for his name is entered as that of the publisher in the Stationers' Registers, under the date of the 20th of May, 1609.

It is hardly possible to doubt that the author of this quaint address could have told us much that would have contributed to remove the obscurity in which the history of these most remarkable poems now lies enveloped; but, as his dedication stands, nearly every line of it has been made the subject of elaborate conjecture and controversy. The " Mr. W. H." is still the representative of an unknown name. Some of the commentators maintain that we ought to reverse those initials, and that the person thus obscurely indicated is Henry Wriothesley, Earl of Southampton; while others are more disposed to adopt the opinion first put forward by Mr. Boaden, that the solution of the problem is to be found in the person of William Herbert, Earl of Pembroke. A less obvious, but perhaps quite as probable a guess, is that made by Tyrwhitt, one of our most learned critics and antiquaries, who suggests that the line in the twentieth Sonnet—

"A man in hue, all hues in his controlling"—

may help to light us in this darkness, and that a W. Hewes, or Hughes, was probably here introduced by Shakespeare, under his favourite form of a verbal quibble.* Chalmers brought to the consideration of this question an originality of extravagance which will probably remain for ever unrivalled. According to his reading of the Sonnets, the object of Shakespeare's passionate admiration was no less a personage than Queen Elizabeth. The prevailing opinion among the most recent commentators seems to be that those strange compositions

---

* The fact that the word *Hews* is printed in the original edition in italics, and with a capital letter at the commencement, seems to give some additional countenance to this conjecture; but we cannot place any absolute reliance upon that evidence, inasmuch as italics are somewhat arbitrarily scattered over the whole volume.

were, for the most part, produced by the poet in a purely fanciful and fictitious character.

With the Sonnets was published a short poem, called "A Lover's Complaint." It is written in that vague, restless, longing, morbid mood, and with that want of condensed vigour of thought, and of a perfect mastery of the resources of rhyme, which seem to us to form the principal characteristics of all the minor and more personal compositions of its author.

The dramatic labours of our great poet were continued, in all probability, throughout the first ten or eleven years of the seventeenth century; and we can hardly entertain a doubt that it was during this period he composed almost all the greatest of his tragic masterpieces. We feel justified in assigning to it the production of "Hamlet," of "Othello," of "Macbeth," of "King Lear," and of all, or nearly all, the Greek and Roman plays.

We learn little or nothing of the poet's place of residence in the city in which he first gave those great creations to the world. In the year 1596 he lived in Southwark, "near the Bear Garden," according to a statement Malone found in a paper which once belonged to Alleyn, the player, but of which no trace can now be discovered. In a subsidy roll, dated October 1st, 1598, he is assessed on property of the value of £5 in the parish of St. Helen's, Bishopsgate; but we cannot, therefore, conclude that he ever resided in that district; and most probably he did not long retain the property itself, whatever it may have been, as his name does not appear in a similar document drawn up two years afterwards. We think we may fairly assume that any establishment he maintained in London was always of an unpretending and inexpensive description, and that throughout his life, but more especially from the period of his purchase of New Place, in 1597, he did not consider the metropolis as his settled place of abode, but wished to be known as William Shakespeare, gentleman, of Stratford-upon-Avon.

The poet's daily habits during his stay in the busy centre

of English life, and the friendships which he there formed, must now be regarded as another of the unknown episodes in his history. Of his personal demeanour we learn little more than that he was a man of courteous and flowing address, and of an easy and sociable temper. It is some proof of his companionable character that he was known among his associates, in their more unrestrained moments, under the familiar name of "Will," and that in their more serious moods he was for them the "gentle" Shakespeare. No one is so much associated in our minds with his hours of social gaiety as Ben Jonson. It is very probable that the tradition which unites the names of the two dramatists may to a great extent be the result less of any reliable evidence, than of that general reputation for wit and humour which is common to them both; but it is hardly conceivable that the following lively account of their "wit combats," given by Fuller in his "Worthies," which was published in 1662, should be wholly unfounded:—

> Many were the wit combats betwixt him and Ben Jonson, which two I behold like a Spanish great galleon and an English man-of-war; Master Jonson, like the former, was built far higher in learning: solid but slow in his performances. Shakespeare, with the English man-of-war, lesser in bulk but lighter in sailing, could turn with all tides, tack about and take advantage of all winds, by the quickness of his wit and invention.*

It is commonly supposed that those verbal encounters took place at the Mermaid Club, in Bread Street; but we have no direct proof that Shakespeare was ever a member of that social circle, although it seems very unlikely that his name was not enrolled in its brilliant ranks.

The personal appearance itself of the poet seems almost wholly to elude our curiosity. Davies, of Hereford, in his "Microcosmos," published in 1603, commends in Shakespeare and Burbadge, their—

"Wit, courage, good shape, good parts, and all good."

---

* We give a notice of Shakespeare and Ben Jonson in Appendix, Note 7.

Aubrey says that Shakespeare was a "handsome, well-shaped man." These words proceed from no high authority; and yet they are the only distinct tradition that has reached us with respect to the form which once enclosed this potent spirit.

There are a few passages in the Sonnets which have naturally given rise to a suspicion that Shakespeare, like more than one of our great modern poets, laboured under the physical defect of lameness:—

"As a decrepit father takes delight
To see his active child do deeds of youth,
So I, made lame by fortune's dearest spite,
Take all my comfort of thy worth and truth;
For whether beauty, birth, or wealth, or wit,
Or any of these all, or all, or more,
Entitled in thy parts do crowned sit,
I make my love engrafted to this store:
So then I am not lame, poor, nor despis'd,
Whilst that this shadow doth such substance give," &c.
Sonnet xxxvii.

"Say that thou didst forsake me for some fault,
And I will comment upon that offence:
Speak of my lameness, and I straight will halt;
Against thy reasons making no defence," &c.
Sonnet lxxxix.

This language is throughout so vague and so figurative that we do not think we should be justified in giving to any portion of it a literal interpretation. The "lameness" in the eighty-ninth Sonnet seems even to be treated as purely imaginary, and only to be accepted as a reality because anything might be accepted from the friend whom he addressed.

We cannot place much confidence in the fidelity of either of the only two likenesses of the poet which we can feel at all certain have descended to us from his own time. Ben Jonson, in his verses attached to the engraving in the Folio of 1623, bears decided testimony to its accuracy; but he, perhaps, wrote from his own fancy; and the mode in which the work is executed compels us to doubt the power of the artist to catch the light lines, and fix the expression, of any face. The Stratford bust seems to us to be singularly deficient in spirituality. We learn, upon the authority of Dugdale, writing in 1653, that it was executed by "Gerard Johnson," who was a distinguished sculptor of that period; but we do not know whether the artist had any authentic likeness of his original to guide his hand.

Shakespeare in his private life was, most probably, no very rigid moralist. Such a character would be hardly compatible with all that we know of his personal history, or with the general tenour of his writings. Two petty scandals are among the traditions which attach to his memory; and it is, of course, possible that they may have had some partial foundation in reality.*

---

* One of those stories was first mentioned by Aubrey, and was afterwards told, with additions, by Oldys. The purport of it is, that Shakespeare, in his many journeys between London and Oxford, was accustomed to put up at the Crown Inn, in the city of Oxford; that he there easily won the favour of Mrs. Davenant, the wife of the host, a beautiful and clever, but light and frivolous, woman; and that Sir William Davenant, her son, had afterwards no objection to have it supposed that Shakespeare was his father. The second of those stories rests wholly on the following entry in the Diary of a member of the Middle Temple, named John Manningham, which now forms a portion of the Harleian Manuscripts in the British Museum:— "March 13, 1601-2. Upon a time when Burbadge played Richard III., there was a citizen grew so far in liking with him, that before she went from the play, she appointed him to come that night to her by the name of Richard III. Shakespeare, overhearing their conclusion, went before, was entertained, and at his game ere Burbadge came. Then, message being brought that Richard III. was at the door, Shakespeare caused return to be made, that William the Conqueror was before Richard III., Shakespeare's name William. Mr. Tooley." This "Mr. Tooley" or "Touse" as some persons think the manuscript ought to be read, is no doubt meant for the name of Manningham's informant; and a Nicholas Tooley was one of the Lord Chamberlain's company of players. The whole passage looks so like a mere "good story," that we do not think it at all probable that it is a true one.

Shakespeare, it is absolutely certain, spent the last few years of his life at Stratford-upon-Avon. A variety, and a perfect concurrence, of testimony leave no room for doubt upon that point. But we have no means whatever of ascertaining the precise period of his complete removal from London. The final departure of the great dramatist from the principal scene of his wonderful achievements was, apparently, as unostentatious and as unnoticed as the arrival there of the obscure and needy young man who was to win by the labour of a few years the greatest name in literature. It is very likely that for some time before his death he ceased to have any personal interest in the fortunes of his former fellow-actors. We have no reason to suppose that he suffered any loss by the burning of the Globe Theatre in the year 1613; and no mention is made of any theatrical property in his will. His income at Stratford, from land, houses, and tithes, is computed to have amounted to between £200 and £300 a year, which would then have been nearly equivalent to between £1,000 and £1,500 of our money. If he still felt—which seems very doubtful—any strong interest in theatrical pursuits, he must have found himself, in his retreat, surrounded by a somewhat uncongenial society. On the 17th of December, 1602, the Corporation of Stratford passed a resolution to the effect that "no play or interlude should be performed in the Chamber, the Guildhall, nor in any other part of the House or Court, from henceforth, under pain that whatever bailiff, alderman, or burgess, should give leave or licence thereunto, should forfeit, for every offence, ten shillings;" and the threat of this penalty not having been attended, as it appears, with the desired effect, the fine which a disobedience of the order was to entail, was raised in the year 1612 from 10s. to £10.[*]

---

[*] We find in the records of 1622, a still more curious proof of the growth of the puritanical spirit among the corporate authorities at Stratford. In that year the King's Players were paid for *not* playing in the hall. The sum allowed them on this account was 6s.—*Malone's Shakespeare, by Boswell*, vol. ii., page 153.

We meet with no indication that Shakespeare himself ever took any part in the management of any public office or business of any kind. From one of the recently published Calendars of State Papers, it appears that in a " Certificate of the names and arms of trained soldiers within the hundred of Barlichway, county Warwick," dated September 23rd, 1605, " William Shakespere " was returned in the list of soldiers of the town of Rowington; and it has been supposed that it is the name of our great dramatist which figures in this entry. But that supposition, from the distance which separates Stratford from Rowington, is, on the face of it, extremely improbable, and we believe we can, upon very distinct evidence, find in this soldier or militia-man another William Shakespeare.*

The silence which followed the poet's footsteps throughout a busy and a glorious career, in the centre of a great city, was

---

* Rowington, which is little more than a village, is fourteen or fifteen miles from Stratford, and between them lies the county town of Warwick. Mr. Halliwell, in his "Life of Shakespeare" (p. 4, ed. 1848), tells us that Rowington was one of the head-quarters of the Shakespeare race; and he then adds, in a note:—" A MS. copy of the customs of the manor, dated 1614, exhibits a William Shakespeare as one of the jury at that period." Mr. Collier, in page 40, of the " Life of Shakespeare," which he has prefixed to his edition of the poet's works, (1858), seems to afford us a further light in this matter, and to make us actually acquainted with the names of the father, of the brothers, of the sister, and of the mother of this William Shakespeare, of Rowington:—" Respecting the Shakespeares of Rowington, we have some additional information, which proves that there was a Richard Shakespeare resident there before 1591. On the 6th of September in that year he made his will, which was proved in the court of the Bishop of Worcester, on the 31st of March, 1592; and from it we learn that his youngest son was William, and that he had other sons, of the names of John, Roger, and Thomas, and a daughter Dorothey, married to a person of the name of Jenkes: the Christian name of his wife was Johane or Joan." With such facts as these before us, it is manifest that we need not go from Rowington to Stratford in search of the armed and trained William Shakespeare, of the year 1605.

naturally not interrupted amidst the unlettered ease and obscurity of a remote country town. A small jest is the only record which tradition pretends to have preserved of his relations with the world around him during the closing years of his life at Stratford.*

In the year 1614 we obtain a further glimpse of the active life of Shakespeare; and here again it is as an earnest man of business, and not as the great poet to whom our thoughts are for ever reverting, that we are made aware of his presence. In the course of that year William Combe and a number of other persons sought to enclose a portion of the common land in the neighbourhood of Stratford. The Corporation opposed the scheme, and Shakespeare, whose property, purchased in the year 1602 of the Combes, as well as the tithe property which he purchased in 1605, would thus, as he thought, have been injuriously affected, joined them in this opposition. In the month of November their clerk, Thomas Greene, who appears to have been in some way related to Shakespeare, was in London transacting their business; and among some memoranda which he then wrote of his proceedings, we have the following entry:—

1614. Jovis, 17 No. My cousin Shakespeare coming yesterday to town, I went to see him how he did. He told me that they assured him they meant to inclose no further than to Gospell Bush, and so up

---

* The story was first told by Rowe, and is to this effect:—An old gentleman named Combe, noted for his wealth and his usury, asked Shakespeare what epitaph he would write upon him, in the event of his surviving him; and the poet at once gave him these verses:—

"*Ten in the hundred* lies here ingraved;
'Tis a hundred to ten his soul is not saved.
If any man asks, 'Who lies in this tomb?'
'Oh! ho!' quoth the devil, ''tis my John-a-Combe.'"

Rowe adds that "the sharpness of the satire is said to have stung the man so severely that he never forgave it." But this addition to the story seems to deserve little credit. The jest does not appear to overstep the ordinary limits of social humour; and we know that Combe remembered Shakespeare in his will by making him a present of £5.

straight (leaving out part of the Dingles to the field) to the gate in Clopton hedge, and take in Salisbury's piece; and that they mean in April to survey the land, and then to give satisfaction, and not before; and he and Mr. Hall say they think there will be nothing done at all.

Greene appears to have returned to Stratford about a fortnight afterwards. He continued there the writing of his notes, and we find from them that the Corporation addressed a letter to a gentleman of the name of "Manyring," or Mainwaring, Lord Ellesmere's domestic auditor, and another to Shakespeare, who must, therefore, have still been staying in London. The first of those two communications has been preserved, but we have now no trace of the letter to Shakespeare.

We possess, however, another piece of evidence which shows, in a curious way, the anxiety which he continued to feel about this threatened encroachment upon his property. Greene makes this further entry, under the date of the 1st of September, without giving the year; but we can have no doubt that he must have been writing in 1615:—

Mr. Shakespeare told Mr. J. Greene that he was not able to bear the enclosing of Melcombe.

The poet did not live long enough to obtain the desired release from this petty trouble. The point in dispute was not decided until the year 1618, or two years after his death, when an order was issued by the Privy Council prohibiting the proposed enclosures.

In the Stratford records we have the following curious entry among the Chamberlain's accounts for the year 1614:—

Item, for one quart of sack and one quart of claret wine, given to a preacher at the New Place, xx. d.

This "New Place" is supposed by the commentators to be Shakespeare's house, and that is, no doubt, the most obvious interpretation of the passage; but, at the same time, we think it possible that it relates to the chapel of the Holy Cross, which immediately adjoins the Guildhall, as well as the poet's place of residence. We should not be surprised if the open space in front of those different buildings was known by the name of "New Place," although we can adduce no evidence to support that conjecture.

We find no notice whatever of Shakespeare during the year 1615, beyond the entry made by Greene, which we have already copied. On the 10th of February, 1616, his daughter Judith was married to Thomas Quiney, a vintner at Stratford, and son of the Richard Quiney who addressed the application to his fellow-townsman for the loan of £30, in the year 1598.

We have already seen that the father and the mother of the greatest of our poets were unable to write their names. That circumstance was not by any means one of a very extraordinary character. But we cannot help feeling some surprise at finding that his own daughter, Judith, when required to sign a deed, which is still extant, had to attach to it her mark. Her sister, Mrs. Hall, must, for some reason or another, have received the advantage of a better education, and she wrote, as appears from her signature, a good hand.

On the 25th of March, 1616, Shakespeare signed his will. It was drawn up on the 25th of the January preceding, and the necessary change was afterwards made in the name of the month. It is very probable that it was framed with a special reference to the approaching marriage of his daughter, as it contains a number of provisions which appear to have been introduced in the expectation of that event. He is there described as in "perfect health and memory;" and so he was, perhaps, at the time the document was actually written; but the three signatures of his name seem to indicate that they must have been traced by an invalid. The end, at all events, was now at hand. On the 23rd of April, 1616, just as he had completed the fifty-second year of his age, the great poet passed from the scene on which his genius had shed so astonishing a light.

The only evidence of any kind that has reached us with

respect to Shakespeare's last illness is the following sentence in a manuscript of the Rev. John Ward, who was appointed Vicar of Stratford in 1662:—

> Shakespeare, Drayton, and Ben Jonson, had a merry meeting, and, it seems, drank too hard, for Shakespeare died of a fever there contracted.

According to a note at the end of Ward's manuscript, "this book was begun February 14th, 1661–2, and finished April the 25th, 1663, at Mr. Brooks's house in Stratford-upon-Avon, in Warwickshire." * Ward must, unquestionably, have had very rare opportunities of obtaining correct information with respect, at all events, to what had been commonly supposed to have been the cause of the poet's death at the time when that event had taken place. Judith Quiney, Shakespeare's daughter, died in Stratford only a few days before the writing of those notes was begun; and there must still, of course, have been several people in the town to whom the poet had been personally known. It may be, no doubt, that the popular rumour had been from the commencement exaggerated, and, to a great extent, erroneous; but it appears not unlikely that there had been some social meeting of the kind to which Ward refers; and, however that may be, we think it extremely probable that Shakespeare died of a fever. Ward's informants could hardly have been mistaken upon such a point; and this was a malady which could not have been uncommon in so uncleanly a town as we know that Stratford must have been at that period.†

Dr. John Hall, who, we may feel assured, attended the death-bed of his father-in-law, has left manuscript notes of

---

* The whole passage from Ward's manuscript relating to Shakespeare is given in Appendix, Note 6.

† Garrick, who visited Stratford in 1769, describes it as "the most dirty, unseemly, ill-paved, wretched-looking town in all Britain." But Stratford no longer deserves this unenviable distinction. It now presents as cheerful and healthy an appearance as any town of its class.

remarkable cases which came under his observation in the course of his professional practice; but the curious in Shakespearian lore are here pursued by their usual ill-luck; those notes do not begin until the year 1617, the year immediately following the poet's death.

There is another singular tradition with respect to the closing scene of this wonderful life. "He died a Papist," says the Rev. Richard Davies, rector of Sapperton, in Gloucestershire, whose own death took place in the year 1708. This is one of the many statements relating to Shakespeare which only serve to perplex inquirers at the present day, and from which we can draw no kind of positive conclusion. Davies may have had access to sources of good information respecting Shakespeare. He communicates his intelligence in the most unhesitating form; and we have not the slightest reason to suspect his personal truthfulness. But, on the other hand, the whole tenour of Shakespeare's history leads us to infer that he and his family conformed to the established religion of the country. His children were, no doubt, baptised in the parish church; and no solitary tradition can outweigh the testimony of such apparently unmistakable facts.

On the 25th of April, 1616, two days after the poet's death, his remains were interred in the chancel of Stratford Church. Over them has been placed a flat stone, bearing the following inscription :—

> "Good frend for Jesus sake forbeare,
> To digg the dust encloased heare :
> Bleste be the man that spares thes stones,
> And curst be he that moves my bones."

The old parish clerk with whom Dowdall was in communication in the year 1693, stated that this epitaph was written by Shakespeare himself, "a little before his death." He is, however, by no means, a decisive authority upon such a subject. The lines certainly afford no indication of Shakespeare's genius; but we do not, therefore, feel absolutely certain that they did not proceed from his hand. At all events, the injunction which they so emphatically convey has hitherto been, and will, no doubt, for ever continue to be, scrupulously obeyed. Undisturbed and unseen, he " sleeps well " through the long night of time.

In the north wall of the chancel of Stratford Church a monument is erected to the poet's memory. It consists of a half-length figure, in which he is represented with a cushion before him, and a pen in his right hand, while his left rests upon a scroll. It must have been erected before 1623, as a reference is made to it by Leonard Digges, in some verses prefixed to the edition of the plays published in that year.*

Beneath this memorial the following inscriptions are engraved :—
"Judicio Pylium, genio Socratem, arto Maronem,
Terra tegit, populus mæret, Olympus habet."

"Stay Passenger, why goest thou by so fast?
Read if thou canst, whom envious Death hath plast,
Within this monument Shakspeare with whome
Quick nature dide: whose name doth deck this Tombe
Far more then cost: sieh† all, that He hath writt,
Leaves living art, but page, to serve his witt.
                        Obiit anô do¹ 1616
                        Ætatis, 53. die 23 Ap."

The only near relatives of Shakespeare, as far as we can now learn, who survived him, were his wife ; his daughter Susanna, who was married to Dr. John Hall; his grand-daughter, Elizabeth Hall; his daughter Judith, who was married to Thomas Quiney; and his sister Joan, who married a hatter in Stratford, named William Hart.

---

* The bust of the poet was originally coloured, in imitation, we may assume, of nature. The eyes were light hazel ; the hair and beard auburn ; and the different articles of the dress were also painted. The colouring was renewed in 1749. Malone caused the whole work to be covered over with white paint in 1793; but it has been re-painted within the last few years, and it bears now, no doubt, the same appearance which it bore at the period of its first erection.

† For sith, or since.

The poet's wife died on the 6th of August, and was buried on the 8th of the same month, in the year 1623. The bequest which he makes to her in his will, of his "second-best bed," is one of the many small circumstances in his history which at once attract our notice, but of which we have no real explanation to offer, and which, very probably, have no important meaning of any kind. We know that she was entitled, by law, to a jointure, and that it was not, therefore, necessary he should have made any express provision for her maintenance.

Dr. Hall died on the 25th of November, 1635, and Mrs. Hall on the 11th of July, 1649. Their only child, Elizabeth, was married, first, in 1626, to Thomas Nash, who died in 1647, without issue; and, secondly, in 1649, to John (afterwards Sir John) Barnard, of Abingdon, in the county of Northampton, by whom, also, she had no family. She herself died in the year 1670, and with her was extinguished the lineal descent from Shakespeare.

Judith Quiney, the poet's second daughter, had three sons, all of whom she lost in their infancy or their early youth, while her own life was prolonged until the commencement of the month of February,* 1661-2.

Joan Hart, the only child of John and Mary Shakespeare, who appears to have survived their eldest son, William, died in the month of November, 1646. She had several children, and there were, not many years since, descendants of hers at Stratford, where they lived in very humble and even indigent circumstances.

The above brief statement sums up all the fortunes of the family for which the great poet had once so earnestly laboured, and for whose continued worldly prosperity he had, by the last act of his life, most carefully provided. But "all flesh is grass," and glory is but an idle name. His freehold estates, which he devised in the first instance to his eldest daughter, were strictly entailed; but the entail was afterwards barred, and the property passed into the hands of strangers.

---

* She was buried on the 9th of that month.

SHAKESPEARE'S CHARACTER.

> "We are such stuff
> As dreams are made of, and our little life
> Is rounded with a sleep."
> THE TEMPEST, *Act IV., Scene I.*

ANY minute account of the life of Shakespeare must form a source of perpetual disappointment and perplexity to the ordinary reader of Shakespeare's works. There exists, at first sight, no conceivable relation between the insignificance of these petty details and the magnitude of the intellectual achievements which this name represents. We are persuaded, however, that if we will only carefully examine all the evidence which is easily accessible, and if we will frankly accept the conclusions to which it obviously leads, we shall find, after all, that in the poet's whole history, amidst many strange complexities, a self-consistent and an intelligible nature stands revealed.

We have no wish whatever to deny the singular incompleteness of our Shakespearian information. We readily admit that a special infelicity here perpetually irritates and disappoints our curiosity. The poet lived in a busy but an uncritical age. Our civil convulsions, and the ascendency of the puritanical spirit during a large portion of the lifetime of the two or three generations which immediately followed, left them but little time or inclination to collect the light threads of literary biography, and, above all, of the biography of a writer for the stage. The limitation of his family to the female line, and its early extinction, prevented the existence of any certain centre round which the traditions of his life might have gathered. The most destructive of natural agencies, too, may have contributed to throw into deeper shadow this wonderful figure; and it is now impossible for us to say what memorials of Shakespeare we may have lost through the destruction of the Globe Theatre by fire in the year 1613, of Ben Jonson's house some seven or eight years later, and of a large portion of the city of London itself in the year 1666.

But the main cause of the scantiness of the evidence in this case remains still, we believe, to be told. That cause, we have no hesitation in stating, must have been the absence of any very marked incidents in the poet's career, and of any very imposing personality in the poet himself. We have learned so many petty details of his history that we feel persuaded we should have heard something of its greater events, if there had been in it any really great events to be made known.

We are confirmed in this conviction by the uniform result of a variety of testimonies. The evidence which helps to guide us to a general knowledge of the life and character of Shakespeare, in spite of many unexpected interruptions in its links, is far more diverse and more reliable than we usually allow ourselves to believe. We are acquainted with a number of the facts themselves in his career; we find many allusions made to him in the works of contemporary authors; we have before us his own writings, all instinct with thought and passion, all coloured with the splendour of the most striking and the most original genius; and it would require nothing less than the suspension of a general law of nature to prevent all those manifestations of a vital energy from largely reflecting the central living principle from which they flowed.

The personal history of the poet, as far as it is known to us, will admit of but one general interpretation. It all leads us to see in him a man of easy temper, intent on securing the advantages of worldly independence; entirely free from any love of personal display; astonishingly indifferent to the fate of the creations of his genius. The impression formed of him by his contemporaries readily harmonises with this character. They approach him, they see him, they converse with him, and they evidently leave him unimpressed with any feeling of special wonder.

We have already quoted a few of the references made to him by the writers of his own generation; but there is, necessarily, a special interest, as well as a special certainty, in any revelations of character which are the result of direct personal communication; and we are, naturally, more than usually anxious to concentrate the feeble but steady light which thus gleams for us, from a distant age, over the strange and shadowy form of William Shakespeare.

In seeking to collect those scanty records we meet, at the very outset, one of those petty doubts and controversies which seem inseparable from every attempt to seize and measure this Protean figure. The earliest contemporary notice of the dramatic labours of Shakespeare proceeded, as many of the commentators are disposed to believe, from the most splendid and romantic poet that had yet risen in England; and we should all naturally feel that this would have been the most fitting tribute that could have been paid to a still imperfectly developed and unrecognised genius. But, on an impartial examination of the evidence, we are driven to the conclusion that we cannot safely indulge in this vision. In Spenser's "Tears of the Muses," a poem published in the year 1591, we find *Thalia*, or the Muse of Comedy, thus lamenting the decay of her art in England:—

> "And he, the man whom Nature's self had made
> To mock herself, and Truth to imitate
> With kindly counter under mimic shade,
> Our pleasant Willy, ah! is dead of late:
> With whom all joy and jolly merriment
> Is also deaded, and in dolour drent.*

---

* Drenched.

> " Instead thereof, scoffing Scurrility,
>   And scornful Folly, with contempt, is crept,
> Rolling in rhymes of shameless ribaudry
>   Without regard or due decorum kept;
> Each idle wit at will presumes to make,
>   And doth the learned's task upon him take.
>
> " But that same gentle Spirit, from whose pen
>   Large streams of honey and sweet nectar flow,
> Scorning the boldness of such base-born men,
>   Which dare their follies forth so rashly throw,
> Doth rather choose to sit in idle cell,
>   Than so himself to mockery to sell."

The very first words in these lines—" the man whom Nature's self had made to mock herself "—supply one of the most appropriate images ever given of the distinguishing qualities of Shakespeare's genius; they now seem to us to form, at the same time, too magnificent a eulogy for any other poet of his age; and we cannot wonder that any one who was not conversant with the details of the literary history of that period should at once and unhesitatingly have believed that it was to him only they must have been applied. This was the conclusion at which Dryden had arrived, and it had also been for a time adopted by Rowe; but this latter writer expunged from a second edition of his Life of the poet the passage in the first one in which he had expressed this opinion; and we may therefore fairly suppose that he had in the interval found some reason to doubt its correctness. The modern commentators are divided upon the point. Malone entered into an elaborate argument for the purpose of showing that Spenser was referring in those verses to John Lily, who was undoubtedly looked upon at that time as one of the most graceful and the most accomplished of English dramatic writers. Other critics think it more probable that the lines were meant for Sir Philip Sidney, who is known to have been the author of some masks. The introduction of the name of " Willy," affords no certain reason for rejecting either of these conjectures, for we find that this word was employed in Spenser's day as a sort of conventional designation for a poet, and it was certainly applied to Sidney, in a copy of verses by another writer.

The more eager admirers of the two great Elizabethan poets still hold by the belief that Spenser here celebrates the genius of the greatest of his contemporaries; but the modern critics generally do not adopt that conclusion; and there are many strong grounds for questioning its accuracy.

The " Tears of the Muses " form portion of a volume which the publisher states is made up of divers productions of Spenser's, " embezzled and purloined " from him " since his departure over sea." The composition of the poem we are now considering is thus thrown back to some distant and unknown period ; and it cannot, in any case, be supposed to have been written before the end of the year 1590, or the very commencement of the year 1591. The tendency of all the evidence which has reached us in reference to Shakespeare's first connection with the stage leads us to think that he had not written anything previously to that period which gave any decisive proof, or even any certain promise, of the supremacy of his dramatic genius. But the language of Spenser carries us still further back, and naturally implies that the writer to whom he is referring had distinguished himself in the composition of comedy at some period more or less remote ; and that he had subsequently withdrawn in disgust from a profession on which a mass of impure productions had brought down a merited disgrace. He was, it seems, too, an accomplished scholar, capable, probably, of undertaking the " learned's task," and his place of retirement was some " cell," which, as Malone observes, it is not unfair to suppose must have been an academic or some other learned retreat. Shakespeare can hardly be said to come within the limits of any one of these allusions ; and it seems utterly incredible that, in consequence of some shock given to his moral sensibility by the excesses of other writers, he had renounced—though for ever so brief a period—in the luxuriant vigour of early manhood, a profession in which he must already have found so welcome a profit, and in which he had just began to feel his way to the mastery of his own powers. Those critics who adopt this very extravagant conclusion probably forget that the three or four years which immediately preceded the year 1591 formed the very period of the rise of the new and improved English drama, and that nearly all its more remarkable writers seem to have avoided any grossness of language more carefully than Shakespeare himself.

In another poem of Spenser's—" Colin Clout's come Home again "—which appears to have been written during the year 1594, we find the following passage:—

> " And there, though last not least, is Ætion;
> A gentler shepherd may nowhere be found;
> Whose Muse, full of high thoughts' invention,
> Doth, like himself, heroically sound."

We think it very probable that these lines refer to Shakespeare. They are portion of a long passage written in praise of a number of the author's literary contemporaries, most of whom are more or less disguised under that veil of allegory which was Spenser's favourite form for the exercise of his luxuriant fancy. It is not likely that we can be mistaken in applying the closing line to the sound of Shakespeare's name. The " gentler shepherd," too, seems to help us to identify him. The whole passage, indeed, is in perfect harmony with all the contemporary allusions to our great dramatist. It is pitched in a much lower tone than the lofty eulogy on the " Willy " of the previous poem; but we are not, on that account, at all the less disposed to accept him as the subject of this more temperate commendation.

We have, perhaps, dwelt at excessive length upon a literary problem which involves no important practical issue; but it may be, too, that many of our readers will feel that they could hardly hear too much of an episode which enables us perhaps to connect, through the ties of a direct personal recognition, the great names of Edmund Spenser and William Shakespeare.

All the remaining contemporary notices of our great dramatist may be disposed of in a much more summary form. Richard Barnfield, in a copy of verses entitled, "A Remembrance of some English Poets," inserted in a work of his, published in 1598, refers as follows to Shakespeare:—

> " And Shakespeare, thou, whose honey-flowing vein
> (Pleasing the world) thy praises doth obtain;
> Whose ' Venus,' and whose ' Lucrece ' (sweet and chaste),
> Thy name in Fame's immortal book have plac'd;
> Live ever you, at least in fame live ever;
> Well may the body die, but Fame dies never."

Among the " Epigrams " of Weever, published in 1599, but which appear to have been written at a somewhat earlier period, we find the following strange lines addressed to Shakespeare:—

> "AD GULIELMUM SHAKESPEARE.
>
> " Honey-tongued Shakespeare, when I saw thine issue,
> I swore Apollo got them, and none other;
> Their rosy-tainted features clothed in tissue,
> Some heaven-born goddess said to be their mother:
> Rose-cheek'd Adonis, with his amber tresses,
> Fair, fire-hot Venus charming him to love her,
> Chaste Lucretia, virgin-like her dresses,
> Proud lust-stung Tarquin seeking still to prove her;
> Romeo, Richard, more whose names I know not;
> Their sugred tongues and power—attractive beauty
> Say they are saints, although that saints they show not,
> For thousand vows* to them subjective duty.
> They burn in love, thy children, Shakespeare, let them:
> Go, woo thy Muse; more nymphish brood beget them."

We have already given the important extract from the " Palladis Tamia," in which Meres mentions a number of Shakespeare's productions, and (page 47) Chettle's appeal to him to offer some poetical tribute to the memory of Queen

---

* (?) Thousands vow.

Elizabeth. In a work entitled "Microcosmos," published in 1603, John Davies, of Hereford, thus alludes to Shakespeare and Burbadge, as we can have no doubt, although he only gives the initials of their names:—

> "Players, I love ye, and your quality,
>   As ye are men that pass-time not abus'd;
> And some [W. S., R. B.] I love for painting, poesy,
>   And say fell Fortune cannot be excus'd,
> That hath for better uses you refus'd;
>   Wit, courage, good shape, good parts, and all good,
> As long as all these goods are no worse us'd;
>   And though the stage doth stain pure, gentle blood,
>   Yet generous ye are in mind and mood."

The same rude rhymer, in his "Humours," &c., published in 1605, speaking of the followers of Fortune, again pays a compliment to Shakespeare and his fellow-actor:—

> "Some followed her by acting all men's parts:
>   Those on a stage she rais'd (in scorn) to fall,
> And made them mirrors, by their acting arts,
>   Wherein men saw their faults, though ne'er so small:
> Yet some [W. S., R. B.] she guerdon'd not to their desarts;
>   But othersome were but ill-action all,
> Who, while they acted ill, ill stayed behind,
> By custom of their manners, in their mind."

Another reference made by Davies to Shakespeare will be found quoted in page 49.

In a work entitled the "Return from Parnassus," published in 1606, but which appears to have been written about the end of the year 1602, we find this strange estimate of the value of Shakespeare's labours down to that period:—

> "Who loves Adonis' love or Lucrece' rape,
>   His sweeter verse contains heart-throbbing strife,
>   Could but a graver subject him content,
>   Without love's foolish, lazy languishment."

Gabriel Harvey, a friend of Spenser's, made the following entry (early, no doubt, in the seventeenth century), in one of his books:—

The younger sort take much delight in Shakespeare's "Venus and Adonis;" but his "Lucrece" and his tragedy of "Hamlet, Prince of Denmark," have it in them to please the wiser sort.

In a poem entitled "The Ghost of Richard III.," written by " C. B." (supposed to be Christopher Brooke), and published in 1614, Richard is made to utter the following lines :—

> "To him that imp'd my fame with Clio's quill,
> Whose magic raised me from oblivion's den,
> That writ my story on the Muses' hill,
> And with my actions dignified his pen;
> He that from Helicon sends many a rill,
> Whose nectared veins are drunk by thirsty men;
> Crown'd be his style with fame, his head with bays,
> And none detract, but gratulate his praise."

These are, we believe, as far as can now be learned, nearly the whole of the direct literary tributes, exclusive of mere incidental allusions, paid to the genius of our great dramatist in his lifetime; and the style in which nearly all of them are written leaves us no room for regretting that they were not further multiplied.

We now pass to a notice of Shakespeare from one of the most vigorous writers of his age, and one by whom he must have been known familiarly. In Ben Jonson's " Timber; or, Discoveries," a sort of common place book, consisting of a series of his detached thoughts and observations, we find the following most interesting passage :—

> I remember the players have often mentioned it as an honour to Shakespeare, that in his writing (whatsoever he penned) he never blotted out a line. My answer hath been, Would he had blotted a thousand! Which they thought a malevolent speech. I had not told posterity this, but for their ignorance, who chose that circumstance to commend their friend by, wherein he most faulted; and to justify mine owne candour, for I loved the man, and do honour his memory, (on this side idolatry), as much as any. He was (indeed) honest, and of an open and free nature; had an excellent phantasy, brave notions, and gentle expressions, wherein he flowed with that facility that

sometimes it was necessary he should be stopped: *Sufflaminandus erat*, as Augustus said of Haterius. His wit was in his own power; would the rule of it had been so too! Many times he fell into those things could not escape laughter; as when he said, in the person of Cæsar, one speaking to him, "Cæsar, thou dost me wrong." He replied, "Cæsar did never wrong but with just cause," and such like; which were ridiculous. But he redeemed his vices with his virtues. There was ever more in him to be praised than to be pardoned.

Jonson has often been accused of a malignant jealousy of his astonishing contemporary. But the charge is not, we think, sustained, in any large sense, by the evidence. There can be no doubt that, even more than the other writers of his age, he overrated the value of that classical learning in which Shakespeare was so deficient, and in which he himself so much excelled. But we have ample proof that his vigorous, incisive intellect enabled him, to some extent, to apprehend the matchless resources of Shakespeare's fancy, and that his rugged, impetuous temper yielded more or less freely to the fascination of the facile, unostentatious grace of Shakespeare's character. In the extract we have just quoted he tells us, with a vehemence in the sincerity of which we are all the more disposed to believe from the frankness with which he enunciates critical judgments from which we must in some degree dissent, that "he loved the man, and honoured his memory on this side of idolatry, as much as any" one. The commendatory verses which he wrote for the folio of 1623 contain a still more enthusiastic acknowledgment of the splendid powers of his "beloved" friend and companion.

"Soul of the age,
Th' applause, delight, the wonder of our stage.
* * * *
And tell how far thou didst our Lily outshine,
Or sporting Kyd, or Marlowe's mighty line:
And though thou hadst small Latin and less Greek.
* * * *
Triumph, my Britain! thou hast one to show,
To whom all scenes of Europe homage owe.
He was not of an age, but for all time.
* * * *

Shine forth, thou star of poets, and with rage,
Or influence, chide or cheer the drooping stage."

Jonson, it will be seen, makes a special reference to the facility with which Shakespeare wrote, and to the absence of any corrections in his manuscripts; and we find a very remarkable testimony to the same effect in the address prefixed to the folio of 1623, by the poet's fellow actors, Heminge and Condell:—

Who, as he was a happy imitator of nature, was a most gentle expresser of it. His mind and hand went together. And what he thought he uttered with that easiness, that we have scarce received from him a blot in his papers.

We meet with another personal allusion to the poet in the statement made by these, his first editors, that they had undertaken their task "only to keep the memory of so worthy a friend and fellow alive, as was our Shakespeare."

All these writers, it is manifest, approached the great dramatist without any extraordinary sentiment of personal veneration. For the greater number of them he was merely a man of gentle address and character, who had written some fine plays, and two, at least, equally fine poems. There was nothing else about him that was specially noticeable. He was never "gazed on like a comet." They never dreamed of him as the paragon of nature. No suspicion ever crossed their minds of the breathless interest with which countless millions in distant ages would have followed the slightest movement of that unpretending figure—would have caught the faintest echo of that low voice. It is true that, for the most part, these men fill no high place in literature. But we may feel assured that they reflect faithfully enough the general feeling of the poet's companions; and Jonson himself, although he could, to no inconsiderable extent, appreciate the astonishing excellence of the dramas which he helped to bring under the notice of the world, was unable to see behind this prodigious work any prodigious workman. We must also remember that many of

Shakespeare's greatest contemporaries appear never to have had their attention directed in any marked manner to his writings, or even to his very existence. His name is never mentioned in the voluminous works of Lord Bacon. There is one conclusion clearly deducible from this slight notice, or this complete silence. Shakespeare mixed noiselessly and unobtrusively with the world around him. He was animated by no visible and striking energy of purpose; he had no firm, commanding originality of character; he pressed himself on no man's admiration. We feel convinced that the slightness of his personality served in no small degree to veil from his contemporaries the splendour of his genius.

But, after all, Shakespeare's inmost nature will, in all probability, be best revealed in his writings. Here we have the great advantage of being able to survey him from a variety of aspects; and we may in some sense find the poems and the sonnets even more instructive than the dramas, inasmuch as in them he addresses the world more immediately in his own personal character.

The poems—namely, the "Venus and Adonis," the "Lucrece," and the "Lover's Complaint," but more especially the two first of these compositions—were regarded by many of Shakespeare's own companions as his best and most distinguishing works; and it is not impossible that he was himself not much disposed to dispute this judgment. They were published at his own desire, and we take it for granted that they were the only productions of his that in their passage through the press received the advantage of his personal supervision. In the year 1593, at a time when many of his dramas must have been acted, he styles the "Venus and Adonis" the "first heir of his invention," believing, no doubt, that he had never before done anything to entitle him to a place in the world of letters. In the following year appeared the "Lucrece," and this work, too, he took care to place under the protection of his chief friend and patron, Lord Southampton. It is evident that productions such as these must directly reflect the special literary tastes, at all events, of their author; and in reflecting his literary tastes, they must, to some extent, disclose the general bias of his whole nature.

But the sonnets of Shakespeare are necessarily the most direct revelations which he has left us of his actual thoughts and feelings. They were not only written by him in his own character, but they were written by him directly with a view to his own gratification, for it seems certain that he had himself no connection whatever with their publication. We are aware that the great majority of modern critics incline to the belief that they were altogether, or in the main, composed by him in a purely fanciful humour. But those writers, we feel persuaded, are in a great measure led to adopt this conclusion from an unwillingness to associate with their profound admiration of Shakespeare's genius those manifestations of a weak and an erring emotional and moral nature, which nearly every page of the sonnets conveys. Our judgment is entirely free from any such influence. We not only do not find any difficulty in reconciling this extravagant impressionability with this airy imagination, but we think the existence of the one helps us to account for the existence of the other. They coalesce and they harmonise as readily and naturally as the warmth and the light of the external world.

It may be said that the attachment which the poet here displays for a male friend is at once humiliating and repulsive, and that is, no doubt, the point on which the whole of this controversy turns. The greatest imaginative genius the world has ever known prostrates himself before some obscure idol, and, in the frenzy of a tremulous devotion, renounces his self-respect, and abdicates the commonest rights of humanity. This is, no doubt, a singular, but it is by no means an impossible spectacle. No man who has had any large experience of life can doubt that such a passion is within the limits of nature; and, in a being so plastic and so emotional as Shakespeare, it found the most congenial field for its rise and its development. There is, necessarily, perhaps, in creative imagination, as in all creative power, a feminine element. It is through a yearning tenderness, through an unsatisfied want, through a vague and insatiable sensibility, that the genius of the poet is most nearly allied to the mighty forms of the world around him. We readily admit that in the sonnets of Shakespeare this restless passion is exhibited in a peculiarly exaggerated and unwelcome form. But its very extravagance renders it the more unlikely that it was chosen, without any personal reference, as a theme for the most detailed and elaborate illustration. It was neither obvious, nor inviting, nor susceptible of any very varied or very brilliant treatment; and we are very much disposed to believe that the man who, out of mere wantonness of fancy, should select such a subject for the indulgence of his literary tastes, and should then continue for years to employ it as a medium for the confession of the most painful weakness and the most brooding self-reproach, must have been reduced to a far more unaccountable and more morbid mental condition than the poet in whose airy, yielding temperament these uncontrollable irregular impulses had actually been implanted.

The dedication of the publisher tends strongly to confirm our belief in the direct personal inspiration of these compositions. The vivid or capricious fancy which, it is supposed, led Shakespeare to create an ideal hero could hardly have extended its influence to Thomas Thorpe, and prompted him to wish to this imaginary personage the immortality promised by the poet. The language of Thorpe seems to us peculiarly pointed and significant. He dedicates his volume to " the only begetter" of the sonnets; thus clearly intimating—what an examination of them most distinctly establishes—that, although some of them seem to be immediately addressed to a woman, it was another friend who was always most present to the poet's thoughts, and who throughout inspired the poet's fancy.*

---

* We have no means of knowing who was the object of Shakespeare's admiration. We place the strongest reliance on the language of Thorpe, and we believe that the unknown "Mr. W. H." was simply a gentleman, and not a nobleman whose name bore those initials. It appears to us,

We find that the sonnets as well as the poems of Shakespeare indicate throughout precisely the same imaginative and emotional tendencies; and this circumstance considerably strengthens our suspicion that we can trace in them some natural direction of the poet's own taste, and some habitual condition of his character. They are all filled with the same theme—with love—unrequited, ardent, longing, lingering, agitating, helplessly consuming love. They deal, too, with the various phases of the passion with an extravagant minuteness of detail; and, unless we are to regard them as—what we certainly do not think they can be—the mere accidental creations of a perfectly

---

too, upon the internal evidence, that the poet's friend was not a man of the very highest rank, and that they lived upon terms of much greater intimacy, and even much more nearly resembling an equality, than any that could have prevailed between Shakespeare and the Earl of Southampton, or between Shakespeare and the Earl of Pembroke. M. P. Chasles, the distinguished French critic, has recently put forward a very singular conjecture upon this subject. According to his solution of the problem, the sonnets were originally addressed by Shakespeare to the Earl of Southampton; the Earl of Pembroke ("Mr. W. H.") got possession of the collection, and inscribed it to his noble friend in the language of the dedication down to the word "wisheth;" Thorpe then appeared upon the scene, and completed this strange composition by adding to it all its remaining portion. This would, indeed, have been a most extraordinary transaction. Why should the Earl of Pembroke be introduced here at all in so very improbable a character? or why should he have disguised his name, unless the work was intended for publication? But if that was his intention, where was Shakespeare himself during the preparation for the press of a volume which was to be brought before the world under such complicated, but still illustrious, patronage? It seems somewhat remarkable, too, that M. Chasles, who believes that Thorpe would not have presumed to address the Earl of Pembroke in so apparently inoffensive a form as "Mr. W. H.," should not feel any surprise at his not only intruding himself into this partnership, but monopolising its honours, and signing the deed by which it was completed. But the whole theory hardly admits of any serious discussion; and nothing but our respect for M. Chasles' high literary reputation has induced us to bestow upon it even this passing notice.

G

disengaged fancy, we must maintain that they bear throughout the marks of a nature strangely impressionable, swayed by vague and subtle impulses, without any proud reserve, without any immovable, all-controlling self-dominion.

There is another remarkable feature in the whole of these compositions. They exhibit throughout a teeming, unchecked, more or less disordered profusion of thought and imagery in the mind of the writer. Diffusion is their most striking characteristic; and we believe that it must have formed a special element in the fancy of the poet whenever his fancy was not removed into the larger and freer life of his dramas. We trace this personal mood in a portion of the dramas themselves—in their conceits, their quibbles, and their occasional prolixities. The same quality seems to have distinguished him in his intercourse with the world; and we receive without any misgiving Jonson's statement, that the flow of his thoughts and his language was sometimes so ready and so inexhaustible that it became necessary to put upon him the drag-chain,—*sufflaminandus erat*.

The great drama of Shakespeare is another revelation of his essential nature. But it is a revelation subject to its own special conditions; and if we lose sight of the qualifications under which it is to be accepted, it may serve to perplex and to mislead, rather than to illumine and to guide, us in our researches into his personal character. Every man is necessarily, no doubt, represented to some extent in his work. It cannot exhibit any capacity which he does not in some way or other possess. All that it is he, too, is potentially. But we need not expect to find the imaginative energy of the poet embodied in his character or in his daily life. In the world of mind, as in the world of matter, nothing grows of necessity with perfect completeness and uniformity in every possible direction. Our gifts and our accomplishments may be endlessly diverse. It is not less true, however, that the human mind is for ever seeking, throughout every object in nature, for a complete growth and a perfect symmetry. This instinct too, seems founded upon an essentially just intuition, and our only error arises from the feeble impatience which prompts us to transfer to the infinitely diversified details of nature the harmony which pervades her larger or her general laws.

The obscurity which has gathered over the details of Shakespeare's life, partly from accident, and partly from its own essential conditions, has afforded his commentators an opportunity of investing his personal character with attributes proportioned to the magnitude of his genius. But, on any careful and impartial inquiry, their efforts will be found to have utterly and even signally failed. Shakespeare, we have the most direct evidence, was the greatest of poets; and upon evidence almost equally direct, and, for every reasonable purpose, equally conclusive, we believe that Shakespeare lived no great life; that he presented to the world without, no imposing, substantial image of the genius which inspired his literary labours. And there was here no real anomaly of any kind— no exception to a common condition of human existence. No circumstance, perhaps, in our life, or in the life of the beings around us, forces itself more distinctly upon our observation, as we advance in years and in knowledge, than the infinite variety of modes in which nature bestows and qualifies her gifts. Our possession of any one faculty affords no guarantee for our possession of any other, however closely or however inextricably they may seem to be related; and the power even of manifesting a particular capacity in one direction does not, by any means, necessarily imply the power of manifesting it in another where apparently no new vital energy need be brought into action. The great painter, or the great musician, is frequently a man of the most limited range of general intellectual vision; or he may be a man who has no greatness to exhibit beyond some special branch of his own art. The great writer may, in speaking, have no language in which to clothe his thoughts, or he may have no thoughts which he requires language to clothe; and the poet, or the philosopher, or the novelist, may have nothing to tell the world outside of some particular form of poetry, or philosophy, or prose fiction.

The great orator, in sitting down to write, may find his hands fettered, his inspiration chilled; or his command of vigorous and impassioned language may desert him in the absence of the audience to whom it could most suitably be addressed. There may, we believe, be yet another phenomenon in the manifestations of mind. A man of the highest and noblest impulses, of the firmest and most comprehensive intelligence, of the finest and most sensitive taste, may find no outward expression for his inward life, either in sound, or in form, or in colour, or in words.

Special genius, it has been said, will usually be found to be general intellectual power specially applied. We do not see how it is possible to accept such an axiom. The man of talent—the merely clever man—may, indeed, be able to manifest his capacity in a diversity of pursuits; and even here we must exclude from the domain of his power every art in which the main agent is the quickened and creative imagination. But the man of genius—and, above all, the man of the highest creative genius—is usually, and perhaps necessarily, a man of some special endowment, within the limits of which all his distinguishing energy is singularly confined. All the work, since the world began, that has most powerfully contributed to irradiate the forms of our mortal existence has been done by men who passed like shadows over the earth. The inventor of letters disappeared in the utter night of elder time; and, in a comparatively recent age, the inventor of printing transmitted to the race he had helped to illumine no history of his own to transcribe. Homer; the morning-star of Western civilisation, " sole-sitting by the shores of old Romance," sank in lonely splendour; and the resounding ocean murmurs to us for evermore a mere melodious name. The earnest and holy spirits that raised the Gothic minsters left in their works the only memorials of their lives. The bold or pathetic ballad poetry of England, of Scotland, or of Spain, seems to have sprung from its native soil in the popular heart with the spontaneity of wild flowers—all fresh with the first early sweetness of morning. The drama of Shakespeare was at least as distinct from the personality of its author as any other of the greatest of human achievements. It was impossible that he should, like Homer, have escaped all recognition or all record; but his ethereal essence, if not wholly unknown and unnoticed, seems to have pressed as lightly and as noiselessly as the light and the air of heaven on the thoughts and the memories of men. The ordinary conditions of individual selfishness are, perhaps, incompatible with the accomplishment of labours which transcend all the ordinary conditions of individual capacity. Genius is here but a half-unthinking instrument in the hands of Nature, in her most unreserved and most propitious hour; and it is her impalpable, unimpeded, mystic influence that alone has wrought this wondrous work.

All imaginative art is the result of a special inspiration. The artist passes into a more impassioned and a more luminous form of life. In it his soul is transfigured, as fire transmutes and etherealises the grosser elements of nature. He cannot, by any possibility, be directly identified with his work. He is necessarily outside of it, beyond it, independent of it. The quickening excitement which is the immediate instrument of his power is, perhaps, much less a sympathy with the object which he reproduces than a sympathy with the charm which the mere reproduction itself exercises over the feelings of those to whom it appeals. The statuary, or the painter, cares, in all probability, as little as ordinary men for the forms or the colours of the external world; he only values the subtle art which unveils the finest secrets of nature by the perfect imitation of the visible conditions under which her inmost life can alone subsist. The poet, too, and above all the dramatic poet, must stand apart from the passions which he evokes. He must survey from a remoter and a more commanding ground the beings whom his fancy calls into momentary life. Hamlet would perhaps have formed a more splendid figure than Shakespeare at the court of Queen Elizabeth. But

Hamlet could not have written the play of "Hamlet." The great drama could only have been the work of some one who was able to seize on all the moods and thoughts of the Danish prince, to see all that he saw, and to see it in the larger and clearer form of the thousand contrasting lights and shadows by which it was encompassed. Hamlet himself would have been too much engrossed by the contemplation of his personal wrongs and sufferings, too much intent on his own individual purposes, to have produced any work presenting the variety, the harmony, the absolute truth and completeness of creative art.

But, although the dramatist stands apart from each detail of his work, it will, in all probability, if it deals largely with the innumerable aspects of life, afford ample means of ascertaining not only his general intellectual capacity, but the general tendency of his thoughts and his feelings, the meditations with which his mind is most familiar, the images on which his fancy most willingly dwells; and we believe that the essential conditions of Shakespeare's nature, and the habitual forms of Shakespeare's life—his airy impersonality, his unobtrusive temper, his utter absence of self-assertion and self-complacency, his endless perplexity and wonder at the fretful vanity and the irremediable littleness of all mortal existence, his profound sense of the omnipotence and the enduringness of death—shine through all the great creations of his genius, as visibly as the stars shine through the azure depths of night.

That very imaginative faculty which was the talisman of his art is itself a revelation of character. He who passed so readily and so completely into the personality of others had no strong, tenacious personality of his own to maintain. We can, however, it is manifest, have no difficulty in accepting as Shakespeare's view of any of the conditions of life, the view in which it presents itself to personages in his drama who speak the language of universal nature, who are not themselves exhibiting the mere caprices of passion; and, above all, we can so accept it, if it be the unvarying expression of the thoughts and feelings of a number of his dramatic characters, acting in harmony with the ordinary intelligence of men.

We believe we can now catch many bright glimpses of the noiseless currents in which this wonderful life flowed.

How beautiful the youth of Shakespeare must have been! All nature smiles her welcome to her young adorer. The face of creation sparkles in the rapt beauty of a new-risen day; a light, as of Paradise, streams over the gliding river, the flowing outline of the purple hills, the soft verdure of earth, the bright expanse of the all-enfolding heavens. There never, perhaps, was a man of great imaginative and emotional genius who had not in boyhood some foretaste, half-solemn, all-entrancing, of the glory that awaited him; who, in the mysterious rapture of some waking-dream, did not seize the prophetic tones of a divine harmony, laden with the promise of a joy unutterable, thrilling and quickening his spirit to its inmost depths, as it floated from afar over the loving summer air. In earliest youth we have all, in momentary flashes, seen or felt our terrestrial ideal; and all the more ambitious efforts of our age are inspired by the passion to give life and form to the loveliness and the splendour of this remote, radiant image.

But human life is no mere unbroken vision of bright enchantment; and he who knows not sorrow knows but little of its deeper mysteries and its wider purposes. This further knowledge, too, soon came to Shakespeare, and helped to restore the perfect balance of his faculties. The misfortunes which in his boyhood fell upon his family rudely awoke his spirit to a sense of the darker realities of life, steadied his volatile imagination, gave to his rapid emotional sensibility the depth and intensity of a meditative wonder. His marriage, we also feel persuaded, was not a happy one. His marvellously tolerant and unexacting temper enabled him, no doubt, to conform with apparent ease to the unavoidable requirements of his condition; but the mature woman, the daughter of a small farmer, whom he had won so early and so cheaply, could hardly, by any possibility, have satisfied the quick perception and the refined taste of the great painter of female loveliness.

"Poets are all who love." Genius is largely influenced by all the circumstances by which it is surrounded. It is essentially an organism, and it is inevitably modified by all the elements which in its growth it embraces and assimilates. But it must also necessarily possess within itself all its originating vitality. We believe that the essential condition under which the genius of Shakespeare unfolded itself was a large, vague, restless love, or, perhaps we should rather say, a yearning for love. All the works which he wrote in his own character—the "Venus," the "Lucrece," and above all the Sonnets—overflow with this passion. It there becomes extravagant, and almost cloying, in its dreamy, moody repetition. Then love, quickening his faculties, drove him to look out into the universe for sympathy, and for an expression of the restless longing by which his soul was surprised; and this out-look introduced to his astonished vision the shadowiness, the fleetingness, the inevitable decay of every object of enchantment. In this meditative passion his genius expanded; he grew in its warmth; he saw all nature, large and clear, in its luminous ether. If his emotional faculties alone had been developed, he must have lost all originating power in the vain, unconcentrated diffusion of feeling; but his spirit of inquiry was at the same time intensely stimulated; and his inspired apprehension—unobstructed by any absorbing self-reference, and united to an unparalleled gift of expression, which is one of nature's own impenetrable secrets—enabled him to become the great dramatic poet of humanity.

Shakespeare reaped with astonishing facility the great harvest of his genius; but it was impossible that he should not have risen from his work another kind of man. No one who has not tried can be aware how steadying is the effect upon the human mind of any earnest thought of any kind. The poet's early plays still reflect much of the changeful vivacity of youth; but the ever-present sense of an impenetrable mystery broods over all his later and grander creations. Our passions are vain illusions; our life is a fevered dream; there is nothing mighty, or certain, or abiding upon earth, save the omnipresence and the mystery of death. This was, we cannot doubt, the general spirit in which, throughout all his deeper self-communings, our "glassy essence" was summed up by the author of "Hamlet" and of "King Lear." His profession as an actor contributed, perhaps, in some degree to bring more frequently and more directly home to his memory the incurable littleness of this our mortal destiny. The mimic representation of passion upon the stage must have a natural tendency to recall the hollowness of the hardly less unsubstantial realities which it mocks. Talma said he never could look an audience in the face without the continually recurring thought—where will all these heads be in another hundred years? A very startling question, most assuredly. We believe that some such idea must often have arisen in the teeming, meditative, mind of Shakespeare. To his rapid apprehension we are all but a troop of poor players. His own life was, after all, but a hurried, perplexed show; and he, too, in spite of the miracles of his genius, had but a shadowy passage over this mysterious stage of time.

But this skyey being had his own firm hold of the fixed, solid earth. How small may be the threads which bind the mightiest and the most discursive spirit to the shores of this mortality! Shakespeare was a most careful man of business, as we are perpetually reminded by nearly all the petty incidents in his career with which we have become acquainted Here alone he is for us an actual, living, unmistakable man. The direct controlling influence in his daily life, the special incentive to all his labours, was the desire to accumulate a fortune, and to secure those social advantages by which the possession of wealth is naturally accompanied. This was the counterpoise to the extravagant emotional and meditative tendencies of his nature. It was by this practical instinct that he held on to the realities of human existence—that, in its agitations and its struggles he was a steadfast actor, and not a mere amazed observer and a passionate dreamer—that he resisted the ceaseless pressure of a restless imagination—that he offered a determined front to the ever-rushing invasion of the wonder and the mystery of this changeful world of time and place. It was the familiar landmark that fixed for him his own little home in the infinite ocean of life.

We do not wonder to find that the great poet selected Stratford as the scene of the tranquil close of his days. It must have been inexpressibly endeared to him by the memories of boyhood; and, in all probability, his connection with it was never for any time wholly suspended. From the moment he purchased New Place it is manifest that he must have regarded his native town as his principal place of residence, and this purchase was made at a very early period in his dramatic career. This circumstance contributes very considerably to strengthen a suspicion, which other reasons lead us to entertain, that the popular tradition which associates with his memory a jovial, riotous life in London is in the main and essentially unfounded. We do not believe that a careless frequenter of taverns could ever have exercised the vigilant prudence which enabled an actor and a writer for the stage in the days of Queen Elizabeth to become, before he had yet passed the rich autumn of his years, the founder of a considerable fortune. All that we learn, too, of the poet's own tastes is opposed to such a supposition. He appears to have been by nature a careful observer of the external decorum of life. He had evidently a decided predilection for gentle blood and gentle manners. That he was no admirer of the mob is one of the few conclusions with respect to his personal feelings which we can draw with a reasonable certainty from his dramas; and, with the unanimous concurrence of the commentators, we may infer, from the sonnets, that he felt pained and humiliated by his connection with the stage, because it excluded him, as he believed, from familiar intercourse with a refined and congenial society. With such a nature, he must have instinctively shrunk from habitual convivial excesses. We do not mean to say that he was not a man of social temper, but we believe that that temper was very considerably under the restraint of a cautious sagacity and an innate refinement of feeling.

Shakespeare's determined renunciation of London society leads us to the adoption of another conclusion. The general character of his conversation is a subject on which we have received no decisive evidence of any kind, but on which we are all naturally led to speculate with a special interest. The best conjecture we can form is that it only very partially reflected the magnificence of his genius. He never took any deep root in the great centre of English social life, and this circumstance seems hardly compatible with his possession of any transcendent conversational powers. We think it very probable, too, that he had naturally no special aptitude for such a pre-eminence. We cannot help suspecting that at the Mermaid Club, or at any other social gathering, he would have recalled the author of the poems, and of the early comedies, rather than the creator of any of his greater and more characteristic dramas. He would have shown wonderful fluency, no doubt, but he would also, not improbably, have shown a tendency to run into extravagant and ineffective conceits. This is a conclusion which, as it seems to us, is also implied in the friendly notice of Jonson. We consider it not at all unlikely that of the two dramatists Jonson himself was the more vigorous talker. Amazed as he must have felt at the manifestations of a mighty and an utterly unaccountable genius, he evidently thought he possessed some sort of personal advantage over Shakespeare; and this impression very probably arose in some degree out of the general result of their more social and familiar intercourse.

There are several points in the history of our great poet which have become the subjects of very lengthened and very elaborate discussions among his critics and biographers. Those controversies are not, perhaps, in any instance worth the time and the industry which have been bestowed upon them, and indeed, in any just estimate of his character and his genius, some of them, as it seems to us, could hardly ever have arisen.

The amount of Shakespeare's learning is one of those debatable topics. We confess that, even if he were still alive, we do not see how it would be possible for us to know much more than we already know upon this subject, by any process short of subjecting him to a direct examination. We believe that the plays themselves afford perpetual evidence that they could not have proceeded from the hand of an exact scholar. In the early comedies the poet betrays a manifest disposition to imitate the classical displays of the most distinguished of the contemporary dramatists; but he never proceeds beyond the resources of the young scholar in this direction; and, before long, he renounced altogether the uncongenial effort. Ben Jonson's evidence, too, upon this point may be fairly regarded as absolutely conclusive. Shakespeare had "small Latin, and less Greek"—the "less Greek" being here, for all practical purposes, fairly translatable into "no Greek." But he cannot therefore be considered, in any just sense of the expression, an unlearned man. He had far more learning of every kind than any of the great founders of the literature of antiquity. He lived in a larger society; he saw life under more diversified aspects; he breathed the atmosphere of a more spiritualised civilisation; and his mind was enriched with a much greater amount of even mere book-reading. The very limitation of his classical knowledge was attended with its own great compensating advantages. He had learned just enough of the genius of antiquity to find his fancy stimulated by the grandeur of its history, or the charm of its fable; and it was, perhaps, on the whole, a positive gain to him that his first rapt vision of this world of remote enchantment had never been disturbed by a minute and an exhaustive acquaintance with its details, obtained through the slow and painful process of mere verbal research.

The variety of knowledge displayed by our great dramatist has been another fertile source of conjecture and discussion. Innumerable attempts have been made to prove, upon evidence of this description, that he was a lawyer, or a sailor, or that he had travelled in foreign countries, or that he had obtained some special acquaintance with statecraft, or that he had, in some unknown way, become initiated into the secrets of some one of a number of other arts and accomplishments. The very diversity of these suggestions goes far to furnish a refutation of each of them in succession; and we do not believe that any one of them has ever been supported by arguments which would deserve a detailed examination.

There are, however, two other points involved in the poet's history, which possess a real literary interest. Was Shakespeare's genius adequately recognised by his contemporaries? Was Shakespeare's genius fully known to himself? We think we can arrive at distinct conclusions upon both of these subjects with considerable certainty.

The extraordinary imaginative powers of Shakespeare were manifestly but very imperfectly known to the men of his own generation; and this partial ignorance may be traced to a variety of causes. They looked upon the productions of the stage with strong suspicion or absolute contempt; and it was impossible that, with such a feeling, they should have assigned a high place in literature to any particular dramatist. But, independently of this general and most powerful influence, there were many special reasons why the wonderful genius of Shakespeare passed away, in a great measure, unnoticed by his contemporaries. They naturally judged of him by all that they saw of him; and they saw him not merely as a great dramatic writer, but also as a man of unimposing personality, and as an undistinguished actor. It is only right, too, we should remember that we have been trained to an admiration of Shakespeare, and that we readily adopt the lesson; while his contemporaries were brought up in another school, and just as naturally remained faithful to its traditions. Classical literature was then the standard of all literary excellence; and Shakespeare certainly did not, in his dramas, conform to its examples or its precepts. He was an unexpected phenomenon in the intellectual world; and it was hardly possible that his wonderful dimensions should at once have been accurately measured. The human mind is a palimpsest. All kinds of characters have been traced upon it in all kinds of ways, and nothing is often more difficult for us than to spell out, amidst this strange complexity of forms, the original and eternal instincts impressed upon it by the hand of nature.

The very airiness of his drama, with its complete freedom from all personal emphasis, must have contributed to prevent the immediate recognition of its astonishing vitality. His genius, like the light of day, stole upon the world. It rose silently and imperceptibly; and no one cared to notice, and no one could tell, when its splendour first overspread the firmament.

We need not, then, feel any great surprise if his contemporaries did not fully appreciate this prodigy. We must all be aware how little we are disposed to value the strangest Apparitions, if they come to us gradually and noiselessly, and mix with us naturally and carelessly. Their immediate presence is unfelt or unnoticed; and it is only when they are gone, and we are led to look with an awakened interest at the wonders which they wrought with an air of so little wonder, that we are led to suspect the true character of our heavenly visitants.

But was Shakespeare himself fully conscious of the extent of his own genius? "Yes," or "No," it has been said, never answered any question. We believe that it is not so much that he was unconscious of it, as that he seldom or never thought about it. We take it for granted, however, that he did not value as highly as we now do his dramatic writings. It was impossible that he should not have acquiesced, more or less completely, in the judgment which his contemporaries formed of such compositions. It is clear that he felt no pride in his connection with the stage. His profession as an actor was absolutely distasteful to him; it humbled him in his own eyes, as well as in the eyes of the world. The 111th Sonnet, which is held by all the commentators to be a genuine expression of his own feelings, is conclusive upon this subject:—

> "Oh! for my sake, do you with Fortune chide,
>   The guilty goddess of my harmful deeds,
> That did not better for my life provide,
>   Than public means, which public manners breeds:
> Thence comes it that my name receives a brand;
>   And almost thence my nature is subdued
> To what it works in, like the dyer's hand.
>   Pity me, then, and wish I were renewed,
> Whilst, like a willing patient, I will drink
>   Potions of eysell,* 'gainst my strong infection;
> No bitterness that I will bitter think,
>   Nor double penance, to correct correction.
>   Pity me, then, dear friend, and I assure ye,
>   Even that your pity is enough to cure me."

We think it not at all improbable that Shakespeare had an absolute dislike to look back upon the work he had once accomplished. This is an opinion which we cannot defend by any conclusive arguments. The state of mind which it implies is one, however, not wholly unknown among men of great imaginative genius, and it is one to which we can conceive that, with his special temperament and his special faculties, he may have been peculiarly exposed. He appears to have at all times written hurriedly; he "never blotted a line;" and we find perpetual indications throughout all his productions that he could not have bestowed upon them any kind of revision after they had once passed from his hands.

The religion of Shakespeare is a topic on which we have little beyond mere surmises to offer, but it is, at the same time, one of too much interest to allow us to let it pass wholly unnoticed in any general estimate of his life and his character. His whole drama appears to us to be singularly free from any

---

* Vinegar.

partiality for any special traditional conviction; and, judging him by this highest manifestation of his genius, we must conclude that he looked with the same toleration, and, perhaps, with much of the same distrust, on every form of faith. His whole nature, so wide and so disengaged, was, we believe, essentially and fundamentally sceptical. The calmer and more reflective class of Englishmen must have looked with a curious perplexity at the religious struggles and oscillations of successive governments and parties throughout the whole of the middle and the latter portions of the sixteenth century; and the rapid, searching intellect of Shakespeare found, not improbably, in this agitated scene no place for any fixed and abiding religious belief. We may, however, at the same time take it for granted that he placed himself in no direct opposition to the religious convictions of the world around him, and that he readily conformed to the social usages which those convictions imposed. We know that his children were brought up in the Established Church; and it is impossible to put any real trust in the wholly unsupported statement of Davies, that "he died a Papist." But the truth of the statement is still not utterly inconceivable. John Shakespeare, his father, took the usual Protestant oath in the year in which he was elected an Alderman of Stratford; but it is remarked that he took it at an unusually late period; and in the curious return made by Sir Thomas Lucy and other commissioners, in 1592, we find him included among those "recusants" who had been "heretofore presented for not coming monthly to church." Mary Arden, the poet's mother, must have been brought up a Roman Catholic, for we find that that was clearly the religion of her father when he made his will, a very short time before her marriage. It is very possible that, under those circumstances, Shakespeare was taught from the commencement to look with tenderness on the same faith. But we can arrive at no certain decision of any kind upon this subject; and we may add that, even if we could, that decision could not be claimed as a triumph by the members of any church. Shakespeare very probably died, like other men, in the faith of his childhood, whatever that faith may have been; but the Shakespeare of the dramas—the Shakespeare of fame and wonder—manifestly belongs to no sect.

We believe that the great poet need not now remain wholly unknown to us in any sense in which we know other men. It is true that the details of his history have not been transmitted to us by his contemporaries; and we are now much more perplexed about them than they were, partly because we know much less about him, but partly, also, and in a far greater degree, because we know a great deal more. They saw no indication of a wonderful energy in his character and in his daily life, and that was a point on which it was impossible they could have been deceived. We see the magnitude of the work he has accomplished, and that is a subject on which we are equally competent to judge. The unpretending character of his personality concealed from them the greatness of his genius, and the greatness of his genius blinds us to the slightness of the forms under which it was revealed.

Shakespeare was not only a man of slight personality, but he was singularly unobtrusive of the personality which he possessed. What an unparalleled indication of character do we find in his almost total isolation from the wonderful work which has given him his solitary place in the history of the human mind! It illumines his whole individuality as with a flash of preternatural light. Another revelation of the same kind may be found in the fact, that the poems which were fashioned to his own immediate tastes, or in which he gave expression to his own immediate feelings, are the productions of an ordinary mind, and that he passes under the influence of a wholly new and distinct inspiration in the dramas, which are, perhaps, the least personal work that ever issued from human hands. That infinite imagination, which seizes, with the force and the freedom of Nature itself, on all the conditions of this mortal scene, is " cabin'd, cribb'd, confin'd," within

H

the petty limits of the poet's personality; and it is only in its own element of boundless life that it can truly live.

This wonderful being died as he had just completed the fifty-second year of his age. He might, in the ordinary course of nature, have still retained for many a day the full possession of his prodigious faculties. But in all probability there remained for him no further work to accomplish. "The long day's task is done, and we must sleep." It may be that his fancy was still capable of any achievement to which it could have been earnestly applied. But he had already embodied in the most splendid forms all the grandest incidents in human annals, and all the strongest passions of the human heart; and he would have been one of the most unlikely of men to return to the representation of any aspect of life on which his genius had already shed its fullest lustre. We believe, too, that by the gradual exhaustion of the mere romance of existence, he must have been to a great extent prepared for the end when it came. It was impossible that the closing years of a career like that of Shakespeare the dramatist could have been years of mere easy contentment. Nothing dries up the fountains of unthinking enjoyment like the impassioned imagination. It uses, and in using it seems to exhaust, not only reality and possibility, but hope and infinitude. As we lose its bright illusions, and only retain its piercing insight, the enchanted light of life gleams fitfully and uncertainly; this old familiar earth is but a strange scene, on which to "play out the play;" and "there is nothing left remarkable beneath the visiting moon." Youth and love had long since faded; and those delicate flowers grow but once in the keen air of this unrelenting world. "All unavoided is the doom of destiny." The great poet passed away as he knew that he would pass, leaving us in our hour to turn round in the sunshine, and dream out our little dream.

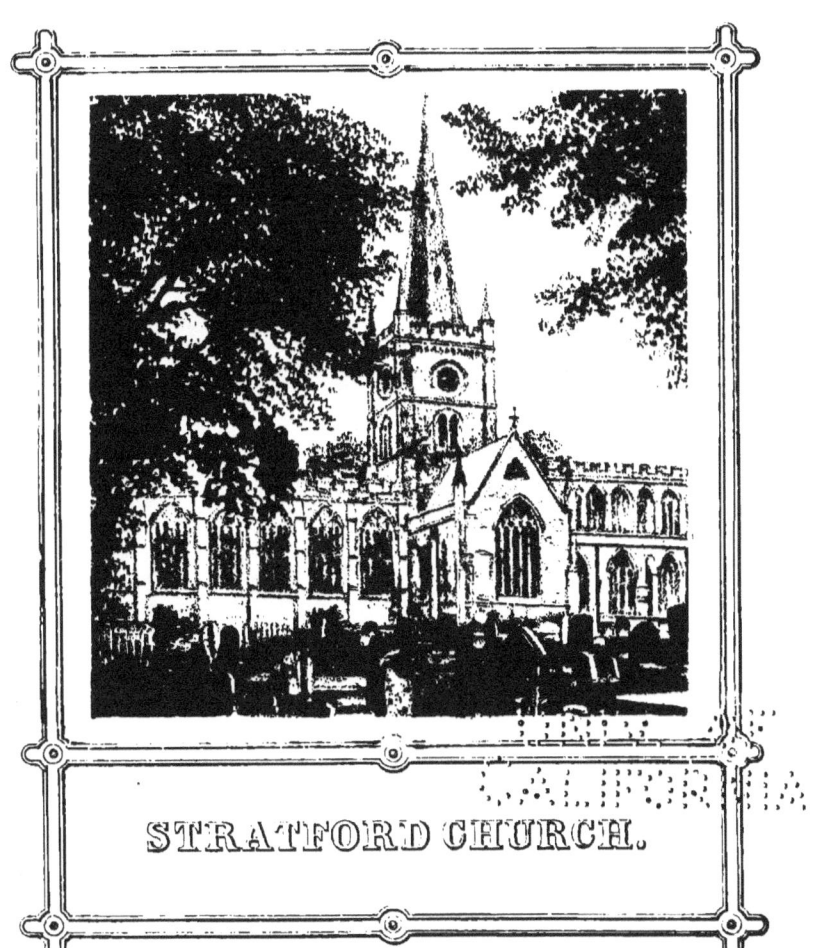

STRATFORD CHURCH.

UNIV. OF
CALIFORNIA

THE GENIUS OF SHAKESPEARE.

> The light that never was on sea or land,
> The consecration and the poet's dream.
> WORDSWORTH.

In attempting to form even the most general estimate of the genius of Shakespeare, we find that we are not yet wholly removed beyond the narrow region of doubt and controversy. That wonderful faculty was developed under two very different conditions, and, as we believe, with two very different results. The author of the poems and of the sonnets, yielding to his personal tastes, and writing in a purely imitative form, gave the world a new and faint echo of the poetry of longing, plaintive desire; the creator of the dramas, freed from the trammels of a perplexing personality, and left without any over-mastering guide or model, seized, by the undisputed right of a disengaged and an illimitable imagination, on the whole domain of human passion, and appropriated all its shows, and all its realities, to the purposes of his art with matchless truth and splendour. There are many critics, however, who regard the poems as extraordinary compositions, and there are a few who even believe that they are essential manifestations of Shakespeare's special genius. Coleridge quoted passages from the "Venus" and the "Lucrece," which he ranked among the fine inspirations of poetry. But Coleridge himself seems to have exhausted his powers in the facile and idle flow of conversation. We can find nothing in the writings he has left behind him to justify the extraordinary reputation he acquired among his contemporaries; and, we believe, that throughout his Shakespearian criticism, amidst occasional indications of a fine perceptive faculty, he has made himself, by his vague idolatry, and his intolerant dogmatism, combined with the innate feebleness or incompleteness of his intellectual apprehension, as useless a guide as it would be possible to follow in any careful and impartial inquiry into the complex phenomena of our great poet's genius.*

We are by no means prepared to adopt the petulant observation of Steevens, that it would be idle to publish "the sonnets, &c., of Shakespeare, because the strongest Act of Parliament that could be framed would fail to compel readers into their service." The poems and the sonnets of Shakespeare are, we believe, decidedly inferior in breadth of imaginative conception, and in the flow and harmony of their numbers, to the best works of Spenser; but in all the essential qualities of poetry they seem to be at least equal to any other portion of the rhymed versification of that epoch. They bear distinct traces of a remote, airy grace; they are distinguished by great sweetness of language and of imagery; and, above all, they display that rapid, acute sensibility which is the very life-breath of imaginative genius. They shed an unmistakable light, too, on one large element in the poet's nature; and the sonnets in particular form, perhaps, the most striking revelation of individual character which the whole world of letters supplies. But they never ascend into the higher and wider regions of passion and invention. They are marked by no originality or vigour of conception, by no special brightness or rapidity of expression. The poet is dominated by his subject, or by the remembrance of the models he is more or less unconsciously following; and, measured by any high standard, his whole work is feeble, diffuse, indistinct, without any con-

---

* Coleridge ("Biog. Lit.," vol. ii., p. 21) states that "in Shakespeare's poems the creative power and the intellectual energy wrestle as in a war embrace." It is not easy to put upon this judgment any distinct interpretation; but, as far as it can be supposed to mean anything, it must, we think, be regarded as a great exaggeration.

centrated interest of thought or feeling. He writes, too, in rhyme, and of the resources of that form of poetical expression he never, we believe, became thoroughly master. In reading the poems we are perpetually reminded that the ends of the lines have been forced into the sounds which they bear for the purpose of meeting the requirements of a mere mechanical contrivance, and not because these are the most easy, natural, harmonious forms in which the thoughts they convey could have been embodied. The mere fact that those compositions have obtained no firm hold in any way of the minds of men, affords the most conclusive evidence of the vast space which separates them from the poet's dramas. There is not a single sonnet, or a single passage in the poems, which the world greatly cares to remember. We do not even find in them all one phrase or image on which our memory perpetually lingers. They wear the light of none of those "jewels, five-words long," that are for ever flashing from the depths of true poetic inspiration. They were, no doubt, much admired by the poet's contemporaries; and among them they earned for him, and not altogether unreasonably, the appellation of the English Ovid; but this must appear to us now a strange distinction for the author of "Macbeth" and of "King Lear."

Shakespeare not only failed to give to his undramatic productions the impress of his highest genius, but that failure, we are persuaded, was an inevitable result of the essential conditions under which his work was accomplished. With his self-distrust, his light, easy temper, his neglect of finished, harmonious workmanship, he could never have found his way to the free, vigorous exercise of his powers in any species of composition in which he came before the world in his own immediate character. The poems reflect the vague and unimposing conditions of his personality. In the dramas he is "broad and general as the casing air;" and his very want of a firm, distinctly-marked individuality enabled him the more readily to restore its own boundless life to the wonderful universe beyond him.

The world will now judge the poet by his greatest work. There seems to be no possibility of mistaking the special genius in which it originated. Shakespeare possessed the most unconfined imaginative sympathy with the whole wide movement of human passion; and a magnificent power, blended with a wild, airy sweetness, and a large unostentatious negligence, in the expression of his rapid apprehension of this most picturesque form of our life.

He probably derived many great advantages from the conditions under which his work was achieved. The very obstacles which prevented the immediate development of his powers may, perhaps, be reckoned among the happy accidents of his position. He had to wait, and to observe life before he could attempt to delineate life; he was thus unspoiled and unexhausted by a too facile and too early success; and he acquired during the period of his long growth the wide materials on which his fancy was to draw in raising its enduring structures. A nature so large required a large development. He made his way gradually to the mastery of his inspiration. He was none of those smaller shrubs which yield all their fruit in the first warmth of their youth's summer; and, to the last, he wrote but little in comparison with some other men of great spontaneous genius.

We believe there can be no doubt that he began his dramatic career in a purely imitative temper. He must at once have been led by his want of any large early training, and even by the very conditions of his own plastic, unassuming nature, to copy the writers whom he found successfully ministering to the great popular want of the age. They were wholly unable to struggle through the tentative, chaotic rudeness and irregularity of an early agitated energy into the ease, harmony, and completeness of creative art. But the spirit by which they were inspired afforded an admirable model to the great genius who was to sum up and complete all their labours, and gather in the whole rich harvest of their glory. The one great object of all their efforts was to reproduce in sweet or glowing language the light, the grace, the power, all the endless life of Nature, and to reproduce them with a breadth and freedom which had been unknown to their supposed teachers of an earlier and simpler world. He had but to carry out this purpose; and, by a most happy fortune, his easy, plastic genius was from the first directed to the very work for which he had received from Nature the most unparalleled aptitude.

But Nature herself—wide, free, universal Nature—was the final and abiding object of Shakespeare's imitation. He saw and felt, with the force of a direct intuition, that in the vital reproduction of her forms begins, continues, and ends the whole business of the dramatist. He has himself found a memorable expression for this belief in Hamlet's advice to the players. The passage refers immediately to the actor only; but the lessons which it conveys evidently embrace every operation in the mimic representation of life. It is written with the direct, uncompromising truthfulness of prose, and it is impossible to doubt that the author himself shared the intense conviction by which this critical utterance is inspired:—

But use all gently; for in the very torrent, tempest, and (as I may say) whirlwind of your passion, you must acquire and beget a temperance, that may give it smoothness. * * * * Be not too tame neither, but let your own discretion be your tutor: suit the action to the word, the word to the action; with this special observance, that you o'erstep not the modesty of nature: for anything so overdone is from the purpose of playing, whose end, both at the first, and now, was, and is, to hold, as 'twere, the mirror up to Nature; to show virtue her own feature, scorn her own image, and the very age and body of the time, his form and pressure.

The poet himself follows these counsels with an unhesitating fidelity. His drama is a great work because it is, under its own conditions, a sincere work. He really desired to copy Nature, and he desired nothing more. He had no self-love and no personal prepossession of any kind to unfold. He looked at Nature through a direct imaginative intuition, and he was thus enabled to follow her in all her changeful shapes and hues. He met her not only in her grander manifestations, but he tracked her most solitary foot-prints, and saw her in her coyest, her subtlest, her most guarded hours. It is his adherence to his great model that gives to his drama its perpetual freshness and charm; for Nature, after all, as Dryden said, "is the chief beauty." That which is most natural is that which is most refined, most true, most removed from the petty caprices and falsehoods of our momentary personality. How often the favourite writers of one generation are forgotten by another! It is because, instead of reproducing Nature, they only minister to some passing taste, and only mimic some passing fashion of the world in which they move. Shakespeare copied universal Nature; and, with a rare felicity in a popular poet, he is far more highly valued at the present day than he was valued by the generation to whom his works were immediately addressed.

But it is Nature in her largest or most expressive forms, and not in her accidental details, that our great dramatist most perfectly copied. All men who work from an innate creative faculty are perpetually impelled to exercise it under its most congenial conditions; and this tendency is inevitably manifested with peculiar intensity in people of his airy genius and temperament. Those free, imaginative natures shrink from that minute care which requires a perpetual appeal to their own individual consciousness. Shakespeare always experienced a difficulty about the perfect construction of his plots, and he frequently declined to take upon himself the slow, patient labour by which alone that difficulty might have been surmounted. He possessed, at the same time, the most wonderful power in developing the larger or subtler incidents or passions which were once presented to his fancy, and he accepted them as they chanced successively to arise, without any very distinct reference to their absolute probability, or their obvious connection with one another. He had, no doubt, a vast command over the realities of the actual world, but it is over its realities in those more general aspects in which they most mingle with universal life. Many of his finest passages bear no marked relation to the circumstances under which they are uttered. His genius has often a lyrical dash and rapture; it soars at a bound into the highest regions of passion and imagination, and forgets to notice, in passing, the intermediate space which it has traversed. The petty sequence of events seems to have been felt by him as a clog to his generalising imagination; and, if we give ourselves time for reflection, we are frequently tempted to doubt the probability of the immediate conditions under which he finds his way to the highest and the most absolute truthfulness.

The greatest even of human works, it has been said, can only consist of a greater or a lesser number of fine conceptions or fine forms, each springing separately into harmonious life under the fire of imaginative apprehension, but all united with one another through more or less lifeless contrivances, supplied by the toilsome, mechanical process of a conscious and calculating reflection. Shakespeare often treats those embarrassing links in his composition with a freedom or a carelessness which, among great poets, is wholly unexampled. The very accuracy with which he is supposed to draw character, and which has been so frequently eulogised, has, we think, been misunderstood and misrepresented; and, besides, we are not sure that this quality would in any case be entitled to all the credit which is claimed for it by many critics. Fidelity to mere character in a work of art is but a means to an end. The artist has, through individuality, to preserve the illusion of his creations; but that individuality itself is of no value to the illimitable world beyond it, except in as far as it serves to disclose a wider and a more abiding form of existence. The individual personages in Shakespeare's dramas are constantly revealing thoughts and feelings which are common to all humanity; but in doing so, the large imagination of the poet himself frequently raises them above the level of their own uninspired personality. He represents, with astonishing truth and force, the particular mood through which the individual is at the moment passing, but he frequently leaves us without any means of ascertaining how the transition from one mood to another was effected; and any attempts we may make to solve the problem must end in little more than mere vague conjectures. Here, we think, we can find the true answer to many questions which have perplexed the poet's commentators. The precise origin of each of the various impulses to which Hamlet successively yields is unknown to us, and in all probability was unknown to Hamlet himself, and even to the creator of Hamlet. In the same way we can give no adequate explanation of the fiendish malignity of Iago. We attribute some portion of the mystery which hangs over occasional details in this magnificent drama to a certain large carelessness in the poet's own temper and imagination; but, in many cases, that mystery is not by any means wholly inconsistent with all that we know of the actual world. In real life we are perpetually meeting with contradictions of character, and we are perpetually witnessing actions produced by influences, for which we are utterly unable to account; and we can hardly refuse to the dramatist the right to imitate this among other forms of the world which he seeks to revive. It is, of course, a right which he may abuse, and Shakespeare undoubtedly avails himself of it most largely. We feel ourselves no disposition in so small a matter to limit his freedom; but we cannot help remembering that any general conclusions rigorously drawn from some special incident in his unconfined, boundless drama, would often be wholly unfounded. He used, without hesitation, any fact or any passion which was in any way conceivable, if he could only turn it to any striking account; and we must not now expect to meet at all times with a strict adherence to small probabilities in this grand negligent work.

The question has been more than once raised, whether each separate character in the poet's dramas is to be looked upon as a mere individual, or as the representative of an entire species; and we are not surprised to find that that question has been differently answered. Pope held the former, and Dr. Johnson held the latter of these positions. It is manifest, we think, that there is in both one and the other of them a certain amount of truth. Each of the poet's dramatic personages has necessarily an individuality, and that individuality is often very finely marked; but it is also undeniable that each personage frequently wears his personality lightly, that he is easily led to exhibit the workings of our common nature under aspects which are universally interesting and universally true; and that, in the exaltation of passion, characters that, in their ordinary moods, are comparatively feeble, pass into the highest form of life to which the poet's own imagination can ascend. It would, perhaps, be unreasonable to expect that Shakespeare, who thinks so little of his own personality in his dramas, should bestow any very minute care on the mere personality of the shadowy beings his fancy calls into momentary life. Macbeth is not essentially the mere brutal murderer and usurper of a petty community and a barbarous age; Hamlet is no mere early Danish prince, or even no mere accomplished Englishman of the sixteenth century, with a soul unstrung by the supernatural revelation of a tremendous crime; Lear is not mainly an irritable old man, cursed with unnatural daughters. These wonderful impersonations may be all that their immediate destinies imply; but they are, at the same time, each in his own way, something immeasurably greater and more enduring than the forms and circumstances under which they move for the hour: they are the highest manifestations of the greatest imaginative genius the world has yet known, laying bare the innermost life of humanity, as it rushes wildly onwards to a supreme struggle with doubt, terror, anguish, love, ambition, madness, fate, or guilt.

Mr. Hallam, after having praised Ben Jonson's "Every Man in his Humour" for the truth of its comic representation of every-day life, and after having stated that it was the first work of the kind ever attempted among us with anything like the same success, proceeds to say that, "for some reason or other, Shakespeare had never yet drawn his story from the domestic life of his countrymen." That reason may, perhaps, without much difficulty, be discovered. There was always something remote, undefined, unrestrained in the genius, as well as in the character, of Shakespeare. He did not like dealing with hard, fixed details. He instinctively shunned them. They could only have been rendered effective or probable through a minute and patient attention to their connection and development which it was not in his nature to bestow upon anything. He passed instinctively into the delineation of large general passions, or of strange caprices, which left him unencumbered by the trammels of petty realities. His free imagination required large sea-room. His genius was not at all immediate and personal, even in its imaginary heroes. How readily he escapes into the free world of romance and enchantment, where he can deal as he may please with mere probabilities! But in the comedy of manners those probabilities must be closely watched, and must bind together the whole composition. The truth of his drama is that highest truth of a wide and an unforced intuition, and it was not at all in his way to trace out laboriously the minute lines of the remote border-land of his ideal dominion.

In the great domain of poetry, the genius of Shakespeare was incomparably the sweetest, the freest, and yet the strongest and the most vital ever displayed by man. With the truth of Nature he combined all the outward conditions under which that truth finds its manifestations in the passions of the human heart. Her forms are his forms, her life is his life. Her unconscious ease, her mighty power, her endless variety, are for ever brightly mirrored in his wonderful drama, and give to it its most distinguishing characteristics; or, if any one should find in it any more expressive quality, it will probably be because he is himself more impressed by some other aspect of that world of thought and feeling which it reveals.

The ease of Shakespeare has no parallel in literature, and

constitutes a main element in the spell which he exercises over our spirits. It is, perhaps, the most constant and the most obvious accompaniment of his genius; it is, in the form of his work, that which is most "Shakespearian." "The light touches of his pencil," says Mr. Hallam, "have ever been still more inimitable, if possible, than its more elaborate strokes." This facile grace is the most decisive test of dramatic genius, or of a genius for art of any kind. It is given to it alone to imitate the unforced vitality of Nature. It pervades all the finest of human works; it is through it that they seem to blend with an ideal and an illimitable world. It still breathes from the sculpture of Greece. As we gaze on this speechless marble we feel as if some unerring instinct had guided the hands which fashioned its deathless beauty. Complete harmony and complete strength form the charm of all art, and they can only be perfectly combined by an apparently spontaneous inspiration, while there is no object in Nature to which this bright power may not lend life and loveliness. Give us the free light of heaven, and the whole universe is beautiful. The sweetest and, perhaps, the truest poets were the most content with simple Nature.

We are all impelled, by an irresistible instinct, to prefer ready productiveness to toilsome labour, for man was made to be the master, not the slave, of the world around him.

The bright ease of the highest art is true not only to the forms of Nature, but to all that we know of Nature's inmost reality. It best harmonises with that volatile, imponderable essence which seems to lie at the heart of all things. All that is most magnificent in Nature and in life presses lightly on our spirits—the all-canopying heavens, the distant mountain-tops, the fresh play of the winds, the sweet hues of flowers, grey morning, and dewy evening, and the starry night, hope, and youth, and love itself—happy and enduring love—not tumultuous, transitory passion; and the most inspired genius in reviving all this wondrous air-woven world, brings it back to us in all the completeness of its light joyousness or negligent grandeur. The finest truths are ever stated without effort and without emphasis. The forms through which they are conveyed partake of their own airy, remote infinitude.

The ease of Shakespeare pervades his whole composition. We find it in his strongest passion as well as in his lightest phantasy. It is a condition of all the highest life; and to the laws of that life his genius, in all its most expressive moods, remains constantly faithful.

But he was not "too tame" either. His strength is another evidence of the absolute plenitude of his dramatic imagination. It is apparently as illimitable as the strength of Nature itself. It is necessarily the most vital and the most splendid expression of his genius. He is always strongest in everything that most tests strength—in the vehemence of passion, in the recklessness of objurgation, in the prostration of anguish, in the fury of madness and despair.

The variety of Shakespeare affords us another wonderful aspect of his genius. All other poets give us, with a special grace or power, partial images of the world around them; the "myriad-minded" Shakespeare alone reproduces the whole medley of life, and reproduces it through all its phases with the same freedom and the same truthfulness. In his populous drama we find the figures, all moving with an equal impartiality, and an equal vitality, of kings, courtiers, statesmen, citizens, clowns, ardent youth, intriguing manhood, helpless age, magicians, ghosts, witches, and all the "shadowy tribe of mind." Hamlet, Lear, Macbeth, Othello, Iago, Hotspur, Shylock, Timon, Coriolanus, Brutus, Antony and Cleopatra, Falstaff, Justice Shallow, Prospero, Ariel, and Caliban, rise at the touch of the light wand of this greatest of enchanters, and live the whole essence of their agitated lives in a few brief scenes and a few hurried hours.

The ease, the strength, and the variety of our great poet are, from the very conditions of his art, most strikingly displayed in the whole texture of his dialogue. In the works of the great tragic or comic writers of antiquity, as in those of their modern followers, the personages are constantly speaking in the stiff, formal style of measured declamation, and they never, therefore, fully reflect the free, wide, changeful life of Nature. Over the shot-silk web of Shakespeare's dialogue, the quick breath of passion plays with the freedom of the light winds that agitate the bending corn-field or the nodding forest. In all his greatest and most characteristic productions the thoughts and emotions of the interlocutors rise, fall, change, return, or pass away at the wild will of their own unconscious spontaneity. With the strong flow of passion he gives us all its starts or all its pauses; and his language, while it assumes the most endlessly diversified forms, is wonderfully faithful to the only real order—the order of truth and nature.

Our spiritual and our material worlds are bound together by countless remote affinities; and the links which thus subsist between them often afford us the safest guidance in our attempts to penetrate their mutual mysteries. The universal genius of our great poet, in its grand, careless movement, bears a perpetual resemblance to all the most potent agencies in the external universe. But, above all, it reminds us of that unconfined element which seems to dispose of and to inherit all terrestrial life. In its freedom, and its spontaneity, and its power, it is most like the " all-encasing air," the least resisting, and yet the most pervading of all the forces in Nature; penetrating into all recesses, piercing through all disguises, more flexible than the osier wand, yielding to the touch of the lightest feather, and yet laying low the forest oaks, stripping the mountain summits, lashing into frenzy the untamed ocean, and bearing without an effort in its broad bosom the great globe itself.

Shakespeare was the only man that ever displayed a genius commensurate with the infinite variety of Nature in the play of human passion. No frenzy was too strong, no caprice was too fine, for this nimble, all-searching faculty. At the touch of this spear of Ithuriel, each impulse of our life starts into shape, and no falsehood can endure its " celestial temper." The very forms under which this strange power was manifested to the world seem to partake of its own wonderful remoteness from all ordinary human experience. In the light of its presence the poet's personality disappears, and nothing stands before us save the image of that universal Nature which he summons for a moment into a more vivid state of being. Many persons have endeavoured to find in the dramas traces of the special feelings, or even of the special pursuits, of their author. But, on a larger examination, we find that we can place no reliance in any conclusions that may be drawn from such vague or such self-contradictory testimony. "Shakespeare," says Hazlitt, "never committed himself to his characters." Like that Nature which was the constant object of his imitation, he was not enslaved to any particular form of thought or feeling; he has no hatreds, and no predilections; and he has also, in all his highest moods, no weaknesses or self-indulgences; but produces, with the same earnestness or the same indifference, his diverse images of life's infinite variety. Nearly every page in his writings gives proof of his vast power of creating living, breathing, palpitating men and women, and of his incomprehensible facility in dismissing them from his regards, and even from his thoughts, the moment they have served the special purpose of his rapid fancy. This remote personality, combined with this creative energy, forms one of the marvels of his dramatic genius. But it was, perhaps, after all, the only condition under which that genius could have found its perfect development. Shakespeare was in no way self-engrossed; he grew not out of the narrow soil of his self-love. He grew out of his unforced sympathy with universal Nature; and he necessarily grew all the larger, the truer, the stronger.

It is to no small extent because Shakespeare was nothing in his drama that his drama was everything. We have most what we seize least. He who loses his soul shall find his soul. If we would possess, in the highest degree, any gift, we must not jealously seek to make it all our own. As we press it to our hearts, we find that its volatile essence disappears. It is easy for us to look at an object so closely, that our view of it and of everything else becomes lost or impaired. The greater impersonality of Shakespeare's genius, as compared with that of other writers, enabled him to seize far more vividly on absolute and permanent truth, and not on merely relative and accidental truth. He never wrote for himself, and he never copied himself; and he saw Nature all the more clearly, and all the more completely, because it had not to pass through the refracting and distorting medium of fitful, bewildering idiosyncrasies. He looked at life through the transparent atmosphere of a light, unenthralled imagination; he offered no resistance to the skyey influences which inspired him. He remained open, with his plastic personality, to all the impressions of Nature. He was none of those solid, opaque bodies which are strong because they shut themselves up in their own individuality, and resist the pressure of the external world, while, "dark within, they drink no lustrous light." The free, disengaged mind is the great mind in the world of creative art. He who sees in the mighty universe around him but a mirror which reflects his own image, will not dwarf its immensity to his petty dimensions, while he prevents his own distorted figure from expanding towards its infinitude.

Shakespeare's dramatic impersonality left his imagination free to copy with the same ease and the same truth all the varieties of human character. It removed the limitations and the perplexities which are inseparable from all intense individuality. It left nothing between him and the life which he reproduced. It was not itself the result of any effort; it came to him easily, naturally, inevitably. He must have felt instinctively that without it he would have lost all his truth and all his power, and he had no difficulty in applying this lesson. If the author of the sonnets had always carried into his work his own momentary experiences and passions, he would have been one of the most unlikely men of genius that ever lived to produce the great Shakespearian drama.

The impersonality of Shakespeare's genius was perhaps the

grand condition of its truthfulness. Every reader of his dramas must often have felt startled by the deep, strange flash with which he lights up the recesses of the human heart. It is like some unexpected and unaccountable manifestation of a remoter spirit-land. We believe that this effect is produced, to a considerable extent, by the conditions under which the truth he has to tell, whatever it may be, is conveyed, as well as by its own force, or largeness, or originality. Other poets are constantly displaying an interest in their subject, or a sympathy with their heroes, which enables us to account in some degree for the labour which they have undertaken and the result which they have achieved. In Shakespeare, as in Nature itself, this link between the workman and his work seems wanting. He mimics human life with the most extraordinary force and completeness, without caring apparently for himself, or for us, or for the life which he is reviving. With Nature's creative power, he seems to possess her unsympathising impartiality or indifference. He lays before us the secrets of the human heart, without displaying himself any of the passion out of which all life is created. We then wonder as we seem to stand under the spell of some disembodied spirit; and the feeling with which we regard this unwonted, incomprehensible power is hardly a welcome one. The jealous, all-grasping human mind recoils from the contact of anything that it cannot account for, of anything that it cannot wholly make its own. It does not like spectres. It is chilled by the presence of agents it cannot perceive, and of influences it cannot measure. There is an element in the imaginative intuition of Shakespeare which we feel that we cannot by any possibility master. We can never assimilate it; we can never exhaust it; fuse it as we will, there remains a residuum, which all our alchemy cannot transmute. Like all the highest creative genius, it has that absolute, illimitable truth of Nature, which seems independent of the passing accidents of man's individual existence.

There is another striking condition of this great manifestation of imaginative power. Shakespeare is still largely and demonstratively human in the magnificent language in which the life of his dramas is arrayed. His spirit here kindled at a new fire:—

> For that fine madness still he did retain,
> Which rightly should possess a poet's brain.

Throughout all his more characteristic moods, there is no indifference, or mistrust, or languor, in the form of his work. He was himself deeply sensitive to the charm of flowing, harmonious rhythm. He had received from Nature the most astonishing faculty of imaginative expression; and, in obedience to a law of universal life, he readily and freely used this splendid gift, in his large and rapid delineation of the capricious humours and passions of this airy scene of our mortal destiny.

THE IMAGINATION AND EXPRESSION OF SHAKESPEARE.

> The poet's eye, in a fine frenzy rolling,
> Doth glance from heaven to earth, from earth to heaven;
> And, as imagination bodies forth
> The forms of things unknown, the poet's pen
> Turns them to shapes, and gives to airy nothing
> A local habitation, and a name.
> A MIDSUMMER NIGHT'S DREAM, *Act V., Scene I.*

THE conditions under which the genius of Shakespeare was unfolded afford us no adequate conception of the essential character of that genius itself. An innate, independent faculty was necessarily the immediate instrument of his dominion over the world of dramatic emotion; and that faculty was manifestly the large, creative imagination which enabled him to summon into an ideal life the complex passions that agitate universal humanity. This was "the master-light of all his seeing." Behind the slight, unimposing forms of his personality, he "had that within which passeth show." The rainbow Daughter of Wonder threw open to him the secret chambers of the human heart, and then gave him the most vivid and the most truthful colours to paint the changeful images which this magical introduction to Nature's inmost recesses disclosed.

Imagination is the poet's supreme gift. It is through it that he conceives and expresses the forms of the world within him and around him. Language would without it be an utterly ineffective representation of Nature, and would possess in comparison with Nature no life and no purpose. Poetry of any kind must be larger and more vivid than reality; it must supply by an ideal beauty, or force, or grandeur, the absence of that direct effect which reality readily and without an effort produces. The passing phenomena of ordinary existence, from their immediate personal relation to ourselves, or from the mere intensity of the impression with which we seize on actual objects, have often an interest in our eyes that the highest creations of genius can with difficulty awaken. Art is therefore not a mere literal copy of the details of Nature, but addresses itself to man's sympathetic apprehension of the most expressive forms in which Nature's soul is revealed. It is thus the largest and the most enduring truth. It is, at the same time, the most powerful agent in shaping the spiritual life of man. The great poets, and not the great philosophers, are the main teachers and reformers of the world. Imaginative genius exercises over the human mind a special influence, from which mere intellect is almost wholly excluded. The work which it accomplishes is more bright, more vital, more like a distinct creation. It gives us a species of new life, and not a mere definition of the laws of a possible or an already existing life. It interests us by appealing to our sense of wonder and of beauty, and, in interesting us, it gains our most willing and complete assent to the truths which it reveals. The philosopher lays before us mere thought, but thought only makes known to us the conditions of life; the poet shapes our feeling, and feeling is our life itself.

Imaginative sympathy connects and harmonises the whole unseen world of spirit, as gravitation links together every solid substance within the frame-work of visible Nature. Nothing is more certain than the existence of this special inspiration in man—subtle, capricious, which we cannot account for, which may be little in itself, but which seems to give to our transient being its nearest link to creative infinitude.

The true poet must not be the mere slave of his inspiration, however unknown may be the source from which it comes. He must select its images; he must know how to adapt them to the special purposes of his art; he must be able to employ them with a large, easy freedom and power. There are poets of an exclusively passionate imagination, who, with the absorbing intensity of passion, display all its inevitable narrowness. There are other men in whom the imagination is slowly constructive. These are the inferior poets. They love fine forms, and indirectly, through that sensibility, they find their way to the beauty which remotely allures them. In the great poets the passion is directly creative. It supplies of itself, and at once, the glowing life for which it longs:—

> Bright Rapture calls, and soaring, as she sings,
> Waves in the eye of Heaven her many-coloured wings.

The imagination of Shakespeare, in its fullest development, and in its most characteristic flights, seems to possess the most absolute mastery over all the moods of human passion. It gives us the brightest reflection of Nature in her grandest or most expressive forms. It is through it alone that he became the great interpreter and illustrator of humanity. Many people are inclined to think that he must have possessed some unknown and extraordinary opportunities of acquiring the familiar acquaintance which he displays with the deeper motives that influence the lives of men or the policy of nations. But we are unable to find in his whole drama any wisdom which can be considered to be at all removed beyond the reach of his searching imagination, following the common light of human experience. With this wonderful faculty alone we can account for all that he is and all that he has done. In it he found all the life he has embodied in his populous drama. His own imaginative insight was his only possible guide through this mighty labyrinth. It gave him all his knowledge, and all his command of the conditions under which that knowledge was displayed. To it he owed all his ease and all his power. There is no such light worker as the imagination. Compared in its operations with the mere intellect, it is what flying is to ordinary motion: it has nothing to encounter but the buoyant, yielding, sustaining air. Its power, too, is resistless and unresisted. Simply and noiselessly it seizes on all life, and then revives, under a more luminous image, all life's essence.

The finest dramas of Shakespeare, although written in an age so distant, and in many respects so different from our own, still preserve the most admirable freshness and vigour; and we have here a most striking proof of the pure, native inspiration of his genius. The highest imagination alone transcends the petty limits of time and place; it reproduces, not the accidental forms, but the permanent spirit of Nature; it passes from the narrow scene of our fleeting caprices into the region of universal truth. All the latter portions of "Othello" are as fresh to-day as if they had but just come from the hand of their creator.

Imagination is at once the great levelling and the great combining faculty in the world of mind. It humbles or it exalts at its will all objects in Nature; it allies our differences, or it separates our affinities, just as suits the purpose or the feeling of the hour. To its comprehensive vision the momentary glance of the human eye is the flash of the eternal stars; the stars themselves are but the candles of night.

Macbeth. The wine of life is drawn, and the mere lees
    Is left this vault to brag of.

"This vault" is the concave heaven above us, and the earth over which it bends, and this image suffices for the all-embracing imagination, which thus seizes on the external world, in one at least of its aspects, more vividly than it could have done through the most elaborate description.

Hamlet. What may this mean,
    That thou, dead corse, again, in complete steel,
    Revisit'st thus the glimpses of the moon?

In this magnificent reverie "the glimpses of the moon" are the whole starry night, with all its countless fires; and this, too, is enough for the glancing disdain of the impassioned imagination. In this melancholy rapture Hamlet himself may be nothing, but the whole visible universe is at least equally finite and equally worthless.

The wide, free imagination of Shakespeare was naturally led to avoid hard, definite details, and to escape into the large region of the strongest and the most unconfined passion; and we find this tendency constantly displayed throughout his dramas. His genius is visibly cramped in dealing with well-known, rigidly-fixed historical events and personages; while, on the other hand, he exhibits the perfection of his power and of his freedom in following the wildest and the most unrestrained impulses of our nature through the storm of terror, or agony, or despair, or madness. It is here that he hurries us onward with the most unhesitating trust in the truth and the splendour of his inspiration. Over the whole region of his own "ecstasy" he rules with the most absolute dominion. The sleep-walking scene of Lady Macbeth, the "obstinate questionings" of Hamlet, the wild, fitful raving of the rash, fretful, bewildered King Lear, stand out to all time in the light of the most unerring imagination. He never mistakes or exaggerates real madness or any other real passion. But we are by no means equally sure that he does not exaggerate feigned madness; and, at all events, he was here unable, from the fictitious character of the mood which he was representing, to afford us the same bright insight into truth and Nature.

Shakespeare himself knew well the perilous affinity of unchecked imagination to absolute mental alienation:—

> The lunatic, the lover, and the poet,
> Are of imagination all compact.

The eager Hotspur became the dupe of his own dazzling phantasies:—

> And so, with great imagination,
> Proper to madmen, led his powers to death.

Imagination was so much the predominant faculty in the poet himself, that, were it not for his freedom from any self-absorption, it would perhaps have pressed upon him with a despotic ascendancy, and destroyed his whole intellectual balance. There can be no doubt that many men of imaginations far less vivid have had the controlling power of reason wholly overthrown. His large, intuitive vision was healthy, because it was not turned curiously inwards on his own little personality, but looked out freely on the whole infinite world beyond him.

Poetry is the natural form of imaginative passion. All free, quick impulses instinctively seek to find for themselves some appropriate expression. In all ages, and under all conditions, men's bright and fanciful conceptions have struggled for a bright and fanciful utterance; and hence the origin of poetry and its rhythm. There is no legitimate feeling of our nature, whether it be joyous, or painful, or timorous, that does not appeal by its own characteristic cry to the sympathy of universal humanity. It is only the guilty and gloomy passion that uniformly desires concealment. There is no place for its stealthy selfishness in the frank, out-spoken life of Nature.

This language of the imagination ministers in many ways to our deepest wants and desires. A strange sympathy binds together the whole sentient universe; and this pervading power is for ever tending to bring into harmonious union the incomprehensible diversities of the world of mind and the world of matter. We are perpetually striving to invest our fleeting being with the enduring magnificence of the external world, and to lend to its silent, mysterious life our own throbbing, tumultuous consciousness. We love to see the remote affinities that subsist between us and the universe set forth in the inspired pages of the poet. The two forms of our intellectual vision illumine one another. The poet delights or instructs us by exemplifying the deeper truths of life through the direct reality of visible objects, and he irradiates those objects themselves with the inward light of spirituality. He adheres to the little actualities of our existence, while he clothes them in the forms of a larger life, and gives to them a more enduring beauty. He seems, too, to interpret for us our own more hidden wisdom. "We are wiser than we know;" and he enables us to seize on the dimmer apprehensions of our consciousness. He gives to the life we have most realised a form suited to its essential grandeur or its essential loveliness. He invests the memories on which we would most willingly dwell with a new radiance; he brings them more distinctly home to our hearts or our understandings; he echoes our joys, hopes, longings, or disquietudes, from some more harmonious and more resounding sphere.

Language, like thought, is an immediate emanation from heaven. It is the light and the splendour in which the unknown substance of thought is arrayed. There is no form of our life which it does not directly and vividly reflect and revive. In the hands of the great masters of composition it is arrayed in a glory which no depth or energy of mere conception can eclipse. It partakes of the vitality of every passion which it reveals. It is the grand elixir which gives to all the finest creations of imaginative genius their eternal youth. It finds in our own hearts willing accomplices of its seductive grace. Give us the lovely form, and, amidst the passion which it inspires, we create in it of ourselves a soul of loveliness. This deep charm of felicitous expression is one of the latest illusions to leave us; it is even, perhaps, only in advanced age that it is most fully appreciated and enjoyed. It derives its main influence from memory, and memory is the last refuge of enjoyment in age. The hard realities of life may have disappointed and betrayed us, but beauty is still a power and a mystery, and holds its everlasting dominion over the human heart.

We can never determine, with any approach to rigorous exactness, how far thought and language are separable, and award to each of them its special influence and value. It is in her vital combinations that Nature is at once most potent and most mysterious. Here "she is cunning past man's thought;" and we are never admitted into that innermost laboratory in which all her finest forms of life are compounded.

The power of conception and the power of expression seem more or less distinguishable from one another, but they are also more or less inextricably blended; and it is in the greatest creations of genius that their union is most completely accomplished. The sense of style, however, seems to be usually the most direct source of inspiration in the most brilliant imaginative compositions. Thought and language are life and the form of life; and it is form that most vividly affects the sensibilities of man. It is the condition under which we seize on every object of sympathy; it is the home of that bright illusion which invests Nature in our eyes with all its interest and all its splendour. It is through it that the innate essential harmony of all things is revealed. It is, perhaps, what is truest to our deepest apprehension of reality itself. All individuality has for mortal vision no essential substantiality. In any minute inquiry it fades under our gaze. It is but the fleeting impalpable condition of the infinite, ever-changing energy of Nature. Death itself, which we regard as the cessation of existence, is but a new mode of existing. Our earthly being is but a passing accident of universal being; and the form of our life is our life's essence.

The energy of the thought, no doubt, often inspires the style, but it is quite as often the sense of style that inspires the depth or the felicity of the intellectual conception. The sense of language is a distinct faculty, and we believe that sufficient allowance for its special influence has not been generally made in philosophical criticism. Some men are great writers, mainly, or even exclusively, because they possess a subtle command over the wonderful power that resides in the sound and the meaning of words. Other men, who seem capable of mastering the grandest subjects, are, nevertheless, unable to communicate to the world any truth to which it cares to attend, because they can impart to the forms of thought no beauty and no vitality. In them the real and the ideal seem unable to coalesce. It is the great expresser alone, however, that is the great practical genius in the world of art.

There is no writer who does not often reject thoughts and images he would otherwise adopt, merely because he feels that they are not susceptible of brilliant and harmonious fashioning. His sense of language affords him his safest and least perplexing guidance; and it is manifestly far less liable to be influenced by individual caprices and delusions than our mere judgments or desires.

Shakespeare's gift of poetical expression was not absolutely free from all limitation. He had, as it seems to us, no perfect command over the difficulties of rhyme. He frequently employs this form of versification in his dialogue; but he does so, not in the exercise of the large freedom of his highest imagination, but in obedience to some petty personal taste; and he never yields to such an influence without some loss of his dramatic vitality. The finest rhymes in his dramas are the brief lyrical pieces scattered over them with so free and careless a hand. The distinguishing quality of these light effusions is the perfect adaptation of their sound to the thoughtless, frolicsome mood in which they are spoken or sung. They are for the most part curiously negligent, and look as if they had been produced in pure imitation, if not even in partial mockery, of the flowing, wandering meaninglessness of the words which are usually allied to popular airs. They are instances of his accurate—perhaps his occasional unnecessarily accurate—adherence to Nature. There are a few of them, however, that possess an essential grace and beauty, and that directly reflect the aerial side of his fancy. In addition to their own wild, wayward caprice, they have the sweetness—and more than the sweetness—of his poems and his sonnets:—

> *Puck.* How now, spirit! whither wander you?
> *Fairy.* Over hill, over dale,
>   Thorough bush, thorough brier,
>   Over park, over pale,
>   Thorough flood, thorough fire!
>   I do wander everywhere,
>   Swifter than the moonè's sphere;

> And I serve the fairy queen,
> To dew her orbs upon the green:
> The cowslips tall her pensioners be;
> In their gold coats spots you see;
> Those be rubies, fairy favours,
> In those freckles live their savours:
> I must go seek some dew-drops here,
> And hang a pearl in every cowslip's ear.
> A MIDSUMMER NIGHT'S DREAM, Act II., Scene I.

This is not, perhaps, to our fastidious modern ears, the very perfection of rhymed versification; but the whole passage has still the true wild-flower freshness of fairy poetry. And here we have a momentary glimpse of a world of still deeper enchantment:—

> ARIEL *sings*.
> Full fathom five thy father lies;
> Of his bones are coral made;
> Those are pearls, that were his eyes:
> Nothing of him that doth fade,
> But doth suffer a sea-change
> Into something rich and strange.
> THE TEMPEST, Act I., Scene II.

But it is only in the blank verse of his most characteristic imaginative scenes that Shakespeare has exhibited his wonderful command of all the highest forms of language. Here he rules as absolutely as in any other region of his enchanted dominion. All ordinary men usually find the finest essence of their first vague conceptions disappear in the narrowing process of composition. It was probably the very reverse with Shakespeare. His thought, we believe, must almost always have gained in beauty, in vigour, and even in imaginative largeness, in the effort to express it. Thought and language were, no doubt, with him rapidly and completely fused; they were produced through no laborious operation of distinct faculties, or of the same faculty acting under different conditions; they were both the work of the same creative imagination. But his power of expression was very probably his most natural and most immediate inspiration. We take it for granted that he had to look out not only for his plots and his characters, but for his thoughts and his images; while mere words seem to have come to him at will. He wrote rapidly and even negligently; and yet his language is at the same time the most vital and the most magnificent that man has ever employed. In it his imaginative apprehension of life is clothed as in a vesture of light.

We can only apply this description, however, to his finest combinations of conception and expression, and there are many portions of his dramas to which it cannot be fairly extended. Dryden tells us that in his time the language of Shakespeare had begun to grow obsolete. Such a statement would hardly be made at the present day; but it is very possible that our more ready understanding of the phraseology of the poet is owing, in no inconsiderable measure, to the many improvements which have been effected in his text since the date of the early quartos to which alone the contemporaries of Dryden could have had access. Mr. Hallam and some other modern critics have complained that Shakespeare's language is frequently involved, ungrammatical, full of strange words, or of words strangely applied; and this complaint cannot, we think, be held to be wholly unfounded. The large, free carelessness of the poet's whole temperament and genius was necessarily reflected in his style; and, as we read his pages, we often miss the presence of pure, sustained poetry, although we never wholly cease to feel that we continue under the spell of the greatest master of imaginative expression the world has ever known.

The rhythm of Shakespeare's versification is as varied as any other manifestation of his genius. It adapts itself, with the ease and the certainty of mere musical expression, to every mood he has to recall.

In the works of most poets language is a series of long smooth sweeps, arising out of some special and ever-recurring train of thought and feeling; in the dramas of Shakespeare it has all the bounding, changeful elasticity of light and air. He displays at once the most careless audacity, and the most ethereal sweetness. In the impassioned form of his thought every object lives, moves, acts, and all Nature helps to interpret his rapid vitality. Unlike the classic poets, he has few formal similes; but his language is all metaphorical; and this is one of its most characteristic as well as most frequent conditions. The soldier "seeks the bubble reputation even in the cannon's mouth;" the poor houseless wanderer "bides the pelting of the pitiless storm," in "loop'd and window'd raggedness;" the orbs of night circle through space "still quiring to the young-eyed cherubim." This grand, swelling, animated, and ambitious style seems hardly consistent with our conceptions of the poet's own unobtrusive personality, and it is possible that he might never have originated it himself. But he inherited it from those dramatic predecessors whom he had no hesitation in imitating; and this was, perhaps, the one great advantage he derived from their teaching or their example. They were themselves unable to wield, with any efficiency, so mighty a weapon; in his hands it became an instrument of the most unparalleled achievements.

The mere bravura form of expression was never carried further than in Hotspur's splendid dream of young and maddening gallantry, or this "proud boast of the bloody Richard":—

Hotspur. By heaven, methinks, it were an easy leap,
To pluck bright honour from the pale-faced moon.
    FIRST PART OF KING HENRY IV., *Act I., Scene III.*

Gloster. Good counsel, marry;—learn it, learn it, marquis.
Dorset. It touches you, my lord, as much as me.
Gloster. Ay, and much more: But I was born so high,
Our aiery buildeth in the cedar's top,
And dallies with the wind, and scorns the sun.
    KING RICHARD III., *Act I., Scene III.*

What pagan poet has ever rivalled the magnificent effect

with which Shakespeare, in his larger mood, uses the images of ancient mythology?—

> See, what a grace was seated on this brow :
> Hyperion's curls ; the front of Jove himself ;
> An eye like Mars, to threaten and command ;
> A station like the herald Mercury,
> New-lighted on a heaven-kissing hill ;
> A combination, and a form, indeed,
> Where every god did seem to set his seal,
> To give the world assurance of a man.
>
> HAMLET, *Act III., Scene IV.*

The rapture is again upon him ; and here is the most brilliant throng that trumpet ever summoned to the fiery charge of battle :—

> *Hotspur.*   Where is his son,
>   The nimble-footed, mad-cap Prince of Wales,
>   And his comrades, that daff'd the world aside,
>   And bid it pass ?
> *Vernon.*   All furnished, all in arms,
>   All plum'd like estridges, that wing the wind ;
>   Bated like eagles having lately bath'd ;
>   Glittering in golden coats, like images ;
>   As full of spirit as the month of May,
>   And gorgeous as the sun at Midsummer ;
>   Wanton as youthful goats, wild as young bulls.
>   I saw young Harry,—with his beaver on,
>   His cuisses on his thighs, gallantly arm'd,—
>   Rise from the ground like feather'd Mercury,
>   And vaulted with such ease into his seat,
>   As if an angel dropped down from the clouds,
>   To turn and wind a fiery Pegasus,
>   And witch the world with noble horsemanship.
>
> FIRST PART OF KING HENRY IV., *Act IV., Scene I.*

There are mere descriptive passages in Shakespeare, in which, through the divine energy of imaginative expression, he seems to strip the veil from the face of Nature, and to lay bare the soul of her grandeur or her loveliness. The wild lonely beauty of the cliff of Dover, in "King Lear," even more, perhaps, than in the scene itself, startles and enchains our spirits. The firm, sinewy frames of Theseus' hounds, in the "Midsummer Night's Dream," still sweep for us over the old classic plains; the deep echo of their musical cry still resounds "in the western valley." The flowers of Perdita bloom for ever in the impassioned imagery of the "Winter's Tale;" the lines seem to faint upon the air, " enamoured of their own sweetness:"—

> *Gloster.* There is a cliff, whose high and bending head
> Looks fearfully in the confined deep:
> Bring me but to the very brim of it.
> * * * * * *
> *Edgar.* Come on, sir; here's the place;—stand still.—How fearful
> And dizzy 'tis, to cast one's eyes so low!
> The crows, and choughs, that wing the midway air,
> Show scarce so gross as beetles: Halfway down
> Hangs one that gathers samphire; dreadful trade!
> Methinks he seems no bigger than his head:
> The fishermen that walk upon the beach,
> Appear like mice; and yon tall anchoring bark,
> Diminish'd to her cock; her cock, a buoy
> Almost too small for sight: The murmuring surge,
> That on the unnumber'd idle pebbles chafes,
> Cannot be heard so high:—I'll look no more,
> Lest my brain turn, and the deficient sight
> Topple down headlong.
> KING LEAR, *Act IV., Scenes I. and VI.*

> My hounds are bred out of the Spartan kind,
> So flew'd, so sanded; and their heads are hung
> With ears that sweep away the morning dew;
> Crook-knee'd, and dew-lapp'd like Thessalian bulls;
> Slow in pursuit, but match'd in mouth like bells,
> Each under each. A cry more tunable
> Was never holla'd to, nor cheer'd with horn,
> In Crete, in Sparta, nor in Thessaly.
> A MIDSUMMER NIGHT'S DREAM, *Act IV., Scene I.*

J

>   Daffodils
> That come before the swallow dares, and take
> The winds of March with beauty; violets, dim,
> But sweeter than the lids of Juno's eyes,
> Or Cytherea's breath.
> THE WINTER'S TALE, *Act IV., Scene III.*

Here are a number of passages touched with Shakespeare's deeper philosophy, and all steept in the finest colours of his genius :—

> Put out the light, and then put out the light!
> If I quench thee, thou flaming minister,
> I can again thy former light restore,
> Should I repent me: but once put out thine,
> Thou cunning'st pattern of excelling nature,
> I know not where is that Promethean heat,
> That can thy light relume.
> OTHELLO, *Act V., Scene II.*

>   Better be with the dead,
> Whom we, to gain our place, have sent to peace,
> Than on the torture of the mind to lie
> In restless ecstacy. Duncan is in his grave;
> After life's fitful fever he sleeps well;
> Treason has done his worst: nor steel, nor poison,
> Malice domestic, foreign levy, nothing,
> Can touch him further.
> MACBETH, *Act III., Scene II.*

> To-morrow, and to-morrow, and to-morrow,
> Creeps in this petty pace from day to day,
> To the last syllable of recorded time;
> And all our yesterdays have lighted fools
> The way to dusty death. Out, out, brief candle!
> Life's but a walking shadow,—a poor player,
> That struts and frets his hour upon the stage,
> And then is heard no more: it is a tale
> Told by an idiot, full of sound and fury,
> Signifying nothing.
> MACBETH, *Act V., Scene V.*

All this transcendent display of the power of conception

and expression is a new revelation in the world of mind. It is, at once, all nature and all rapture. The imagination of the poet, " ascending the brightest heaven of invention," lights up, as with a preternatural lustre, the remoter recesses of human consciousness. There is nothing else in the creations of genius comparable to the absolute truth of this deep vision, that instinctively pierces to the heart of all the strangest forms of our mortal existence, and the airy splendour of this inspired language, that " prouder than blue iris bends"—nothing so far removed from the ordinary limitations of reality—nothing so wholly free, bright, rapid, universal. " Shakespeare alone is ' high fantastical.' " Through his wonderful drama the genius of humanity, freed as it were from the narrowing restraints of personality, seems to have found a medium for embodying, once and for ever, the whole essence of its agitated, impassioned life in the divine form of words.

THE DEFECTS OF SHAKESPEARE'S DRAMAS.

> Thus we play the fools with the time; and the spirits of the wise sit in the clouds and mock us.
> SECOND PART OF KING HENRY IV., *Act II., Scene II.*

WE believe that the drama of Shakespeare is incomparably the largest creation of imaginative genius. Its surpassing greatness has not, however, by any means obtained a universal recognition throughout the world of letters. For a period of two centuries the admiration which it awakened even in England was mixed with many qualifications; and among some of the most refined nations of Europe it still remains almost wholly unnoticed, or it continues to be regarded as the strange and hardly welcome manifestation of a wild and an ill-regulated energy. Nearly all the modern critics of this country and of Germany, on the other hand, proclaim its almost absolute perfection with an enthusiasm that overbears all opposition and all remonstrance.

No other great work of man has given rise to anything resembling this singular conflict of opinions. The poetry of Homer, the sculpture of ancient Greece, the painting of Italy in the fifteenth and sixteenth centuries, appeal to all cultivated minds with an immediate and an irresistible charm; while a far greater work, as we confidently regard it, has only partially won the admiration of the civilised world. Mere national peculiarities will not wholly account for this diversity of tastes, for whole generations of Englishmen remained more or less insensible to the transcendent merits of the greatest of our poets. Under these circumstances we are naturally led to think it extremely probable that the greatness of his genius has dazzled the imaginations of his unqualified admirers, and that the real imperfections by which the manifestations of that genius are accompanied have perverted the judgments of his extreme depreciators; and a careful inquiry into the subject tends strongly to confirm our belief in the truth of this supposition.

We think it is quite possible to strike a fair general balance between the merits and the defects of Shakespeare's dramas.

His dramatic genius itself, in its larger and more characteristic mood, seems to possess in an almost absolute form every conceivable element of vitality and splendour. If he is deficient in any dramatic gift, it is in the power of constructing stories; and very probably this was an operation in which his highest imaginative energy could find no room for its development. Such a limitation of his faculties was perhaps inevitable; it certainly seems to have had a real existence; and we may, perhaps, even take it for granted that the very airiness of his genius contributed to give to it a specially prominent manifestation. The poet took his plots—and often took them with their improbabilities and exaggerations—from the popular stories of his time. He seems to have needed this support for his buoyant imagination. He was thus brought into more certain contact with the actual world. He possessed naturally but little confidence in the creations of his own fancy. He was like the large soaring eagle, which finds its first bound from the heavy tenacious earth the most difficult portion of its flight.

But there is a far more pervading defect in the dramas of Shakespeare. In the execution of his work, he had no power of close, continuous attention; he had no haunting passion for ideal perfection; he was indisposed to incur the anxious labour by which alone the highest harmony in creative art can be constantly attained. His genius only appears in its true form in those great scenes in which it is called forth without any effort; and then it seems to stand apart from every other faculty which the human mind has ever displayed.

There is another mood in which this intuitive and illimitable power finds no place in the poet's work. We often meet him in the smaller forms of his own personality; we find him indulging his taste for petty conceits, and frivolous or coarse jests and allusions; we have to follow him in that prolixity or diffusiveness which formed a marked characteristic of the less firm and less largely imaginative element in his nature. A man earnestly engaged in his work might have successfully combated this petty tendency; but he felt no pride in his connection with the stage; and he clearly only wrote for the direct purpose of meeting the requirements of the theatrical audiences of his time.

The very freedom of his whole nature, and the largeness of his intellectual vision, seem to have contributed to the creation of this careless workmanship. He knew nothing of which man could feel vain; and he made no steady effort to give a fictitious grandeur to the fleeting littleness of our life.

With these diversities in Shakespeare's genius and temperament, we think we can account for all the diversities and inequalities in Shakespeare's dramas. He is manifestly the most negligent of all the great poets that ever existed. Throughout a large portion of his writings we find a capacity for splendid work, rather than splendid work actually performed. He is frequently diffuse and purposeless; he trifles with some mere remote aspect of his subject; he seeks to supply the place of innate, essential vitality by vague extravagance; he wants firmness, exactness, deep, vivid earnestness. Nature did not make him a complete and an all-accomplished prodigy. To the wondrous breadth and freedom of his expansive imagination she did not unite a rigorous exacting taste, irresistibly impelling him to undertake, throughout the whole process of composition, the labour of careful selection and revision. He felt, personally, a strange indifference to the fate of the one grand achievement of his life; and this indifference must often have checked the fervour of his inspiration. No human being can ever accomplish any great work, and above all any great imaginative work, in which he does not feel some sort of living interest. We have no doubt that, in Shakespeare's grander scenes, the rapture of his genius filled him with its own passion and its own energy. But this quickening impulse deserted him in dealing with any topics that were not fitted immediately to call forth its inspiration. No writer, in reproducing the less idealised details which must enter into every complete reproduction of life, could by any possibility sustain himself, through the mere force of imagination, at the height to which Shakespeare frequently ascends. Those details could only be brought into harmony with the finer achievements of his genius by patient, thoughtful labour; and that labour he seems never to have been prepared to bestow upon any subject. There is, we think, some truth in the statement of the older critics, that he wanted art. He had, no doubt, the supreme art of genius, passing unerringly in its highest flights to the highest truths; but he had not the art of elaborate workmanship—the art which vigilantly awaits the happiest moments of inspiration, or which, by attentive comparison and repeated efforts, seeks to supply the deficiencies arising out of the occasional languor to which all inspiration, from the very conditions under which it works, is inevitably exposed.

When Shakespeare ascended into the higher regions of his imagination he could sustain himself there almost without an effort, but he did not always find opportunities for attaining to this elevation, and he sometimes did not avail himself of the opportunities he might easily have found. We could all do many most desirable things, if we would only earnestly undertake them, which we leave for ever undone, from some unwillingness, or it may be from some incapacity, to make this originating effort.

Whatever Shakespeare could not do rapidly and readily—at least, in the more mechanical and less impassioned portions of his work—he seems not to have tried to do in any way; and wherever he is not freely and largely dramatic, the inspiration of his genius partially disappears. The long formal speeches in which his characters sometimes indulge, are instinct with none of his electric life. The conclusions too, of his dramas are often very imperfectly managed. He had here to deal with rigorous realities; he had to submit to the definite limitations of his art; he had to satisfy the known expectations of his audiences; and he did not always find his way to his own grand imaginative truthfulness amidst the restraints to which he had thus to submit.

We do not find in the dramas of Shakespeare any indications that he was at all disposed to pander to the tastes of the more ignorant and unintelligent portion of his audiences. We think we can even plainly see that he looked upon the turbulent and changeful multitude with feelings very nearly akin to distrust and dislike. But the dramatist can never wholly dissociate himself in his works from what he knows to be the wants and wishes of the great mass of the audiences whom he is addressing; and no man would have been less likely than our great poet himself to retire into this proud and immovable isolation. He is perpetually recurring to the mode of thinking and of writing that generally prevailed among his contemporaries; and it was impossible that that mode could always be perfectly acceptable to more refined and more critical generations. His idea of imitating Nature itself was in some measure the imitation of what in his own day passed for Nature upon the stage; and he was thus almost necessarily led into extravagances and exaggerations, as in his romantic plots, of which it is now impossible for us to approve. The passion of credulous wonder is the first developed among men; the more complex sense of truth and beauty is a later and a finer growth.

Shakespeare, we believe, had an overruling naturalness. His grand, negligent genius copied even the actual forms of Nature with a minuteness which a very fastidious taste would have instinctively avoided. He gives us carelessly the commonplace failures, as well as the essential poetry, of life. In his pages the intemperate lover addresses intemperate verses to his mistress. The play within the play, as in the "Midsummer Night's Dream," and in "Hamlet," faithfully reflects the tumid extravagance of the great mass of the dramas of the time. There is an easy flowing truthfulness in this imitation of actual forms, and we have no right, perhaps, to assign any strict limits to its exercise. But it is hardly compatible with the very highest art; and when it merely copies passing customs or caprices, it is necessarily less interesting to the readers of distant ages than it was to the generation to whose special knowledge or to whose special tastes it directly appealed.

Shakespeare's wonderful gift of expression is itself but very imperfectly manifested in many portions of his dramas. We often find in his language the same faults which we find in his conceptions, and we have no doubt that they may be traced to the same sources. Every writer must be aware of the constant difficulties he has to encounter from the unaccommodating limitations of the sense or of the rhythm of the words which first present themselves for his selection. Shakespeare often overleaped those restraints by forcing his language to assume the proportions which his immediate purpose required, or by attaching to it some strained and unusual meaning. This, too, was a result of hurried, slovenly workmanship. But there is in his language, throughout his more languid or more careless moods, a more striking defect. We feel that it is often purposeless and extravagant; and the reason, we believe, why it wears this form is that he extends to it in his tamer passages the same imaginative amplitude which so naturally and so magnificently accompanies the manifestations of his higher inspiration; or he, perhaps, even exaggerates this intensely figurative style for the purpose of supplying the want of any deep truth and energy in the substance which it embodies. The language, however, will not bear this strain. There is no harmony between it and the thought, and in the absence of that harmony it loses much of its fascination and its power. The poet was thus abusing, in his negligent way, the impassioned form of expression which prevailed among the dramatists of his time, and which gives so unparalleled a glory to his drama in its grander scenes. We will cite an instance of the extravagance into which he is, by this means, occasionally betrayed. In the first act of "Othello" we find Othello himself thus seconding the prayer of Desdemona, that she might be allowed to accompany him to the scene of his new command :—

> *Othello.* Your voices, lords :—'beseech you, let her will
> Have a free way.
> Vouch with me, Heaven; I therefore beg it not
> To please the palate of my appetite ;
> Nor to comply with heat, the young affects
> In my defunct and proper satisfaction ;
> But to be free and bounteous to her mind :
> And Heaven defend your good souls, that you think
> I will your serious and great business scant,
> For she is with me : No, when light-wing'd toys
> Of feather'd Cupid seel with wanton dulness
> My speculative and active instruments,
> That my disports corrupt and taint my business,
> Let housewives make a skillet of my helm,
> And all indign and base adversities
> Make head against my estimation !

This is strange language to meet in one of the finest works that Shakespeare ever wrote. It may serve to show how powerful was the influence which the example of his contemporaries exercised over his easy temper and his pliant fancy. There is, after all, a striking consistency between his character and the forms in which his genius was unfolded. He seems to have but imperfectly known how far he could trust his own powers in any departure from the usages established by his earliest models; he was, perhaps, in some moods, disposed to shrink from the isolation of his own astonishing imagination; and he easily returned, as to a safe refuge, to the settled habits of the more certain world by which he was surrounded.

We have all many moments in which we do not turn to the pages of Shakespeare for our wisest guidance, or even for our most welcome distraction. He is not the poet of lingering, sympathetic tenderness. In his unsparing dramatic truthfulness, he hurries over the changeful forms of our mortal life with the unrelenting certainty and rapidity of fate itself. This was, however, an essential condition of the art which he practised; and we feel that we have no right to quarrel with him for the very completeness with which his special object was thus attained. We may often think, too, that he wants deep spirituality. But here again he was only following his absolute apprehension of the world which he sought to revive. He felt it to be no business of his to transform our vague longings into living realities. He was the poet of Nature; and Nature—it is vain to deny it—as far as she reveals herself in human life, is often essentially earthy.

We are aware that it is now the fashion to claim for the dramas of our great poet an absolute exemption from every kind of qualifying criticism. But we can hardly conceive a more extravagant pretension. There have been, ever since the days he first wrote, numbers of men, of large as well as of cultivated understandings, who believed that his wonderful work is a very unequal work; and we cannot help suspecting that the vast majority of his readers, either secretly or openly, share this conviction. "But was there ever," said George III. to Miss Burney, "such stuff as great part of Shakespeare? only one must not say so." Everybody that thinks so has a perfect right to avow his opinion; and the mere fact that any restraint has been placed upon that right shows that our common Shakespearian criticism is framed in a very narrow, and probably a very erroneous, spirit. There is, we believe, little fear that any man of large intelligence will now adopt the blunt conclusion of the shrewd but narrow-minded royal critic, in all its completeness. But in any free inquiry we do not see how it is possible to deny that no small amount of idle diffusiveness accompanies a considerable portion of the manifestations of Shakespeare's wholly unparalleled genius. Men who themselves possessed the most piercing imaginative intuition, or the finest poetical feeling, seem to have found something to censure in the frequent negligences of these wonderful creations. The diffuse, illimitable imagination of Shakespeare had no special fascination for the powerful and searching humour of Swift; and it appears, too, to have but partially attracted the admiration of the vigorous manly nature and the finely harmonised genius of Burns. But we may, perhaps, call a still more illustrious witness to bear testimony against the supposed absolute perfection of Shakespeare's dramas, and that is Shakespeare himself. The great poet, it is manifest, was not one of the fanatical admirers of his own works. He looked upon them with but little interest; and it is impossible not to believe that he attached to them but little value.

There is perhaps in all literary criticism no such perplexing task as that of adequately appreciating the essential magnificence of Shakespeare's dramas, and at the same time freely acknowledging the frequent faults by which they are evidently defaced. The double effort appears at first sight to involve the most startling contradiction; and even upon the most careful examination, that seeming contradiction will not by any means wholly disappear. The contrast, however, lies, we believe, in reality in the conditions under which the work of the poet was accomplished. At one moment he copies Nature through the force of an imagination which in absolute truth and splendour has had no parallel among men; at another, in an apparently almost complete disregard of this divine faculty, he follows carelessly and thoughtlessly the habits of his contemporaries, or the caprices of his own natural or acquired tastes; and in either mood he takes so little interest in the labour in which he is engaged that he seems hardly to distinguish between his boundless inspiration, and the petty conventionalities to which he is pleased to submit. His wonderful genius, however, is necessarily the form under which he is finally known to the world, and we inevitably find the petty qualifications of criticism speedily lost in its overpowering radiance. He is for ever passing beyond the limits of our narrow jurisdiction by the privilege of a higher life. The bright, unforced flow of his fancy disarms our very censure, not only of all bitterness, but even of all reality and all meaning; his airy impersonality gives to his genius an unknown and an inaccessible life :—

> We do it wrong, being so majestical,
> To offer it the show of violence;
> For it is, as the air, invulnerable,
> And our vain blows malicious mockery.

He cannot still, however, destroy the conditions of our consciousness, and we continue to believe that, through some mere special carelessness, his wonderful drama is subject to those inequalities from which, through some more direct innate feebleness, none of the other great works of man have ever been wholly exempt.

THE TRAGEDY AND COMEDY OF SHAKESPEARE.

> All the world's a stage.
> As You Like It, *Act II., Scene VII.*

The drama, like every other form of art, seeks to reproduce the finest or the most expressive forms of Nature. It finds overwhelming suffering and anguish at one extremity of human life, and at another, light mirth or whimsical extravagance; and it embodies in Tragedy and in Comedy these two most striking conditions of our changeful existence.

Tragedy appeals to that intense sympathy which is the widest element in the life of humanity. In developing the larger passions of our nature it insensibly softens and subdues our lower and more selfish instincts. The awe which it inspires is solemn and refining; it is no mere helpless terror, but a profound sense of the invisible affinities which bind together the whole sentient universe. "We have one human heart, all mortal thoughts confess a common home."

Comedy is of a more remote and a more complex origin. Its essential spirit is well expressed in our English word "humour;" and humour is the unreasoning and capricious expression of our sense of the inexplicable contradictions of our own nature. Its source seems to lie in the deep conviction which we entertain of the littleness and the falsehood of all continuous and absorbing abstraction. The comic helps to restore us to the truth and freedom of nature; it redresses the folly and the extravagance which all sustained earnestness sooner or later engenders. We are complex beings, and we cannot in any single mood express that complexity.

Humour, however, is singularly limited in the range of its influence. In its largest form it is essentially unfeminine. It is a defiant sense of our own isolation and our own impotence; and there is no strongly defiant element in the nature of woman. She has not the vices which would require this corrective. There is in humour a whim, an audacity, a recklessness, which are incompatible with her tranquil truthfulness, her guarded refinement, her resigned humility. In many men, and even in many great poets, it is almost equally unknown; but these are men of specially fastidious tastes, or men of confined natures growing in only one particular direction. We do not, however, it must be admitted, associate humour with our conceptions of higher and purer Intelligences. We find no trace of it on the face of external Nature itself. It is never reflected from the mountain, or the plain, or the ocean, from the star or the flower. It is man's special expression of his own special incongruity in the universe; but being essentially human, we naturally conclude that those are the largest and the most complete men who, without any consequent limitation of other faculties, possess it in the readiest and the most unmeasured abundance.

The genius of Shakespeare was displayed with equal force and equal freedom in the highest tragedy and the highest comedy. He was the only man that ever attempted, in any large measure, to reproduce these two extreme manifestations of human passion, and in each of them he possesses the same unconfined power over all their changeful phenomena. His comedy, however, seems to have been usually with him the result of a more personal mood, and it is often, on that very account, the result of a weaker mood. The taste which in his earlier labours impelled him to run unseasonably and intemperately into comedy was a petty personal caprice and weakness; it was the taste that gave rise to those conceits and quibbles which form the most frequent blemishes of his wonderful drama. We think it very probable, however, that there were also many occasions on which he was disposed to exercise even his freer and larger fancy in comedy rather than in tragedy. There is in all strong emotion a self-display which men of bright, unaffected temperament instinctively avoid, except under the pressure of some very exceptional influences. In communing with the world at large our first impulse is to meet life with an air of light, cheerful carelessness; we seek to exhibit under this playful disguise our personal unobtrusiveness; and we shrink from appearing in that deepest and most serious mood which is also of necessity our most personal and most solitary mood.

But whatever may have been Shakespeare's personal taste for comedy in his less impassioned moments, there seems to be no reason to doubt that he found in tragedy the most complete expression of his highest genius. The comedy was principally the work of the earlier period of his dramatic career, while all his greatest tragedies were produced in the maturity and the very plenitude of his powers. In tragedy he had to trust more exclusively to the force of his own imaginative insight; he was less tempted to appeal to the accidental tastes of his contemporaries; and his work was naturally more sustained and more harmonious. There are no long series of scenes in his comedy in which his genius shines with the same unchanging lustre as in all the concluding portions of "King Lear" and of "Othello." Tragedy, too, is, after all, the loftiest manifestation of passion, and it necessarily furnishes the grandest subject for the exercise of poetical inspiration. We have not only a higher life, but we think we have also a larger and a more varied life in the tragedy than in the comedy of Shakespeare; and the tragedy thus becomes a grander creation. Tragedy, too, has essentially a deeper and a more abiding reality than comedy. It seems to be less an accident and an exception in the universe. Our final conception of all life is profoundly and steadfastly earnest. The extremity even of joy "is serious; and the sweet gravity of the highest kind of poetry is ever on the face of nature itself."

The tragedy of Shakespeare embraces nearly all his greatest works. It is the general form which the passion assumes in "Hamlet," and "King Lear," and "Othello," and "Macbeth," and "Romeo and Juliet," and "Julius Cæsar," and "Antony and Cleopatra," and throughout the whole series of his historical dramas. All those great productions are perpetually representing life under its more agitated aspects; and their tragic interest is the poet's most direct revelation of the enduring and inevitable conditions of existence. It is the image of Destiny bending, through the presence of external influences, the heart of humanity.

His comedy is necessarily a lighter, and, in some sense, a more personal creation. In it he could more readily indulge the caprices of his own fancy; he was more master of the moods and the incidents which it reproduced; and it thus serves to establish something more like a direct relation between him and his readers. But he never, in his larger and more imaginative moments, obtrudes upon us his own individuality; and it is in his finest comic, as in his finest tragic compositions, that he most escapes from the narrow restraints of accidental tastes or predilections into the free region of universal life.

In the comedy of Shakespeare—and this circumstance alone affords a sufficient proof of the more limited range of comic as compared with tragic characterisation—we find one overshadowing figure. Falstaff is here the undisputed representative of the poet's widest genius. It is curious to observe out of what slight materials this great comic figure has been formed. Falstaff is one of the least complex characters it is possible to imagine. He is an incomparable mass of the broadest and the richest humour, developed through a few unimposing conditions. He is a huge, unwieldy, unscrupulous old sensualist, flowing all over with drollery, living only for careless animal enjoyment, or the gratification of his inexhaustible capacity for extravagant merriment. His few personal vices sit loosely on him, and only serve to bring into more prominent relief his inexhaustible humour. His love of drinking, and of loose company, are more or less real weaknesses; but his boasting and his lying are only used by him as mere instruments for the purpose of creating diversion. But with what wonderful force the comedy of this simple character is developed! The very simplicity of the materials with which the poet had to deal left his fancy the more vivid and the more unconfined in the delineation of this most vigorous of all comic figures. Falstaff offered the largest conceivable subject for the display of innate imaginative humorous power. He is, from his very nature, never doing anything but acting comedy; he is always a more or less self-conscious jester; he is perpetually playing a part, mainly from an easy, unforced propensity, but, in some degree, also, from a shrewd desire to promote his own interest and convenience. Hazlitt states that Falstaff " shakes his fat sides with laughter." But there seems to be some mistake in this observation. Falstaff is too self-conscious a humourist to abandon himself unrestrainedly to the diversion which he is creating. He was himself better acquainted with the surest resources of the art which he so successfully practises:—

I will devise matter enough out of this Shallow to keep Prince Harry in continual laughter. . . . Oh, it is much, that a lie, with a slight oath, and a jest, with a sad brow, will do with a fellow that never had the ache in his shoulders.

We never see Falstaff except in one mood; but that mood is a perfectly conceivable one. We never get a glimpse, behind the extravagance of his drollery, at a more real and a more earnest nature. We believe that he had no such nature; or, at least, that he had none which it would have been possible for him to bring into actual and visible operation. We know nothing of him beyond his amusing vices, and their most amusing exhibition. His only distinguishing quality is his fine insight into the sources and influence of humour in human character. This is his genius; it is through it alone that he has learnt all that he knows of the world around him.

It is manifest that a character so free and so reckless as

Falstaff offered a constant inducement to exaggerate his whimsical peculiarities; and we do not believe that the poet always resisted that temptation to indulge in an excessive display of his own lighter fancy to which he was thus directly exposed. There was in the very conception of such a character a large element of riotous extravagance; and we are not prepared to say that we do not, throughout the embodiment of that conception, find introduced here and there some small improbabilities or contradictions, and even a certain amount of coarseness and caricature. But when we remember the whole history of the period at which Shakespeare wrote, and the perilous latitude allowed him by his subject, we cannot help feeling that he has exercised much strong sense and fine discretion in this greatest manifestation of his comic powers.

The poet, at the close of his labours, treats this great comic figure with little favour; and we see in this circumstance one of the many proofs we obtain of the small amount of sympathy that bound him to the creations of his fancy. The readers, however, of his works will look upon the whole of this dramatic episode in a more indulgent temper. We must all feel for ever indebted to "old Jack" for that exuberant drollery which forms our strongest and most enduring comic remembrance; and we doubt whether there is any other character we should be more unwilling to lose in the whole Shakespearian drama. The poet is so rich in great tragic creations, that in the absence of any one of them we could still, perhaps, form an adequate conception of his more impassioned powers; but the removal of Falstaff would leave unrevealed to us a large and distinct region in his world of phantasy, and would create a void in our most familiar acquaintance with the less serious aspects of life which all the other comedy that was ever written could never enable us to fill up.

Falstaff is not only "witty in himself, but the cause that wit is in other men." He has a number of companions who serve to bring into play his riotous humour. Foremost among them we must rank the Prince; but we do not quite share the manifest predilection of the poet himself for his favourite hero. We should have liked the young "madcap" much better if he had yielded more freely to the contagious influence of Falstaff's wonderful merriment. It seems to us that he is only half the good fellow he ought to have been in such matchless company. Bardolph has no important part to perform. But Pistol, although a slight, is a truly Shakespearian figure. He goes through his stage-rant with a most unrestrained and a most incomprehensible truthfulness. We find in the dramas of Shakespeare many indications of a disposition to imitate, in a half-mocking tone, the tragic extravagance of his age, or of the age which immediately preceded; and, in Pistol, he indulges the propensity with all the mysterious ease and freedom of his larger imagination.

Justice Shallow is another admirable comic creation. He is, in his way, as curiously natural as anything that ever came from the magic hand of Shakespeare. While Falstaff is acting comedy, Justice Shallow is unconsciously presenting it; and we are very much disposed to think that it is through this more helpless agent we obtain our deeper and surer glance at the innermost life of humanity.

Shallow. O the mad days that I have spent! and to see how many of mine old acquaintance are dead!

Silence. We shall all follow, cousin.

Shallow. Certain, 'tis certain; very sure, very sure: death, as the Psalmist saith, is certain to all; all shall die. How a good yoke of bullocks at Stamford fair?

Silence. Truly, cousin, I was not there.

Shallow. Death is certain. Is old Double of your town living yet?

Silence. Dead, sir.

Shallow. Dead! See, see! he drew a good bow; and dead! He shot a fine shoot. John of Gaunt loved him well, and betted much money on his head. Dead! He would have clapped i' the clout at twelvescore; and carried you a forehead shaft a fourteen and fourteen and a half, that it would have done a man's heart good to see. How a score of ewes now.

Silence. Thereafter as they be: a score of good ewes may be worth ten pounds.

Shallow. And is old Double dead?

This wandering, incoherent helplessness is the very perfection of the widest and airiest comedy. It is that startling mockery of nature which forms the essential and enduring mystery of all the finest creations of Shakespeare's genius. It is, perhaps, in its way, as great an imaginative effort as the disordered raving of King Lear; and we may no doubt learn, from an attentive observation of Lear and of Shallow, how close are the affinities between the deeper lights or shadows of the highest tragedy, and the highest comedy in the flickering flame of human passion.

The clowns play no small part in the drama of Shakespeare. They are of various kinds, and they are drawn with different degrees of truthfulness and of interest. If we include under the appellation the whole class of confused, bewildered chatterers, we shall find among them some of the most curiously touched sketches of his lighter fancy. The Nurse in "Romeo and Juliet" is one of their most remarkable representatives; and Mrs. Quickly, in her more hasty mood, may be taken as a fitting companion-picture. Dogberry and Verges are also wonderful specimens of inconsistent and amusing loquacity. Shakespeare must have observed this class of people with a curious interest, and he betrays a marked inclination to exhibit them in the lighter scenes of his comedy.

The clowns are the introduction of the grotesque into the drama. Shakespeare often employs them even in his most impassioned creations; and then they are the extravagant comic relief from the extravagant intensity of tragic emotion. They are on the stage what the fantastic carved figures are in the solemn forms of Gothic architecture. They give a more striking relief to the conceptions of the poet; they invest them with a less refined, but a freer and a larger life.

The supernatural world forms another element of vitality and interest in the poet's drama; and here, too, he displays all the unconfined resources of his genius. His versatile imagination uses with the same readiness and the same facility all the more gloomy, and all the more fantastic, images that have sprung from the capricious fears or fancies of mankind :—

> 'Tis now a Seraph bold, with touch of fire,
> 'Tis now the brush of Fairy's frolic wing.

We do not, however, believe that he found in these airy shapes any of the larger elements of his world of enchantment. All the finest human work must be essentially human; and it is only by their affinities with our own nature that the beings of an unknown spirit-land obtain their holds on our hearts and our imaginations. Hamlet is a far grander creation than the ghost of Hamlet's father; the witches in "Macbeth" owe their main interest to the fatal influence which they exercise over Macbeth's own stormy destiny; the "tricksy" Ariel is but an embodiment of our own lighter fancies; and Caliban himself is nothing more than an accidental perversion of elements that lie deep in the origin of humanity. These air-born forms have for us all a solemn or a frolicsome existence; and they impart to the work of the poet the charm of a remoteness and a diversity of imaginative phantasy.

Shakespeare, unlike the dramatists of classic antiquity, unhesitatingly mingles the elements of tragic and comic emotion. He was originally led to this large freedom by the tastes and habits of his time; but it was also, we believe, essentially suited to all the tendencies of his own character and his own genius. It was not in the way of his easy open temper to push the pursuit of any object to an absolute extremity. He shrank from the narrow and fallacious indulgence of any engrossing abstraction. That imaginative insight, too, which was the secret of all his art, had the rapid and undefinable movement of the world of passion, which it so harmoniously seized and revived. With the subtle truth of nature it combined nature's inexhaustible variety. It taught him the bound and the rebound of life; it impelled him to the manifestation of its own mysterious truthfulness; and it has given to the light creations of his fancy a more distinct and a more familiar place than that of the beings of history itself, in the faith and the memory of men.

THE MEN AND WOMEN OF SHAKESPEARE.

> And all the men and women merely players.
> AS YOU LIKE IT. *Act II. Scene VII.*

MEN and women are the special study of the dramatist, and their relations and their contrasts form one of the most certain elements of interest in his compositions. Shakespeare seems to have seized with equal completeness on the essential characteristics of each of these two great divisions of humanity; but in representing them his genius necessarily appears under two different aspects, from the different conditions under which it was developed.

The male figures in his drama comprise nearly all his greatest creations, and this was an inevitable result of the truthfulness of his imitation of nature. It is in man alone that all the strongest and most agitating passions are unfolded in their most unrestrained intensity. The more refined and more timid, the less selfish and less adventurous, character of woman, instinctively evades the extremity of rash reckless action. There is no female Falstaff, or Hamlet, or Othello; and even if such a being were to arise out of some unaccountable caprice of nature, we should withhold our sympathy from the monstrous combination; and the dramatist would find in it no subject on which his art could be successfully employed.

The great creations of Shakespeare's genius are never his model heroes and heroines. Like other dramatists, it is through the working of violent and irregular impulses that he affords us the deepest glance at the springs of human action. In all love stories the lovers must be made too amiable to be completely striking and original characters. The writer of impassioned fiction must not, on the one hand, give a shock to our trust in his impartiality and truthfulness, by investing his favourite figures with novel and astonishing attributes; and, on the other hand, he must not distract our interest in their persons and their fortunes, by presenting them with the drawbacks of unwelcome vices or follies. He must not help to destroy the illusion which he seeks to create. In real life the lover will forget, or altogether ignore, the existence of great defects in the object of his love; in our more impartial observation of the mimic representation of life, those defects would at once become clearly visible, and would rudely shake our sympathy with the passion which their presence cannot moderate or extinguish. Romeo, and Ferdinand, and Orlando, and Florizel, are all brave, generous, and accomplished, and are all equally destitute of any very salient or very perplexing characteristics.

Hamlet, also, is a lover; but in the great crisis of his life love is not the prevailing influence to which he yields. He is saddened and amazed; he is intensely meditative and bewildered; in him the familiar light of love pales before the lurid glare of grief and horror; and he becomes the strangest and most complex figure the genius of the great dramatist ever delineated. Lear is another of Shakespeare's largest creations. In both those characters his imagination expatiates in the wide realm of meditative passion, with a freedom which seems hardly compatible with the limited conditions of distinct individual consciousness; and the partial or complete frenzy of Hamlet and of Lear alone seems to give even an appearance of truth to the wild variety of moods through which they are passing.

In Richard III. and in Iago we meet with another source of perplexity. The fine intelligence which they display affords the most startling contrast to the remorseless villainy with which they seek the attainment of the most worthless objects;

and we should perhaps be disposed to question the possibility of such a combination of calm clear sense and frenzied passion, were it not that the imagination of the poet, hurrying us onward in its own rapid flight, leaves us no time and no desire to measure the petty changes in the great panorama of life which he unfolds to our wondering vision.

We know, too, that he possesses the most admirable power of delineating less complex characters. There is a class of men who unite to a very limited amount of intelligence the most inflexible firmness of purpose; and this class has been represented by the creator of the wavering Hamlet with the most absolute truth and distinctness. Faulconbridge, in "King John," affords a remarkable type of their direct, untroubled resolution. Othello, with a larger and a finer nature, is another of those strong men whom nothing can subdue that does not utterly shatter. How clearly we see that it is with the fixedness of fate itself he has formed his last tremendous resolution:—

> Never, Iago. Like to the Pontic sea,
> Whose icy current and compulsive course
> Ne'er feels retiring ebb, but keeps due on
> To the Propontic, and the Hellespont;
> Even so my bloody thoughts, with violent pace,
> Shall ne'er look back, ne'er ebb to humble love,
> Till that a capable and wide revenge
> Swallow them up. Now, by yond' marble heaven,
> In the due reverence of a sacred vow
> I here engage my words.

It is perhaps in men of this simple conformation that we find the most complete models of pure unfaltering courage. The highest genius even for action—the genius of a Cæsar or of a Napoleon—may become for a moment perplexed by that imaginative sensibility which is perhaps a necessary accompaniment of genius of any description; while some comparatively small and narrow mind, throughout all the conjunctures of life, never knows either fear or vacillation. The greatest men, however, are the complex men; and it is in the agitating conflict of thought and feeling the dramatist finds the elements of his finest revelations of human character.

The women of Shakespeare can hardly, from the essential conditions of their nature, be ranked among the strongest manifestations of his genius. "No one," says Hazlitt, "ever hit off the true perfection of the female character, the sense of weakness leaning on the strength of the affections for support, so well as Shakespeare." We believe we may find in this observation a clue to the true character of woman. The perfection of her nature consists in the tenacity of her affections, counteracting the shrinking timidity which disinclines her to all violent and original action; and in this combination of amiable strength and amiable weakness lies her deepest fascination.

But this perfect womanhood affords an opportunity for the display of the grace rather than of the power of dramatic genius. Cleopatra is perhaps the finest female figure Shakespeare ever drew, because she is the most complex, the most fanciful, the most changeful. A large amount of native impulsiveness magnificently blends with her consummate acting, and this union of spontaneous passion and subtle artifice derives an inexhaustible charm from the depth of its vague mysteriousness. "Age cannot wither her, nor custom stale her infinite variety." She is the very model of the splendid, abandoned, triumphant syren. She was already in her own class the most famous woman in history; and the genius of Shakespeare, without in any way altering the familiar conditions of her character, has again revealed her to the world with all the force and splendour of an absolutely new creation. The spell which she and the whole fatal tribe of which she is the most conspicuous representative, exercise over so large a portion of mankind, seems to lie mainly in their brilliant capriciousness. "The wiser the waywarder." Their love of fitful excitement renders them perhaps incapable of any earnest and enduring attachment. But this very fickleness inflames the vanity of their victims, who idly hope to attain what is partially seen to be unattainable. They are the women who understand best the weaknesses and follies of men, and who, in their own way, profit by these weaknesses and follies most largely.

The next most striking female characters, perhaps, in Shakespeare's dramas, are Lady Macbeth and Margaret of Anjou. They both belong to another type of character. They have all the boundless ambition and the unconquerable resolution of which the nature of man is susceptible. But they still hold on to their own sex by their special weaknesses. They do not possess man's sustained energy, or they are accessible through their feelings to the prostration of the most helpless failure and disappointment in their exaggerated audacity. The demoniac ambition of Lady Macbeth outrages nature. It is only conceivable as a most remote possibility; and the fine sense of the poet instinctively shrinks from pressing to an extremity this perilous extravagance. The preternaturally strong woman perishes in her frightful triumph, and is again brought within the pale of human faith and human sympathy, while the imagination of the poet, regardless of the double mood through which she has passed, only seeks to create through either phenomenon images of an ideal grandeur and terror. This is, we believe, the true solution of the supposed mystery of the character. Queen Margaret never wholly ceases to be a woman, although a bold and a bad one; and it is the loss of her son alone that consummates the quenchless agony that burns out her heart to a dismal remnant of bitter ashes.

The special pattern heroines of Shakespeare, like his corresponding male figures, are never strongly marked characters. They very closely resemble one another, although some slight shades of difference in their natures, harmonising with the different influences to which they are subjected, may, no doubt, be discovered. Thus, we have the bright temper and the loving heart of Rosalind; the rash, rapid, devouring passion of the young Southern Juliet; the consuming, untold devotion of Viola; the gentle loveliness and the sad perplexity of the "fair Ophelia;" the delicate reserve of the truthful Cordelia; the sweet, sorely-tried constancy of Imogen; the artless, liquid tenderness of Miranda—the child of solitude and of nature.

The late Mrs. Jameson devoted a whole work to the illustration of these and of a few other distinguishing characteristics of the women of Shakespeare. It required all the ingenuity and all the delicacy of observation of an accomplished female writer to create a book out of such slight materials; and it was impossible that, coming from any hands, the result of so minute a labour should not have appeared somewhat diffuse and unsubstantial.

The poet's own taste in the representation of his female heroines underwent a very perceptible and a very remarkable change in the course of his dramatic career. In his earlier comedies he displayed a strong tendency to invest them with a talent for clever repartee, which is perpetually running into mere petulance and shrewishness. This is the distinguishing quality of the women in "Love's Labour Lost," and in "Much Ado About Nothing." But his finer genius enabled him to effect a complete escape from this petty extravagance; and he soon learned to yield to the charm of a more delicate and more refined reproduction of nature. The new influence, too, visibly grew upon him as he advanced in the mastery of his art. The love of Juliet, and of Viola, and even of Ophelia and Desdemona, seems more or less perilous and disordered; but Cordelia, and Imogen, and Miranda move in an atmosphere of as untroubled purity as can be ever known in any mere human passion; and it is no small testimony to the supreme charm of a delicate reserve in the female character, that this is the last consummate grace in which the genius of Shakespeare arrayed its ideal type of woman:—

> The chariest maid is prodigal enough,
> If she unmask her beauty to the moon.

Shakespeare possessed an astonishing command over the grace and the tenderness of young love. Nothing in art, or perhaps even in nature, has ever equalled the thrilling transport, the entrancing gladness of the passion of his youths and maidens. There is, however, a very distinct naturalness in his representation of this electric rapture. The poet's heroines are sweet, refined, tender; but they are also beautiful, and their beauty is their first and most universal attraction. Here also he was, no doubt, perfectly true to the conditions of the actual world. The purest and the deepest love may exist in the absence of beauty; but that love must want immediate, irresistible enchantment; and it is not the rapid and contagious passion by which the dramatist most surely leads captive the sympathies of mankind. There is no wider dominion than that of mere form in this world of types and shadows. It is the lovely face that "rules like a wandering planet over us."

But neither beauty nor love need be confined to the grosser region of sense. They may even, by the very ardour which they inspire, serve to evoke the larger and deeper elements in the soul of humanity. Beauty readily passes into the higher form of grace, and grace becomes a refining element in our purer and freer life. It is the nearest link between spiritual and material enchantment; it is the finest expression in form and in motion of abstract loveliness; it is the harmony of the real and the ideal world; it is the delicate substance of visible nature fading into the pure essence of the invisible mind. Love is a still mightier and more expansive agent. With its first roots in earth, it has the whole boundless universe for its ultimate dominion. It grows with all growth; it changes with all change; and wherever our true life may be, we may trust that we shall not fail to be guided by its light and kindled by its warmth.

THE PLAYS OF SHAKESPEARE.

> Or sweetest Shakespeare, Fancy's child,
> Warble his native wood-notes wild.
> MILTON.

ANY minute examination of the plays of Shakespeare must necessarily embrace a multiplicity of obscure details, and will often fail to lead us to any very certain and very definite conclusions. The negligent largeness of the poet's own genius is more or less impressed on all his writings, and opens a perpetual field for the widest and most diversified criticism. We find, too, that we have been left singularly destitute of external aid in our attempts to solve the minor problems of Shakespearian scholarship. We have received from the writers of the poet's own age no special notice of his wonderful career, and modern critics, in attempting to trace even the most general outline of his literary labours, are often unable satisfactorily to supply this absence of direct contemporary testimony.

In the midst, however, of these elements of doubt and embarrassment, we believe that we can not only learn the great characteristics of his genius, but that we can also seize, more or less completely, on the main conditions under which his work was accomplished. The great dramatist occupied no isolated and wholly independent position in the domain of literature. He drew his intellectual aliment largely and freely from the world around him. He readily accepted the theatrical traditions, and conformed to the theatrical tastes of his contemporaries. We have the most direct evidence of the enor-

UNIV. OF
CALIFORNIA

mous, and even, as we occasionally cannot help thinking, of the too hasty and undiscriminating receptivity of his genius. In some cases he imitates old plays which are still extant;* and he borrows from history or from fable the ground-work of a large portion of the remainder of his dramatic presentment of character and passion. Thus we see that for the substance of his Roman plays he has recourse to North's translation of Plutarch; that in his English historical dramas his usual guide is Holinshed's "Chronicle;" and that in his more fanciful compositions he finds his materials in the tales and romances—generally of Italian origin—which had become the common working-stock of the dramatists and story-tellers of his generation.† These discoveries, however, in no way diminish our admiration of his transcendent powers. It was his own genius alone that gave to the materials on which it was employed all their special interest and all their special vitality. His thoughts, his sentiments, his language, his characters themselves, are almost uniformly drawn from his own resources; it is to himself that he is indebted for many of the finest and the most expressive of the minor details of his plots; and it is in his grandest and most characteristic labours that he trusts most to his own unaided inspiration.

The chronology of the plays is a subject which involves some of the more minute and more obscure points in Shakespearian criticism. In this, as in nearly all our other Shakespearian inquiries, our difficulties begin at the very beginning. All the circumstances of the poet's first connection with the

---

* Shakespeare's imitations of old plays will be found enumerated in the title-page of a work published in 1779 by J. Nichols, with the assistance, apparently, of G. Steevens. It is entitled—"Six Old Plays, on which Shakespeare founded his 'Measure for Measure,' 'Comedy of Errors,' 'Taming the Shrew,' 'King John,' 'King Henry IV.' and 'King Henry V.,' 'King Lear.'"

† The principal tales employed by Shakespeare in the composition of his dramas have been published by Mr. Collier in his "Shakespeare's Library."

stage are involved in the most complete obscurity; and we can only attempt to determine from general, and more or less incomplete evidence what was the period at which he began to be known as a dramatic writer. The great majority of the commentators think that period may be fixed about the year 1590; and that seems to be a very reasonable conjecture. He must certainly have written for the stage before Greene composed his pamphlet in 1592, and it seems almost equally evident, from that work, that he must then have been but a new candidate for the honours or the emoluments of dramatic authorship. Neither are we left to the unsupported testimony of Greene upon this subject. It is manifest from a variety of contemporary allusions that Marlowe's fame had preceded that of Shakespeare. But Marlowe himself does not appear to have produced his earliest known play, "Tamburlaine the Great," until the year 1586 or 1587; and we are thus enabled to bring, with considerable probability, the commencement of Shakespeare's dramatic career within a very narrow compass. The passage in Greene's pamphlet, the early fame of Marlowe, and the obscurity in which the name of Shakespeare was at the same time involved, all lead us here to the same conclusion, and it is hardly conceivable that it should be an erroneous one.

No positive information has reached us with respect to the date at which any one of the plays of Shakespeare was written. But the order of their production is not therefore involved in complete and unbroken obscurity. We know that by a certain period, which is sufficiently early in his career to afford us an important chronological resting-place, a considerable number of them had become known to the world. Meres, in a passage which we have already quoted* from a work published in the year 1598, mentions six of Shakespeare's comedies—the "Two Gentlemen of Verona," the "Comedy of Errors," "Love's Labour's Lost," "Love's Labour's Won," "A Midsummer Night's

---

* Page 36.

Dream," and the "Merchant of Venice;" and six of his tragedies—"Richard II.," "Richard III.," "Henry IV.," "King John," "Titus Andronicus," and "Romeo and Juliet." This mention of the dramatic productions of our great poet removes our inquiries into the probable order of their succession beyond the region of mere helpless and interminable conjecture; and it serves, too, to inspire us with increased confidence in the conclusions which mere internal evidence leads us to form upon this subject, for there is not one of these plays which we cannot readily believe might have been written at this somewhat early stage in his literary labours. A greater absence of conceits and quibbles, and a more sparing employment of the undramatic expedient of jingling couplets, seem to afford us a further means of distinguishing Shakespeare's later from his earlier compositions; and we meet in a few of the plays themselves allusions to contemporary incidents, or "notes of time," as they are called by the commentators, which enable us to fix their date with a reasonable certainty. But our researches are still often at fault. We have no exactly defined chronology of any portion of the drama of Shakespeare, and in attempting to follow its course we have sometimes to encounter insoluble doubts and perplexities. There are many of the plays which we feel assured could only have been produced by him in the very plenitude of his powers; there are some of them which seem to bear almost equally unmistakable indications of an immature and purely tentative origin; but there are others again in which the manifestations of his strength and of his weakness are so singularly blended, that we are almost completely at a loss to decide to what precise period in his career they ought most probably to be assigned, or even whether we are to look upon them as wholly the work of his own hands.

Many critics think they can find in Shakespeare indications of a first, a second, and even of a third manner. But distinctions of this description are necessarily somewhat arbitrary, and do not admit of any very rigorous and uniform application. The genius of the poet seems throughout his whole career to have unfolded itself under a variety of aspects. It is, we think, just possible that, writing in a purely imitative temper, he produced first of all the tragedy of "Titus Andronicus," and, it may be, some other drama or dramas marked by the same crude and repulsive extravagance. But his earliest free workmanship is most probably to be found under the two very different forms of the light early comedies and the English historical dramas. It was from the latter works mainly, we may suppose, that he passed on to the composition of his greater tragedies and of his Greek and Roman plays. The first productions of his lighter fancy made way for the deeper and brighter comedy of his middle period, and this comedy itself seems to have been succeeded by those sterner and less imaginatively expressed romantic stories, such as "Measure for Measure" and the "Winter's Tale," which afford us, we believe, the only decided indication of what can be called in him a third manner.

There is unquestionably a striking difference often observable between his earlier and more feeble, and his later and grander performances; but that difference is, we believe, nothing more than the natural result of increased intellectual power, and of a more complete mastery of the forms under which that power was developed. The poet gradually learned to reproduce nature in a more free and a more independent temper; he stood more aloof from the play of humour or the conflict of passion; he wrote less under the influence of his own accidental tastes or of the accidental tastes of his audiences; he acquired more ease and more power; and it is this wider and more disengaged vision, under a larger inspiration, that chiefly marks the final reach of his genius.

It was, perhaps, in comedy that Shakespeare first displayed any original capacity for dramatic composition. Here he found the most natural field for the indulgence of the luxuriant fancy of his early manhood; and many of the comedies themselves bear internal testimony to the young and immature inspiration in which they originated. It was apparently upon them, too, that his fame among his contemporaries was first founded. Thus we find that Henry Chettle, when apologising for his own share in the publication of Greene's pamphlet in the year 1592, selects as a special subject of commendation in Shakespeare "his facetious grace in writing that approves his art." Those early works never exhibit the completeness of the poet's genius. They are, even to a greater extent than is usual with him in any of his other writings, defaced by extravagant conceits and quibbles; the characters in them are slight and shadowy; the stories are constructed with little regard for probability or consistency; and the closing scenes are specially abrupt and inartificial. These faults, however, are in a great degree redeemed by an unstudied grace and rapidity of fancy. The poet, it is evident, can pass lightly and readily into a wide diversity of humours, and can allow the airy beings he calls into momentary life to reveal themselves in the flexible and vital form of imaginative expression.

The "Two Gentlemen of Verona," the "Comedy of Errors," and "Love's Labour's Lost" are the works first mentioned by Meres, and they were all, no doubt, among the very earliest productions of Shakespeare. We have no kind of certainty that they were written in the order in which they are thus enumerated, but that is as likely to be the real course of their succession as any other chronological arrangement which we could adopt.

THE TWO GENTLEMEN OF VERONA.

This play is the most lightly and the most gracefully executed of these early works, but it displays at the same time the least variety of incident and the least breadth of character. There is still a very remarkable amount of freshness and correctness observable in its language. Pope expresses his surprise at finding that "the style of this comedy is less figurative, and more natural and unaffected, than the greater part of this author's, though supposed to be one of the first he wrote."

We believe this special sobriety of expression may be attributed to the simplicity which distinguishes the general design of the work, to the absence of any bewildering complexity in its details, and to the unusual pains taken by the poet to give to his slender materials the charm of a refined and graceful vivacity. That portion of its plot which relates to the adventures of Proteus and Julia must evidently have been taken by him, either directly or indirectly, from the "Story of the Shepherdess Felismena," which itself forms an episode in the "Diana" of George of Montemayor. The earliest English translation of this Spanish romance now known to us was not published until the year 1598; and Shakespeare's comedy must have been written before that period. We should very probably be now pursuing a false track if we were to attempt to conjecture how he might have obtained any direct acquaintance with the work of Montemayor. It seems very likely that he here copied a play no longer extant, which we may fairly suppose, from its title, was founded on the Spanish story, and which we learn, from the following entry in the "Accounts of the Revels at Court," was acted before Queen Elizabeth in the year 1584-5:—

The history of Felix and Philiomena, shewed and enacted before her Highness, by her Majesty's servants, on the Sunday next after New Year's day, at night, at Greenwich.

The "Two Gentlemen of Verona" betrays, in many ways, the immature hand of its author. It has but little sustained interest or distinct meaning of any kind. The only passion which the poet appears as yet capable of distinctly realising is the special passion of youth—capricious, restless, disordered love; and it is principally in the glimpses which he gives us of this subtle impulse, that his genius holds out any certain promise of its future depth, and truth, and airy freedom. The jests in the comic scenes are often puerile and extravagant; and Launce himself exhibits the overcharged farce quite as much as the fine humour of the Shakespearian drama. There are several small improbabilities, or inconsistencies, throughout the work, which serve to show how natural to Shakespeare was that neglect of the details of his plots which, more or less, accompanies all the manifestations of his dramatic genius. The most remarkable proof, as it seems to us, of this free, easy workmanship, is to be found in the unexplained and unexpected rapidity with which his characters pass from one state of thought or feeling to another of a very different or of a totally opposite description. The perverse fickleness of Proteus, in this comedy, is almost wholly unaccountable, and the suddenness of his repentance is, perhaps, still more incredible. The readiness, too, of Valentine, in the closing scene, to part with his mistress in favour of his friend, is an instance of somewhat extravagant generosity, and looks like a mere hasty concession to some supposed theatrical conventionality. Silvia's consent to send her portrait to Proteus creates for us another small perplexity. We cannot account for it by supposing that she entertains for him some secret preference, for it seems impossible to doubt the sincerity of her detestation of the treachery he has practised, or the depth of her devotion to Valentine. Sir Eglamour, if he could only make himself heard, would seem to have good ground for complaining of the facility with which his honour is sacrificed to the dramatic exigencies of the poet. He is the generous companion and protector of Silvia in her adventurous flight from her father's court, but, the moment she becomes exposed to the worst peril by which she could have been overtaken, he runs away and leaves her to her fate. Was this the "fair Sir Eglamour" whom Julia had before mentioned as one of her admirers? We have no means of knowing. Shakespeare seldom enters into any explanatory details in his dramas. He seems never to have written with any view to meet the requirements of a minute criticism. His unparalleled genius is displayed in the representation of large interests and passions, and hardly ever troubles itself with the perfect harmony of·the separate incidents in his general design.

THE COMEDY OF ERRORS.

The researches of the commentators have thrown considerable light upon the probable date and origin of this play. In Act III. Scene II., one of the Dromios, when asked in what part of Luce he could find France, replies :—

> In her forehead;
> Arm'd and reverted, making war against her hair (heir).

There can be no doubt that we have here an allusion to the civil war which raged in France towards the close of the sixteenth century. On the death of Henry III., who was assassinated in the month of August, 1589, Henry of Navarre became the legitimate inheritor of the French throne; but he did not succeed in finally establishing his right until the month of July, 1593; and the "Comedy of Errors" must have been written during the progress of the contest in which he thus became engaged.

In all probability, this is the play which, we learn from the following entry in the "*Gesta Grayorum*," was performed at Gray's Inn, in the month of December, 1594 :—

> After such sports, a Comedy of Errors (like to Plautus his Menechmus) was played by the players.

The "Menæchmi" of Plautus must, of course, have formed the more or less remote foundation of Shakespeare's play; but the special circumstances of the connection between the two works are somewhat complicated, undetermined, and uncertain. We may take it for granted that the Latin comedy was not known to the English poet, through the idiomatic and very difficult language in which it was originally written. But, on the other hand, the earliest English translation of the "Menæchmi" does not appear to have been published until the year 1595. Another antiquarian discovery, however, seems to supply the missing link between the two works. Among the "Accounts of the Revels at Court," we have the following entry, under the date of 1576-7:—

> The History of Error, shown at Hampton Court on Newyear's day, at night, enacted by the Children of Paul's.*

The "Comedy of Errors" is the only one of Shakespeare's plays which affords any large traces of the imitation of a classic composition; and one of the reasons, perhaps, why that imitation is so deficient in closeness is, that it was itself made at second hand. Nearly all the details in Plautus are altered by Shakespeare; and there is little in common between the two works beyond their general design.

The English dramatist, following his usual practice, gives much greater breadth and variety to his scenes than his Latin original. But, in the present instance, at all events, this larger effect is obtained, to some extent, by a more unlimited use of the licence of fiction. Plautus has but one pair of twins, to give rise, by their perfect resemblance to one another, to the extravagant confusion of his incidents. Shakespeare introduces a second pair; and, by this means, he not only makes another large demand on our credulity, but he creates in our minds a perplexity so complicated, and so intricate, that it is hardly quite compatible with the light, easy movement of frolicsome humour. One of the curious characteristics of the "Comedy of Errors" is the employment of those long doggrel rhymes in which some of its more farcical scenes are expressed. This is a form of language which Shakespeare adopted in imitation of some of his dramatic predecessors; but we find it introduced in a few only of his early comedies.

The "Comedy of Errors" is manifestly one of the poet's inferior works. Here and there, no doubt, it presents traces of the large play of his humour, and of the vital structure of his versification. But, in the greater portion of its scenes, we can

---

* "The "Children of Paul's" were the singing boys at St. Paul's Cathedral.

only recognise his presence through the tendency of his fancy, in its lower moods, to minister to the popular taste of his time by the careless accumulation of petty jests and extravagant conceits. The whole play is, in truth, but a farce; and a farce distinguished more by its whimsical ingenuity than by the overflowing richness of its humour; and in so artificial and so exaggerated a work, it was impossible that he should have found a fitting subject for the exercise of the finer qualities of his genius.

LOVE'S LABOUR'S LOST.

This play is one of the characteristic works of Shakespeare, but it is characteristic of a still early and imperfect stage in the development of his powers. No play or tale can now be discovered which could have formed the foundation of its plot. But it is by no means improbable that such a work formerly existed; and, at all events, it is clear that this comedy, in its general form and spirit, strongly reflects the lighter and more fantastic mood of the genius of old romance. We have no external testimony to enable us to decide on the date of its composition; but it bears on every page of it unmistakable indications of an early origin. We find in it nearly all the comic elements on which the fancy of the poet, at the commencement of his dramatic career, was most apt to run riot; and we are at once struck by the undecided, and, at the same time, the extravagant form in which they are produced. The whole light, wide scene is perpetually hovering between the bewildering visions of airy romance and the fated shapes and hues of the real world.

The work unquestionably displays considerable variety and movement. But there is in its diversity no small amount of indistinctness and confusion. The poet appears throughout to be unable to see his way to the clear and full development of his incidents and his characters. Biron and Rosaline, the two most marked personages in these scenes, are but early sketches of the Benedick and Beatrice of " Much Ado About Nothing." The young King of Navarre may, perhaps, pass as a specimen of the gay and yet not undignified head of a Court; but the Princess of France seems an unnecessarily pale and undecided figure. The very first words she utters (Act II., Scene I.) are purposeless and feeble; and a little further on, in her interview with the king, the poet still fails to present her under the expected charm of fine sense and high-bred refinement. In the specially comic portions of the work—as, for instance, in the scene in which the princess and her attendants baffle their young suitors, who have come to them in the disguise of Muscovites—the dialogue overflows with trivial conceits, and is so far deficient in true comic wit and spirit. Don Armado, Holofernes, and Sir Nathaniel are perhaps the most original creations in the whole play; and the few scenes in which they figure seem most directly to reveal the subtle ease and strength of Shakespeare's genius. The rhyming generally throughout this comedy is careless and infelicitous, and seems to show that, in this form of versification, Shakespeare's command of poetical expression was subject to some special limitation. Throughout the whole work the gentlemen meet with more than their matches. They are everywhere foiled by the superior ingenuity and vivacity of the ladies. This triumph seems to be continued to the very close of the piece; but we cannot help doubting whether the sentence which condemns the whole party to separation and to solitude for a year and a day, must not have been very unwelcome to the fair victors themselves.

"Love's Labour's Lost" shows, we think, that Shakespeare was naturally a negligent writer. But it still recalls more or less frequently, and more or less distinctly, his wonderful and most peculiar genius. The fancy of the poet moves light and buoyant amidst the frequent confusion and extravagance of his scenes; and, whatever may be the shortcomings we think we can discover in this play, we have no difficulty in seeing that the workman is here greater than his work.

MUCH ADO ABOUT NOTHING.

This play was first printed in quarto, in the year 1600. Unlike the early copies of many other of Shakespeare's plays, this quarto does not seem to have been followed by any similar edition. The general opinion of the commentators is that "Much Ado about Nothing" was written shortly before the period of its publication. There exists no direct evidence, however, to support this conclusion. We have no wish to multiply idle conjectures in reference to the mere antiquarian details of Shakespearian criticism; but we cannot help observing that this is one of the plays for which some claim to the place occupied by Meres' doubtful "Love's Labour's Won" might not unreasonably be advanced. It unquestionably bears a striking resemblance to "Love's Labour's Lost;" and it is hardly possible to imagine that the poet should have written the later and more vigorous of those comedies without having had his recollection specially directed to its feebler predecessor. They are both conceived in the same vivacious temper; the "labours" of their "love" are of the same easy, unexacting description; and Biron and Rosaline, and Benedick and Beatrice, who are in each of them the central figures round which the whole light play of repartee and passion gathers, are as nearly as possible the same characters developed under somewhat different conditions, and with some change in the strength and freedom of the poet's own genius.

But, whatever may be the date of this play, we believe that it forms in its very essence one of Shakespeare's early comedies; it belongs to them by the romantic and improbable cast of its story, by the profusion and the extravagance of the quibbling witticisms in the dialogue, by the frequently careless and imperfect drawing of the characters; and we should, therefore, include it among them for the purposes of our present classification, even though we should discover upon the most incontestible evidence that it had in reality a later origin.

We find that the main incident in its plot—that which

relates to the love adventures of Claudio and Hero—is but a dramatic version of the story of Ariodante and Genevra, as told in the fifth canto of Ariosto's " Orlando Furioso ;" and it is very probable that we can point out the immediate source from which Shakespeare derived his knowledge of this episode. Here the " Accounts of the Revels at Court" seem to come again to our assistance. In them we find entered, under the date of 1582-3:—

A History of Ariodante and Genevora, shewed before her Majesty on Shrove-Tuesday, at night, enacted by Mr. Mulcaster's children.

We believe that we have in this extract another of those partial revelations which so often come to light us in our Shakespearian researches, but which seldom or never supply us with any complete and conclusive information. We have no means of forming even a conjecture whether the poet drew from the same source that other portion of his work, in which he disposes of the fortunes of Benedick and Beatrice. We do not know of any book which could have suggested to him that lively episode, and we see no reason to think that it may not have been of his own creation.

In modern times "Much Ado About Nothing" has been commonly held to occupy a high place in the Shakespearian drama. We do not think, however, that, if it be tried by any rigorous critical standard, it will be found to have any strong claim to this distinction. We can perceive in it hardly any trace of the rarer and finer powers of its author. The whole story of Claudio and Hero is melodramatically conceived, and is throughout melodramatically rendered. Hero is one of the poet's feeble and shadowy female figures. She accepts, without an effort, whatever fate is prepared for her by others, and in all the changes of her fortune she affords hardly any indication of an individual character. Claudio, too, seems drawn with an irresolute and uncertain hand. There is no appearance of probability in his resolution to leave the prosecution of his suit to the prince. This would, under any circumstances, have been an extravagant device, and in this case there seems to be no reason whatever for its adoption. We find ourselves again somewhat removed beyond the world of probability throughout the scenes which relate to the supposed death of Hero. Her father, Leonato, and her other friends who are parties to the propagation of the false rumour, are compelled, in the presence of those other personages in the drama who have not been admitted into the secret, to refer to her memory with an insincerity which seems scarcely consistent with the existence of the deep grief they must feel at the real injury she has suffered. We cannot, too, but look with some surprise at the readiness with which Claudio consents to marry some supposed cousin of the mistress whom he believes to have been lost to him for ever; and we are not reconciled to this improbability by any special exhibition of force or tenderness in the treatment of the scene in which his misapprehension is removed, and Hero is restored to him in happiness and honour. He seems, however, throughout the whole play to be but a cold and careless lover; and even in the midst of his regret for the great injury he has unwillingly inflicted on his hapless mistress, we find him occasionally talking and acting with a levity which creates in us an unwelcome suspicion of the truthfulness of the whole of this creation of the poet's fancy.

Benedick and Beatrice are drawn much more spiritedly. But the hard, sharp form of their repartee runs, as is usual with Shakespeare, into frequent excesses, and necessarily wants the grace and gaiety of his larger humour. Benedick, in the indulgence of his wit, is sometimes petulantly coarse; and Beatrice is a still more unamiable, or, perhaps, we should rather say, a still more unintelligible personage. She invariably out-talks Benedick; but she obtains this triumph over him mainly because she is more unscrupulously acrimonious and railing. The last resource of her wit is invariably some outrageous personal insult. In the greater part of the scenes in which she figures, she is little more than a bitter and an unsparing shrew. It is manifest that, if she maintained this character throughout the whole play, we should feel little or no interest in her fate; and the poet has, therefore, endeavoured to soften, here and there, the harder lines of this figure; but we are not sure that, in doing so, he has drawn her with perfect consistency. Leonato tells us that Beatrice is naturally so disposed to be merry that, as he has heard his daughter say, she has "often dreamed of unhappiness, and waked herself with laughing." But we find it very difficult to attach perfect credit to this statement. The stinging vivacity of Beatrice seems never inspired by the genius of joyous, irrepressible laughter. She shows unexpected warmth and generosity of feeling in advocating the cause of the injured Hero; but we think she is somewhat precipitate and unreasonable in her demand that Benedick should at once "kill Claudio." The pair of witty rebels to love are ultimately brought under the dominion of the passion, and there is considerable humour in the representation of the mode in which this change is effected. It is manifest from the very commencement of the play that they have been thinking a good deal about one another, and the very vehemence of their denunciations of marriage helps to show that they are by no means perfectly secure against the perpetration of the supposed folly. We feel no surprise, therefore, at the immediate termination of this episode; but, at the same time, we cannot look forward without some slight misgiving to the nature of the domestic relations which are afterwards to prevail among a couple so strangely assorted.

A few of the smaller details in this comedy seem also to have been somewhat hastily and loosely constructed. Don John is one of the many unaccountable villains in the dramas of Shakespeare. Borachio, too, is more or less vaguely represented. He exhibits a strange readiness to confess his guilt under circumstances in which he might easily have persisted in asserting his innocence; and he subsequently appears in so undecided a character, that we are at a loss to determine whether we are to regard him as a sincere penitent or as an unreclaimed criminal. At the commencement of the second scene of the first Act, Leonato asks Antonio:—"How now, brother? Where is my cousin, your son?" But we hear no more of this son; and in the first scene of the fifth Act, Leonato is made to say:—"My brother hath a daughter, and she is heir to both of us." The first of these passages was in all probability forgotten by the poet when he was writing the second; and even a small contradiction of this kind may serve to show how little he was prepared to bestow any very scrupulous care on the perfect consistency of the minor incidents in his dramas.

But, after all, perhaps, the most truly fanciful and original portions of "Much Ado About Nothing" are to be found in the delineation of the strangely and elaborately blundering constables, Dogberry and Verges. These are, in their way, unmistakable and inimitable Shakespearian characters. They even stand out throughout his whole drama as the most striking and amusing representatives of their own peculiar class. The intricate absurdity of their language must have been devised through some more or less conscious labour on the part of the poet; and yet it often wears the easy, absolute truthfulness of the most rapid imaginative inspiration. Some of their mere verbal paradoxes have the charm of the widest and the freest humour, and have naturally passed into the universal language of proverbial comedy.

A MIDSUMMER NIGHT'S DREAM.

We find in the four preceding comedies no special manifestation of Shakespeare's finer poetical power. In them he is more or less conventional; he is ministering to the immediate tastes and humours of his audiences, or to the caprices of his own lighter temper. In the "Midsummer Night's Dream" he enters the wide realm of thought and fancy, with much of the unconfined ease and grace of his lightest and airiest inspiration. This bright work is, no doubt, a creation of the poet's rapidly maturing powers. It was very probably written in the year 1594. The detailed enumeration made by Titania, in Act II., Scene I., of the elemental convulsions which followed her quarrel with Oberon, seems to contain an unmistakable allusion to the unseasonable and disastrous weather with which we know that England had been visited during that year:—

> Therefore the winds, piping to us in vain,
> As in revenge, have suck'd up from the sea
> Contagious fogs; which falling on the land,
> Have every pelting river made so proud,
> That they have overborne their continents:
> The ox hath therefore stretch'd his yoke in vain,
> The ploughman lost his sweat; and the green corn
> Hath rotted, ere his youth attain'd a beard:
> The fold stands empty in the drowned field,
> And crows are fatted with the murrain flock;
> The nine men's morris * is filled up with mud;
> And the quaint mazes in the wanton green,
> For lack of tread, are undistinguishable:
> The human mortals want their winter here;
> No night is now with hymn or carol blest:—
> Therefore, the moon, the governess of floods,
> Pale in her anger, washes all the air,
> That rheumatic diseases do abound;
> And thorough this distemperature, we see
> The seasons alter: hoary-headed frosts
> Fall in the fresh lap of the crimson rose;
> And on old Hyems' chin, and icy crown,
> An odorous chaplet of sweet summer buds
> Is, as in mockery, set: The spring, the summer,
> The childing autumn, angry winter, change
> Their wonted liveries; and the 'mazed world,
> By their increase, now knows not which is which.

This picturesque delineation of the disastrous caprices of the seasons had its counterpart in the world of reality. Dr. Simon

---

* A game played by boys.

Forman, in his manuscript notes, preserved in the Ashmolean Museum, makes the following entry, under the date of 1594:—

This months of June and July were very wet and wonderful cold, like winter, that the 10th day of July many did sit by the fire, it was so cold; and so was it in May and June; and scant two fair days together all that time, but it rained every day more or less: if it did not rain, then was it cold and cloudy: there were many great floods this summer, and about Michaelmas, through the abundance of rain that fell suddenly, the bridge of Ware was broken down.

The floods of this year are mentioned by several other writers. Stowe, the chronicler, tells us:—

This year, in the month of May, fell great showers of rain, but in the months of June and July much more; for it commonly rained every day or night till St. James's day.

Dr. King, in certain lectures which he delivered at York, gives a similar account of a visitation, from which it seems that no age is necessarily exempt:—

Remember that the spring was very unkind by means of the abundance of rains that fell: our July hath been like to a February; our June even as an April. * * * We may say that the course of nature is very much inverted; our years are turned upside down; our summers are no summers; our harvests are no harvests; our seed-times are no seed-times; for a great space of time scant one day that hath not rained upon us; and the nights are like the days.

We find that there was thus a foundation in reality for what would otherwise appear to be the meaningless and extravagant passage in the drama, and with it that passage presents a poetical and an appropriate allusion to what must have been at the time a notorious and a remarkable phenomenon. We believe, too, that the introduction further on in the "Midsummer Night's Dream," of "the thrice three Muses, mourning for the death of learning, late deceased in beggary," refers to the death of Robert Greene, in the month of September, 1592. That event obtained a publicity in which the name of Shakespeare himself became involved; and he could hardly help bearing in mind that those lines would recall its remembrance. No one doubts that the verses (Act II., Scene I.) which celebrate the happy escape of the "fair vestal throned by the west," contain a compliment—the most exquisite compliment ever offered by genius at the shrine of royal vanity—to the maidenly pretensions of Queen Elizabeth.

> *Oberon.* My gentle Puck, come hither : Thou remember'st
> Since once I sat upon a promontory,
> And heard a mermaid, on a dolphin's back,
> Uttering such dulcet and harmonious breath,
> That the rude sea grew civil at her song;
> And certain stars shot madly from their spheres,
> To hear the sea-maid's music.
> *Puck.*   I remember.
> *Oberon.* That very time I saw (but thou could'st not),
> Flying between the cold moon and the earth,
> Cupid all arm'd : a certain aim he took
> At a fair vestal thronèd by the west;
> And loos'd his love-shaft smartly from his bow,
> As it should pierce a hundred-thousand hearts :
> But I might see young Cupid's fiery shaft
> Quench'd in the chaste beams of the watery moon,
> And the imperial votaress passèd on,
> In maiden meditation, fancy free.[*]

---

[*] Many of the poet's biographers believe that this passage refers in a special manner to the reception given by Leicester to Queen Elizabeth at Kenilworth Castle, in the summer of 1575; and as Kenilworth is only fourteen miles distant from Stratford, they have further conjectured that Shakespeare himself, who was at the time in his twelfth year, was very probably a witness of that splendid ceremonial. G. Gascoigne states, in his account of it, published in 1576, that "Triton, in likeness of a mermaid, came towards her Majesty," and that "Arion appeared sitting on a dolphin's back;" and Laneham, in a descriptive "Letter," written in the preceding year, makes special mention of a "ditty in metre aptly indited to the matter, and after by voice deliciously delivered." Those passages might have furnished Shakespeare with the allusions in the drama, but we have no means of knowing whether he was himself one of the crowd who witnessed the magnificent pageants prepared by Leicester.

Shakespeare seems to have derived from the "Canterbury Tales" of Chaucer, and more especially from the "Knight's Tale," a few of the less characteristic incidents in the "Midsummer Night's Dream;" and the name, at least of the interlude, is to be found in the "Piramus and Thisbe" of Ovid. Oberon and Titania, and Puck, or Robin Goodfellow, were already old and universally accepted denizens of the Fairy world of England. But apart from these general forms, the work is essentially his own creation, and is throughout suffused with the special colours of his imagination. The approaching marriage of Theseus and Hippolyta furnishes the general framework, or, in musical language, the "motive," for the whole composition. Oberon and Titania, with their attendant elves, hasten from the extremities of the earth to assist at the celebration of this splendid ceremony. A set of illiterate actors—"a crew of patches, rude mechanicals"—prepare a dramatic entertainment for the same occasion; and the most prominent member of this company becomes an accidental and unconscious instrument in the development of the frolicsome humour of the fairy king, and is thus led to display, in a new and most exaggerated form, his extravagant folly. Two pairs of lovers, already more or less at cross purposes with themselves or with the world, become involved in the unintentional misapplication of the same supernatural agency, which thus further strangely complicates their troubles and perplexities. The mistakes and delusions of the scene, however, are of course ultimately removed. The lovers find for once that the "course of true love" has "run smooth;" the interlude of the poor players is "played out;" and the "dream" naturally ends with all the pomp and festivity of marriage. These are, perhaps, the slightest and the most fantastic materials on which the imagination of man ever raised a dramatic structure. A wide, careless humour is the soul of the whole light creation. The work is throughout steeped in the rainbow colours of the most capricious poetry. It is perpetually revealing to us long vistas of fairy land, with fresh dews, delicate flowers, soft moonlight, the "spangled star-light sheen," and the depths of mystic forest glades. It contains some of the airiest and most graceful poetry Shakespeare ever wrote. The very atmosphere, peopled with its light phantasies, is resonant of magic and of music:—

> "And never, since the middle summer's spring,
> Meet we on hill, in dale, forest, or mead,
> By pavèd fountain, or by rushy brook,
> Or on the beachèd margent of the sea,
> To dance our ringlets to the whistling wind,
> But with thy brawls thou hast disturb'd our sport."

> "Come, now a roundel, and a fairy song;
> Then, for the third part of a minute, hence;—
> Some, to kill cankers in the musk-rose buds;
> Some, war with rere-mice for their leathern wings,
> To make my small elves coats; and some, keep back
> The clamorous owl, that nightly hoots and wonders
> At our quaint spirits."

> "Be kind and courteous to this gentleman,—
> Hop in his walks, and gambol in his eyes;
> Feed him with apricocks and dewberries,
> With purple grapes, green figs, and mulberries;
> The honey-bags steal from the humble bees,
> And, for night-tapers, crop their waxen thighs,
> And light them at the fiery glow-worm's eyes,
> To have my love to bed and to arise;
> And pluck the wings from painted butterflies,
> To fan the moonbeams from his sleeping eyes:
> Nod to him, elves, and do him courtesies."

The "Midsummer Night's Dream" is Shakespeare's most characteristic invasion of the world of pure enchantment. In it he has found a voice and a form for the idlest and most undefinable movements of the human fancy. But there are manifest, and perhaps to some extent inevitable, limitations to the success with which he has accomplished this wonderful task. The versification, more particularly in the rhyme, is often more or less languid and negligent. The human characters are for the most part feebly drawn, and the incidents through which they pass seem occasionally, as in the case of Bottom for instance, unnecessarily mean and trivial. We are unprepared, too, to feel any magical interest in the unrelieved humiliation of the poor players amidst scenes so generally playful. We are aware, however, at the same time, that the wonderful ease and freedom with which this incident is managed has given to it an enduring place in the world's comedy. The fancies of the poet are no doubt bright and vivid, but they still seem wanting in some expected charm. They are hardly, after all,

> " Such sights as youthful poets dream
> On summer eves by haunted stream."

Most probably, however, those were not the sights that Shakespeare sought to recall. He had to produce an acting, and not a purely lyrical work; and he had to submit to the somewhat hard conditions which this design necessarily imposed. The light, careless temper in which he regards his characters helps to maintain the dramatic illusion of the whole fairy scene. The "human mortals" are throughout treated by the poet with a distant and half-mocking disdain: "Lord, what fools these mortals be!" This self-possessed impartiality saves him from the enfeebling languor and insipidity which the passionate indulgence of any mere dreamy sensibility must almost inevitably have entailed. The "Midsummer Night's Dream" is not, perhaps, the perfection of frolicsome grace. It certainly is not the most rapt form of "harmonious madness" which it is possible to conceive. But in it we find the world of phantasy and the world of reality brought together with an ease and a truthfulness which had previously been unknown in any work of human hands. It was a new phenomenon in the manifestations of genius. It showed that a poet had at length arisen who, by the unaided force of imagination, and apparently without any intellectual effort, or the gratification of any personal predilection, could give an outward form to the most shadowy and fugitive images of the mind; and in this bright power he had neither predecessor nor follower among men.

THE MERCHANT OF VENICE.

This play is another creation of Shakespeare's growing genius. Malone thought that this was probably the " Venesyon Comedy" entered by Henslowe in his Diary as a new play, under the date of the 25th of August, 1594. We find, however, that we can place no certain reliance on this conjecture, although we may reasonably suppose that Shakespeare's drama was written about that period.*

The two main elements in its plot—the incident of the casket and the incident of the bond—are to be found in the collection of mediæval romances known as the " Gesta Romanorum;" but the special version of the latter story adopted by Shakespeare seems to have been first given in the " Pecorone" of Giovanni Fiorentino. We have now no knowledge of any English translation of the tale as told by Giovanni. But it is a singular

---

* If we are to believe that Henslowe's Diary (printed for the Shakespeare Society, under the editorship of Mr. J. P. Collier, in 1845) was drawn up with rigorous accuracy, we must conclude that the Lord Admiral's company of players, of which he was himself one of the chief managers, and the Lord Chamberlain's company, of which Shakespeare was a member, were acting together at the Newington Butts Theatre, from the 3rd of June, 1594, to the 18th of July, 1596, for we find him entering under the following heading all the performances which took place during that interval :—" In the name of God, amen: beginning at Newington, my Lord Admiral's and my Lord Chamberlain's men, as followeth, 1594." But it is impossible to believe that the two companies continued united throughout that period. We do not find in all Henslowe's entries a single piece which can with any certainty be assigned to Shakespeare, and this could hardly have occurred if his company had acted with Henslowe's during the whole time which elapsed from the month of June, 1594, to the month of July, 1596. It is, besides, extremely improbable that the Lord Chamberlain's company did not perform in the winter seasons of these two years at their own house in the Blackfriars. Henslowe drew a line under the date of the 13th of June, 1594 ; a remarkable increase took place in his receipts after that period; and it is very possible that the connection between the two companies, whatever may have been its nature, was then brought to a close.

circumstance that in nearly every instance in which we are unable to lay our hands on any English work that could have made Shakespeare acquainted with a foreign author whom he imitated in the production of his own dramas, we meet with indications of the existence of some old English play which might have supplied him with this information; and in endeavouring to ascertain the origin of the plot of the "Merchant of Venice," we seem to find this resource again available. Stephen Gosson, in a tract published in 1579, and entitled "The School of Abuse," bestows special commendations upon certain plays, one of which he calls "The Jew shown at the Bull, representing the greediness of worldly choosers, and bloody minds of usurers." It is easy to conceive that from these "worldly choosers" and "bloody-minded usurers" Shakespeare may have taken the episodes both of the casket and of the bond in his "Merchant of Venice;" and while we know that in his day such a play as this "Jew" existed, it would be idle for us to enter into any discussion as to the possibility of his having derived from some foreign source the materials of his drama.

In the "Merchant of Venice" we see the poet, steadily passing into the larger truth and freedom of his dramatic representation of life. But his genius still wears some remnants of the fetters which impeded the strength of its first flight. The incidents of his story are complex and improbable; they hold somewhat loosely together; the whole work forms no perfect and harmonious combination, rising naturally out of the play of intelligible accidents or passions. The tale of the casket is closely allied to the idle devices of romance; and our faith is quite as hesitatingly given to the cardinal incident of the bond, with all its extravagant details. The actors in the scene, as might readily be expected, from the melodramatic cast of its general conception, are not always naturally and consistently exhibited. Shylock, no doubt, forms in the main an admirably vigorous and striking figure; but some portions of his motives, or of his character, seem involved in considerable obscurity. We do not see the precise ground of his insane malignity to Antonio; and, indeed, from the peculiarly gentle character of the latter, it is hardly conceivable that he should have heaped upon any one the indignities to which the Jew complains that he has himself been subjected. The engagement ultimately extracted from him that he should become a Christian as the condition on which his life was to be spared, seems to be a mere careless concession of the poet to the extravagance of popular taste, or of stage conventionality. The marriage of Gratiano with Nerissa is another of Shakespeare's hasty devices; and it may be worth while to point out a further slight deviation in the play from absolute dramatic consistency. In the second scene of the second act Gratiano, after undertaking to observe a greater sobriety in his language for the future, carefully exempts from the period of this engagement the coming evening, when he is to be allowed full license for his humour at the promised convivial entertainment. He does not, however, appear at all at such a festival; and the expectation we were led to entertain of some unusual merriment seems to be by this means somewhat unfairly disappointed. The special heroine of the play does not yet exhibit Shakespeare's complete mastery of female character. Portia displays at first some of the liveliness of the Rosalind of "As You Like It," and subsequently some of the persuasive eloquence of the Isabella of "Measure for Measure;" but in one or two of her allusions she appears somewhat to overstep the bounds of the most perfect maidenly delicacy; and she hardly ever quite realises the grace and the charm of those two later female creations of the poet. Jessica plays an inferior and a more questionable part, and Shakespeare appears to have felt no desire greatly to commend her to our favour.

The fifth act of this play is but a light and fanciful addition to its main plot. The real story of the piece had already been fully told. But no one could wish on that account to lose this graceful and brilliant afterlude. It is the least dramatic, but it is, at the same time, the most poetical portion of the whole work. The dreamy charm of the moon-lit avenue of Belmont on that bright night for ever haunts our memories; the echo of the distant harmony still steeps our senses in its enchanted languor:—

> How sweet the moonlight sleeps upon this bank!
> Here will we sit, and let the sounds of music
> Creep in our ears; soft stillness, and the night,
> Become the touches of sweet harmony.
> Sit, Jessica: Look, how the floor of heaven
> Is thick inlaid with patines of bright gold;
> There's not the smallest orb which thou behold'st,
> But in his motion like an angel sings,
> Still quiring to the young-ey'd cherubins:
> Such harmony is in immortal souls;
> But, whilst this muddy vesture of decay
> Doth grossly close it in, we cannot hear it.

This remote music of the spheres is no unfitting accompaniment to the rapt beauty of the scene; and for the moment, at least, we can hardly desire any less aërial sounds to disturb this soft trance of nature:—

> Peace, ho! the moon sleeps with Endymion,
> And would not be awak'd.

The "Merchant of Venice," in spite of the general extravagance of its plot, is one of the distinctive works of Shakespeare. He does not yet, it is true, display the fulness of his powers. Shylock is not one of his largest and most harmonious creations; but Shylock, from his wholly exceptional individuality, and the special vividness with which he is represented, is still one of the poet's most marked and most expressive types of human character.

AS YOU LIKE IT.

We believe that we can fix within very narrow limits the date of this fine comedy, and there can be no doubt about the source from which its story was derived. It was entered in the books of the Stationers' Company on the 4th of August, 1600, together with "King Henry V.," "Much Ado about Nothing," and Ben Jonson's "Every Man in his Humour;" but to this entry was attached a "stay," or an injunction against their publication. That prohibition, however, seems to have been soon evaded or removed in the case of the three last works, as they were all published in the course of that year, or of the year succeeding; while "As You Like It" does not appear to have been printed until its insertion in the folio of 1623.

This play is not included in Meres' list of the year 1598. It is very probable, therefore, that it was not produced before that period. There are other circumstances which tend to strengthen that conjecture. Stowe, in his "Survey of London," tells us that in the year 1598 there had been set up, near the Cross in Cheapside, "a curious wrought tabernacle of grey marble, and in the same an alabaster image of Diana, and water conveyed from the Thames, prilling from her naked breast." Malone felt confident that Rosalind, when she says, in Act IV., Scene I., of "As You Like It," "I will weep for nothing, like Diana in the fountain," is alluding to this statue. Mr. Collier, however, thinks that we can draw no such inference from these words, as Stowe expressly states that the water was "prilling from the breast" of the figure; and the point is one on which we can hardly feel any absolute certainty. We believe we can rely with more confidence, as an indication of the date of this play, on the quotation made in it (Act III., Scene V.) of a line from Marlowe's "Hero and Leander."

" Dead Shepherd! now I find thy saw of might;
Who ever lov'd, that lov'd not at first sight?"

"Hero and Leander" was entered in the Stationers' Registers in 1593, and again in 1597; but it does not appear to have been published until 1598; and although, as Mr. Dyce observes, " in those days, poems by distinguished writers were often much read in manuscript before they reached the press," we think it very unlikely that Shakespeare would have made a distinct reference of this description to a passage in a still unpublished work of a deceased poet. Under these circumstances, we may fairly assume that it was at some period between the commencement of the year 1598 and the summer of the year 1600, " As You Like It " was composed.

The plot of this comedy is clearly founded on a novel by Thomas Lodge, called " Rosalynd. Euphues' Golden Legacie," &c., which was first published in 1590, and was re-published in 1592, and again in 1598.* The characters of Jaques, of Touchstone, and of Audrey are entirely of Shakespeare's own invention ; but, in every incident in which they do not figure, he has followed the novel with considerable, and often with minute, fidelity ; and it is evidently to the closeness of the copy we are to attribute the improbabilities which his work occasionally presents. The horrible malignity, for instance, of Oliver, his extraordinary conversion, and the sudden attachment which springs up between him and Celia, are all to be found in the original story. But the whole of the dialogue, and all the admirable gaiety and movement of the scene, are the work of the dramatist ; and it is curious to observe what a wholly new life he has infused into the extravagant adventures narrated by Lodge, with a certain eloquence and passion, it is true, but with a much more remarkable amount of tedious and elaborate circumlocution and formality.

" As You Like It " is one of the most popular creations of the poet's lighter fancy. " In no other play," says Mr. Hallam, " do we find the bright imagination and fascinating grace of Shakespeare's youth so mingled with the thoughtfulness of his maturer age." The fresh, youthful charm of the work is mainly centred in the brilliant vivacity and the passionate tenderness

---

* It is inserted in Mr. Collier's "Shakespeare's Library."

of the disguised Rosalind; while the more serious relief to this romantic foreground is supplied by the subdued and contemplative temper in which the banished Duke, and the moralising Jaques, and their companions, survey those vicissitudes and contrasts of life which their experience of courts and of solitude has presented. In this portion of the work, we find, we think, more than is usual, even in Shakespeare, of the deeper irony of life; and the light and fantastic form itself of the " humorous sadness" of the principal characters, seems only more completely to reveal the depth of that abyss of distrust and scepticism with which they regard the idle illusions of this " universal theatre."

The charm of the work lies in its brighter passion. Over the whole scene is spread the light grace of a half-enchanted forest land. This was the favourite retreat of Shakespeare in his more airy comic mood. It was a reminiscence of his own early joy in the streams, and the meadows, and the woodlands of leafy Warwickshire. This remembrance readily coloured and inspired his fancy throughout all the labours of his after life. But there was always a certain amount of extravagance, and even of unmeaningness, in the form in which he displayed his more purely sportive powers, and his more purely personal predilections. Touchstone is one of his characteristic creations; but the wit of Touchstone, whenever he passes out of that stage of vague and curious mental incoherency which is his most admirably comic condition, is apt to be over-strained, obscure, comparatively purposeless, and deficient in ideal truth and refinement; and all the mere verbal fencing of the other personages partakes, more or less, of the same characteristics. The real power of the work is shown in its fresh and graceful exhibition of the growth and play of feeling, in the fine harmony of its versification, and in the rapid flow of its dialogue. The great difficulty in this, as in any other drama, was not the discovery of striking thoughts, or sentiments, or images, but it was the faculty of imparting to its varied scenes, under imaginative forms, the subtle life and truth of Nature. Shakespeare has given to this charming comedy no small share of this bright vitality. In the heart of the Forest of Arden, "under the shade of melancholy boughs," we are never wholly removed beyond the reach of a busy and an immediate human interest; and it is this ever-changeful yet ever-present dramatic energy that lends to the magical illusions of "As You Like It" their most certain and most enduring hold on our hearts and our memories.

THE MERRY WIVES OF WINDSOR.

This play was published very imperfectly in a quarto volume in 1602,* was re-published in the same form in 1619, and was printed for the first time in a perfect shape in the folio of 1623.

In looking over these early editions the question at once meets us whether we are to regard the quarto of 1602 as a mere mutilated copy, made up from memory, or from loose notes of the comedy as it was originally written by the poet, or whether we are to suppose that it reproduced with general accuracy his own first imperfect sketch of his work. We have little or no doubt that we must place it in the first of these two classes. The quarto wants, throughout, the fulness of the complete edition. It is distinguished by a baldness and a poverty in its whole form, which are utterly unlike the true manner of Shakespeare. There is not, at the same time, the smallest improbability in the supposition that many of his works were thus imperfectly committed to the press. On the contrary, we should consider it almost wholly incredible that the greatest and most popular of all dramatists should have escaped a species of literary piracy, to which we know, upon direct evidence, that some of his contemporaries were exposed.

---

* This edition has been reprinted for the Shakespeare Society, under the editorship of Mr. Halliwell.

We draw our conclusion in this case from the whole form of the quarto version of the play; and we are confirmed in it by one minute and special testimony. The quarto does not contain a word of the opening dialogue between Justice Shallow, Slender, and Sir Hugh Evans, with the remarkable introduction of the coat-of-arms and the white luces of the Shallow family. This whole passage must have appeared almost wholly meaningless to any old copyist who did not possess a special knowledge of one of the obscure details in Shakespeare's history. We believe that it contains a distinct allusion to the Lucy family, and we do not think it at all probable that Shakespeare, on a revision of his work, would have made to it so unnecessary an addition, or at all events that he would have made it after the death of Sir Thomas Lucy, which took place in the month of July, 1600.

Dennis, the critic and dramatist, has handed down to us a tradition, which, if we could only place in it any absolute trust, would undoubtedly afford a fair presumption that the "Merry Wives of Windsor" proceeded in an unfinished state from the author's own hands. In the year 1702 this writer published an alteration of Shakespeare's play, and in an address prefixed to his work, after alluding to the favour which the "Merry Wives of Windsor" had found with Queen Elizabeth, he proceeds as follows:—"This comedy was written at her command, and by her direction, and she was so eager to see it acted, that she commanded it to be finished in fourteen days; and was afterwards, as tradition tells us, very well pleased at the representation." Rowe, in his "Life of Shakespeare," written in 1709, relates a similar story, with some change in its accompaniments. He states that Queen Elizabeth "was so well pleased with that admirable character of Falstaff, in the two parts of Henry IV., that she commanded him to continue it for one play more, and to show him in love. This is said to be the occasion of his writing the 'Merry Wives of Windsor.'" It is supposed that the tradition thus set forth was transmitted from Sir William

Davenant, either through Dryden or through Betterton the actor, and it may be that it is not wholly unfounded. But we do not think that we can attach any credit to the statement of Dennis that Queen Elizabeth commanded that the work should be finished in fourteen days. That allegation is in itself utterly improbable, and we can never rely upon a distant tradition for the perfect accuracy of small details of this description.

The probable date of this comedy affords another perplexing problem, and one on which a great diversity of opinion prevails among the commentators. It must, of course, present a double aspect, if we are to assume that the poet himself produced two different versions of his work. It has been generally taken for granted that the play, in its original shape, must have been written some time between the year 1597 and the year 1602, when the quarto edition was published. But Mr. Charles Knight is of opinion that this is one of the very early compositions of Shakespeare, and that it was probably first produced very shortly after the year 1592. He is led to the adoption of this conclusion by the internal evidence of immaturity which the whole work, as it appears in the quarto, seems to him to afford, by the absence of any immediate connection between it and the historical dramas in which the same characters are introduced, and by one curious piece of external testimony which he believes that he has discovered. In the earlier, as in the later edition of the play, several allusions are made to certain depredations which the landlords of the inns along the line from Brentford to Reading sustained at the hands of some Germans, or supposed Germans, who, it was said, were about to visit the Court; and Mr. Knight thinks that those passages refer to the Prince of Würtemberg and his suite, who, as he finds from an old German tract, came to England and visited Queen Elizabeth at Windsor Castle, in the year 1592. It appears that this prince had been furnished with a sort of passport, addressed to all justices of the peace, mayors, &c., in this country, informing them that he was to be furnished with shipping and post-horses, "he paying nothing for the same." We must confess that, even with this additional piece of evidence, we can place no kind of trust in Mr. Knight's supposition. If Shakespeare was alluding to this event, we do not see why he might not have done so a few years after its occurrence. But we must, besides, very much doubt whether Mr. Knight has not mistaken the real nature of the whole transaction on which his conjecture is founded. The probability is, we think, that these supposed Germans were but cheats and impostors. In both versions of the play they throw the servant who accompanied them into the mire, they ride off with the horses which had been lent to them; and the whole episode is treated as "cozenage, mere cozenage."

The "Merry Wives of Windsor" is not mentioned by Meres in 1598, and the omission of so remarkable a work from his list affords a strong presumption that it was not in existence at that period. It seems, besides, extremely improbable that this comedy was written before the First Part, at all events, of " King Henry IV." In that drama Falstaff was originally introduced under the name of Oldcastle; and in one of the rhyming lines in the first edition of the " Merry Wives of Windsor "—" How Falstaff varlet vile "— which stands in the same words in the amended copy, the metre would not admit of the employment of that name. Malone thought, plausibly enough, that the line uttered by Falstaff (Act I., Scene III.)—" Sail like my pinnace to these golden shores," or "the golden shores," as it runs in the quarto, shows that this comedy must have been written after Sir Walter Raleigh's return from Guiana, in 1596. But this is, perhaps, an argument on which we cannot very strongly insist.

The " Merry Wives of Windsor" occupies an almost entirely independent position in Shakespeare's drama; it bears no immediate relation of any kind to the historical plays in which several of the same characters are introduced.

But if we are to attempt to take it in the order of its composition, we are strongly inclined to think that it must have been written either immediately before or immediately after "King Henry V.," and it seems to us much more probable that it followed, than that it preceded, that drama. Nym, who is one of the companions of Falstaff, both in the "Merry Wives of Windsor" and in "King Henry V.," does not appear at all in either part of "King Henry IV." There are some other striking resemblances between the characters in the two first-mentioned works. In each of them a Welshman makes a somewhat prominent figure; and in each of them, too, we have one or more Frenchmen speaking English after the imperfect manner of their countrymen. Shakespeare was led, by the very nature of his subject, to introduce French characters into his "King Henry V.;" and it seems likely that, finding they afforded there a certain description of amusement, he again brought forward a specimen of the class in the "Merry Wives of Windsor," in which the presence of such a person as Dr. Caius would, in the first instance, have been a much less obvious contrivance. The probability is, we think, that after having promised in the prologue to the "Second Part of King Henry IV." a continuation of the humours of Falstaff in "King Henry V.," he found, in representing the great contest which ended in the field of Agincourt, that he could not fittingly redeem this engagement; and, after that disappointment, he was naturally disposed to fulfil as far as possible his original design, by reviving as many of the personages of the histories as he could conveniently bring together in a new and purely comic performance.

We believe we have a fair right to infer that "King Henry V." was produced in the summer of 1599; and if the "Merry Wives of Windsor" followed that drama, we think it very probable that it was written in the winter of the same year, or in the spring of the year succeeding. The satire directed against the Lucy family was probably composed before the death of Sir Thomas Lucy, to which we have already adverted.

Shakespeare himself has created one of the perplexities we have to encounter in an examination of this play. We find it wholly impossible to reconcile the circumstances under which some of the characters are here presented to us with those under which we know them in the three historical dramas. Falstaff, in the "Merry Wives of Windsor," may, without any great effort of imagination, be supposed to be living at Windsor at any period, in his old age. Pistol, Nym, and Bardolph are brought before us at some still more indefinite epoch. In "King Henry V." we are told that Falstaff died a natural death, and that Nym and Bardolph were hanged. It would, we think, be manifestly unreasonable to debar the poet, on this account, from the right of taking them up again at any time or under any circumstances he might think proper to select. But we should not be at all surprised to find that, after having finally disposed of them in another drama, he should now "fight shy," as we think he does, of their well-known antecedents. In Act III., Scene II., of the folio copy, we find Page objecting to Fenton as a son-in-law, on the ground that "he kept company with the wild Prince and Poins;" and in Act IV., Scene V., Falstaff alludes to the ridicule to which he would be exposed, if it should "come to the ear of the Court how he had been transformed." But these are the only allusions, we believe, in the present play to that wonderful comedy in which Falstaff figures in other company and in other scenes.

Justice Shallow, like Falstaff, is here introduced to us at some unknown period towards the close of his life. He himself says (Act III., Scene I.) that he has "lived fourscore years and upward." But we can never feel safe in interpreting with literal exactness the chronological allusions in the dramas of Shakespeare.*

---

* Ritson, a critic and antiquary, who wrote towards the close of

Mrs. Quickly, however, is the most shifting character in the whole of these four plays. In the "First Part of King Henry IV." she is the wife of the host of the Boar's Head Tavern; in the "Second Part of King Henry IV." (Act II., Scene I.) we find her suddenly changed into a "poor widow of Eastcheap;" in "King Henry V." she is married to Pistol, and she afterwards dies "at the Spital." In the "Merry Wives of Windsor" (Act II., Scene II.) she and Falstaff meet as perfect strangers to one another, although in the "Second Part of King Henry IV." (Act II., Scene IV.) she had known him "these twenty-nine years." We are aware that these detailed references may seem little better than the idle pedantry of criticism. But they serve to show how freely the poet takes up the incidents of which he finds it for the moment convenient to avail himself in the construction of his dramas. We believe that in writing this comedy he was perfectly prepared to conform to the wish of his audiences that he should again bring before them characters with which they had already become familiarised; and, as the Mrs. Quickly of the historical plays would have been in his way in the "Merry Wives of Windsor," he retained her name, but gave her a wholly new part to perform. And this was done entirely in the spirit in which his whole drama was produced. He never at any time had any anxious retrospect to bestow upon his own past achievements; and the rapid variety and the careless freedom of his genius are perpetually reflected from every page of his writings.

We believe there can be no doubt about the sources from

---

the last century, entered into a series of elaborate calculations for the purpose of showing that we must read "threescore" instead of "fourscore" years in this passage. Malone, however, in a note which affords a very favourable specimen of his useful research, clearly points out the folly of applying to the chronology of Shakespeare the test of a minute comparison of facts, and cites various passages which prove that the poet habitually used the term "fourscore years" as a mode of designating extreme old age.

which Shakespeare derived any incidents in this play that were not of his own invention. In the "Piacevoli Notti" of Straparola there is a tale in which a young gallant unknowingly makes a betrayed husband the confidant of his intrigues, and in which he escapes through various stratagems, somewhat resembling those employed in the adventures of Falstaff, from the danger of detection to which he is, under those circumstances, naturally exposed; and, again, there is a tale of the same general design in the "Pecorone" of Giovanni Fiorentino. This story of Giovanni was copied almost literally in "The Fortunate, the Deceived, and the Unfortunate Lovers," a collection of tales of which we have no edition of an earlier date than 1632. The other version of the adventures given by Straparola is freely translated in "The Tale of the Two Lovers of Pisa," which forms a portion of Tarlton's "Newes out of Purgatorie," a work which, although it bears no date, was in all probability published about the year 1590. We think we may take it for granted that this latter story is the only one now known from which Shakespeare could have taken any hints for the composition of the "Merry Wives of Windsor."

The estimation in which this play has been held has undergone some considerable changes. We have no evidence to show what was the nature of the reception which it met among the poet's own contemporaries. But in the days of the Restoration it appears to have enjoyed an extraordinary amount of favour. Dennis tells us that "in the reign of King Charles the Second, when people had an admirable taste of comedy, all those men of extraordinary parts, who were the ornaments of that Court, as the late Duke of Buckingham, my Lord Normandy, my Lord Dorset, my Lord Rochester," &c., "were in love with the beauties of this comedy;" and then this writer expresses his own belief that "as the Falstaff in the 'Merry Wives' is certainly superior to that of the 'Second Part of Harry the Fourth,' so it can hardly be said to be inferior to that of the First." We need not, perhaps, much wonder at this strange criticism when we remember that it was written at a period when the really great works of Shakespeare were but little known or valued; but we cannot help feeling some surprise at finding a man of refined taste, like Warton, in the middle of the last century, characterising this play as the "most complete specimen of his [Shakespeare's] comic powers."

The modern critics, for the most part, judge the work differently, and, in our opinion, much more correctly. We believe that the comic power in the "Merry Wives of Windsor" is strikingly inferior to that displayed in either of the two Parts of "King Henry IV." It is, to some extent, different in kind, and not merely in degree. Falstaff is, of course, the great comic figure in the three productions; but Falstaff in the "Merry Wives" is brought before us in a new character and with greatly diminished effect. He is removed from that careless tavern life and from that brilliant companionship in which alone his boundless and vivacious humour could naturally and fully unfold all its resources. He is not playing, half consciously, a large part in all the strength and freedom of the highest comic genius; he does not command, by his inimitable, inexhaustible drollery, the wonder and amazement of his audience; he is no longer master of the situation. He is a butt and a dupe, and not mainly a triumphant wit and humourist. He is enfeebled and subdued, and the genius by which he was created is somewhat subdued with him. The poet seems throughout the play to labour unwillingly and dispiritedly, upon more or less uncongenial materials.

All the principal characters in the scene are, like Falstaff, reduced below their former levels; and by this means, no doubt, they hold towards him their old relative positions. Justice Shallow is no longer the wonderful chatterer we have known elsewhere, feebly leaning for support on the equally feeble Davy, or, as far as his helplessness will allow him, sorrowfully recalling the distant memory of the supposed happy days he had once spent in the distant city. Slender is one of Shakespeare's stupid clowns; but he is somewhat more stupid, and certainly not more amusing, than many other members of his class. Mrs. Quickly is so absolutely changed that, but for her name, we should hardly suspect that we had ever heard of her before. Bardolph, Pistol, and Nym have all lost something of their old originality and vigour. Pistol still draws largely upon his interminable store of dramatic bombast; but the fantastic ranting is now less needed and less happily applied.

The whole play is manifestly deficient in that large freedom of imagination which usually distinguishes the works of Shakespeare. Nearly all the principal characters are made up of a few idiosyncrasies which they are perpetually displaying under some peculiar form of expression. We cannot help suspecting that the plastic fancy of the poet may here have caught for the moment the special tone of Ben Jonson's comedy of "Every Man in his Humour," in which we know that he sustained one of the characters about the period of the composition of the "Merry Wives of Windsor;" and that he was thus led to introduce for once this narrow imitation of life into his own more imaginative drama. We see this peculiarity further manifested in the host of the Garter Tavern, in Sir Hugh Evans, and in Dr. Caius. There is, unquestionably, in the whole work a considerable amount of broad, strong humour; and we are not sure that any other writer could have presented his characters with the wonderful ease which distinguishes some portions of its dialogue. But we do not find revealed under that ease the poet's finest and subtlest insight into Nature; and we believe that there is little or nothing in this exceptional production which could have enabled us to form any complete conception of the depth, and truth, and freedom of all his highest comic as well as tragic creations.

TWELFTH NIGHT; OR, WHAT YOU WILL.

This comedy was first printed in the Folio of 1623. Malone supposed, from some slight allusions which he thought it contained, that it was written in 1607; and Tyrwhitt, from evidence of a similar description, was led to assign to it the probable date of 1614. A modern discovery has entirely disposed of both those conjectures. In the Diary of John Manningham, a member of the Middle Temple, we find the following entry:—

1601-2, Febr. 2.—At our feast we had a play called "Twelfth Night; or, What You Will," much like the "Comedy of Errors," or "Menæchmi" in Plautus, but most like and near to that in Italian called "Inganni." A good practice in it to make the steward believe his lady widow was in love with him, by counterfeiting a letter as from his lady, in general terms, telling him what she liked best in him, and prescribing his gesture in smiling, his apparel, &c., and then when he came to practice, making him believe they took him to be mad.

"Twelfth Night" was, therefore, acted early in 1602, according to our present computation of the year, and in all probability it was composed not very long before that period. It was not mentioned by Meres in 1598, and this circumstance affords a strong presumption that it was not at that time in existence. There is in the play itself a passage which seems to favour this conclusion. In Act III., Scene II., Maria says of Malvolio, "He does smile his face into more lines than are in the new map, with the augmentation of the Indies." The commentators in general are disposed to believe that this passage refers to one of the maps in an English translation of Linschoten's "Voyages," which was first published in the year 1598. That map, as Steevens observes, "is multilineal in the extreme, and is the first in which the *Eastern Islands* are included." Mr. Dyce, however, thinks it likely that Maria is speaking, not of a map inserted in a book, but of some separate print; and we have no means of offering a decided contradiction of his opinion. But the map in Linschoten's "Voyages" so completely fulfils, by the number of its lines and the country which it for the first time depicts, the special conditions of

Maria's comparison, that we believe we may fairly suppose it is to it she is referring. In any case we should take it for granted, on the internal evidence alone, that " Twelfth Night " is not one of the poet's very early works.

The plot of the more serious part of this play may have been derived from any one of a number of sources. The cross-purposes to which the Duke, and Viola, and Olivia are exposed resemble the incidents in a variety of old tales and dramas; but their first origin is most probably to be traced to one of the stories of the Italian novelist, Bandello. There are three Italian comedies, each of them published before the time of Shakespeare, in which the same incidents are embodied. It is not necessary, however, nor would it even be reasonable, to suppose that he was acquainted with any one of them. The tale of Bandello is closely imitated in a story which forms portion of a work by Barnaby Rich, published in 1581, under the title of " Rich, his Farewell to the Military Profession." The whole substance of the complicated love adventure in " Twelfth Night" was here available for Shakespeare's use. But all the more broadly comic incidents in his drama seem to be entirely of his own creation; and it is hardly necessary to add that it is his own genius that imparts to the more romantic adventures he has employed all their charm and all their vitality.

The central incident in the play is the complication of the loves of the Duke, of Viola, of Olivia, and, at a later stage, of Sebastian, whose presence helps so materially to the production of the final escape from this series of perplexities. With the fortunes of these more distinguished personages are more or less closely interwoven the misadventures and the humiliation of Malvolio, and the knavery, dupery, and rioting of the two disreputable but truly comic figures of Sir Toby Belch and Sir Andrew Aguecheek; while the whole scene is further enlivened by the humour of the clown, and by the natural tact and cleverness of the lively and astute Maria.

The grace and the vigour of Shakespeare's genius are

frequently observable throughout his delineation of the whole of these incidents; but we cannot class this work among his highest achievements, and the admiration with which we regard it is by no means free from any qualification. There is much of extravagance and improbability in the development of its more romantic incidents, and it thus frequently becomes less purely creative and less absolutely truthful than less striking productions of the poet's genius. The treatment of the story is sometimes manifestly melodramatic, as, for instance, in the appearance of Antonio, and his arrest by the officers, in Act III., Scene IV.; and, we think we may add, in the hurried and strange marriage contract between Olivia and Sebastian. The disguise of Viola is one of those artifices which are only possible in the large domain of poetry; and the freedom of poetry itself seems somewhat abused in the representation of the supposed complete likeness between her and her brother. The merely comic business of the play is more naturally executed. Many people will probably regard the misadventures of the befooled and infatuated Malvolio as its most vigorous and amusing episode.* But we cannot help thinking that the punishment to which the vanity of Malvolio is exposed is somewhat coarse and excessive. In spite of the bad character which he bears in his very name, there is nothing in his conduct, as far as we can see, to justify the unscrupulous persecution of his tormentors. The poet himself, when the pressure of dramatic necessity is removed, seeks to treat this incident in his usual easy temper; but we doubt whether such an outrageous practical joke could ever be

---

* King Charles I. seems to have been of this opinion. In his copy of Shakespeare's Dramatic Works, he inserted "Malvolio," with his own hand, as the title of this play. In the same way he called " Much Ado About Nothing," " Benedick and Beatrice;" "A Midsummer Night's Dream," "Pyramus and Thisby;" "As You Like It," "Rosalind;" and "All's Well that Ends Well," "Mr. Paroles."—*Malone's Shakespeare, by Boswell,* Vol. XI., p. 500.

forgotten or forgiven by its victim. We confess that, as exemplifications of Shakespeare's wonderful comic power, we prefer to this humiliation and discomfiture of Malvolio the scenes in which Sir Toby and Sir Andrew make the welkin ring to the echo of their uproarious merriment. It is often in lighter sketches of this description that the hand of Shakespeare is most distinguishable and most inimitable; and this triumphant protest against the pretensions of a narrow and jealous austerity will no doubt last as long as social humour forms one of the elements of human life :—

Sir Toby. Dost thou think, because thou art virtuous, there shall be no more cakes and ale?
Clown. Yes, by Saint Anne; and ginger shall be hot i' the mouth, too.

We find in "Twelfth Night" no striking indication of Shakespeare's power in the delineation of character. Such a display was, perhaps, hardly compatible with the general predominance of the lighter romantic element throughout the whole work. The passion of the Duke for Olivia is neither very deep nor very dramatic. It is merely dreamy, restless, longing, and enthralling desire. It is the offspring of a mood which, we cannot help thinking, was specially familiar to the poet himself; and it seems directly akin to the state of feeling which he has revealed in his sonnets. We do not believe, however, that he required for its delineation the light of a personal experience. His airy imagination, aided by his general human sensibility, enabled him truly to reproduce this, and perhaps all other conceivable passions; and it may be that it was when his fancy was most disengaged, it was most readily and most vividly creative. Neither Viola nor Olivia can be ranked among his finest female characters. The former has a difficult and a somewhat unnatural part to sustain; and although she fills it with considerable brilliancy and spirit, she scarcely enlists our strongest sympathies in her favour. The allusion, however, to her untold love is one of the bright passages in Shakespeare's drama, and will for ever form for tender hearts a cherished remembrance. The character of Olivia suffers much more from the perplexities or temptations to which she becomes exposed, and she certainly fails to display, amidst those trials, the highest maidenly purity and refinement.

"Twelfth Night" is, we think, on the whole, one of the bright, fanciful, and varied productions of Shakespeare's less earnest dramatic mood; but it possesses neither complete imaginative nor complete natural truthfulness; and it seems to us to be more or less deficient throughout in consistency, in harmony, in the depth and firmness of touch, which distinguish the finer creations of his genius.

ALL'S WELL THAT ENDS WELL.

The probable date of this play forms one of the minor problems of Shakespearian criticism. Dr. Farmer, in his "Essay on the Learning of Shakespeare," published in 1767, was the first who expressed a belief that this is the comedy which Meres, in 1598, mentions under the title of "Love's Labour's Won;" and nearly all the succeeding commentators have adopted this conjecture. It does not seem to us, however, that the evidence is by any means conclusive in its favour. Coleridge believed that "All's Well that ends Well" was "originally intended as the counterpart of 'Love's Labour's Lost.'" But we can discover no indication of any such intention, and there is, we think, as little resemblance between the two works as between any other two comedies of their author. The present title, too, of "All's Well that ends Well" seems indicated, with a distinctness which is very unusual in the Shakespearian drama, in several of its concluding passages. At the end of Act IV., Scene IV., we find Helena telling us—

All's well that ends well: still, &c.

In Act V., Scene I., she repeats the same sentiment:—

> All's well that ends well; yet, &c.

The last line but one of the whole play is—

> All yet seems well; and, if it end so meet.

And the second line of the epilogue still recurs to this idea:—

> All is well ended, if this suit be won.

We may observe, however, that the termination of this last line recalls the title of Meres' play of "Love's Labour's Won;" and it seems just possible that we may find another echo of the same designation in the language addressed by Diana to Bertram, towards the close of Act IV., Scene II. :—

> You have won
> A wife of me, though there my hope be done.

And again, a few lines lower down, we have—

> Only, in this disguise, I think't no sin,
> To cozen him that would unjustly win.

And, finally, in one of Helena's last addresses to Bertram, Act V., Scene III., she asks him—

> This is done:
> Will you be mine, now you are doubly won?

Tieck and Coleridge thought they could discover in this comedy traces of two different styles; the one belonging to Shakespeare's earlier, and the other to his later manner; and several of the more modern commentators are disposed to accept this judgment, and to conclude that the work was first produced, under the name of "Love's Labour's Won," at a very early stage in the poet's dramatic career, and that it was many years afterwards brought out by him in an altered and amended form, and under the name by which it is now known. We are not sure that this conjecture will derive any very substantial support from the passages we have above quoted, and which seem to recall each of the two titles. But a more solid presumption in its favour may be found in the contrast that appears to exist between different portions of the play as it stands. There are in it some scenes which contain more of Shakespeare's loose, negligent rhymes than we usually find in any works which we can with perfect certainty assign to the maturity of his powers. We allude more particularly to the dialogue in Act II., Scene I., between the King and Helena, on the occasion of their first interview, and to the language of the King, Act II., Scene III., in remonstrating with Bertram on his refusal to accept Helena as a wife. On the other hand, we think we can perceive in many portions of this drama a firmness of conception, a steady insight into Nature, a personal freedom on the part of the poet, an absence of any readiness to enter into a compromise with the weaknesses and vices of the world, which do not naturally belong to the imagination or the passions of early life, and which we do not find displayed in his undoubted earlier dramas. We do not, however, believe that this evidence is to be found in any single passage so much as in the pervading spirit of the work; and we certainly cannot follow Malone in thinking that the words quoted by the King in Act I., Scene II., "'Let me not live,' quoth he, 'after my flame lacks oil,'" &c., taken by themselves, might not have been written by Shakespeare at a comparatively early period in his dramatic career. But still less can we agree with the same critic that "the satirical mention made of the Puritans (Act I., Scene III.), who were the objects of King James's aversion—'Though honesty be no Puritan,'" &c., affords a reasonable ground for concluding that this play must have been written after that sovereign's accession to the throne. We have no evidence that "All's Well that ends Well" was ever acted before King James, and the whole character of Shakespeare's drama is utterly opposed to the supposition that he was in any way disposed to court royal favour by humouring royal passions.

We must add, however, that the dramas of Shakespeare

were always apt to contain great inequalities, and that we can never feel perfectly safe in concluding from their existence that any particular play was written at any definite period in his career. We doubt, too, whether he ever engaged in any careful revision of any of his works; and we are perfectly convinced that any such revision must have been with him a very unusual and exceptional operation.

Under these circumstances, we must leave the date of this play a subject of mere conjecture. We can have no doubt, however, on the other hand, as to the sources from which the main incidents in its plot were derived. Those incidents are closely copied from a tale which forms part of the "Decameron" of Boccaccio, and which 'was translated under the title of "Giletta of Narbona," by William Paynter, in the first volume of his "Palace of Pleasure," which was published in 1566. This information is of some use in qualifying our judgment of the poet's workmanship. There is much in the general outline of his drama of which we must decidedly disapprove; but we find that all his most objectionable episodes are taken from the old tale; and we must, therefore, hold him less directly answerable for them than we should have done if they had been entirely of his own invention. In the pages of Boccaccio and of Paynter, the King of France is suffering from the same malady which we find mentioned in the drama; he is cured by Giletta, who answers to Shakespeare's Helena; the latter obtains, as her reward, the unwilling hand of the young Count of Roussillon, who immediately leaves her for Florence, where she afterwards finds him attempting to intrigue with the daughter of a widow, and where she has, through the aid of this young woman, got possession of his ring, and has herself become a mother; and having thus fulfilled the two conditions on which alone he had engaged to recognise her as his wife, their reconciliation is ultimately effected. But the characters of the Countess, of the Clown, of Parolles, and of Lafeu, are wholly created by Shakespeare himself; and it is easy to see how much they contribute to give variety and animation to the worthless and extravagant story into which they are so naturally introduced.

The unamiable character of Bertram seems to constitute the great defect of this drama. He is young, brave, handsome, and high-born; but he is, at the same time, petulant, arrogant, cold, and selfish, and his very vices present no feature of impressive interest. The unwelcome part which he plays is, no doubt, in some measure, the result of the false position in which he has been unfairly placed by the understanding between the King and Helena; but his own character appears to have been made unnecessarily repulsive. We lose all trust in him when, immediately after his apparent repentance, we find him insolently untruthful in his account of his relations with Diana; and this unexpected aggravation of his demerits seems to be somewhat unaccountably introduced, as we have no such scene in the original tale of Boccaccio. The poet most certainly has treated his hero with no indulgence; and we must further admit that the vices which Bertram exhibits are by no means, in themselves, improbable or untrue to the common experience of the world. But in the hero of a romantic episode they are out of place, and they are here essentially undramatic. The disagreeable character of the young Count tends greatly to diminish the interest which we should, under other circumstances, be disposed to feel in the adventures of the beautiful and afflicted Helena. We can entertain no very intense desire that she should succeed in the pursuit of an object which seems hardly to deserve her devotion; and, besides, we cannot quite conceal from ourselves that she only attains it by the employment of an extravagant and a not very delicate stratagem. She is herself brought before us with some drawbacks from the general beauty and elevation of her character. She has clearly no very strong regard for rigid, unequivocating truthfulness. She does not really mean to go, as she announces, on a pilgrimage to the shrine of St. Jaques. It is not true, as she states to Diana, that she does not know Bertram's face. And, again, we find that she does not hesitate to cause false intelligence of the accomplishment of her pilgrimage and of her death to be conveyed to the camp at Florence. These departures from strict veracity harmonise, no doubt, readily enough with the rude spirit of old romance; but they contrast somewhat disagreeably with that general ideal perfection with which Shakespeare has invested many of his female characters, and Helena herself, in no small degree, among the number. But a scrupulous truthfulness is a virtue on the practice of which the poet hardly seems to have been disposed at any time very rigorously to insist.

It is not, however, in purely romantic adventures that we must expect to meet with the higher manifestations of Shakespeare's genius. The most admirable passages in this play are those in which he represents less extravagant aspects of life with his own curious fidelity to Nature. How finely Helena reveals to us the depth and the infatuation of her attachment to Bertram:—

> I am undone; there is no living, none,
> If Bertram be away. It were all one,
> That I should love a bright, particular star,
> And think to wed it, he is so above me:
> In his bright radiance and collateral light
> Must I be comforted, not in his sphere.

And in her subsequent dialogue with Parolles, with what subtle power she is made to play with the passion which consumes and all but over-masters her.

All the scenes in which Parolles figures are more or less characteristic of the hand of Shakespeare; but they cannot be ranked among his most felicitous comic efforts. Parolles has been compared to Falstaff; there is, however, we think, no very strong resemblance between the two characters. The humour of Falstaff is self-conscious and intellectual; the humour to which Parolles gives rise is the result of the involuntary exhibition of his insolence, cowardice, falsehood, and folly. The cool, sharp sagacity and the contemptuous frankness of the old lord, Lafeu, are admirably employed in the unmasking of this shallow impostor. The "drum" scene will perhaps be generally regarded as the culminating point of these humorous sketches. But in the hardness of its form and in the completeness of the savage triumph over the unhappy braggart, we cannot recognise the finer genius of Shakespeare. He seems, however, to have been always ready to push to the utmost extremity the exposure of worthless and shallow pretenders, as we think we can see in the ultimate fate of Pistol, Nym, and Bardolph in "King Henry V.," of Malvolio in "Twelfth Night," and of Parolles in the present comedy.

The language in "All's Well that Ends Well" is often rude and harsh. The whole work is deficient in easy flow and in fine harmony of fancy. It is certainly not the least vigorous, but we believe that it is one of the least graceful and least interesting of all the comedies of Shakespeare.

CYMBELINE.

This play is another of the works which we owe to the Shakespeare folio of 1623. It is there inserted among the tragedies, and it is even called the "Tragedie of Cymbeline." We cannot, however, adopt that classification. "Cymbeline" is not a tragedy in any sense in which the word is usually employed. But neither can it be regarded as a comedy in the natural acceptation of that term. We believe it must merely be called a drama, which is the only epithet we can with any propriety apply to many of the plays of Shakespeare, founded on romantic tales, or even on actual historical events.

No direct evidence of any kind has reached us with respect to the period of the composition of this work. Dr. Simon Forman, the astrologer, in a diary which is preserved in the Ashmolean Museum, states that he assisted at a performance of "Cymbeline," and gives a detailed account of its plot. He does not assign any date to this entry; but it seems likely that it was made either in 1610 or 1611. The general form of the versification in this drama, it has often been observed, bears a marked resemblance to that of the "Tempest" and of the "Winter's Tale," which were both most probably among the latest of the poet's works. Malone thought that "Cymbeline" was written about the year 1609. Nearly all the later commentators have coincided in this opinion, and we take it for granted that it must be substantially correct.

Cymbeline, King of Britain, and his sons, Guiderius and Arviragus, are briefly mentioned in Holinshed; but there is no trace in the "Chronicle" of any of the adventures through which they are made to pass in the play. Those adventures, which are of the most romantic and improbable description, do not, however, look as if they had been invented by Shakespeare himself; and it is quite possible that he copied or imitated them from some work which is now unknown. The other portion of his plot, which relates to the fortunes of Posthumus and Imogen, with the wager and the treachery of Iachimo, evidently had its origin in one of the tales of Boccaccio. But we have no means of determining how that tale became known to Shakespeare. It is not at all likely that he had recourse to a rude and imperfect translation, or rather imitation, of it, published in this country at so early a date as the year 1518. The whole "Decameron" was translated for the first time into English in 1620; but it is stated, in an introduction to that translation, that many of the novels had before appeared separately in an English dress; and it is easy to conceive that Shakespeare might in many ways have become acquainted with a story which must have long been popular throughout Europe, and which we find was used as the foundation of an old French miracle play that is still extant. The substance of it is embodied in a collection of tales which was published in this country at the commencement of the sixteenth century, under the title of "Westward for Smelts." Steevens says that the first edition of this publication is of the date of 1603, but no earlier copy than one of 1620 can now be discovered, and it is not improbable that Steevens was led into some mistake upon this point. It is certain, at all events, that Shakespeare must have consulted some other version of the incident, inasmuch as this tract contains no mention of the mole on Imogen's breast, to which such marked reference is made both in the Italian novel and in the drama of "Cymbeline." In the pages of Boccaccio, all the personages who take any direct part in the wager scene are merchants; and we cannot now find any work from which the dramatist could have directly copied any of his characters, except in as far as he might have learned from Holinshed the mere existence of Cymbeline and of his two sons.

This is another extravagant tale thrown into the form of a drama. Its plot is most singularly complicated, and, in the frequent succession of surprises and perplexities which it creates, it leaves little room for the development of real dramatic emotion. And yet "Cymbeline" is throughout written with much of Shakespeare's earnestness and vigour. It is by no means one of his more careless and hasty works. His special imagination is distinguishable in the whole of these scenes, although never, perhaps, in its largest and freest mood. The actors are almost exclusively princes, or courtiers, or the leaders of armies; and the language is not only imaginatively coloured, but is animated by a tone of sustained elegance and dignity. The dialogue, it is true, contains none of Shakespeare's more wonderful manifestations of the beauty or the power of expression, but we find in it many passages which could have come from no other hand. Imogen's desolation of heart, on learning the frightful change of feeling in Posthumus, is indicated with pathetic delicacy and grace; and the charm of a less agonising tenderness is finely thrown over the lamentations of the young princes on the loss of Fidele. In the interview between Imogen and Iachimo, the wily Italian exhibits wonderful dexterity, volubility, and rapidity of fancy in the various devices to which he is driven; and it may be worth while to remark how perfectly the poet has in this case given to a purely feigned state of mind the same appearance of intense earnestness with which he elsewhere invests real moods and passions. It seems to us that this inexhaustible versatility affords a striking proof of the independence and impersonality of his own genius.

But we must still regard this drama as one of Shakespeare's comparative failures. In it he never rises to his finer and more imaginative presentment of life. All the higher purposes of dramatic composition are here more or less sacrificed to the necessities of mere romantic narration. The most rapid examination of "Cymbeline" will show, we think, that it is not largely distinguished by vivid characterisation. The King is old and feeble, and has no striking part to perform. The two young princes are also comparatively unimportant figures; true enough to the very exceptional circumstances in which they are placed, but in no sense great dramatic creations. The Queen is a sort of diminutive Lady Macbeth, but without any opportunity, throughout these intricate and improbable episodes, of distinctly developing her character. Cloten is a more original portraiture; and although he is but slightly sketched, and in spite of some apparent contradictions here and there, which make him sometimes better and sometimes worse than we are prepared to expect, we seem to catch in his brutal but not wholly unmanly nature, glimpses of a real unmistakable human being of a very unconventional type. The "yellow Iachimo" is one of the many villains in Shakespeare's dramas who sin without any intelligible motive, and who afterwards, at the desired moment, appear to renounce their wickedness with an equally unaccountable facility.

The mode in which Posthumus himself is represented in these scenes is open to some objection. He appears to have been conceived by the poet as a perfectly complete and harmonious character, and, on the whole, perhaps he realises this conception. But he sometimes seems very strangely to fall short of this ideal standard. His consent to accept the wager, with all its conditions, is an absurd and unnatural resolution;

the solicitation which he addresses to Pisanio to kill his mistress is still more out of place, and is absolutely cruel and treacherous; and in Act V., Scene I., he could not have been prepared to pardon such a crime as that of which he still believes his wife to have been guilty, and he could no longer have spoken of her as "the noble Imogen." These may be that slight inconsistencies; they were, no doubt, introduced by the poet to meet his immediate dramatic requirements; but they disturb the harmony of the impression which we are disposed to form of the all-accomplished Posthumus. We are aware that Shakespeare manages the wager scene with more skill and delicacy than Boccaccio, who makes the offer of the extravagant test of female fidelity to proceed from the merchant whose own wife is to be tempted; but we are not satisfied with merely finding that a mediæval romance presents less of ideal truth and grace than the Shakespearian drama.

Imogen is the redeeming figure in this work; it is she alone that gives to it any deep vital interest. Without any apparent effort, or any straining after effect, the poet places her before us in the light of the most natural and engaging loveliness. The charm of her divine purity and tenderness is finely blended with the rapid but enchanting glimpses we obtain of her personal grace and attractiveness. She is undoubtedly one of the most exquisite of all Shakespeare's female creations. But we still cannot class such a figure among the greatest achievements of his genius, for it is evidently one that arose out of a refined sensibility rather than out of the highest creative imagination.

We have still to notice what seems the most curious passage in "Cymbeline." This is the vision of Posthumus, with the rhymes of the ghosts of his dead relatives, and of Jupiter himself, who "descends in thunder and lightning," together with the strange scroll which the dreamer finds before him on awaking. We feel utterly perplexed in attempting to reconcile the employment of this extravagant stage trick with our knowledge of the wonderful imagination and the fine sense of the poet. Some critics have taken it for granted that the scene was not written by himself, but that it was foisted into the work by the players. There does not, however, seem to be the slightest ground for attributing it to such a source, and, indeed, the episode appears to form an essential link in the conclusion of the drama. Our surprise at its introduction would be considerably diminished if we could find that it was only an imitation by Shakespeare of a passage in some work which he was generally copying in his play—for such a circumstance would be in complete accordance with a practice which he very frequently adopted; and we think it not at all improbable that it was in this way a large portion of " Cymbeline " was written. The only other mode in which we can attempt to account for the selection of so grotesque a show is by supposing that the dramatist was here yielding, in one of his careless rhyming moods, to what he knew to be the taste of his audiences. But, on either of these suppositions, we should still find a singular want of harmony between the weakness and extravagance of this episode and the clearness and strength which more or less characterise the rest of his composition. We are specially struck by this contrast on reading immediately afterwards, in the same scene, the singular comic dialogue between Posthumus and his gaolers—a dialogue so strangely natural, so wild and reckless, so replete with the careless, impersonal power of the poet. In it, as in many other portions of his dramas, he seems to allow the characters to speak absolutely for themselves; he has no interest in them; he knows nothing of them; he does not even appear disposed to indulge, through the medium which they afford, in any bitter and concealed irony; he is wholly passive and indifferent, and Nature follows, through the unforced play of his fancy, her own capricious, unaccountable will. The poet himself is no more to be found here than in the rhymes of Jupiter, or in any of the more serious incidents of his drama. But this impersonality is a constant and special accompaniment of the whole of these wonderful creations. We can never perfectly comprehend the nature of Shakespeare as it is revealed in his work. In his heights and in his depths he is still removed from us by the exceptional conditions of his personality and his genius; and we can never fully account for such wholly unconcerned and apparently illimitable power, or for the strange and even worthless uses to which that power is frequently applied.

THE TEMPEST.

This very remarkable creation of Shakespeare's fancy has given rise to a variety of inquiries and discussions. All that we know of it previously to its insertion in the Shakespeare Folio of 1623 is that, as we learn from the " Accounts of the Revels at Court," it was performed before James I. at Whitehall, on the 1st of November, 1611. The commentators in general are disposed to think that it was in that year a new work, and the whole character of the composition seems strongly to favour that supposition. There is also some external evidence which points more or less distinctly in the same direction.

Malone wrote a treatise for the purpose of proving that the opening incident in this play, and the one from which it receives its title, was suggested by the dreadful tempest which in July, 1609, dispersed the fleet of Sir George Somers and Sir Thomas Gates on its passage to Virginia, and by which the "Admiral-ship," as it was called, with both those officers on board, was wrecked on the Island of Bermuda—"the still vex'd Bermoothes" of the poet. It seems very probable that Malone was right in this conjecture. There can be no doubt that, after the lapse of some time, the loss of the vessel became known in this country, and attracted a considerable amount of public attention. We find that it was made the subject of special mention in two tracts, published in 1610, the one entitled, " A Discovery of the Bermudas, otherwise called the Isle of Devils," by " Sil. Jourdan;" and the other, " A true Declaration of the Estate of the Colony in Virginia." It appears, from both these tracts, that the ship was driven in and " fast lodged and locked" between two rocks, and that, although she was there at some distance from the shore, not a soul on board perished. Malone very reasonably infers that this latter circumstance was known to Shakespeare before he commenced to write the "Tempest." But as the first intelligence of the safety of the crew did not reach England until August or September, 1610, and as neither the "Discovery of the Bermudas," nor the "True Declaration," &c., was published until a month or two later, we seem justified in further assuming that no portion of this comedy was composed until the close of that year or the commencement of the year following.

In the third scene of the third act of the "Tempest" there are some allusions to the extravagant narratives of travellers; and here it is supposed by some of the commentators that the dramatist had specially in view the account published by Sir Walter Raleigh, in 1596, of his voyage to Guiana in the preceding year.

Another attempt to fix the date of this play from a reference which it is supposed to contain to a contemporary incident was made by Chalmers. In Act II., Scene II., Trinculo exclaims, on discovering the grotesque form of Caliban—" Were I in England now (as once I was), and had but this fish painted, not a holiday-fool there but would give a piece of silver: there would this monster make a man; any strange beast there makes a man: when they will not give a doit to relieve a lame beggar, they will lay out ten to see a dead Indian." Chalmers thought that the poet, in this bantering allusion to the capricious tastes of his countrymen, was thinking of the exhibition of one of a party of five Indians who were brought over to England in the year 1611. But this supposition rests on the most shadowy foundation, and cannot be said to be entitled to any serious credit.

There is another antiquarian discovery which seems to fix with much more probability a limit to the period within which this drama must have been written, and which, besides, possesses a special interest, from the momentary light which it throws on the course of Shakespeare's own reading. In a translation of Montaigne's Essays, by John Florio, published in 1603, we find the following passage, Book I., chap. xxx., page 102:—

It is a nation, would I answer Plato, that hath no kind of traffic, no knowledge of letters, no intelligence of numbers, no name of magistrate, nor of politic superiority; no use of service, of riches, or of poverty; no contracts, no successions, no dividences, no occupation but idle; no respect of kindred but common; no apparel but natural; no manuring of lands, no use of wine, corn, or metal. The very words that import lying, falsehood, treason, dissimulation, covetousness, envy, detraction, and pardon, were never heard of amongst them.

There can be no doubt that the above passage must have been present to the mind of Shakespeare while he was writing in the "Tempest" (Act II., Scene I.) the lines in which Gonzalo announces the state of society which he would establish in his imaginary island:—

> I' the commonwealth, I would by contraries
> Execute all things: for no kind of traffic
> Would I admit; no name of magistrate;
> Letters should not be known; no use of service,
> Of riches, or of poverty; no contracts,
> Successions; bound of land, tilth, vineyard, none:
> No use of metal, corn, or wine, or oil:
> No occupation; all men idle, all;
> And women too; but innocent and pure:
> No sovereignty.
>   *   *   *   *   *   *
> All things in common Nature should produce,
> Without sweat or endeavour: treason, felony,
> Sword, pike, knife, gun, or need of any engine,
> Would I not have; but Nature should bring forth,
> Of its own kind, all foizon, all abundance,
> To feed my innocent people.

A comparison of these two extracts brings Shakespeare before us as a reader of one of the shrewdest and liveliest, and yet the most naively and negligently discursive and gossiping books which the genius of philosophic observation has ever produced; and it, of course, seems to justify the inference that the "Tempest" must have been written subsequently to the publication of this translation of "Montaigne" in 1603.*

But the restless spirit of antiquarian inquiry seems to leave nothing absolutely settled in the history of our great dramatist. In the year 1839 the Rev. Joseph Hunter published a "Disquisition on the Scene, Origin, Date, &c., of Shakespeare's 'Tempest,'" in which he endeavoured to show that this work was written at so early a period in the poet's literary career as the year 1596. He seems to have arrived at this conclusion, mainly upon the very unsatisfactory grounds that Ben Jonson, in the prologue to his "Every Man in his Humour," which he supposed was acted in 1596,† directed his censure against the "Tempest" among other dramas; and that this play must have been produced immediately after the publication of Sir Walter Raleigh's account of his voyage to Guiana. He thinks it probable that this is the "Love's Labour's Won" mentioned by Meres in 1598; and he disposes of the argument in favour of a later date for the work, which is deduced from the imitation of the passage in Florio's "Montaigne," by the supposition that Shakespeare read that translation in manuscript, or that he saw this particular portion of it in some separate publication. Mr. Hunter further enters into a series of minute inquiries, for the purpose of showing that the island of Lampedusa was the scene of the "Tempest." His principal reasons for adopting this conclusion are, that Lampedusa lies on the route between Naples and the coast of Africa; that it is a small and an uninhabited island; that it had the reputation of being

---

* A further interest attaches to this imitation by Shakespeare of the old French essayist. There is now in the library of the British Museum a copy of Florio's "Montaigne," containing what good judges believe to be a genuine autograph of the poet. This volume cost the trustees of the British Museum £120; its intrinsic value without the autograph would not have been more than about 15s.

† Mr. Hunter was here mistaken. Jonson's play seems to have been first acted in 1597.

haunted; that it contains a recluse's cell, which "is surely the origin of the cell of Prospero;" and that while we are told Ferdinand was employed there in piling logs of wood, we find that it still supplies fire-wood to Malta. This elaborate trifling is manifestly the mere abuse of ingenuity and learning, and can only serve to show the folly of attempting to apply the petty results of antiquarian research rigorously and indiscriminately to the airy creations of poetry.

No tale is known to exist from which Shakespeare could have drawn the principal incidents in the "Tempest." Warton, in his "History of English Poetry," says that Collins, the poet, told him that this play was founded on a romance called "Aurelio and Isabella." But this romance has since been discovered, and an examination of it does not in any way justify this statement. Warton thought it probable that Collins, whose memory failed him in his last calamitous indisposition, was merely mistaken in substituting the name of one novel for that of another; and Boswell was told by a friend that he had read a work answering to Collins's description. But such a work has not been found, and we do not think it at all likely that it ever existed. Many of the commentators still take it for granted that Shakespeare must have borrowed from some now unknown source the general plot of the "Tempest;" but we can see no necessity for adopting that conclusion. There was very little room for the invention of mere incidents in this play. We think, too, that we can perceive a special harmony between the whole substance and the whole form of the work, and that they both, in all probability, sprang readily and completely from the same airy fancy.

The "Tempest" has long been one of the most admired of all the works of Shakespeare. There is undoubtedly great originality in its whole conception; and that novelty of design, through the happy art of the poet, is formed into a scene of free ideal truthfulness. But this drama does not, we believe, display the highest kind of creative inspiration. Its story is slight, and is slightly developed. The whole composition is removed beyond that region of probability and nature within which alone, perhaps, the highest imaginative work can ever be achieved. The poet, it is true, has happily overcome the difficulty of reconciling this dream of enchantment with the reality of dramatic art, but he has overcome it by one of the lighter and less sustained efforts of his fancy; and the whole scene presents but few revelations of that special grace or strength, or splendour of imagination, which could alone entitle it to a foremost place in the great Shakespearian drama.

Caliban is the most original creation in the "Tempest," and it is this character in particular that has attracted the admiration of Shakespeare's critics. Caliban, however, is but a slight sketch, and we must confess that we admire the skill quite as much as the power displayed in its production. A few rude elements make up the character, and the poet wisely abstains from bringing them before us in any marked detail or with any marked prominence. The charm of poetical expression is finely employed to temper the unwelcome impression of the ferocity of the character, while at the same time it perfectly harmonises with our conception of Caliban's supernatural origin; and we just accept this strange figure as at once truly fanciful and truly natural, as it rises under the free, rapid touches of the poet's pencil. Ariel is the other purely superhuman agent in this scene of enchantment. He offers in many respects a direct contrast to Caliban. He is all air, and life, and movement. He flies, he swims, he dives into the fire, he rides "on the curl'd clouds." But Ariel, like Caliban, is drawn with a prevailing observance of the ordinary conditions of nature. All his thoughts and all his desires are essentially and even narrowly human. He seeks to regain his freedom, and this simple and natural feeling is the motive of all the activity with which he is endowed by the poet.

The human characters in the scene do not appear to be in any way beyond the reach of Shakespeare's less elevated imagination. Prospero has nothing to distinguish him but that magic which he ultimately renounces. The two worthless princes, Sebastian and Antonio, serve, by their jibes, and even by their villany, to give a certain amount of variety and animation to the scene, but they certainly add nothing to its airy enchantment. Gonzalo, the " honest old counsellor," is drawn with the usual indistinctness of his class in the pages of Shakespeare, and we are to the last unable quite to make up our minds whether we are to regard him as a feeble chatterer or as a benevolent sage. Stephano and Trinculo are amusing specimens of Shakespeare's clowns. They belong to a type of character which he seems to have curiously observed, and which he always represents with the most natural humour.

The loves of Ferdinand and Miranda, however, form the most charming, and, it may be, the most truly fanciful, episode in the whole drama. "At the first sight they have chang'd eyes." Miranda is, perhaps, the most ideal of all Shakespeare's impersonations of delicate and gentle maidenhood. Her artless tenderness, and the anxious yet exquisite awakening of her spirit to the new and unknown passion that enchains her, come upon us fresh from the very fountains of nature. There is nothing, perhaps, in all poetry simpler and yet sweeter than the image that she gives us of that conflict of emotions which, as she first learns that she is loved, constitutes her overflowing happiness :—

> *Ferdinand.* I,
> Beyond all limit of what else i' the world,
> Do love, prize, honour you.
> *Miranda.* I am a fool,
> To weep at what I am glad of.

But we do not find in the "Tempest" many of those indications of Shakespeare's command over the finest forms of emotion and expression. The language is here usually somewhat strained and involved, and the general management of the dialogue is more or less abrupt and irregular. The poet seems to have been desirous of avoiding the risk of giving an air of too much unreality to his fanciful creation by a minute attention to the harmony of his versification, or to the perfect connection of thought in the development of his characters. He believed, perhaps, that a certain ruggedness and apparent negligence of form would facilitate his imitation of nature; and there would, no doubt, be some ground for such a notion. But he also appears to have somewhat abused the licence of his art, and to have often left his work inharmonious and incomplete from a mere desire to save himself time and trouble. There are, we think, some instances in this play in which he has contented himself with producing a general effect through means which will not bear the test of a rigid examination. Thus in the very first scene it seems to us that the rudeness of the boatswain—perfectly truthful and dramatic as it is in itself— is somewhat extravagantly exhibited; while Gonzalo dwells at what under the circumstances must be considered excessive length on the jest that the unmannerly seaman is not likely to be drowned, as he must naturally be reserved for another fate; and towards the close of the same scene, as the ship is sinking, we find it impossible to persuade ourselves that we are listening to the real voice of either Antonio or Sebastian in the following exclamations:—

> *Antonio.* Let's all sink with the king.
> *Sebastian.* Let's take leave of him.

This is the sketchy and hasty imitation of nature. In the next scene Prospero, while recounting to Miranda the circumstances which led to their arrival in the island, frequently breaks the narrative for the purpose of arousing the attention of his supposed listless auditor. This, too, is in itself a very dramatic expedient; but it seems here out of place, for Prospero could not have thought that Miranda remained indifferent to so strangely interesting a disclosure, and her own words show that she listens to it with the most absorbing interest. Again, in the same scene we meet with a manifest instance of Shakespeare's inattention to the minor details of his story. Ferdinand states that among those who perished in the wreck of the vessel were "the Duke of Milan and his brave son." But, as Theobald remarked, there must here be some slight mistake, for we are expressly told that no one was lost in the shipwreck, and yet we find in the subsequent scenes no such character as the son of the Duke of Milan. The poet seems in this case to have fallen into much the same forgetfulness as in "Much Ado About Nothing," where Leonato asks Antonio about a "son," who cannot, as it afterwards appears, have ever existed. We are aware that these are very minute criticisms; but it is only by such criticisms that a general negligence in the construction of any work can be shown; and we think that negligence is perceptible throughout the whole of the "Tempest."

There is no more famous passage in the dramas of Shakespeare than that in which Prospero in this play recalls the fate that awaits all the works of man and the very universe that we inhabit:—

> Our revels now are ended: these our actors,
> As I foretold you, were all spirits, and
> Are melted into air, into thin air:
> And, like the baseless fabric of this vision,
> The cloud-capp'd towers, the gorgeous palaces,
> The solemn temples, the great globe itself,
> Yea, all which it inherit, shall dissolve;
> And, like this insubstantial pageant faded,
> Leave not a rack behind. We are such stuff
> As dreams are made of, and our little life
> Is rounded with a sleep.

All the first portion of the above passage seems to have been suggested to Shakespeare by the work of a contemporary writer. In the year 1603 Lord Sterline published a play called "Darius," which, as Steevens first pointed out, contains the following lines:—

> Let greatness of her glassy sceptres vaunt,
>   Not sceptres, no, but reeds, soon bruis'd, soon broken;
> And let this worldly pomp our wits enchant,
>   All fades, and scarcely leaves behind a token.
> Those golden palaces, those gorgeous halls,
>   With furniture superfluously fair,
> Those stately courts, those sky-encount'ring walls,
>   Evanish all like vapours in the air.

If the "Tempest" was written, as we certainly believe that it was, subsequently to the year 1603, we can hardly doubt that Shakespeare imitated to some extent the above passage. But that very imitation would only serve to show the special magnificence of his genius. He has clothed his image of the dissolution of Nature with a wholly new splendour, and his concluding and most striking expression of the fleetingness and the illusiveness of this mortal scene is entirely of his own creation.

The "Tempest" offers in one respect a curious exception to the general form of Shakespeare's dramas. The whole of its action is expressly stated in the play itself to have passed within a period of three hours. This information is conveyed to us twice in the concluding scene: first, when Alonzo states that he and his companions "three hours since were wreck'd upon these shores;" and next, when he says of Ferdinand and Miranda that their "eld'st acquaintance cannot be three hours." We have no objection to accept these assurances; but in order to do so, we must suppose that the progress of the story has been extremely hurried and crowded; and we confess that in any case we are not disposed to attach any kind of importance to the accomplishment of the alleged feat. In the picturesque illusions of the stage we have no desire to insist on the observance of the ordinary limitations of time and place; and we should have been more than usually prepared to forget them in a drama of light enchantment, with such personages for the chief agents in its scenes as Prospero, and Caliban, and Ariel, and Miranda.

This play has often been compared to the "Midsummer Night's Dream;" and there exists this obvious resemblance between them, that they are the only works of the poet in which the power of enchantment is the special instrument of the action. But they also differ in some important respects, and as mere works of art they can hardly be said to admit of any close comparison. The form of the "Midsummer Night's Dream" is more loose and more languid; its humour is lighter and more frolicsome. The fancy of the poet in the "Tempest" is comparatively serious or restrained. In the "Midsummer Night's Dream" the counterpoise to the extravagance of the fable is supplied by the light mockery with which the human characters are treated. In the "Tempest" the balance of Nature seems restored by the firmness of the form in which the whole fantastic scene is cast. The entire conception and execution of this latter drama show that it was written in the calmness and the maturity of advanced age. But though a late, we do not think it is a very great or very vigorous effort of the poet's genius. It appears to us to be such a work as he might have readily and rapidly written; and we see no indication that he bestowed upon it any very earnest labour. It does not in any large measure reveal to us his finest insight into life. It is to some extent removed beyond the ordinary limits of human experience; and it is, after all, only in the reproduction of Nature in her subtlest, or brightest, or most passionate moods, that his imagination puts forth all its illimitable power.

KING HENRY IV.—PART I.

This great historical drama is one of the most popular of all the works of Shakespeare. The first mention we find made of it consists of the following entry in the books of the Stationers' Company :—

25 Feb., 1597-8.

ANDREW WISE.—A book entitled "The History of Henry the

iiiith, with his battle at Shrewsbury against Henry Hotspur of the North, with the conceited Mirth of Sir John Falstaff."

In pursuance of this notice the play was published in quarto in 1598, and was re-issued in the same form in 1599, in 1604, in 1608, in 1613, and in 1622. It was next inserted in the Folio of 1623; but two other quarto impressions followed in 1632 and 1639. The first edition, like the earliest copies of several other of Shakespeare's plays, did not contain the name of the author. The edition of 1599 is stated in the title-page to have been "newly corrected by W. Shake-speare;" but we can attach no credit to announcements of this description; and we find that in this particular case the edition of 1598 is generally regarded as the most correct of all the early impressions.

We have no external testimony to enable us to determine how much sooner than the commencement of the year 1598 this drama may have been written; but, from the whole character of the composition, we may take it for granted that it must have been preceded by most of the plays to which we have any ground for assigning a very early origin; and we believe that its date may, without hesitation, be assigned to the year 1596 or 1597.

There is no reason to doubt that Shakespeare, throughout the composition of this play, as well as of the "Second Part of King Henry IV." and of "King Henry V.," must have had his attention directed to an old drama entitled "The Famous Victories of Henry the Fifth." It is true that he might have found the general outline of his story in the Chronicles; but he appears to have borrowed a few names from the "Famous Victories," &c., and he has even imitated the treatment of some of its incidents. The principal companion of the Prince in the old piece is called "Ned," which is the familiar appellation given by him to Poins in Shakespeare's work; the spy, or petty thief, of the party is called Gadshill; and there is also introduced a Sir John Oldcastle, who, however, makes but a very unimportant and subordinate figure in the scenes. Four editions of this old drama have come down to us. One of them was published in 1598, and another in 1617; the other two are undated; but one of them was very probably issued in 1594, as such a work was entered in that year in the Stationers' Registers. We learn that Tarlton, the celebrated low comedian, who died in 1588, performed in it the parts both of the Clown and of the Chief Justice; and we may fairly conclude, from the general form of its language, that it was not composed many years before that period. This is perhaps the play to which Thomas Nash refers in the following passage in a tract entitled "Pierce Penniless," &c., published in 1592:—

What a glorious thing it is to have Henry the Fifth represented on the stage, leading the French king prisoner, and forcing both him and the Dauphin to swear fealty!

We find that Henslowe enters in his Diary (p. 26, edition Shak. Soc.), a performance of "Harey the Vth," under the date of the 14th of May, 1592. It appears certain that the "Famous Victories" was once a very popular drama; but we can now only account for that circumstance upon the supposition —a supposition which the whole of the internal evidence seems strongly to warrant—that we have received it in a miserably mutilated and imperfect condition. Its only characteristic, as it now stands, is its tame and feeble stupidity. A few lines taken from its opening scene will convey a fair idea of the style in which it is throughout written:—

Enter the young Prince, Ned, and Tom.

Henry V. Come away, Ned and Tom.
Both. Here, my lord.
Henry V. Come away, my lads.
  Tell me, sirs, how much gold have you got?
Ned. Faith, my lord, I have got five hundred pound.
Henry V. But tell me, Tom, how much hast thou got?
Tom. Faith, my lord, some four hundred pound.
Henry V. Four hundred pounds; bravely spoken, lads.
  But tell me, sirs, think you not that it was a villainous
  part of me to rob my father's receivers?

Ned. Why no, my lord, it was but a trick of youth.
Henry V. Faith, Ned, thou sayest true.
   But tell me, sirs, whereabouts are we?

It is manifest that Shakespeare could have found no source of inspiration in such a work as this. It could not even have suggested to him any large portion of his incidents or characters. It embraces in one short play the historical epoch which he has illustrated in his two parts of "King Henry IV." and his "King Henry V.;" and it has no Hotspur, or Glendower, or Falstaff; for Sir John Oldcastle, who is usually supposed to have been the original of the latter character, does not here even attempt to display any wit or humour of any kind, and forms one of the most insignificant figures in the whole production. The principal business of the Prince in its earlier scenes is systematic robbery. Shakespeare commences his drama with a partial imitation of this strange exhibition of the habits of the heir to the crown, but he seems to have soon found it wholly incompatible with his larger and more truthful representation of the character.*

The principal discussion to which this play has given rise among the commentators is one that relates to a subject which may awaken some interest from its associations, but which can of itself possess little or no importance. Rowe, in his "Life of Shakespeare," written in 1709, states that the "part of Falstaff is said to have been written originally under the name of Oldcastle: some of that family being then remaining, the Queen was pleased to command him to alter it; upon which he made use of Falstaff;" and most of the succeeding commentators have adopted this supposition, which seems to be confirmed by a variety of testimony. Steevens and Malone, however, dissented from it, and believed that it owed its origin to the fact that Falstaff fills the same part in Shakespeare's plays

---

* The "Famous Victories," &c., is printed in Nichols', or Steevens' "Six Old Plays," &c.

which had previously been filled by Sir John Oldcastle in the "Famous Victories," or, perhaps, in some other drama, no longer extant, dealing with the same portion of English history. But a mass of evidence,* some of which has only been brought to light since the time of those critics, seems to prove, beyond the possibility of doubt, that not only was Falstaff first known as Oldcastle, but that the latter name continued to attach to the character long after it had been changed by Shakespeare himself. Nathaniel Field, who, as we learn from the Folio of 1623, was at that time an actor in the company of which Shakespeare had previously been a member, in a play entitled "Amends for Ladies," published in 1618, and again in 1639, makes one of his characters ask:—

>   Did you never see
> The play where the fat knight, hight Oldcastle,
> Did tell you truly what this honour was?

This passage seems clearly to allude to Falstaff's speech at the end of the first scene of the fifth act of the present drama. Mr. Halliwell has published, for the first time, an equally decisive testimony upon this subject. In a dedication prefixed to a manuscript work preserved in the Bodleian Library, Dr. Richard James, who is known to have been a friend of Ben Jonson's, states, "that in Shakespeare's first shew of 'Harry the Fifth,' the person with which he undertook to play a buffoon was not Falstaff, but Sir John Oldcastle; and that offence being worthily taken by personages descended from his title, as peradventure by many others also who ought to have him in honourable memory, the poet was put to make an ignorant shift of abusing Sir John Falstophe, a man not inferior of virtue, though not so famous in piety as the other." It is manifest that for "Harry the Fifth" we should read "Harry the Fourth" in this extract. We find that Fuller,

---

* This evidence has been fully set forth by Mr. Halliwell in his Essay "On the Character of Sir John Falstaff."

in two passages in his works, complains very much in the same tone as James has done of the employment of the honourable names—first of Sir John Oldcastle, and afterwards of Sir John Fastolf—for the ludicrous or discreditable character assigned to the Falstaff of Shakespeare. There are also a few tracts, published in the early years of the seventeenth century, in which "Sir John Oldcastle," and his unwieldy frame, are referred to in terms which seem only applicable to Shakespeare's great comic character.

We have further, in the poet's own plays, a number of passages that naturally lead to the conclusion which all this external testimony seems unmistakably to establish. In the very first scene (First Part of "King Henry IV.," Act I., Scene II.) in which Falstaff appears, the Prince addresses him as "my old lad of the castle"—an address which seems to have originated in his name. In the early copies of the Second Part of "King Henry IV.," *Old* is given as the prefix to the speech of Falstaff to the Chief Justice (Act I., Scene II.), beginning, "Very well, my lord, very well;" and this slip may reasonably be supposed to be the result of the name under which the character was first introduced. The epilogue to the same drama furnishes a still more striking testimony to the same effect. A promise is there made that the same comic character will be continued in another play, of which the scene will be laid in France—"where, for anything I know, Falstaff shall die of a sweat, unless already he be killed with your hard opinions; for Oldcastle died a martyr, and this is not the man." This address would, apparently, be wholly out of place if Oldcastle had never filled the part which was afterwards assigned to Falstaff.

Malone observed, in support of his opinion, that in the verses in which the name of Falstaff is introduced, Oldcastle could not be substituted without destroying the metre, and that Shakespeare was very unlikely to recast all the lines for the purpose of meeting such a change. But this argument was singularly misplaced; for the name of Falstaff occurs in verse but once in the First Part of "King Henry IV.," namely, in the line (Act II., Scene II.), "Away, good Ned, Falstaff sweats to death;" and there the verse is short a foot, which the substitution of the name of Oldcastle would, of course, supply; while in the second of these plays, the name of Falstaff is introduced six times in verse; and Ritson has shown how the lines in these instances might be amended; and, besides, it is quite conceivable that the supposed change was made in the name before the later of the two dramas was produced.

In this play Shakespeare has made a visible progress towards the mastery of his art since the composition of "King John" and of "King Richard II." We now see his genius rapidly assuming all its native amplitude. He moves with a new power and a new freedom. He seizes both on the humorous and on the serious aspects of life with at once an imaginative ease and an imaginative vigour, to which the writings of no other poet can hardly be said to afford any distinct resemblance. His large workmanship is still, no doubt, unaccompanied by any absolute perfection of form; it often looks hurried, and careless, and exaggerated; but, amidst all the minute indications of his negligence, it possesses a free, overflowing vitality, in comparison with which all the other productions of genius in the dramatic presentment of character look shadowy and attenuated.

Falstaff is universally regarded as the poet's largest and most effective comic creation. It may be that elsewhere he has now and then presented the whimsical and incongruous side of life with a more subtle fancy, with a deeper truthfulness, with a finer harmony, with a more purely creative insight; but nowhere else has he evoked the genius of unrestrained merriment with such broad effect, and such apparently inexhaustible variety. We are not by any means prepared to maintain that Falstaff is his greatest production; but it seems to be the one which stands out most alone and independent, with nothing equal to it, or even like to it, in his own or in any other drama. By some happy accident, or it may be by some native instinct, he here found, for once, a figure definite enough to form a clear and unmistakable reality, and yet wide enough to admit of the play of the most unrestrained humour; and he has prodigally lavished upon it all the resources of his fancy. The largeness of the character saved him from the indulgence of that taste for petty conceits which enfeebles or defaces so many of his other comic creations; and we all now readily yield to the contagious influence of its riotous drollery, and willingly forget that, in its unrestrained abandonment to the genius of merriment, it makes no pretension to the representation of an ideal grace, or truthfulness, or harmony.

The more tragic or more serious portions of this work, although they do not by any means occupy the same exceptional position in the poet's dramas, constantly reveal his fine imagination. They display no wonderful originality, but they are, at least, brightly and vigorously coloured. They fulfil with striking effect the first condition of the historical drama, or indeed of a drama of any kind; they bring before us freely and strongly the motives and the passions of the actors in the great scenes which they represent. The King is, perhaps, too equivocal a character to form a great dramatic figure; or, at least, the poet has not bestowed upon his portraiture that elaborate art which alone could have given clearness and firmness to our conception of a nature so reserved and so undemonstrative. The successful but anxious usurper is no longer the brilliant Bolingbroke of "King Richard II." We never penetrate to his inmost feelings, and his personal influence over the march of events is never very distinct or decisive.

We cannot accept the representation of the young Prince himself without some qualifications. He does not, we think, abandon himself with natural frankness to the influence of the scenes which he has himself chosen for his amusement. The poet seems to treat him with too constant a remembrance of his future greatness, and never in this portion of his work fully exercises the large rights of his own genius. His hero, therefore, fails to secure our entire sympathy, or even, perhaps, to win our perfect belief in the reality of the form in which he is presented to our observation.

We believe that we have in Hotspur a much finer dramatic creation. The poet treats this character with more freedom, and, therefore, with more vitality and more truthfulness. Hotspur has manifestly a nature less large and less flexible than that of the Prince; he is more obstinate and more unmanageable, less complete and less harmonious; but the whole figure, with its impulsiveness, its fancifulness, its capricious, uncontrollable restlessness, is eminently original and dramatic, and is rendered by Shakespeare with the finest and most striking touches of characterisation which the whole drama contains. He is, perhaps, after all, a more brilliant and dazzling impersonation than the Prince; he is a rarer being; his loss is apparently more irreparable; and we are disposed to sympathise but very imperfectly in the triumph which his rival obtains by his fall. Indeed, we hardly believe in that triumph. The poet is manifestly so committed to the Prince that we are tempted to doubt the truth of his representation; and thus his partiality in some measure defeats its own ends.

The great characteristic of this drama, considered as a whole, is the fine effect with which its lighter and its graver scenes are blended and harmonised. Its predominant element is undoubtedly the comic; and yet its comedy never for a moment disturbs or overshadows the march of its grander and more stately events. The mirth and the solemnity of the scene seem to follow each other with the most perfect naturalness and the most perfect effect, without any unexpected or unwelcome rapidity, without any surprises or contrasts of any kind. There is, we believe, in this large harmony something more than the triumph of mere conscious art. It is the result of the special genius of the poet. This work, like the whole Shakespearian drama, is the creation of a light and an unforced imagination; it presents no trace of any narrow self-reference or absorbing anxiety. There is nothing, either in its comedy or in its tragedy, to oppress and enchain us; and we turn with the most perfect readiness and the most perfect freedom to all its flexible images of the infinite variety of human life.

KING HENRY IV.—PART II.

The "Second Part of King Henry IV." was first published in quarto in 1600, and was not, as far as we can now discover, again printed until its insertion in the Folio of 1623. The quarto edition appears to have been passed very hurriedly through the press. The whole of the first scene of the third act was omitted from the greater number of the copies, and this omission was supplied by the addition of two leaves in the remainder of the impression.

It seems very probable that this play was written either in the year 1597 or in the year 1598; but we can adduce no direct proof in support of that conjecture. The few scraps of evidence which seem to aid us in our inquiries do not enable us to fix the date within any very narrow limits.

In the second scene of the fifth act, immediately after the death of Henry IV., the new King seeks to raise the drooping spirits of his brothers, telling them:—

> Not Amurath an Amurath succeeds,
> But Harry Harry.

In the month of December, 1574, the Turkish Sultan Amurath III., immediately on his succeeding to the throne, caused his five brothers to be strangled; and on his death, in January, 1595, his son and successor, Mahomet III., perpetrated, on a still larger scale, a similar atrocity, by destroying his nineteen brothers and a number of women of the late Sultan's harem, who were supposed to be in a condition which rendered it possible that they might give birth to new claimants to the crown. It was in all probability to this double tragedy the young English monarch was referring, and the above passage would thus show that this play must have been written some time after the commencement of the year 1595.

In Ben Jonson's "Every Man out of his Humour," which was acted in 1599, we find the following dialogue, Act V., Scene II. :—

Saviolina. What's he, gentle Monsieur Brisk? not that gentleman?
Puntarvolo. No, lady; this is a kinsman to Justice Silence.

This is naturally supposed to be an allusion to Shakespeare's Silence, and, if that supposition be correct, either this play or the "Merry Wives of Windsor" must have been written before the latter part of the year 1599.

The question of the date of this drama seems to us to possess a special interest, from its probable connection with an event in the poet's own history. Justice Shallow—who, if we are not mistaken in the period we have assigned to the composition of the "Merry Wives of Windsor," is here introduced for the first time—has, by ancient and uninterrupted tradition, been held to be a satirical copy of Sir Thomas Lucy of Charlecote, near Stratford; and it seems hardly possible that this belief should be wholly unfounded. In the only passages in which Shakespeare appears to have particularised the character, we find distinct allusions made to the coat of arms of the Lucy family. That emblematical device consisted of "three luces hariant," the luce being a name for the full-grown pike. Near the close of the third act of the present play, Falstaff talks of the "young dace" being "a bait for the old pike;" and a similar allusion is still more distinctly set forth in the opening scene of the "Merry Wives of Windsor," where the "old coat" and the "dozen white luces" become, without this explanation, wholly purposeless or unintelligible. The poet himself could not have forgotten the natural application of his own words; they are introduced in a very marked and a very unexpected form; and we feel convinced that they were employed by him with a perfect consciousness of their obvious meaning. The history of his own life seems at the same time to afford us a ground for suspecting that he may have thought he had some reason for complaining of the conduct of Sir Thomas Lucy, and for manifesting his resentment in this very exceptional fashion. We know that between the years 1596 and 1599 he was himself engaged in procuring a grant of arms for his father, and that in this attempt he met with some unusual opposition. It is true that we have no direct evidence of any kind to show from whom that opposition proceeded; but the whole character and position of Sir Thomas Lucy lead us to think he was a person by whom it would have been likely to be offered. We know that he was often employed as a magistrate or as a special commissioner at Stratford, and that he must have possessed a personal knowledge of the principal inhabitants of that town. He was also a member of Parliament, where he appears to have joined the Puritan party, and to have displayed much more active habits than we should have expected from the prototype of Justice Shallow.* Such a man would probably have been very apt to interfere, for the purpose of preventing an encroachment on the privileges or the honours of gentility in his own immediate neighbourhood; and the satire of Shakespeare appears to have a direct reference to a subject which must have occupied a good deal of his attention, and must have caused him some special annoyance, at the time those plays were written. We are aware that tradition has assigned a different cause for his hostility to Sir Thomas Lucy. But that is just one of those details in which a mere popular rumour is most apt to be at fault. We cannot believe that the poet would have gone out of his way to revive in his

---

* Malone has, with his usual diligence, collected the principal events in the history of Sir Thomas Lucy; and we find from the text and notes of vol. ii., pp. 123 and following, of his "Shakespeare by Boswell," that Sir Thomas was born in the early part of the year 1532, that he died on the 6th of July, 1600, and that for some years he took an active part in the business of the House of Commons.

advancing manhood the memory of one of his own juvenile frolics, or to gratify the long-cherished rancour to which the punishment of his folly had given rise.

The "Second Part of King Henry IV." is but a continuation of the First Part, and is throughout written in much the same form and with much the same power. It seems, however, to want something of the freshness and vivacity of the preceding drama. The brilliant and romantic figure of Hotspur is absent from its scenes, and his place is not supplied in the more serious portions of the work by any new and strikingly original character. The King, however, plays a somewhat more distinct part in the action of the present play; and we have some new and fine effects produced by the glimpses which we obtain of the cares and the weariness that beset the coveted prize of his usurpation. The Prince is passing into a new character, and in one, at least, of the scenes—the interview with his dying father—the transition is finely manifested.

The comic power of the piece is still purely Shakespearian, although it is displayed under somewhat altered conditions. The humour of Falstaff appears less exuberant than in some of the episodes of the earlier play; but it is often represented with the same essential truthfulness and originality.

The comedy of this drama is enlarged by the introduction of some new and admirably drawn figures. Pistol, on his first appearance in the fourth scene of the second act, pours forth his tragic rant with a copiousness and an extravagance which raise him into an unmistakable dramatic creation; and Doll Tearsheet repays his "fustian" with all the richness and freedom of her peculiar vocabulary. But the command which the poet exhibits, in both these plays, over all the forms of the freest tavern-life, is one of their distinct characteristics, and affords a singular proof of the closeness of his observation, or, perhaps, we should rather say, of the power and freedom of his imagination, in dealing with all the more curious and more dramatic aspects of life.

Justice Shallow is another of the poet's original comic personages. The character is finely conceived and finely rendered; and there are a few passages in this impersonation of feeble loquacity which form some of the airiest and the most purely fanciful comedy that Shakespeare has written.

We cannot help feeling struck by the hasty and contemptuous mode in which Falstaff and his companions are dismissed towards the close of the drama. The poet, after having made all the use that he required of those figures, disposed of them with an indifference which in all probability, arose mainly out of the special freedom and impersonality of his own genius; but it may be, too, that he had in reality little sympathy with people of their tastes and habits. It is, besides, quite possible that he was here yielding to much less abstract and less remote influences. There is, we think, some truth in the observation of Dr. Johnson, that his dramas are often brought hurriedly and carelessly to a conclusion; and we seem to find throughout this "Second Part of King Henry IV." many indications that he felt he had exhausted the interest of his subject. There is a languor observable in his representation of some of his later incidents, and more particularly in his treatment of the expedition of Prince John of Lancaster; his wonderfully versatile imagination required perhaps, new fields for its development; and when he had once made up his mind to get rid of any dramatic episode, and of any dramatic personage, he appears to have had no hesitation in disposing of them with an abrupt completeness, which saved him from the necessity of any minute and elaborate workmanship in the execution of his design.

KING HENRY V.

"The Chronicle History of Henry the Fifth" was published in 1600 by Thomas Millington and John Busby. This is the earliest copy of "King Henry V." It was reprinted by

Thomas Pavier in 1602, and again in 1608. These three editions appeared without the name of the author, and they are all so singularly imperfect that we have no doubt they were made up from memory, or from notes taken during the performances at the theatre of the drama as it was written by Shakespeare, and as we find it printed for the first time in the Folio of 1623. They contain no portion whatever of the choruses, which we have the strongest reason to believe must have formed part of the work on the occasion of its first production; they omit whole scenes, including the opening scene between the two bishops; and they do not present a single passage of any length with perfect completeness. Some of the commentators think it probable that Shakespeare produced two versions of this play, and that we have received in the quartos his earlier and less finished work. But we can find nothing to justify this supposition. It is wholly gratuitous and unnecessary, and it is opposed to all the evidence by which its truth can now be tested.

We believe that there is a passage in the quartos which could not have been written by Shakespeare in the shape in which it is there presented; and as that passage will serve to throw a light on one of the special controversies in Shakespearian literature, we shall proceed to examine it in some detail. In the Folio copy of "King Henry V.," Act I., Scene II., the Archbishop of Canterbury expounds at considerable length the right of the kings of England to the French crown. His whole address, which we do not think it necessary to quote, is manifestly copied, and copied as literally as the requirements of the dramatist's special form of expression would permit, from the following passage in pp. 545 and 546 of Holinshed's "Chronicle," Vol. III., ed. 1587:—

Whereupon, on a day in the parliament, Henry Chicheley, Archbishop of Canterbury, made a pithy oration, wherein he declared, how not only the duchies of Normandy and Aquitaine, with the counties of Anjou and Maine, and the country of Gascoigne, were by undoubted title appertaining to the king, as the lawful and only heir of the same; but also the whole realm of France, as heir to his great-grandfather, King Edward the Third.

Herein did he much inveigh against the surmised and false, feigned law Salike, which the Frenchmen alledge ever against the kings of England in bar of their just title to the crown of France. The very words of that supposed law are these, *In terram Salicam mulieres ne succedant;* that is to say, Into the Salike land let not women succeed. Which the French glossers expound to be the realm of France, and that this law was made by King Pharamond; whereas yet their own authors affirm that the land Salike is in Germany, between the rivers of Elbe and Sala; and that when Charles the Great had overcome the Saxons, he placed there certain Frenchmen, which having in disdain the dishonest manners of the German women, made a law, that the females should not succeed to any inheritance within that land, which at this day is called Meisen; so that if this be true, this law was not made for the realm of France, nor the Frenchmen possessed the land Salike, till four-hundred and one-and-twenty years after the death of Pharamond, the supposed maker of this Salike law; for this Pharamond deceased in the year 426, and Charles the Great subdued the Saxons, and placed the Frenchmen in those parts beyond the river of Sala, in the year 805.

Moreover, it appeareth by their own writers, that King Pepin, which deposed Childerick, claimed the crown of France, as heir general, for that he was descended of Blithild, daughter to King Clothair the First: Hugh Capet also, who usurped the crown upon Charles, Duke of Loraine, the sole heir male of the line and stock of Charles the Great, to make his title seem true, and appear good, though, indeed, it was stark nought, conveyed himself as heir to the Lady Lingard, daughter to King Charlemaine, son to Lewis the Emperor, that was son to Charles the Great. King Lewis also the Tenth, otherwise called Saint Lewis, being very heir to the said usurper, Hugh Capet, could never be satisfied in his conscience how he might justly keep and possess the crown of France, till he was persuaded and fully instructed, that Queen Isabell, his grandmother, was lineally descended of the Lady Ermengard, daughter and heir to the above-named Charles, Duke of Loraine, by the which marriage, the blood and line of Charles the Great was again united and restored to the crown and sceptre of France; so that, more clear than the sun, it openly appeareth, that the title of King Pepin, the claim of Hugh Capet, the possession of Lewis, yea, and the French kings', to this day, are derived and conveyed from the heir female, though they would, under the colour of such a feigned law, bar the kings and princes of this realm of England of their right and lawful inheritance.

The version given of this harangue in the quarto editions of " King Henry V." is as follows:—

> *Bishop.* Then hear me, gracious sovereign, and you peers,
> Which owe your lives, your faith, and services
> To this imperial throne:
> There is no bar to stay your highness' claim to France,
> But one, which they produce from Pharamond:
> No female shall succeed in Salique land;
> Which Salique land, the French vainly gloze
> To be the realm of France,
> And Pharmond the founder of this law and female bar.
> Yet their own writers faithfully affirm,
> That the land Salique lies in Germany,
> Between the floods of Sabeck and of Elme,
> Where Charles the Fifth, having subdued the Saxons,
> There left behind and settled certain French;
> Who, holding in disdain the German women,
> For some dishonest manners of their lives,
> Established there this law: to wit,
> No female shall succeed in Salique land;
> Which Salique land (as I have said before)
> Is at this time in Germany, called Meisene.
> Thus doth it well appear, the Salique law
> Was not devised for the realm of France:
> Nor did the French possess the Salique land,
> Until four-hundred one-and-twenty years
> After the function of King Pharamond,
> Godly supposed the founder of this law.
> Hugh Capet also that usurped the crown,
> To fine his title with some show of truth,
> When in pure truth it was corrupt and nought,
> Conveyed himself as heir to the lady Inger,
> Daughter to Charles the foresaid Duke of Loraine;
> So that, as clear as is the summer's sun,
> King Pepin's title, and Hugh Capet's claim,
> King Charles his satisfaction, all appear
> To hold in right and title of the female:
> So do the lords of France until this day,
> Howbeit they would hold up this Salique law,
> To bar your highness claiming from the female,
> And rather chose to hide them in a net,

Than amply to embrace their crooked causes,
Usurp'd from you and your progenitors.

It is clearly impossible that this latter version of the archbishop's address, with all its omissions and all its errors, could have been written by any one who was acquainted with the source from which it must have been copied; and no one doubts that Shakespeare drew this and every other portion of his play from the pages of Holinshed.

The date of the composition of "Henry V." is more certainly and more distinctly defined than that of any other of the plays of Shakespeare. In the chorus at the commencement of the fifth act, the poet gives us the following illustration of the enthusiasm with which the citizens of London received Henry on his return from his French conquests:—

> As, by a lower but by loving likelihood,
> Were now the general of our gracious empress
> (As in good time he may), from Ireland coming,
> Bringing rebellion broachèd on his sword,
> How many would the peaceful city quit,
> To welcome him!

There can be no doubt that these lines refer to the expedition of the Earl of Essex to Ireland, on which he proceeded on the 15th of April, and from which he returned on the 28th of September, in the year 1599. This chorus must therefore have been written between those two dates, and we may fairly assume that the play itself was first brought upon the stage about the middle of the same year. It is very likely that Shakespeare was the more disposed to indulge in this kindly allusion from the fact that his own special patron, the Earl of Southampton, served in the expedition, and held in it the important office of Master of the Horse. The passage was manifestly meant to be of a wholly complimentary character, and we may therefore feel assured that it was not added to the play at a later period; for Essex returned from his command under circumstances which provoked the marked disapproval of his royal mistress, and which directly contributed to precipitate his own ruin. The anticipation expressed in the lines was, therefore, singularly infelicitous; and the very fact that the poet left them unaltered in after years seems to afford a curious proof of the little care that he took of the form of his dramas from the moment they had once passed from his hands.

Henslowe, in his Diary, mentions "Harey the Vth." as having been performed by his company on the 14th of May, 1592; and again, under the date of the 28th of November, 1595, he enters "Harey the V.," and enters it as a new play. This was, we may take it for granted, another dramatic version of the main incidents in the history of Henry V.; and it appears to have been a popular production, as we find that its performance was repeated on several occasions, and with fair profit to the manager. We do not think there is the slightest reason for supposing that it was Shakespeare's play, the date of which must, upon the strongest evidence, be fixed at a later period; and we cannot even believe that towards the end of the year 1595 any connection whatever existed between Henslowe's company and the company to which Shakespeare was attached. The only other fact with which we are acquainted in the early history of the present play is that it was performed before the Court of James I. on the 7th of January, 1605.

The drama of "King Henry V." is, in some respects, deserving of the special notice of the students of Shakespeare's genius. The poet had here a magnificent scene to delineate. The subject was sure to be popular with his audience, and it is evident that he himself felt in it an unusual amount of interest. We do not know any other work of his in which his national or personal predilections have made themselves so distinctly visible: and yet it is impossible to class this play among the great productions of his genius. In all the higher conditions of the dramatic representation of life—in freedom, in variety, in depth, in truthfulness, in imaginative power—it is decidedly inferior not only to his more famous tragedies, but to some even of his mixed dramas. It contains hardly a single passage which can be said absolutely and unmistakably to reveal his distinctive ease and splendour of form, or his distinctive insight into character and passion. The truth is, that the subject itself did not admit of perfect dramatic treatment. It is a heroic history, and such a history, to be dealt with effectively, should be dealt with epically or lyrically. Henry V. is here exhibited as a complete, harmonious, self-possessed character; but such characters are not dramatic. In the epic delineation of great personages and great exploits we are dominated by them. In dramatic representation we are comparatively independent of the agents in the scene. We see them caught in the struggle of passions which we know to be but distant and latent elements in our own nature. In epic narration it is our admiration that is mainly or exclusively awakened; in the dramatic exhibition of life it is our critical, discriminating, illuminating sympathy that is called into action. The play of "King Henry V." is the representation, not of great passions, but of great events, and it naturally fails to attain the highest dramatic vitality and movement. A large portion of its story has to be told, or merely indicated, by the choruses, in which the poet himself has to appear, and to confess the inability of his art to reproduce the march and shock of armies, and, above all, the great scene on the field of Agincourt. It is in some measure, perhaps, in obedience to his sympathy with the inevitable conditions of his work that he here appears for once in his own personality; and it may be that we have in this change another proof of the wonderful harmony of his imagination with every form of life which it seeks to revive. There is much in these scenes that is noble and imposing, and, in particular, it is impossible to witness without admiration the frank and gallant bearing of the king. But the work, on the whole, is forcible, eloquent, and declamatory, rather than vital, passionate, and dramatic.

The comedy in this drama is naturally pitched in a much lower key than that of the two parts of "King Henry IV."

The riotous humour of Falstaff, and his personal disregard of the sentiments of chivalry, would here have contrasted very inharmoniously with the heroic spirit and the wonderful achievements of the English monarch and his followers in France. Fluellen, with his fiery temper and his military pedantry, forms a less amusing, but a more appropriate figure in such a scene. We find again, however, that the poet has treated his older humourists with unexpected severity. Nym and Bardolph are here hanged, and Pistol eats his leek most ingloriously. But the treatment of Mrs. Quickly seems specially unaccountable; for there appears to have been nothing in her former life or character which could in any way justify the disreputable end for which she has been reserved.

Among the comic sketches in this work we are specially struck by the scene (Act III., Scene VII.) in which the fantastic conceit of the Dauphin and the sarcastic temper of the Constable of France are so strangely delineated. The nature of the relations which must have prevailed between the two characters seems to have been utterly disregarded by the poet. It was impossible that a French subject should indulge in this contemptuous banter towards the heir to the French crown; and so far the form of the dialogue is wholly incongruous. But in its substance we are very much disposed to think that this is the most singular and the most distinctly Shakespearian scene in the whole drama. Amidst the light and even coarse indifference of its whole tone it displays throughout that firmness of touch, and that reckless truth to nature, which so often startle us in the manifestations of Shakespeare's genius.

Some of the modern Continental critics think they can see that not only was Henry V. Shakespeare's favourite hero, but that this is the character, in all the poet's dramas, which he himself most nearly resembled. Many people will, perhaps, hardly be able to refrain from a smile on hearing of this conjecture. We certainly cannot see the slightest ground for its adoption. The mere vigour with which the character is drawn by the poet cannot furnish an argument in its favour; for, in that case, we should equally have to identify him with Hamlet, or Othello, or King Lear, or Richard III., or any other of the leading figures in his dramas. Neither will the manifest partiality with which he treats the hero of Agincourt show that he was himself a King Henry. That partiality was, perhaps, in the main a national feeling; and, in any case, it is at least as often those characters that seem to supply our own deficiencies, as those which closely reproduce even our highest endowments, that most attract our admiration. The whole history of Shakespeare's life, and the whole cast of Shakespeare's genius, are opposed to this extravagant supposition. We have no doubt that the poet readily sympathised with the frank and gallant bearing of the king. But we find no indication in all that we know of his temperament, or of the impression which he produced upon his contemporaries, of that firm, rigid, self-concentrated personality which distinguishes the born masters of mankind.

Henry V. was necessarily peremptory, designing, unwavering, energetic, and self-willed; Shakespeare was flexible, changeful, meditative, sceptical, and self-distrustful. This was clearly the temperament of the author of the sonnets; it was, too, we believe, not less clearly the character of the wonderful observer and delineator of all the phases of both tragic and comic passion ; and it was, perhaps, in no small degree, through the very variety of his emotional and imaginative sensibility, and the very absence of that completeness and steadfastness of nature which his injudicious admirers now claim for him, that he was enabled to become the great dramatic poet of the world.

KING HENRY VI.—PART I.

The precise nature of Shakespeare's connection with the three parts of " King Henry VI." forms the most perplexing problem in the history of his dramas. It is a subject which has already undergone considerable discussion, and yet may be said to be still wholly undecided; and it is, at the same time, one which possesses a larger amount of interest than is usual in the questions on which the commentators have been divided, from the special relation which it bears to the early development of the poet's genius, and the history of our dramatic literature at the critical period of the commencement of the last decade of the sixteenth century.

The difficulty which is involved in this discussion does not by any means arise from that almost total absence of evidence which we have to encounter in so many of our Shakespearian inquiries. On the contrary, the details which the research and ingenuity of the critics have brought to bear upon it are unexpectedly numerous; but they are, at the same time, so complicated that they have naturally led to the most opposite conclusions; and we fear that we shall now find it very difficult to discuss, or even to state them without producing in the minds of our readers a considerable amount of perplexity and confusion.

The immediate object of the whole controversy is to ascertain how far Shakespeare was the author of any one, or of the whole, of these dramas, and the main element in the consideration of that question is the publication of two old plays, which look like early versions of the Second and Third Parts of "King Henry VI.," as they have reached us in the Shakespeare Folio of 1623. The First Part of this dramatic series, however, appeared for the first time in that volume; and we shall, therefore, be able to consider it separately, although in doing so we shall find it impossible to abstain from making frequent allusion to the two later parts, and to the two older works on which they are generally supposed to have been founded. Those works are entitled, respectively, "The First Part of the Contention betwixt the two famous Houses of Yorke and Lancaster," which was first published in 1594, and "The True Tragedie of Richard Duke of Yorke," which was first published in 1595.*

---

* We shall use for our quotations from the "First Part of the

The " First Part of King Henry VI." is generally supposed to have been written about the year 1589 or 1590, and we believe that that date may be fairly assigned to its composition. On the 3rd of March, 1591-2, Henslowe enters in his Diary— " Henery the VI.," a play which seems to have been more than usually popular, as it was acted for the fourteenth time on the 19th of June in the same year. It has been thought that this may be the drama which is now known as Shakespeare's " First Part of King Henry VI. ;" but if it was, as it appears to have been, a new play on the 3rd of March, 1592, we must hold it to be very improbable that it was at that period written by Shakespeare for Henslowe's company ; and such a conjecture would, in fact, be opposed to the conclusions which have been generally formed, not only with respect to the date of this play, but with respect to all the circumstances of the poet's early connection with the stage. We have so little perfectly reliable evidence upon those points, however, that we must be content to leave them involved in more or less obscurity; but we ought not to forget that Henslowe and his associates might easily have been induced to get up a play upon a subject which had already been successfully dramatised by a rival company. There seems to be better grounds for supposing that this is the drama to which Thomas Nash alludes in the following passage of his " Pierce Penniless," &c., published in 1592:—

> How would it have joyed brave Talbot (the terror of the French), to think that, after he had lain two hundred years in his tomb, he should triumph again on the stage, and have his bones new embalmed with the tears of ten thousand spectators at least (at several times), who, in the tragedian that represents his person, imagine they behold him fresh bleeding.[*]

We find that the fall of Talbot and of his son forms one of the most striking incidents in the " First Part of King

---

Contention," &c., and from the "True Tragedie," &c., the edition prepared by Mr. Halliwell for the Shakespeare Society.

[*] P. 60, ed. Shak. Soc.

Henry VI.," and it is impossible to doubt that such a scene must have produced on the passionate audiences who frequented the theatres in the days of Queen Elizabeth just such an effect as Nash describes in the above passage.

There is some other testimony which appears to connect this drama more or less closely with the undoubted works of Shakespeare. The Chorus, in the epilogue to "King Henry V.," after a modest allusion to the imperfect attempt made by the dramatist to revive the glories of the hero of Agincourt, proceeds to state that "this star of England" was succeeded by his infant son—

> Whose state so many had the managing,
>   That they lost France and made his England bleed:
> Which oft our stage hath shown; and, for their sake,
> In your fair minds let this acceptance take.

It is clear that the two last of these lines refer to the frequent representations on the stage of the principal events in the earlier part of the reign of Henry VI., and that the author puts forward the success which had attended those performances as a plea for the favourable reception of the new work. In this reference some of the commentators think they can discover a ground for believing that Shakespeare was the author of the play, or plays, describing the history of Henry VI., while others regard the circumstance of his alluding to those works with a certain air of triumph as a proof that they could not have proceeded from his hand. The passage, it must be admitted, is not one of a very distinct and pointed description. In it, as it seems to us, the poet is referring not so much to the author of those productions as to the fact that they had been performed upon the same stage on which the new drama was represented; and, on the general ground of the amusement which they had afforded, he solicits the indulgence of the audience for his company rather than for himself. This is the natural purport of the passage; and we believe that by attempting to deduce from it any argument on the subject of the authorship of the older dramas, we should be attaching to it a meaning which it will not reasonably bear. It will, however, at all events, serve to show that from an early period there must have been a play founded on the history of Henry VI., performed by the company to which Shakespeare was attached.

There are two other items in the external testimony connected with the authorship of this play; but, as we so often find in our Shakesperian researches, they do not lead to the same conclusion. The first is the omission of "King Henry VI.," in any form, from Meres' enumeration of Shakespeare's dramas in 1598. But Meres' list makes no pretension to completeness; he might have forgotten, or he might not have known the poet's earliest works; or he might have been perplexed by the fact that two of these plays had been published under other titles; and, in any case, there seems to be no reason to doubt that the "Third Part of King Henry VI.," at all events, as it was either written or altered by Shakespeare, must have been produced before Robert Greene died in September, 1592. The other fact we have to notice in the history of these three dramas is their insertion in the Folio of 1623; and it certainly must be held to be one of considerable importance in the consideration of the present question. It is true that Heminge and Condell must have been very careless editors; and it is open to any one to suggest that the first of these plays, in particular, was published in the Folio merely because Shakespeare had been engaged in slightly amending it, or in preparing it for representation on the stage. Such a supposition, however, can only be admissible upon the condition that it is supported by valid internal or collateral evidence. There must always exist a strong *primâ facie* presumption in favour of the genuineness of any play inserted in the first Folio; and it is manifest that negligent, but honest, editors would be more apt to omit from their volume a work of their author's, than to ascribe to him one which he could not have legitimately claimed.

Leaving this incomplete and undecisive external testimony, and turning, for some more certain light, to the indications of authorship which the work itself may afford, we find that we have at the outset an unusual conflict of authorities to encounter. Theobald doubted whether these three plays were wholly the productions of Shakespeare; Warburton felt confident that Shakespeare was not the author of any one of them; and Farmer "could not believe" that they were "originally" written by our great dramatist. Johnson and Steevens, however, thought the hand of Shakespeare was discernible in all of them. Malone was at first of this latter opinion; but a more attentive examination of the evidence afterwards led him to the conclusion that the "First Part of King Henry VI." was wholly, or almost wholly, the work of some other dramatist, and that the "First Part of the Contention," and the "True Tragedie," were also not written by Shakespeare, but that he used them as the foundations of his Second Part and Third Part of this dramatic trilogy. Malone maintained this position in a "Dissertation on the Three Parts of King Henry VI.," which will be found printed at length in the eighteenth volume (pp. 557 to 596) of his edition of Shakespeare, as it was brought out under the superintendence of Boswell, in the year 1821. This treatise is his most celebrated contribution to Shakesperian criticism. It met with the marked approval of many of the scholars of his time; it reduced to evidently unwilling silence the opposition of the learned and acute Steevens; and its reasoning seems to have brought conviction to the minds of the great majority of the commentators of the present century. There are still, however, some dissentients from its conclusions; and Mr. Knight, in particular, has not only declined to accept them, but has himself written an elaborate essay to prove that Shakespeare was the author of the Three Parts, as they are now published in his works, as well as of the older plays which Mr. Knight regards as the poet's imperfect sketches of the two last of these dramas.

Malone's dissertation, however, appears still to be generally held to be the most authoritative argument to which this controversy has given rise; and, as we cannot adopt the position which it seeks to establish, we shall bestow upon it a more lengthened notice than it has, we believe, as yet received.

In the earlier portion of this essay, Malone endeavours to show that Shakespeare was not the author of the first of these three plays, although he may have altered or re-written a few of its scenes; and that is the subject to which we shall for the present confine our observation.

His first argument in support of that opinion is derived from the general form of the language used in this drama. He believes that the "First Part of King Henry VI." contains more allusions to mythology and classical authors, and to ancient and modern history, than any other piece of Shakespeare's founded on an English story; he also thinks that the versification of this play is clearly of a different colour from that of the poet's genuine dramas—that it is marked by a certain heavy and stately march, the sense concluding or pausing almost uniformly at the end of every line, and the verse having scarcely ever a redundant syllable. In addition to these larger characteristics of the style of the work, he finds in it single words of an unusual description and of Latin origin, as "proditor," "immanity," and, we believe, he might have added "disanimates," which are not introduced into any of Shakespeare's undisputed writings; and finally he is struck by the circumstance that Hecate is here employed, in conformity with classic usage, as a trisyllable, while it is shortened into two syllables by the author of "Macbeth."

It seems to us that all the more important of these peculiarities can go to prove nothing more than that this was one of Shakespeare's earliest and least mature compositions. Malone himself shows, by a variety of examples, that the classical allusions and the cumbrous versification of this play have many parallels in the great mass of the dramas written by the immediate predecessors or the early contemporaries of Shakespeare. But no student of our great dramatist will be surprised to learn that at first he formed his style, in a great measure, on that of the writers whom he found in possession of the stage; and it may, we think, be doubted whether he ever sufficiently escaped from their influence. That imitative spirit, however, was of necessity most powerful at the commencement of his career. He was by temperament specially averse to all eccentric self-display; and the whole history of his genius shows us that it unfolded itself gradually, and in wonderful harmony with all the immediate conditions of the every-day world around him. We have no hesitation in stating that, if we had had transmitted to us those works only in which his peculiar manner is generally and distinctly traceable, we should take it for granted that the fruits of his earliest labours had perished; while if, on the other hand, we should find that in a number of early productions, to which any credible tradition had attached his name, the manifestations, however imperfect, of his special dramatic power seemed to be mingled with the feebleness and the extravagance which characterised all the dramas of his age, we should at once conclude that they fulfilled all the conditions which would most naturally justify us in ascribing them to his hand. There can be no doubt that, however limited his classical reading may have been, he possessed a general knowledge of the forms of ancient mythology; and we cannot wonder that he should, after the universal fashion of his age, have at first employed that knowledge with a tasteless prodigality. Malone has quoted portions of two passages in the present drama, which are strongly marked with this tumid pedantry:—

> *Charles.* Was Mahomet inspirèd with a dove?
> Thou with an eagle art inspirèd then,
> Helen, the mother of great Constantine,
> Nor yet St. Philip's daughters, were like thee.

> Bright star of Venus, fall'n down on the earth,
> How may I reverently worship thee enough?
> > KING HENRY VI., Part I., *Act I., Scene II.*

> *Charles.* A statelier pyramis to her I'll rear,
> Than Rhodope's of Memphis ever was:
> In memory of her, when she is dead,
> Her ashes, in an urn more precious
> Than the rich-jewel'd coffer of Darius,
> Transported shall be at high festivals,
> Before the kings and queens of France.
> > KING HENRY VI., Part I., *Act I., Scene VI.*

Some of these allusions may now seem to us beyond the reach of a man of imperfect education. But they might, most probably, have been got up without any great effort by a mere English reader, in an age when nearly every kind of literary illustration was drawn from classic antiquity; and we know that one of the most recondite of the number—" the rich-jewel'd coffer of Darius "—might have been found by Shakespeare in Puttenham's "Arte of English Poesie," a work which was published in 1589, and with which we may take it for granted that he must have been acquainted.* There can be no doubt that such passages seem somewhat strangely placed in the Shakespearian drama. But there are undisputed works of the poet in which we may find lines distinguished both by the same pedantic extravagance and the same heavy halting march in the versification:—

> *King Henry.* By this account, then, Margaret may win him;
> For she's a woman to be pitied much:
> Her sighs will make a battery in his breast;
> Her tears will pierce into a marble heart;
> The tiger will be mild, while she doth mourn;

---

* The passage in Puttenham's work is thus quoted by Malone:— "In what price the noble poems of Homer were holden with Alexander the Great, insomuch as every night they were laid under his pillow, and by day were carried in *the rich jewel coffer of Darius,* lately before vanquished by him in battle."

> And Nero will be tainted with remorse,
> To hear, and see, her plaints, her brinish tears.
>
> KING HENRY VI., Part III., *Act III., Scene I.*

> *Warwick.* Our scouts have found the adventure very easy:
> That as Ulysses, and stout Diomede,
> With sleight and manhood stole to Rhesus' tents,
> And brought from thence the Thracian fatal steeds;
> So we, well cover'd with the night's black mantle,
> At unawares may beat down Edward's guard,
> And seize himself; I say not—slaughter him,
> For I intend but only to surprise him.
>
> KING HENRY VI., Part III., *Act IV., Scene II.*

There is not a trace of either of these two last passages in the "True Tragedie of Richard Duke of Yorke," on which the "Third Part of King Henry VI." is supposed by Malone and other critics to have been founded; and they must, therefore, according to Malone's hypothesis, not only have been written by Shakespeare, but they must have been written by him as enlargements and improvements of the work of another dramatist. We readily admit, however, that the "First Part of King Henry VI." betrays greater weakness and extravagance of hand than either of the two succeeding dramas, or than any of the other undisputed productions of Shakespeare; but we believe that the earlier date which may be fairly assigned to its composition will sufficiently account for this inferiority. It is, of course, to a similar cause that we ascribe his employment of a few single words of manifestly foreign origin, and which have never received a settled place in our own language. The poet may not have known much Latin; but that is no reason why we should suppose that he was not, in his immaturity, prepared to make use, after the manner of his models, of the little that he did know, unnecessarily and extravagantly. His elliptical employment in "Macbeth" of the classical name of Hecate is only one of those licences which an English writer might fairly claim a right to exercise, and for which many analogies might be found in our poetry. He may, perhaps, have been more careful to conform to classical restraints at the commencement of his literary career; and we can no more conclude from this difference of pronunciation that he did not write the present drama before "Macbeth," than we can conclude that he did not write the "Taming of the Shrew" before "Hamlet," merely because, in the former play, Baptista is properly employed as the name of a man, while in the latter it is erroneously used as the name of a woman.

The selection of the historical incidents and allusions in these dramas forms no slight element in the consideration of their probable authorship. Malone says the original writer or writers of the "First Part of King Henry VI." and of the two old plays on which, as he believes, the Second and Third Parts are founded, went to Hall and not to Holinshed for their materials; and as he thinks he has proved that Holinshed was the only chronicler whom Shakespeare consulted in the construction of his English historical dramas, he naturally concludes that Shakespeare did not write the present play, or the "The First Part of the Contention," or "The True Tragedie of Richard Duke of Yorke." We believe that upon all the fundamental conditions of this argument he is clearly and completely mistaken. We shall hereafter have occasion to show that the original author or authors of the "First Part of the Contention" and of the "True Tragedie" must have read Holinshed; but for the present we shall confine our attention to the evidence respecting the historical reading of the author of this "First Part of King Henry VI."

Our old chroniclers, Stow, Holinshed, &c., allowed themselves the most complete freedom in turning to account the labours of their predecessors; and their narratives have thus become, in many instances, so similar that it is very difficult to determine which of them a later writer must have followed. There are, however, a number of small details which show that Shakespeare, in his historical plays, usually adopted Holinshed as his authority, while there is, at the same time, no evidence to create even a presumption that he might not have referred to Hall's Chronicle in the composition of the Three Parts of "King Henry VI." Hall is the special historian of the long contest between the houses of York and Lancaster; to that great episode in our national annals his work professes to be confined;* and no author proposing to deal with the same subject in another form would be likely to refrain from consulting his pages. Holinshed, on the other hand, compiled a general history of England, Scotland, and Ireland; and, for the period of our first great civil convulsions, he is but a servile copyist of his predecessor. In spite of the closeness of this imitation, however, it is occasionally possible to discover that the original author or authors of the Three Parts of "King Henry VI." must have used both the one and the other of these chroniclers. Malone has selected a few passages from the present drama which must, he thinks, have been directly copied from Hall. In the opening scene we find the following line :—

What should I say? His deeds exceed all speech.

This phrase, "What should I say?" occurs very frequently in Hall when he wishes to be particularly impressive. This resemblance may be the result of a direct imitation, but the evidence cannot be held to be decisive upon that point. There exists, however, much stronger reasons for believing that the author of the "First Part of King Henry VI." was acquainted with Hall. He seems to have, in a special manner, followed that chronicler in his whole treatment of the character of Talbot, who is spoken of in the play (Act I., Scene IV.) as "the terror of the French, the scarecrow that affrights our children so," and of whom Hall (Fol. 166) says that "this man was to the French people a heavy scourge and a daily

---

* It is called in the title page, "The Union of the Two Noble and Illustrate Famelies of Lancastre and Yorke," &c. It commences with the reign of Henry IV., and ends with the reign of Henry VIII.

terror," and that the "women in France, to fear their young children, would cry, 'the Talbot cometh!'" Holinshed (p. 640) does not imitate this passage, and the only statement which his work contains in any way resembling it is one (p. 597) in which it is said that Talbot's "only name was, and yet is, dreadful to the French nation," a statement which is itself literally copied from Hall (fol. 102). It seems much more likely, too, that the last scene between Talbot and his son was suggested to the dramatist by a corresponding dialogue in Hall (fol. 165-6) than by the mere narrative (p. 640) of Holinshed. But there are other passages in this play which seem, at least, as clearly to have been derived from this latter chronicler.* The whole account of the career of Joan of Arc must be supposed to have been taken mainly from him, and not from Hall, for it is only in Holinshed (p. 600) that we find the specific allusion to her selecting her sword out of a quantity of "old iron," or to her recognition of the Dauphin while he attempted to conceal himself behind his courtiers, or to the revolting avowal of her own profligacy (p. 604) which she makes after her capture.

Malone appears to be equally in error when he tells us (p. 589)—" Holinshed, and not Hall, was his (Shakespeare's) guide, as I have shown incontestibly in a note on King Henry V." When we turn to this note, however, all that we find in it is that Shakespeare appears to have imitated Holinshed in the single passage in which the Archbishop of Canterbury, in Act I., Scene II., of "King Henry V.," gives an account of the genealogy of the royal house of France, and

---

* We shall give our references to Holinshed from the third and last volume of the edition of 1587, the edition, in all probability, which Shakespeare himself used. We shall quote for Hall the edition of 1548. It is, we believe, usually bound as one volume, although it has a new pagination at the commencement of the reign of King Edward V. The pages are only marked by folios—that is to say, each numeral represents both sides of a leaf.

in which the poet has been led, through this imitation, erroneously to substitute King Lewis X. for King Lewis IX., which is the name given by Hall. Upon this single fact, and upon no other evidence whatever, Malone adds:—" Here, therefore, we have a decisive proof that our author's guide in all his historical plays was Holinshed, and not Hall." We are unable to discover that proof, and it is manifest, we think, that such a conclusion cannot be legitimately deduced from such a premise. The poet might surely have consulted different authorities at different periods, or even at the same time, and in reference to the same subject; and we find, upon the most direct evidence, that that was the course which the author or authors of the Three Parts of "King Henry VI." actually adopted.

The more we inquire into the circumstances of this case, the more are we confirmed in our conviction of the inconclusiveness of Malone's reasoning. The Three Parts of "King Henry VI.," if they were written by Shakespeare at all, must have been written by him at the very commencement of his dramatic career. We know that he produced his "King Henry V." some eight or nine years later; and the statement that he must, throughout the whole of this period, have read only one English historian, is one of those extravagant assumptions which carry on the face of them their own confutation.

Malone believed that he was able to furnish, from the historical allusions in this play, a number of proofs that it is not the work of Shakespeare, or of the author or authors of the "First Part of the Contention," or the "True Tragedie of Richard Duke of Yorke." The first argument which he employs, and the one on which he most insists, is that the writer, whoever he was, does not seem to have known the real age of Henry VI. at the time of his father's death; while it is manifest that Shakespeare, as well as the author of the "True Tragedie of Richard Duke of Yorke," possessed that knowledge. In Act III., Scene IV., of the "First Part of King Henry VI.," the King, addressing Talbot, says—

Welcome, brave captain, and victorious lord!
When I was young (as yet I am not old),
I do remember how my father said
A stouter champion never handled sword.

But Shakespeare, as it appears from a passage in the "Second Part of King Henry VI.," Act IV., Scene IX., was aware that Henry was but nine months old when his father died, and that he could not therefore have remembered any thing that his father had said—

King Henry. No sooner was I crept out of my cradle,
But I was made a king, at nine months old.

These lines are not contained in the "First Part of the Contention," and must, therefore, according to Malone's theory, have been added by Shakespeare to the drama he was imitating. There is a similar statement both in the "True Tragedie" (p. 121, ed. Shak. Soc.), and in the "Third Part of King Henry VI." (Act I., Scene I.), which Shakespeare is supposed to have founded upon that play. In both of these latter works we have precisely the same line—

King Henry. When I was crowned, I was but nine months old. *

Malone, after having thus shown, as he believed, that neither Shakespeare, nor the author of the "True Tragedie," each of whom was acquainted with the real age of Henry VI. on his accession to the crown, could have written the "First Part of King Henry VI.," in which an erroneous reference is made to that subject, proceeds to argue that this latter play could not have been the work of the author of the "First Part of the Contention," even supposing that drama and the "True Tragedie" to have been produced by different hands.

---

* This statement is again repeated in Act III., Scene I., of the "Third Part of King Henry VI." The king is there made to say—
"I was anointed king at nine months old."
This line is not in the "True Tragedie."

He adduces two more historical illustrations in support of this position. The writer of the "First Part of the Contention," in a dialogue between the Duke of York and the Earl of Salisbury, makes it appear that the person whose title to the crown the duke has inherited (meaning Edmund Mortimer, although he is ignorantly called the Duke of York), was "by means of that monstrous rebel, Glendower, done to death;" and Shakespeare, in the corresponding scene of the "Second Part of King Henry VI." (Act II., Scene II.), has introduced a similar statement :—

> *Salisbury.* This Edmund, in the reign of Bolingbroke,
> As I have read, laid claim unto the crown;
> And, but for Owen Glendower, had been king,
> Who kept him in captivity till he died.

On this false assertion the Duke of York makes no remark. But the author of the "First Part of King Henry VI." has represented this Edmund Mortimer not as a captive, put to death by Owen Glendower, but as a state prisoner, who died in the Tower in the reign of King Henry VI., in the presence of this very Duke of York, who was then only Richard Plantaganet.

The second argument by which Malone seeks to prove that the author of the "First Part of the Contention" could not have written the "First Part of King Henry VI.," is derived from the fact that a correct account of the issue of King Edward III., and of the title of Edmund Mortimer to the crown, is given in the latter play; while in the "First Part of the Contention," a very incorrect statement is made upon the same subject.

Malone endeavours to strengthen the argument which he deduces from these passages, by producing another contradiction between the historical incidents set forth in this play and in one of Shakespeare's undoubted works. In Act II., Scene V., of the "First Part of King Henry VI.," Mortimer states that the Earl of Cambridge "levied an army" for the purpose of wresting the crown from Henry V. But in "King Henry V.," Act II., Scene II., we find that the Earl of Cambridge did not levy an army, but only engaged in a conspiracy to assassinate the king immediately before his departure from Southampton on his French expedition.

These are somewhat complicated details; but there can be no doubt that they prove the existence of the contradictions on which Malone has founded his conclusions. We believe, however, that he has attached to them an exaggerated importance. He has, as it seems to us, too much lost sight of the licence with which Shakespeare, throughout his whole drama, has treated the minor incidents of history, and, above all, the mere chronological order of events; and he has shown how specially liable he was to be misled, in a question of this description, from his natural tendency to judge, by the standard of his own laborious attention to minute facts, the largest and the most negligent work that ever came from human hands.

We shall now inquire more specifically into those arguments, and we believe we shall find that they will thus lose much of that force which they at first sight seem to possess. The allusion in the "First Part of King Henry VI." to the age of that sovereign at the period of his father's death, is one of those mere slight and incidental illustrations in which a poet like Shakespeare would be specially apt to disregard mere historical accuracy; and the whole course of Malone's own reasoning shows that this particular error must have been the result of mere inattention, or of mere forgetfulness. He believes, upon the internal evidence, that the author of this play was specially conversant with Hall's "Chronicle," and adopted it as the foundation of his drama. But Hall, in the opening sentence of his account of the reign of Henry VI., states in the most marked and distinct manner that the "young Prince Henry, the sole orphan of his noble parent, King Henry V., being of the age of nine months, or thereabout," was proclaimed King of England and France ;* and if we have a right, as we manifestly have, to conclude from this circumstance that the dramatist either accidentally forgot, or more or less systematically disregarded, this information, we know no great writer to whom such free or careless workmanship could be ascribed with so much probability as to Shakespeare. We might, of course, suggest, as a means of accounting for this discrepancy in the poet's dramas, that he had extended his acquaintance with the history of the period of which he was treating before he commenced his later work; but it is precisely from our knowledge of the licence which he allows himself in dealing with his minor illustrations, that we think there is no ground for our here resorting to any such conjecture.

The contradictory accounts given of the end of Edmund Mortimer are of a more striking and more perplexing description. Malone only refers to them for the purpose of showing that the author of the "First Part of King Henry VI." could not have written the "First Part of the Contention ;" but, as we believe that Shakespeare was the author of the latter work, they would prove for us, if they proved anything, that he could not have written the present drama. The evidence, however, would, we think, be insufficient to justify us in arriving at such a conclusion; and we find in the circumstances in which the contradiction appears to have originated, a means of accounting for its occurrence, without supposing that those two plays were necessarily the productions of different writers. The dramatist seems to have constructed the scene in the "First Part of Henry VI." upon a somewhat obscurely-worded statement of Hall, which is repeated by Holinshed. Both those writers (fol. 92, and p. 589), after describing a visit paid by a Portuguese prince to this country, during the period of the sitting of a Parliament, in the third

---

* The first sentence of Holinshed's account of this reign contains precisely the same statement.

year of the reign of King Henry, proceed as follows:—
" During which season Edmund Mortimer, the last Earl of
March of that name (which long time had been restrained
from his liberty, and finally waxed lame), deceased without
issue, whose inheritance descended to Lord Richard Plantagenet, son and heir to Richard Earl of Cambridge,
beheaded, as ye have heard before, at the town of Southampton." This statement, however, is substantially unfounded,
and is opposed to another tradition which connects the name
of Owen Glendower with the fate of Edmund Mortimer, and
which is distinctly mentioned by Hall and Holinshed in
another part of their account of this very same reign of
Henry VI. In each of their works (fol. 178, and p. 656),
we find in what purports to be " the Duke of York's oration
to the lords of the Parliament," a passage in which it is said
that Mortimer was detained " in captivity with Owen Glendower, the rebel in Wales." But this latter tradition is, in its
turn, wholly falsified by the most authoritative testimony,
from which it appears that this personage spent all the
maturer portion, at all events, of his life in a state of perfect
freedom, and in a position of great wealth and distinction,
and that he died in Ireland at the early age of thirty-two.
His history had thus become involved in strange obscurity
and confusion; and we cannot feel surprised if Shakespeare
varied in his treatment of it, just as he found convenient for
his immediate dramatic purposes, or as he was led to follow
any particular passage in the chroniclers.

We have another observation to offer upon this subject.
We find, in a subsequent reference made by the dramatist to the
career of this Earl of March, a remarkable proof of the latitude
which we must allow him in his employment of the obscurer
incidents and personages of history. In the " Second Part of
King Henry VI." it is stated that Mortimer was " kept in
captivity " by Owen Glendower till he died. This statement
must have proceeded from Shakespeare himself, as there is no
mention made of any such " captivity " in the " First Part

of the Contention;" but it is manifestly inconsistent with the representation given of the relations between Glendower and Mortimer in the "First Part of King Henry IV.," where they form a close family alliance, and conspire to deprive Henry of the crown; so that if we were strictly to apply Malone's argument, we should have to conclude that Shakespeare could not have been the author at once of the "Second Part of King Henry VI.," as it was printed in the Folio of 1623, and of the "First Part of King Henry IV." But in this instance, too, a reference to the chroniclers will probably reveal to us the source of our embarrassment. In Hall (fol. 20) and in Holinshed (p. 521) it is stated that in the third year of the reign of Henry IV. the Percies resolved on raising Mortimer to the throne, and "not only delivered him out of the captivity of Owen Glendower, but also entered into a league and amity with the said Owen." We find, therefore, in the writers whom Shakespeare must have used as his authorities in the construction of those dramas, each of the three versions he has given of the history of Edmund Mortimer, and we find them, too, in those very portions of the narratives to which he was at that moment giving his own dramatic form.

But Malone further contends that the contradiction between the accounts given in the "First Part of King Henry VI." and the "First Part of the Contention," of the issue of King Edward III., shows that those dramas could not have proceeded from the same hand. That is an argument which may be met in two different ways. Those who think that Shakespeare was the author of both works as they stand, may attribute the discrepancy to his general inattention to minute historical details. But that is not the position which we are prepared to maintain. We believe that the "First Part of the Contention" is but a mutilated copy of the corresponding play in the Folio edition of the poet's dramas; and the manifest and extravagant errors in the genealogical narration to which we are now referring will supply us with what we regard as a decisive argument in support of that opinion. That is a point, however, on which we must reserve any further discussion until we come to an examination of the Second and Third Parts of " King Henry VI."

The argument deduced by Malone from the erroneous statement made with respect to the part played by the Earl of Cambridge will, we think, after the explanations we have just offered of similar mistakes or negligences in these dramas, at once admit of a sufficiently satisfactory answer. We have already quoted (p. 263) a passage in which it is stated that this Earl was beheaded at Southampton; and the only other allusion, we believe, made to him in either Hall's or Holinshed's account of the reign of Henry VI. consists of the following statement in "the Duke of York's oration" (Hall, fol. 178; and Holinshed, p. 656) :—" Likewise, my most dearest lord and father, so far set forth this right and title that he lost his life and worldly joy at the town of Southampton, more by power than indifferent justice." In writing the "First Part of King Henry VI." the dramatist, having become aware from these passages that an attempt was made to deprive the House of Lancaster of the crown, seems to have been induced to talk hastily of the levying of "an army;" but in passing to the composition of "King Henry V." he was naturally led to make a special study of his authorities, and he there made the conspiracy of the Earl of Cambridge the subject of a distinct scene, and treated it correctly.

We have met by a few special explanations the above four arguments of Malone. We believe that we shall now be able still further to show the inconclusive character of his reasoning by a more general reference to the careless mode in which Shakespeare deals with his historical allusions.

In the "Second Part of King Henry IV." (Act III., Scene I.) the King thus recalls a prediction made by his predecessor, Richard II. :—

> But which of you was by
> (You, cousin Nevil, as I may remember,)
> [*To* WARWICK.
> When Richard, with his eyes brimful of tears,
> Then check'd and rated by Northumberland,
> Did speak these words, now prov'd a prophecy?
> *Northumberland, thou ladder, by the which*
> *My cousin Bolingbroke ascends my throne—*
> Though then, heaven knows, I had no such intent;
> But that necessity so bow'd the state,
> That I and greatness were compell'd to kiss;—
> *The time shall come,*—&c.

Here we are told that Nevil, Earl of Warwick, was present when Richard uttered his prophecy, and that Bolingbroke had at that time no intention of ascending the throne. But when we turn to Act V., Scene I., of "King Richard II.," where the prophecy was made, we do not find that Nevil was one of the listeners—indeed, he does not appear at all in that play—and Bolingbroke was then so far from being free from any intention of making himself king, that he had at the close of the preceding act accepted the offer of the crown, and appointed his coronation at Westminster for the following Wednesday.

In the opening scene of the "Third Part of King Henry VI." it is stated by the Duke of York that the elder Clifford and certain other adherents of the House of Lancaster "were by the swords of common soldiers slain." But in the "Second Part of King Henry VI.," Act V., Scene II., the elder Clifford is killed by this very Duke of York. It is true that these facts are similarly set forth in the "First Part of the Contention," and in the "True Tragedie," on which the Second and Third Parts of "King Henry VI." are supposed by Malone and other critics to have been constructed. We are not prepared to adopt that supposition; but, in any case, it is impossible for us to believe that Shakespeare, in improving the works of other dramatists, would have felt himself bound servilely to follow his models in petty incidents of this description; and we must certainly attribute the contradiction to his own forget-

fulness, or to his own indifference to perfect accuracy in such
a matter. It is perhaps hardly worth while to add that, if
he was led into this error by his readiness to accept the facts
of the writers whom he was generally copying, there would
be nothing improbable in the supposition that the " First Part
of King Henry VI." was also founded upon some preceding
drama, and that he was thus led to introduce into it passages
which do not harmonise in all their details with his later
works.

The different versions which the poet has given of the prediction of Richard II., and of the death of the elder Clifford,
show us how freely he could deal with his lighter incidents
or allusions in his undisputed productions. In the very play
we are now considering we find instances of contradictions not
less direct, and not less characteristic. In Act I., Scene III.,
of this " First Part of King Henry VI." the Bishop of Winchester is called " Cardinal" three times, first by Woodville,
next by Gloster, and afterwards by the Lord Mayor of London; but in Act V., Scene I., he is raised for the first time to
that dignity by the Papal Legate.

Again, in the opening scene of the play a messenger enters,
and brings to the English Council disastrous tidings from
France, telling them that—

> Guienne, Champaigne, Rheims, Orleans,
> Paris, Guysors, Poictiers, are all quite lost.

On hearing this intelligence Gloster asks—

> Is Paris lost? Is Rouen yielded up?

We must, therefore, suppose that Rouen was included by the
messenger in the same line with " Guienne," &c., which, without that addition, is deficiently constructed, and would afford
another instance of the strangest carelessness on the part of
the poet. But, as we proceed with our reading of the play,
we find that Rouen and Paris, at all events, must still have
been held by the English. In Act III., Scene II., the French

lay siege to Rouen, and their attack having been finally repelled, Talbot proposes to go " to Paris, to the King."

> For there young Harry, with his nobles, lies.

In Act III., Scene IV., and in Act IV., Scene I., we accordingly find Henry and his court in the French capital, where he celebrates the great ceremony of his coronation. And in Act V., Scene II., Charles, who has succeeded to the French crown, states that :—

> 'Tis said, the stout Parisians do revolt,
> And turn again unto the warlike French.

Upon which Alençon suggests to him that he should avail himself of this change of feeling—

> Then march to Paris, royal Charles of France.

We believe that we can again find, by a reference to the poet's historical authorities, how these errors originated. Hall (fol. 116), and Holinshed (p. 606), state that Henry, towards the close of the year 1431, and in the tenth year of his reign, was crowned king in Paris; and they afterwards relate (fol. 130-1, and p. 612-13) that in the year 1436, or more than four years later, the English sustained great losses in France, and " in especial," that "of the noble city of Paris;" while " twelve burgesses of the town of Gysors sold it for money." The dramatist, it is manifest, reversed the order of those events, and in doing so destroyed the perfect consistency of his scenes. These small contradictions seem of themselves to create a probability that this is one of the productions of Shakespeare ; and they must, at all events, serve to convince us that the author of the " First Part of Henry VI.," whoever he was, might very easily have been led to adopt in subsequent works passing allusions or petty traditions which would not perfectly harmonise with the statements in that drama.

We have already endeavoured to show that the general character of the diction in this play does not warrant the supposition that it could not have been written by Shakespeare. Malone, however, returns to a more special form of the same argument. He believes that there are minor characteristics in the style of this work which create a strong presumption in favour of his conclusion. That is a point, however, on which we cannot help thinking that he is specially infelicitous. He says that in this drama there are hardly any of those repetitions of the same thought or form of expression which are so often to be met in Shakespeare's undoubted productions. In fact, he finds here only one of those passages. In Act V., Scene V., we have :—

> As I am sick with working of my thoughts.

And in the chorus which precedes the third act of "King Henry V." we read :—

> Work, work your thoughts, and therein see a siege.*

Malone very justly observes that this repetition of a single expression is too slight a circumstance to justify us in concluding that the present play is the work of Shakespeare. But we find in it many more of those resemblances to passages in the poet's acknowledged productions; and we believe that they are of so remarkable a character that they must help to give a new aspect to the whole question which we are now considering :—

> They want their porridge, and their fat bull-beeves;
> Either they must be dieted like mules,
> And have their provender tied to their mouths,
> Or piteous they will look, like drownèd mice.
>   KING HENRY VI., Part I., *Act I., Scene II.*

>   Can sodden water,
> A drench for sur-rein'd jades,—their barley broth,
> Decoct their cold blood to such valiant heat?
>   KING HENRY V., *Act III., Scene V.*

---

* Again, in the fifth chorus of the same play, we find the following line :—

> "In the quick forge and working-house of thought."

Give them great meals of beef, and iron, and steel; they will eat like wolves, and fight like devils.
*Ibidem, Scene VII.**

I love no colours: and, without all colour
Of base insinuating flattery.
KING HENRY VI., Part I., *Act II., Scene IV.*

I do' fear colourable colours.
LOVE'S LABOUR'S LOST, *Act IV., Scene II.*

These eyes, like lamps whose wasting oil is spent.
KING HENRY VI., Part I., *Act II., Scene V.*

My oil-dried lamp, and time-bewasted light.
KING RICHARD II., *Act I., Scene III.*

Done like a Frenchman, turn, and turn again.
KING HENRY VI., Part I., *Act III., Scene III.*

Sir, she can turn, and turn, and yet go on,
And turn again.
OTHELLO, *Act IV., Scene I.*

Thou antic death, which laugh'st us here to scorn.
KING HENRY VI., Part I., *Act IV., Scene VII.*

Keeps death his court; and there the antic sits,
Scoffing his state, and grinning at his pomp.
KING RICHARD II., *Act III., Scene II.*

She's beautiful; and therefore to be woo'd:
She is a woman, therefore to be won.
KING HENRY VI., Part I., *Act V., Scene III.*

She is a woman, therefore may be woo'd;
She is a woman, therefore may be won.
TITUS ANDRONICUS, *Act II., Scene I.*

Was ever woman in this humour woo'd?
Was ever woman in this humour won?
KING RICHARD III., *Act I., Scene II.*

---

* These three passages refer to the English fighting in France. It is Alençon that is speaking of them in "King Henry VI.," and the Constable of France in "King Henry V." The "porridge" may now excite in us some surprise; but this does not appear to have been a mere thoughtless allusion on the part of the writer of the earlier drama.

> Gentle thou art, and therefore to be won,
> Beauteous thou art, therefore to be assail'd.
> > SHAKESPEARE'S SONNETS, *Sonnet XLI.*

> And yet, methinks, I could be well content
> To be mine own attorney in this case.
> > KING HENRY VI., Part I., *Act V., Scene III.*

> Marriage is a matter of more worth,
> Than to be dealt in by attorneyship.
> > *Ibidem, Scene V.*

> Be the attorney of my love to her.
> > RICHARD III., *Act IV., Scene IV.*

We will not undertake to determine how far the above extracts go to create a presumption that the "First Part of King Henry VI." is one of the productions of our great dramatist; but they must certainly be allowed some force in the determination of that question; and we need hardly add that they afford an ample reply to the argument of Malone, that the special absence of such resemblances from these pages indicates the hand of another author.

There is one of this series of repetitions which seems to us to be deserving of special notice. The line—"She is a woman, therefore to be won"—was probably copied from a work by Robert Greene, entitled "Planetomachia," which was published in 1585. But the thought, in its completeness, looks as if it was Shakespeare's; and it is somewhat singular that it should be found in two of his disputed plays. We think the coincidence goes some way to create a probability that both those dramas did not proceed from some other hand. It is a curious proof of the special hold which this light image obtained of the poet's fancy that he introduced it into his sonnets, and that he there applied it to a male friend, and not to a woman, by whom it was no doubt originally and naturally suggested.

There is another characteristic of the style of "King Henry VI.," which, in Malone's opinion, renders it very improbable that this drama should have been written by

Shakespeare. "In this play," he observes, "though one scene is entirely in rhyme, there are very few rhymes dispersed through the piece, and no alternate rhymes; both of which abound in our author's undisputed early plays." He admits that there is also an unusual paucity of rhymes in the Second and Third Parts of these dramas; but he attributes that peculiarity to the fact that Shakespeare, in the two latter plays, was merely engaged in improving the works of other writers, whose style he naturally imitated. We do not believe in the existence of those writers, and we cannot, therefore, accept such a settlement of the question. That is, however, a matter for separate consideration. The main answer we have now to give to Malone's argument is, that Shakespeare throughout this work was manifestly conforming to the manner of his immediate dramatic predecessors, and that from their writings rhyme was at that period in a great measure banished. The successful example of Marlowe had just then contributed to make blank verse almost the only form of language adopted for all the more stately descriptions of dramatic composition; and Shakespeare naturally yielded to the influence of this universal usage. But he yielded to it with a certain incompleteness and with frequent indications of his own natural leaning to a different form of expression. Malone has not failed to remind us that one episode in this play is "entirely in rhyme." But he has not, we think, made sufficient allowance for such a circumstance as an indication of the natural taste of the writer. That episode is one of a very remarkable description; it is the last appearance of Talbot and his son; and the rhyming is not only maintained throughout the whole of it, but is also continued for some time by the characters that follow. We believe, too, that Malone has somewhat overstated the facts on which he founds his conclusion. It is not quite true that there are "very few rhymes dispersed through the piece," or that both rhymes and alternate rhymes "abound in our author's undisputed early plays." The addresses of the personages in this play often close with a rhyme; and there are but few alternate rhymes in "King Richard II.," which Malone believes was written in 1593, and there is not much rhyming of any kind in "King Richard III.," to which he assigns the same date. The fact is, that it is in the early comedies more particularly the poet has recourse to this species of versification; and yet, in the "Two Gentlemen of Verona," which is unquestionably one of those works, there is from first to last less rhyming than in this "First Part of King Henry VI."

We have now noticed all the arguments advanced by Malone in the first part of his "Dissertation." We do not believe that they in any way establish his proposition, that this play could not have been written by Shakespeare. On the contrary, we cannot help thinking that he has in many instances completely mistaken the facts on which his judgment is founded, and that, throughout his inquiries, he has been led into a constant misunderstanding of his subject, by his strange forgetfulness of that special disregard of perfect harmony of detail which distinguishes the whole Shakespearian drama, and of the natural immaturity and imitative character of the poet's genius at the period when this work must have been written.

We cannot forget, however, that we have not yet exhausted the reasons which may be urged against the commonly supposed authorship of this drama. There are passages in it which we must all feel unwilling to associate with the name of our great poet; and this natural feeling exercises, perhaps, a much greater influence over the minds of most readers in the consideration of this question, than the minute reasoning of more formal and elaborate criticism. The feeble and tumid extravagance of many of the addresses greatly contributes to create this impression. That quality is peculiarly distinguishable in the general representation of the character of Talbot. The author of the play, whoever he was, in his anxiety to give prominence to his conception of this "terror of the French," has made of him a sort of ogre, and has drawn the whole figure

s

with a constant disregard of the restraints of nature and of common sense. This was, however, an error which was almost inevitable in an early production, and into which Shakespeare was at least as likely to be betrayed as any other imaginative writer that ever existed.

But the most offensive portion of this play, and the one in which we feel it most difficult to recognise the hand of Shakespeare, is that which relates to the ultimate fate of Joan of Arc. There are reasons, however, why we think he may have been its author. It is manifest that if he wrote this play at all, he wrote it with a constant reference to the tastes and usages of his time, and hardly in any way in the spirit of original and creative genius. But this wonderful enthusiast could hardly as yet have been known in England, except as a sorceress and an agent of Satan; and we doubt whether it would have been possible to present her upon our stage in any other character. The dramatist had here a certain task almost necessarily assigned to him; and we should not feel much surprise at finding that Shakespeare performed it in his usual thorough and even careless fashion.

We shall now proceed briefly to state the reasons that lead us to adhere to the tradition which has ascribed this drama to Shakespeare. We believe that, if we make due allowance for the period of its composition, we shall find that it fulfils all the natural conditions of his workmanship. It contains, amidst all its imperfections, frequent elements of true imaginative vitality. It brings before us the men and times of which it treats with a distinctness and a vigour to which we doubt whether we can find a parallel in the work of any other dramatist of the same generation.

The scenes between Talbot and his son (Act IV., Scenes V., VI., VII.) have been often selected by critics as characteristic indications of the presence of Shakespeare's hand in this production. We confess, however, that, although we can see in them glimpses of true pathos, we do not think they are at all executed in his finer and more unmistakable manner. They are throughout written in rhyme; and the truth, and force, and freedom of his dramatic imagination never find in that jingling form of versification a perfect expression. The scene in the Temple Garden, which furnished the emblem of the fatal quarrel of the Houses of York and Lancaster, seems to us much more decisively Shakespearian. It is distinguished by no small amount of that lightness and rapidity, and yet firmness of touch which give, perhaps, the most inimitable of all its forms to the creations of imaginative genius. The interview between Margaret and Suffolk points, we think, to the same origin. Suffolk displays, in his first approach to the brilliant young beauty, much of the grace of Shakespeare's fancy; and in the subsequent perplexity of his sudden and guilty passion, we seem partially to catch that deep whisper of Nature which so seldom strikes on our ears or our memories in any other pages than the dramas of Shakespeare.

There are even single lines, or short passages, in this work which appear stamped with the sovereign impress of our great poet's genius:—

> Mad, natural graces that extinguish art.
> *Act V., Scene III.*
>
> Spring crestless yeomen from so deep a root?
> *Act II., Scene IV.*
>
> You tempt the fury of my three attendants,
> Lean famine, quartering steel, and climbing fire.*
> *Act IV., Scene II.*

---

* We might have quoted, as a parallel to this line, the following passage in the opening chorus of "King Henry V.:"—

> "And, at his heels,
> Leash'd in like hounds, should famine, sword, and fire,
> Crouch for employment."

Malone observes (p. 584) that the line in the present play was suggested by a passage in Hall's Chronicle:—"The Goddess of War, called Bellona, hath these three handmaids ever of necessity attending on her—blood, fire, and famine." That observation may be well-founded, but it is also true that the poet has given to this familiar imagery a wholly new, and, as we believe, a wholly Shakespearian life and vigour.

> Glory is like a circle in the water,
> Which never ceaseth to enlarge itself,
> Till, by broad spreading, it disperse to nought.
> *Act I., Scene II.*

We must also class the quibbles among the apparent manifestations of Shakespeare's hand in this drama. The general character of the work seemed to forbid their introduction, and yet they are scattered somewhat freely over its pages:—

> Proditor,
> And not protector, of the king or realm.
> *Act I., Scene III.*

> Pucelle, or puzzel.
> *Act I. Scene IV.*

> *Winchester.* This Rome shall remedy.
> *Warwick.* Roam thither then.
> *Act III., Scene I.*

> Our sacks shall be a mean to sack the city.
> *Act III., Scene II.*

> Sell every man his life as dear as mine,
> And they shall find dear deer of us, my friends.
> *Act IV., Scene II.*

The very variety which distinguishes this work seems to reveal to us its true origin. We find in it many faults; but we find them relieved by frequent indications of real imaginative energy. It is crowded with incidents and characters, crudely and extravagantly, but still intelligibly, and even strongly delineated; and throughout all its changeful scenes the fancy of the writer moves with the same unfailing rapidity and freedom. He leaves behind him no trace of lingering, careful, self-reference; he is never oppressed by his labours. This easy, natural movement seems distinctly characteristic of the genius of our great dramatist. The present play has been assigned to him on the only contemporary authority that is now accessible, and we do not think that modern criticism has been able to throw any just discredit upon that testimony.

It seems, at the same time, to fill up what we should without it be compelled to regard as a void in our knowledge of the history of his dramatic labours; and, under these circumstances—although we can never feel any absolute certainty in the decision at which we may arrive in a controversy of this description, in which some authority must always be left to the uncertain element of taste, and in which no appeal can ever be made to any conclusive external evidence—we still think we can receive this "First Part of King Henry VI." with considerable confidence as the very earliest work in which the hand of Shakespeare is largely and readily distinguishable.

KING HENRY VI.—PARTS II. AND III.

The Second and Third Parts of "King Henry VI." seem to bear unmistakable marks of the impress of Shakespeare's genius, and, by the common consent of the poet's commentators, they are entitled to the place they have obtained among his collected dramas. But criticism appears to be still at fault in the attempt to determine whether he ought to be regarded as their sole or original author; and there can be no doubt that however much that very complicated question may have been already discussed, it will still admit of further investigation.

We believe that it would be impossible for us, without a large amount of confusion and repetition, to notice these works separately. They involve the same essential problem, and the evidence upon which that problem must be decided is, in both cases, of precisely the same description, or else is perpetually intermingled; and, under these circumstances, we shall find it convenient to include in the same inquiry any observation with respect to either drama which we may now have to offer.

We shall, first of all, state the facts of this controversy, and we shall afterwards proceed to consider the conclusions which these facts may be supposed to establish. The two dramas, as they are now printed in Shakespeare's works, have only reached us through the Folio of 1623. But two plays were published—the one in 1594, and the other in 1595—which differ from them in so many small details, and yet, on the whole, resemble them so closely, that a doubt has very naturally arisen how far they are to be regarded as substantially the same works. The first of those two old plays was published in a small quarto volume, under the following title :—

The First part of the Contention betwixt the two famous Houses of Yorke and Lancaster, with the death of the good Duke Humphrey: And the banishment and death of the Duke of Suffolke, and the Tragicall end of the proud Cardinall of Winchester, with the notable Rebellion of Jacke Cade: And the Duke of Yorke's first claime unto the Crowne. London Printed by Thomas Creed, for Thomas Millington, and are to be sold at his shop, under Saint Peter's Church in Cornwall. 1594.

The second of those old plays was published in a small octavo volume, which is thus entitled :—

The True Tragedie of Richard Duke of Yorke, and the death of good King Henrie the Sixt, with the whole contention betweene the two Houses Lancaster and Yorke, as it was sundrie times acted by the Right Honourable the Earle of Pembrooke his servants. Printed at London by P. S., for Thomas Millington, and are to be sold at his shoppe under Saint Peter's Church in Cornwal. 1595.*

---

* There is but one copy of this publication known to be extant, and that volume holds a memorable place in the annals of bibliomania. On a fly-leaf Chalmers has made the following entry :—" This very rare volume, of which no other copy is known to exist, was purchased by Mr. Chalmers at Dr. Pegge's sale in 1796 [this appears to be a mis-statement for 1798]. It was then unbound, as it had been neglected by the Doctor, who was unaware of its great value. By an oversight of Mr. Malone, and a singular mistake of Mr. Steevens, Mr. Chalmers obtained it easily for £5 15s. 6d., without much competition; and Steevens was enraged to find that it had gone for less than a fifth of what he would have given for it." At Chalmers' sale, in 1842, it was purchased for the Bodleian Library, for the sum of £130.

These two works were reprinted, although still separately, in small quartos, in the year 1600; and in that year there was also issued another copy of the "First Part of the Contention," &c. All these editions were published by Thomas Millington. At a later period both plays were printed together in a quarto volume, under the following title :—

> The Whole Contention betweene the two Famous Houses, Lancaster and Yorke. With the Tragicall ends of the good Duke Humfrey, Richard Duke of Yorke, and King Henrie the sixt. Divided into Two Parts: And newly corrected and enlarged. Written by William Shakespeare, Gent. Printed at London, for T. P.

This "T. P." is no doubt Thomas Pavier, and, in all probability, the volume was published in 1619. The "True Tragedie" is there inserted as the "Second Part of the Contention."

In the books of the Stationers' Company we find the following entry relative to the first of these plays :—

> 12 March, 1593-4.
>
> Tho. Millington.] A booke intituled the firste parte of the contention of the twoo famous Houses of York and Lancaster, with the Deathe of the good Duke Humphrey, and the Banishment and Deathe of the Duke of Sufk, and the tragicall Ende of the prowd Cardinall of Winchester, with the notable rebellion of Jack Cade and the Duke of York's first clayme unto the Crowne.

It will be seen from this entry that Millington announced his intention of publishing the "First Part of the Contention" in the March of the year in which his edition was actually issued. But no notice can now be found at Stationers' Hall of the publication of the "True Tragedie of Richard Duke of Yorke."

The same registers contain the following entry :—

> 19 April, 1602.
>
> Tho. Pavier.] By assignment from Tho. Millington, *salvo jure cujuscunque*, the 1st and 2nd parts of Henry the VI.': II. books.

This "Tho. Pavier" is, manifestly, the "T. P." who

published, in a single volume, "The Whole Contention," &c.; and we may also take it for granted that that publication took place in 1619; for the signatures, or the letters which indicate the order of the sheets, show that the work was printed immediately before Pavier's edition of "Pericles," which was issued in that year; the last signature of the text of "The Whole Contention" being the letter Q; and the first signature of the text of "Pericles" being the letter R.

We learn, through this last extract from the Stationers' Registers, that in the year 1602, different plays, dealing with the events of the reign of Henry VI., were known as parts of a dramatic series; and the special qualification in the assignment seems to show that Millington's copies had been illegitimately obtained.

The editions of 1594, 1595, and 1600, both of the "First Part of the Contention" and of the "True Tragedie of Richard Duke of Yorke," were published without the author's name, and those works were for the first time attributed to Shakespeare in Pavier's edition of 1619, which was some years after the poet's death. Our readers will also perceive that the "True Tragedie" is stated, on the title-page of the first edition, to have been acted by the "Earl of Pembroke's servants."*

---

* The first editions both of the "First Part of the Contention" and of the "True Tragedie of Richard Duke of Yorke" have been reprinted, with literal exactness, for the Shakespeare Society, from the unique copies in the Bodleian Library, under the careful editorship of Mr. Halliwell. His volume will afford the most valuable aid to the students of the present controversy. He has there pointed out, in a long series of notes, the variations between the texts of the first editions and of the editions of 1600 and 1619. Malone used the editions of 1600 as the basis of his inquiries respecting the two plays. Steevens inserted "The Whole Contention" in the third volume of his "Twenty of the Plays of Shakespeare," &c. Mr. Knight, in his larger editions of Shakespeare, has also printed both works from the copy of 1619, employing, for the first time, the modern spelling and punctuation, correcting the manifest

The omission of any mention of the Three Parts of "King Henry VI." by Meres, in 1598, is a circumstance which will be sure to arrest the attention of every inquirer into this controversy, whatever may be the reason we may think it most natural to assign for the silence of that writer, or however we may feel that we are not called upon to account for it in any way. It is hardly possible, in any case, to entertain a doubt that the Second and Third Parts of these dramas must have been brought out by the poet, in the shape in which they are now known to us, before the date of Meres' work.

We meet with a more important and a more interesting element in the consideration of this question in the passage which we have already quoted (p. 31) from Greene's "Groat's Worth of Wit," published in 1592. It will be seen that Greene there refers in language of special bitterness to Shakespeare, whom he calls " an upstart crow beautified with our feathers, that, with his *tyger's heart wrapt in a player's hide*, supposes he is as well able to bombast out a blank verse as the best of you; and, being an absolute *Johannes Fac-totum*, is, in his own conceit, the only Shake-scene in a country." It has naturally been supposed, from this passage, that Shakespeare was in some way indebted to Greene and his companions for the success he had already achieved as a dramatist; and that inference is manifestly strengthened by the following lines in "Greene's Funeralls, by R. B. Gent," a small tract which was published in 1594 :—

> Greene gave the ground to all that wrote upon him.
> Nay, more; the men that so eclips'd his fame,
> Purloin'd his plumes—can they deny the same?

---

errors in the metrical arrangement of the lines, and dividing the speeches into acts and scenes, corresponding with those in Shakespeare's undisputed Second and Third Parts of "King Henry VI." In our quotations we shall give our references to the reprints of the editions of 1594 and 1595, made by Mr. Halliwell for the Shakespeare Society, and we shall adopt the modern punctuation and spelling, but we shall leave the arrangement of the language unaltered.

The "First Part of the Contention" and the "True Tragedie" had long been regarded as mere imperfect versions, whether as originally written by the author, or as surreptitiously copied by the publisher, of the two plays which have come down to us as the Second and Third Parts of Shakespeare's "King Henry VI." Malone, however, as we have already stated, came to the conclusion that the early plays were the work of some other writer or writers, and that Shakespeare did nothing more than enlarge and amend them in his two dramas.

The arguments which Malone employed in support of this position embrace a great variety of small details, but we shall probably be able, without discussing or even stating them all at length, to do ample justice to their general force and purport. He has endeavoured to furnish his readers with an important help, in the consideration of the question, by printing the Second and Third Parts of "King Henry VI." with marks which might serve to indicate what portions of these works are entirely new, what portions of them are to be found in the same, or nearly the same, words in the "First Part of the Contention," or in the "True Tragedie," and what portions resemble, in a more or less general way, passages in those earlier publications. The value of the curious task in which he thus engaged is, unfortunately, somewhat diminished by the imperfect mode in which it has been performed. His notation abounds in small mistakes, and it will be impossible for any one, who has closely examined any considerable portion of his pages, to place in it any absolute reliance.* It was,

---

* In Malone's "Shakespeare by Boswell," the "Second Part of King Henry VI." begins on p. 167, vol. xviii.; and in pp. 168—9, a speech of Queen Margaret, consisting of eight lines, is given as an imitation of one in the "First Part of the Contention," although the only resemblance between them is that the former begins with—" Great king of England," and the latter ends with—"mighty England's king." In p. 214, the line, "As, like to pitch, defile nobility," is given as an imitation, but there is not a trace of it in the older volume. In p. 240 the two following lines are marked as imitations:—

perhaps, drawn up from the beginning somewhat hastily; and, at all events, it is manifest that, in passing through the press, it did not receive that severe revision which could alone have ensured complete accuracy in so long and so minute a labour. We have no doubt, however, that the work was executed in the most perfect good faith; and we take it for granted that its errors in sometimes attributing too much to Shakespeare are, upon the usual principle of averages, counterbalanced by other errors in sometimes attributing to him too little; so that we are prepared to accept as substantially correct Malone's computation (p. 572) that—

The total number of lines in our author's Second and Third Part of "King Henry VI." is 6,043: of these, as I conceive, 1,771 lines were written by some author or authors who preceded Shakespeare; 2,373 were formed by him on the foundation laid by his predecessors, and 1,899 lines were entirely his own composition.

We repeat that we have no objection to make to this state-

"Ah, that my fear were false! ah, that it were!
For, good King Henry, thy decay I fear."

And yet Malone attaches to them the following note:—"The variation is here worth noting. In the original play, instead of these two lines, we have the following:—

"Farewell, my sovereign; long may'st thou enjoy
Thy father's happy days, free from annoy!"

In p. 537 (Act V., Scene VI., of the "Third Part of King Henry VI.") these two lines—

"Suspicion always haunts the guilty mind;
The thief doth fear each bush an officer."

are inserted as literal transcripts, but there is not a word of the last of them in the "True Tragedie."

We might cite many more errors of the same kind, and we shall have occasion to notice a few as we proceed with our present task; but the above extracts will, in any case, be sufficient to show that the marks in Malone's text have not been made with rigorous accuracy.

ment; but we must add that, taken by itself, it would convey an impression that Shakespeare had a much larger share than could fairly be claimed for him in the production of the amended works; for all the scenes and all the characters must have been created by the original writer or writers; and it is they that must have produced, although in a more or less imperfect shape, nearly every one of those passages in the Second and Third Parts of "King Henry VI." which the readers of Shakespeare have for ages singled out as most specially Shakespearian.

Malone is again more than usually unlucky in the first argument he puts forward in support of his position that our great dramatist could not have written the two older publications. He observes that the name of Shakespeare is not mentioned as that of the author of the "First Part of the Contention" in the entry of that volume (he is mistaken in supposing that the "True Tragedie" was entered at the same time) in the Stationers' Registers in March, 1594, and that his name is not inserted in the title-pages of the editions of these works published in 1594 and 1595; and he then adds:—"Nor, when the two plays were published in 1600, did the printer ascribe them to our author (though his reputation was then at the highest), as surely he would have done, had they been his compositions." This is clearly an error. In the year 1594 or 1595, it was not the universal or even the usual practice to attach the names of even the most celebrated authors to their published plays. Several of Marlowe's dramas, and both parts of his "Tamburlaine" among the number, were at first printed without his name; and we may observe that, if he was the author, as Malone supposes him to have been, of the "True Tragedie," there would have been at least as little reason for omitting any allusion to that fact from the edition issued in 1595, as there would have been for a similar omission of the name of Shakespeare; for there can be no doubt that he continued down to that time to enjoy as high a literary reputation as his greater contemporary, while he was not alive to claim any kind of personal interest in the publication. The first editions of Shakespeare's own "Richard II." and "Richard III.," both issued in 1597, and of his "First Part of King Henry IV.," issued in 1598, appeared without the name of the author; but that name was certainly given in the title-pages of the editions of these plays printed in 1598 and 1599. His "Romeo and Juliet" was first published in 1597 without his name; and no allusion was made to the authorship of that drama in the editions which followed in 1599 and 1609, although they were stated in the title-pages to have been "newly corrected, augmented, and amended." But there is a still more direct and more conclusive answer to Malone's argument. The editions of the "First Part of the Contention" and of the "True Tragedie," dated 1594, 1595, and 1600, were all published by Thomas Millington; and this same publisher, in conjunction with John Busby, issued in 1600 the first edition of "King Henry V." without Shakespeare's name; and that work was re-issued, still without the name of the author, both in 1602 and 1608, by the same Thomas Pavier who published the "Whole Contention," with Shakespeare's name, in 1619, that is to say, some years after the poet's death. It is unnecessary for us to insist on the curious completeness with which these facts meet the statement of Malone, that if Shakespeare had been the author of the "First Part of the Contention" and of the "True Tragedie," his name would certainly have appeared on the title-pages of those works in 1594, 1595, and 1600.*

---

* The "First Part of the Contention," the "True Tragedie," "Romeo and Juliet," and "King Henry V." are the only dramas of Shakespeare's (we are supposing for a moment that he was substantially the original author of the two first of those works) of which more than one edition was published during his lifetime without his name; and they are all at the same time, more or less, imperfect copies, or at least they differ very considerably in many passages from the texts given in the Folio of 1623. Under these circumstances, we cannot help suspecting that it was in consequence of their more

It is quite true, as Malone states, that the old play of the "Troublesome Raigne of King John," on which Shakespeare's drama of "King John" is founded, but with the composition of which he had probably no connection, was published anonymously in 1591, was re-published in 1611, as the work of "W. Sh.," and again in 1622, with the announcement on the title-page that it was written by "W. Shakespeare." These facts, however, can only be used for the purpose of showing that we can place no absolute trust in the announcements of those old publishers. We are not now in any way contending that the statement in the title-page of Pavier's edition of the "Whole Contention," in 1619, affords a proof that the two plays were written by Shakespeare. We only desire to show that the omission of his name from the early editions of the "First Part of the Contention," and of the "True Tragedie" affords us no ground for concluding that he was not their author; and the whole history of the publication of the early editions of "King Henry V." establishes that position beyond the possibility of doubt.

The next circumstance to which Malone adverts furnishes him with a more reasonable argument. He says that, "The 'True Tragedie' (but not the 'First Part of the Contention,' as he supposed), is stated in the title-page to have been performed by the Earl of Pembroke's servants. 'Titus Andro-

---

or less spurious and defective origin, they continued to be anonymously issued from the press. The publishers, in withholding the writer's name, were perhaps influenced either by their own consciousness of the imperfections of the works, or by some dread of exposure if they were to assign them to an author who might be disposed to disavow his connection with them in the shape in which they were produced. The only other plays of Shakespeare's which can be supposed to have been at first printed in the same incomplete form, are the "Merry Wives of Windsor" and "Hamlet;" and both of these, for some reason which we cannot now determine, but which may have been nothing more than the bolder or more unscrupulous character of the publishers, bear the author's name on the title-pages of the earliest editions.

nicus' and the old 'Taming of a Shrew' were acted by the same company of comedians; but not one of our author's plays is said, in its title-page, to have been acted by any but the Lord Chamberlain's, or the Queen's, or King's servants." After having made this statement, he proceeds as follows:— " This circumstance alone, in my opinion, might almost decide the question." That would, we think, be drawing much too large and too distinct a conclusion from so very minute and so very obscure an incident. The fact is, that there does not appear to have been any kind of fixed property in plays at that period, and each company seems to have performed with the most complete impunity any piece of which they could in any way obtain possession. The " True Tragedie " may have been a work of Shakespeare's, and this very version of it may have been surreptitiously prepared for the actors known as the Earl of Pembroke's servants. But, besides, we really know nothing, with the smallest approach to certainty, of Shakespeare's first connection with the stage. It is quite conceivable that he may not have been permanently attached to any particular company when the "True Tragedie" was produced; and the probability is, in our opinion, so strong that he is the original author of that work, that we should have no hesitation in concluding that he was connected with the Earl of Pembroke's servants at the period of its composition, if we should otherwise have to ascribe it to any other writer.

Malone afterwards passes to a consideration of that passage in the " Groat's Worth of Wit " which has acquired so singular a notoriety. He very naturally believes that it contains an allusion to Shakespeare; and he then goes on to say that Greene and Peele were probably the joint authors of the two old plays, or that Greene was the author of one of them, and Peele of the other; that those works had recently been new-modelled and amplified by Shakespeare, who had by that means gained a considerable reputation; that Greene could not conceal the mortification which he felt on finding his own fame and that of his associate eclipsed by an "upstart" writer, and that he naturally quoted a line from one of the pieces which Shakespeare had thus re-written—"a proceeding which the authors of the original plays considered as an invasion both of their literary property and character." This is, we think, a very loose and a very improbable view of the matter, and Malone himself, at a later period, so far altered it that he believed the "True Tragedie" was written principally, if not wholly, by Marlowe. But, however that may be, it is extremely unlikely that the author or authors of the two old plays had any kind of literary property in them; and, even if they had, that property could hardly have been affected by the mere reproduction upon the stage of the remodelled dramas. Neither could this reconstruction of their works, with the adoption of all their incidents, and of a very considerable portion of their language, for two new plays, have inflicted any serious injury on their character.

In considering this question, we are perpetually reminded of the relative merits of the different authors, if there were different authors, of those productions; and we are so strongly convinced of the superior dramatic power of every kind displayed by the original writer or writers, as compared with their imitator, that we believe they could not possibly have found much reason to envy him either his genius or his fame. But if a new and obscure author had written the parting of Margaret and Suffolk, and the death scene of Beaufort, and the comedy of "Jack Cade," and the soliloquy of Richard after the murder of King Henry, we should at once be able to understand the astonishment which his advent appears to have created among the established dramatists of his time, and the special animosity which it awakened in the distempered mind of Greene. It was manifest from that moment that there had arisen a new master of the language of passion and imagination—one who could give to the mimic representation of life a force and a splendour of which his predecessors seem hardly to have even dreamed. The whole tone of Greene's language shows that he was aware of the unwelcome presence of a genius who had already outstripped all competition. It is clear that he was secretly impressed with the conviction that his companions had no longer any marked distinction to expect from their connection with the stage, "*for* there is an upstart crow," &c. ; and this unconscious testimony to the superiority of a writer whom he was anxious to vilify, affords the most striking proof that, in his mind, that writer had displayed some wholly new and unparalleled power.

The modern commentators in general have, we think, made a great deal too much of Greene's allusion to the obligations which Shakespeare owed to his dramatic contemporaries. That allusion is conveyed in the vaguest and the most general terms. The exclamation, "O tiger's heart, wrapt in a player's hide," only leads us to believe that the attention of the writer had been enviously directed to the "True Tragedie," or the additional Part of "King Henry VI.," of the new dramatist, and that he applied to the malignant purposes of the moment one of those vigorous lines in that work which still haunted his memory; while, on the other hand, the supposition that he was here laying claim to the authorship of an unpublished drama, on which another unpublished drama had been founded, appears to us to be one of those extravagant notions which only occur to people who are prepared to find in the most indifferent circumstances arguments in support of a foregone conclusion. The quotation is a parody, and it seems to have been introduced in its manifestly offensive form for the express purpose of at once identifying and insulting its original author.

Malone asks whether, if Shakespeare had originally written these three plays of "King Henry VI.," they would not probably have been found by the bookseller in the same manuscripts? And whether they would not have been procured, whether surreptitiously or otherwise, all at the same time? These questions can in no way affect the conclusion at which we have arrived with respect to the formation of those works. We believe that they were not merely obtained surreptitiously, but that they were made up, in part, at least, from memory,

T

and from notes taken during the performances at the theatre; and in that case they must necessarily have been produced gradually and slowly. But even if the publisher had access to one of the copies, it does not by any means necessarily follow that he could have obtained the remainder of the number; and even if he could, it is quite conceivable that he would have selected for his particular purpose what he believed would be the most popular of the series. It is reasonable to suppose, however, that he actually experienced some difficulty in obtaining his copies, for we find that the "True Tragedie" was not published until 1595, or a year after the "First Part of the Contention," although it must have been in existence when Greene wrote his tract, in September, 1592.

Malone further asks whether, if the three plays were Shakespeare's, they would not have borne in the manuscripts the titles of the First, and Second, and Third Parts of "King Henry VI.?" and whether the bookseller would not have entered them on the Stationers' registers, and published such of them as he did publish, under those titles? But if a piratical bookseller was led, in the first instance, either from choice or from necessity, to publish the second part of the series, it was perfectly natural that he should not have given to it a name which would at once have proclaimed its incompleteness. The fact is that, as we find from numerous entries in Henslowe's Diary, among other evidence to the same effect our old plays frequently passed under a variety of designations. The publishers of those works, in particular, allowed themselves the largest licence in attaching what they may have considered the most appropriate or the most catching titles to their volumes; and we are sometimes very much at a loss to account for the choice which they exercised upon those occasions. When this very Thomas Millington published Shakespeare's "King Henry V.," he not only issued it without the author's name, but he issued it under the title of "The Chronicle History of Henry Fifth;" thus diminishing, as we should now suppose, the chance of its being at once recognised as one of the popular productions of the most celebrated dramatist of the age; and in the same way, when Pavier published, in 1619, these two old plays in a single volume, he called the work " The Whole Contention," &c., and not the First and Second Parts of " Henry VI.," under which name they had, in the year 1602, been assigned to him by Millington.

All the preceding details are manifestly of a very inconclusive character, and it is in the internal evidence that we shall most probably find our surest guidance in this intricate controversy. It is upon that evidence that Malone himself seems most to have relied, although we may observe that it is by a comparison of detached passages, and not by an examination of the large and general characteristics, either of the substance or the form of these plays, that he seeks to establish his conclusion. He is naturally struck by differences between the two versions of the works which seem to show that the " First Part of the Contention " and the " True Tragedie " could not have been the productions of an ordinary copyist, writing from imperfect notes. Amidst the general resemblance of the old editions to the dramas in the Folio of 1623, a few of the less important scenes are transposed; an incident or an allusion is now and then altered, or some entirely new incident or allusion is introduced; and sometimes a speech, as it appears in Shakespeare's plays, is considerably expanded, or is produced with wholly new details. Thus, Warwick, towards the close of Act II., Scene II., of the " Second Part of King Henry VI.," addresses York as follows :—

> My heart assures me, that the Earl of Warwick
> Shall one day make the Duke of York a king.

Instead of these two lines we have in the " First Part of the Contention" (pp. 26, 27, ed. Shak. Soc.), the ten which follow :—

> Then York advise thyself and take thy time,
> Claim thou the crown, and set thy standard up,

> And in the same advance the milk-white rose,
> And then to guard it will I rouse the bear,
> Environ'd with ten thousand ragged staves,
> To aid and help thee for to win thy right,
> Maugre the proudest lord of Henry's blood
> That dares deny the right and claim of York;
> For why, my mind presageth I shall live
> To see the noble Duke of York to be a king.

In the same play (p. 70), young Clifford, while preparing to carry off the dead body of his father, is assaulted by Richard. He puts this enemy to flight, and he then exclaims:—

> Out, crook'd-back villain, get thee from my sight;
> But I will after thee, and once again,
> When I have borne my father to his tent,
> I'll try my fortune better with thee yet.

But in Shakespeare's play no such incident occurs; nor is Richard introduced in that scene; and, of course, it does not contain a trace of Clifford's address.

In one of the scenes between Jack Cade and his followers (pp. 59, 60), which corresponds to the seventh scene in the fourth act of the "Second Part of King Henry VI.," Dick Butcher drags a sergeant or constable on the stage, and at the conclusion of a dialogue, which extends over thirteen or fourteen lines, Cade orders that the officer of justice shall be "brain'd with his own mace." But of this whole sketch there is not a word in Shakespeare's play.

There are many more of the same kind of differences between the two versions of these dramas. We have selected some of the most striking of the whole number, and we believe that we need not further increase our list. The alterations or additions in the old plays are never of much value in themselves; but it is natural that some surprise should be excited by their appearance in mere mutilated copies. It is, however, at the same time, manifest that they cannot finally decide the present question. Those critics who hold that the two early publications were works of Shakespeare's, which he subsequently improved, can have no difficulty in believing that he might have made in them even still more considerable changes. But that is not the conclusion which we are disposed to adopt. We believe that the early volumes are but imperfect copies of Shakespeare's dramas; and, unless we are much mistaken, we can show that that belief is not irreconcilable with the differences which exist between the two editions. A modern critic would, we think, be very apt to misapprehend the circumstances under which such imitations must have been produced by a plagiarist of the close of the sixteenth century. A popular dramatist now enjoys a wide and distinguished reputation; and the publisher of any of his works would naturally be desirous of reproducing it with the most absolute completeness. His volume, indeed, would otherwise be almost wholly valueless. But in the days of Queen Elizabeth the most successful dramatist had hardly any recognised position in the world of letters. His name carried with it little or no authority or credit. The whole history of the literature of the time leaves no room for a doubt upon that point. Shakespeare himself, in the year 1593, dedicated his "Venus and Adonis" to Lord Southampton as the "first heir of his invention;" and that poem and the "Lucrece" were for many years afterwards singled out by his admirers as objects of the most marked commendation. We may feel assured that under such a condition of the public taste, the piratical printer of one of his early dramas would be animated by no strong anxiety to adhere with scrupulous fidelity to his original. He would most probably be only desirous of producing a popular and striking volume; and no reverence for his author would for a moment stand in the way of his pursuit of that object. We very much doubt whether he would not even have regarded a large amount of novelty in the publication, if it could only be introduced with effect, as a positive recommendation in its favour. We know that Henslowe paid poets, whose fame has descended to our times, for altering some of the most popular pieces in his repertory, when their very success had contributed to exhaust the interest they had originally excited. Millington did not in any way profess to reproduce the dramas of Shakespeare—any copyist whom he might have employed would have been utterly unable to attain such a result; and under these circumstances we can have no reason for supposing that they did not both allow themselves a large licence in the accomplishment of the work they had actually undertaken.

We are now enabled to give a further answer—and an answer of the most practical and convincing character—to the argument which Malone has deduced from the variations in the different versions of these dramas. He believed that a copyist would not have reversed the order of the scenes as laid down in the work which he was imitating, and, above all, that he would not have introduced scenes without any authority from his model. But since Malone's time, the first edition of "Hamlet," which was manifestly a mutilated and an imperfect copy, has been discovered; and in it there are some remarkable transpositions in the dialogue, and there is one scene between the Queen and Horatio of which no trace whatever exists in the more perfect edition. There never, perhaps, was a more unlucky casuist than the author of the "Dissertation on the Three Parts of King Henry VI." The very dead seem to rise to testify against his assumptions.

There are a number of historical errors or contradictions in all these works which, Malone thinks, go to prove that Shakespeare could not have been their original author. In the "True Tragedie" (p. 154), and in the "Third Part of King Henry VI.," Act III., Scene II., King Edward states that Sir Richard [John] Grey, the husband of Lady Grey, fell, fighting for the house of York, at the Battle of St. Albans. But in "King Richard III.," Act I., Scene III., Richard states correctly that Sir John Grey followed the fortunes of the house of Lancaster. Again, in the "True Tragedie" (p. 163), and in the "Third Part of King Henry VI.," Act III.,

Scene III., it is arranged that Prince Edward is to marry Warwick's " eldest daughter ; " and further on in both plays (p. 166 of the " True Tragedie," and Act IV., Scene I., of the "Third Part of King Henry VI."), Clarence announces his intention of marrying her " younger " sister. But in reality it was Clarence that married the elder, and Prince Edward that married the younger daughter of Warwick; and those facts must have been known to Shakespeare when he wrote his " King Richard III.," for Richard there states (Act I., Scene I.) that he will marry " Warwick's youngest daughter," " though he killed her husband and her father." All that those passages absolutely prove is, that if Shakespeare was the author of the " True Tragedie," or of the " Third Part of King Henry VI.," he avoided, at a subsequent period, two errors into which he has there fallen ; and such a circumstance could not, in our opinion, present the slightest appearance of improbability.

But that is not the only answer we have to make to Malone's argument. We believe that a reference to the chroniclers will enable us to afford some explanation of those inconsistencies. The only mention, unless we are mistaken, which Hall, in his history of the reigns of King Henry VI., and of King Edward IV., makes of the death of Sir John Grey will be found in the two following passages :—" In this battle [the second battle of St. Albans] were slain 2,300 men, and not above, of whom no noble is remembered, save Sir John Grey, which the same day was made knight, with twelve other, at the village of Colney" (fol. 184). And subsequently (fol. 193) Hall refers to King Edward's first introduction to "dame Elizabeth Grey, widow of Sir John Grey, knight, slain at the last battle of St. Albans, by the power of King Edward." Any one forming his impression from the first of these extracts might easily, and even naturally, have concluded that Sir John Grey fell in the ranks of the party of the Duke of York, who were defeated in that encounter. The corresponding passages in Holinshed seem to afford us still further light upon this subject :—" In which [the second battle of St. Albans] were slain 2,300 men, of whom no nobleman is remembered, save Sir John Grey, which the same day was made knight, with twelve other, at the village of Colney" (p. 660). "The Lady Elizabeth Grey, widow of Sir John Grey, knight, slain at the last battle of St. Albans, as before ye have heard" (p. 668).

It is manifest that, if the original author of the "Third Part of King Henry VI." followed Holinshed in this instance, we should at once be able to account for the mistake into which he has been led; and that he was indebted to the latter chronicler for some of his incidents we shall be able to show upon the plainest and most indisputable evidence. But Shakespeare, in reading, as he must have done before writing his "King Richard III.," the reign of King Edward V., either in Hall or in Holinshed, found there the most distinct mention of the real history of Sir John Grey. We need only give the passage from Holinshed (p. 726), who, in the opinion of Malone, was the chronicler Shakespeare consulted for all his English historical dramas:—" Howbeit this dame Elizabeth herself, being in service with Queen Margaret, wife unto King Henry the Sixth, was married unto one John Grey, an esquire, whom King Henry made knight upon the field that he had on Barnet Heath by St. Albans, against King Edward. But little while enjoyed he that knighthood, for at the said field he was slain." We think it very probable that the above quotations will admit us into the secret history of this portion of Shakespeare's workmanship.

We have no similar conjecture to offer on the subject of the disposal of Warwick's daughters. In both Hall and Holinshed we find the most distinct and even minute information with respect to the marriage of the elder sister to Clarence; and that of the younger one, some years later, to Prince Edward. But here, again, we must bear in mind that the dramatist, whoever he may have been, must have read one or both of the chroniclers. He could not, indeed, otherwise have known that either union was ever accomplished. It is just possible that in the hurry of composition he forgot the order of those events; but it seems to us at least as probable that he more or less deliberately disregarded that petty accident. He was naturally led to bring both those marriages together, and he may have thought proper to assign the hand of the elder sister to the more distinguished of the two princes. We have in these works many instances of the freedom with which he treats the details of chronology; and we find it impossible to determine how far he might knowingly have availed himself of that privilege.

The fact is that it would be the merest delusion to attempt to bind down the author of these dramas in any way to an observance of the literal truth of history, or even to any perfect consistency in his own choice of historical allusions. It is wholly inconceivable that the original constructor of such works should not have read one or other of the historians who relate the incidents he has used for his special purpose; he must afterwards, however, have frequently departed from his authorities, either through forgetfulness, or negligence, or his own deliberate conception of the licence of his art; and we know no writer in the whole history of letters who is so likely to have fallen into this thoughtlessness, or to have exercised this right, as Shakespeare.

We have already referred to the contradictory accounts given of the death of the elder Clifford towards the close of the " First Part of the Contention," and of the " Second Part of King Henry VI." on the one hand, and the commencement of the " True Tragedie " and of the " Third Part of King Henry VI." on the other. In the former case Clifford is made to fall by the hand of York, while in the latter version of the story York himself states that Clifford and other leaders of the Lancaster party were " by the swords [" hands " in the " True Tragedie "] of common soldiers slain." We believe that here, again, the most reasonable mode of accounting for the inconsistency is by supposing that in the fervour of composition Shakespeare's memory was sometimes wholly or almost wholly quiescent in respect of petty details; and we find in the "Second Part of King Henry VI." what appears to be another most singular justification of that solution of the difficulty. In Act III., Scene II., of that play there is a long passage which is not contained in the "First Part of the Contention," in which Queen Margaret three times speaks of herself as "Eleanor," if the old editions of the poet's dramas are to be trusted; and there is some reason to believe that this is not an error of the printers; for King Henry, her husband, had just before addressed her as "Nell" in the following line:—

I thank thee, Nell; these words content me much.

The great majority of the modern editors, struck by the obvious character of these inadvertencies, have changed both the "Eleanor" and the "Nell" into "Margaret;"* but in doing so they have been compelled to spoil the metre of the line we have just quoted.

The above statement would afford, we think, a sufficient explanation of the discrepancy in the accounts of the death of the elder Clifford; but the argument which has been drawn from that circumstance, and which is perhaps the most obvious and the most generally effective one that has been employed to support the conclusion that the old plays could not have been the productions of any single writer, will, we believe, admit of some further answer. No one, we take it for granted, will deny that the end of the "First Part of the Contention," or of the "Second Part of King Henry VI.," and the commencement of the "True Tragedie," or of the "Third Part of King Henry VI.," must have been more or less connected in the mind of the original author. The very first sentence of the two latter plays—"I wonder how the King escap'd our hands"—seems at once to establish this relation. Shakespeare

---

* Capell and Mr. Collier have substituted "Meg" for "Nell." But "Meg" is not used in any other portion of these works.

was certainly at work upon both these dramas; and we cannot discover the slightest reason for believing that he would, out of mere deference to his models, have fallen into an inconsistency which his own memory and his own judgment would have led him to condemn. It is possible for us to suppose that the "First Part of the Contention" and the "True Tragedie" came from different copyists; but we feel assured that there was but one writer for the Second and the Third Parts of "King Henry VI." We know, too, that Shakespeare was specially liable to indulge in this negligent workmanship; and we find another and a precisely similar instance of it in this series of dramas. The commencement of the "Second Part of King Henry VI." appears to be a direct continuation of the end of the First Part. Suffolk relates in the one the result of the embassy which he was in the other ordered to undertake. But while he was told by the king, before his departure, to collect "a tenth" for his expenses, we find from a statement of Gloster's that, on his return, he demanded "a whole fifteenth;" and that statement must certainly have proceeded from Shakespeare himself, for there is no reference whatever made to the subject in the "First Part of the Contention." All these circumstances only confirm us in the belief that an elaborate comparison of small details, for the purpose of identifying the writer, is wholly inapplicable to the dramas of Shakespeare, and that no reliance can be placed on any conclusion that may be deduced from such a labour.

We have now done with these proofs of the carelessness with which Shakespeare treated the minor incidents of his stories. There cannot be the slightest doubt that he fell into manifold contradictions in his undisputed productions; they afford one of the striking characteristics of his workmanship; and there is another circumstance connected with their appearance in his published works which excites our astonishment, and which even seems to us more or less utterly unaccountable. We could perhaps understand, without any great difficulty, that in the ardour of composition he bestowed no rigorous attention on the perfect consistency of his details; but we are still perplexed at finding him leave uncorrected mistakes which must have frequently been brought under his notice, and which he might have removed without any sensible effort. Why did he, for instance, retain the contradictory accounts of the death of the elder Clifford in dramas which he must repeatedly have seen acted, and in the performance of which he himself, in all probability, must have taken a part? Or was it he that introduced not less than four times the name of "Nell" or "Eleanor" for that of Margaret; and if so, could he afterwards have allowed such obvious errors to remain unaltered? These and many similar mistakes in the edition of his dramas published by his fellow-actors, seem to show that he not only wrote negligently in the first instance, but that when his works once left his hands, he must, as far as possible, have ceased to give a thought to the form in which they were brought under the notice of the world, or even to their very existence.

There is a very remarkable instance in which Shakespeare has avoided an inaccuracy into which the author of the "True Tragedie" has fallen. Malone thinks it tends to show that that work was not originally written by our great dramatist; but it seems to us to lead very distinctly to the opposite conclusion. In the "Third Part of King Henry VI.," Act II., Scene III., Richard thus announces to Warwick the death of his brother:—

> Ah, Warwick, why hast thou withdrawn thyself!
> Thy brother's blood the thirsty earth hath drunk,
> Broach'd with the steely point of Clifford's lance:
> And, in the very pangs of death, he cried,—
> Like to a dismal clangor heard from far,—
> "*Warwick, revenge! brother, revenge my death!*"
> So, underneath the belly of their steeds,
> That stain'd their fetlocks in his smoking blood,
> The noble gentleman gave up the ghost.

This passage naturally perplexed the early readers of Shakespeare, inasmuch as Montague, the only brother of Warwick who is introduced into this drama, is made to fall (Act V., Scene II.) at a later period and on another field of battle:—

> *Somerset.* Ah, Warwick, Montague hath breath'd his last;
> And to the latest gasp, cried out for Warwick,
> And said—" Commend me to my valiant brother."
> And more he would have said; and more he spoke,
> Which sounded like a cannon in a vault,
> That might not be distinguish'd; but, at last,
> I well might hear, deliver'd with a groan,—
> " O, farewell, Warwick ! "

The commentators of the last century were enabled to account for this apparent contradiction. They found, on consulting the chronicles, that an illegitimate brother of Warwick was slain in the first action to which the dramatist has referred,* and the statement of Richard is thus shown to be literally true to history. The writer of the " True Tragedie," however, was not so well informed upon this point. He appears to have known nothing of any brother of Warwick's, except the one who is killed in a subsequent scene, and he accordingly substitutes (p. 145) Warwick's " father " for his " brother " in the passage which he attributes to Richard:—

> Ah, Warwick, why hast thou withdrawn thyself?
> Thy noble father, in the thickest throngs,
> Cried still for Warwick, his thrice valiant son,
> Until with thousand swords he was beset,
> And many wounds made in his aged breast;
> And as he tottering sat upon his steed,
> He waft his hand to me, and cried aloud,
> " Richard, commend me to my valiant son ; "
> And still he cried, " Warwick, revenge my death ; "
> And with those words he tumbled off his horse,
> And so the noble Salisbury gave up the ghost.

---

* Hall (fol. 186) and Holinshed (p. 664) mention the fact in precisely the same words:—" The Lord Fitzwater," &c., " was slain, and with him the bastard of Salisbury, brother to the Earl of Warwick, a valiant young gentleman, and of great audacity."

In the same version of the drama (p. 178) Somerset thus relates the end of Montague:—

> Thy brother Montague hath breath'd his last,
> And at the pangs of death I heard him cry
> And say, "Commend me to my valiant brother;"
> And more he would have spoke, and more he said,
> Which sounded like a clamour in a vault,
> That could not be distinguish'd for the sound;
> And so the valiant Montague gave up the ghost.

It is clear that the attention of the writer of the "True Tragedie" had here been specially directed to the similarity of the two incidents he had to describe, and this circumstance would perfectly account for his introduction of the "father" instead of the "brother" of Warwick in the earlier scene. He seems, in his last passage, to have been carefully copying the first passage in Shakespeare, and there can be no doubt that he has carefully copied his own preceding description; for, in both cases, the concluding lines, and the exclamations which he attributes to the dying warriors, are as nearly as possible identical. There is no appearance of any similar constraint in the language of Shakespeare, and the natural conclusion is that he was saved from it by the different conditions under which his work was performed.

There is another circumstance which seems curiously to unmask the special ignorance of the author of the passage in the "True Tragedie." In the account he has given of the death of Salisbury, he has completely misrepresented one of the best known incidents in the history of the period of which he was treating; and, what is more, he has completely misrepresented an incident with which he must himself have been perfectly acquainted if he was the original author of the drama. Hall, after having stated that the Earl of Salisbury was made prisoner at the battle of Wakefield, in which the Duke of York was killed, proceeds as follows (fol. 183):—"After this victory by the Queen and her party obtained, she caused the Earl of Salisbury, with all the other prisoners, to be sent to Pomfret, and there to be beheaded; and sent all their heads, and the Duke of York's head,* to be set upon poles over the gate of the city of York." We find that this insult to the remains of York is three times referred to, both in the "Third Part of King Henry VI." (Act I., Scene IV.; Act II., Scene I.; and Act II., Scene II.), and in the "True Tragedie" (pp. 133, 135, and 139). But the original writer of the work could only have derived his knowledge of this fact from the very sentence we have just quoted, in which such distinct mention is also made of the end of Salisbury. We must, therefore, suppose that the author of the "True Tragedie" knowingly and deliberately indulged in this falsification of history if he was writing from any independent information, and if he was the original framer of the work.

Let our readers now observe the importance of the whole of the above statement as an element in the decision of the present controversy.

It affords the most direct proof that, if Shakespeare was copying the author of the older publication, he did not feel bound to follow him in his errors. It shows not less clearly that, in this instance, at all events, it was he, and not the writer he is supposed to have imitated, that consulted the chroniclers. It creates, at the same time, a presumption so strong as almost to amount to decisive evidence, that he worked with the freedom and the knowledge which naturally accompany original composition, while the writer of the "True Tragedie" was but a timid, and an ignorant copyist.†

---

* "The duke's head of York" in the original. Holinshed (p. 659) tells the same story, and almost in the very same words.

† We are not sure that it is worth while to notice here an argument advanced by Malone in a note (p. 475). Warwick, in Act III., Scene III., of the "Third Part of King Henry VI.," asks—

"Did I forget, that by the house of York
My father came untimely to his death?"

Malone says that this passage, which is also to be found in the "True

There are other passages in these works which furnish Malone with an additional argument. They are certainly of a somewhat peculiar description, and they will, at all events, afford us another instance of that strange carelessness which distinguishes the hand of Shakespeare, and which, we may feel sure, forms no inconsiderable source of the perplexities we have to encounter in any minute examination of his dramas, whatever may be the solution of those perplexities which we may think it most natural to adopt. " Our author," says Malone, " in his undoubted compositions, has fallen into an inaccuracy, of which I do not recollect a similar instance in the works of any other dramatist. When he has occasion to quote the same paper twice (not from memory, but *verbatim*), from negligence, he does not always attend to the words of the paper which he has occasion to quote, but makes one of the persons of the drama recite them with variations, though he holds the very paper quoted before his eyes." Thus, in " All's Well that Ends Well," Act V., Scene III., Helena says:—

> Here's your letter : This it says :—
> *When from my finger you can get this ring,*
> *And are, by me, with child.*

Tragedie " (p. 162), was inserted by Shakespeare, through a mistake, upon his part, in adhering too closely to his model, inasmuch as it refers to the death of Salisbury—an event of which, as we have seen, a distinct, although an erroneous, account is given in the latter play, while no mention is made of it in the " Third Part of King Henry VI." But if Salisbury was made prisoner while fighting for the House of York, and was immediately afterwards beheaded, it would be literally true that it was in consequence of his devotion to their cause that he " came untimely to his death," while it would be a manifest error to suppose that the original writer of the passage could not have made this allusion to an incident which he had not before described ; for, in both versions of the work, we find Warwick, in the very next line, speaking of an "abuse done to his niece," which is mentioned both by Hall (fol. 195) and by Holinshed (p. 668), but of which no notice whatever is to be found in any other portion of these dramas.

But Helena had previously (in Act III., Scene II.) read this very letter aloud, and there the words are different, and are in plain prose :—" When thou canst get the ring upon my finger, which never shall come off, and show me a child begotten of thy body," &c. In the same manner, in the first scene of the " Second Part of King Henry VI.," the Duke of Gloster begins to read the articles of peace concluded between France and England; but when he has gone no further than these words :—" Item, that the *duchy* of Anjou and the *county* of Maine shall be released and delivered to the King her father" —he is seized with sudden illness, and becomes incapable of proceeding; on which the Bishop of Winchester, at the command of the King, reads the whole of the paper, and recites the article in question as follows :—" Item, *it is further agreed between them*, that *the duchies of Anjou and Maine* shall be released and delivered *over* to the King her father," &c. This curious inconsistency is avoided in the " First Part of the Contention," where the reading of Winchester corresponds with that of Gloster in the minutest particulars. We find a precisely similar neglect of the most natural uniformity in Act I., Scene IV., of this " Second Part of King Henry VI." Bolingbroke there reads the following lines :—

>What fate awaits the Duke of Suffolk?
>What shall befall the Duke of Somerset?

But the Duke of York immediately afterwards reads the lines, and from the same paper, somewhat differently :—

>Tell me, what fate awaits the Duke of Suffolk?
>What shall betide the Duke of Somerset?

The existence of this curious discrepancy may be adduced to show that Shakespeare was probably the author of the " Second Part of King Henry VI. ; " but we certainly do not think it can prove anything further; and we are at a loss to conceive how Malone could have supposed that it is " of such weight that, though it stood alone, it might decide the present question." If Shakespeare himself wrote all these works, there would be nothing extraordinary in the fact that in one of them he fell into these small contradictions, and did not fall into them in another; and it would be perfectly natural—we might even say it would be almost inevitable—that they should have been avoided by an ordinary copyist, writing from imperfect notes, and necessarily distrustful of himself at every step that he took in his laborious operation.

The very strangeness of this workmanship, if it betrays anything, seems to betray the hand of an original writer. And this observation will afford a perfect answer to the argument which Malone deduces from the occasional introduction into Shakespeare's two plays of such an unusual form of language as the employing of adjectives adverbially, as in the line in the opening scene of the "Third Part of King Henry VI.,"—"Is either slain or wounded dangerous;" while in the "True Tragedie" the expression used in its stead is the more natural and more usual one, "wounded dangerously."

There is another instance in which we shall, we think, find the same answer again available. Shakespeare, Malone says, has fallen into inconsistencies "by sometimes adhering to, and sometimes deviating from, his original." Thus, in the "Second Part of King Henry VI." (Act IV., Scene IV.,) the King, when asked what reply he wishes to have sent to the supplication of the rebels, says:—

> I'll send some holy bishop to entreat, &c.

This answer, according to Malone, was taken by Shakespeare "from Holinshed's 'Chronicle;' whereas in the old play no mention is made of a bishop on this occasion. The King there says he will himself come and parley with the rebels; and in the meantime he orders Clifford and Buckingham to gather an army. In a subsequent scene, however, Shakespeare forgot the new matter which he had introduced in the former; and Clifford and Buckingham only parley with Cade, &c., conformably to the old play." There appears to be here some misunderstanding. It is obvious that a copyist, who had to perform his task with the greatest caution, would be specially apt to avoid an inconsistency of this kind, supposing—which we doubt—that there is any real inconsistency in the matter; and if Shakespeare, in a work in which he was throughout closely following another writer, made for once what must have been an exceptional reference to the historian, such a circumstance would be likely to impress itself on his memory with more than usual distinctness. He must, at all events, have displayed very much the same species of carelessness or forgetfulness in the one case as in the other; and this fact, combined with so many others of the same description, ought to teach us how unsafe it would be to deduce any rigorous conclusions from irregularities which form marked and frequent characteristics of his whole drama.

Malone afterwards mentions a somewhat trifling circumstance, to which, however, he is disposed to attach considerable weight. The priest who is engaged with the Duchess of Gloster in certain magical operations, is called "Hum" in Hall's "Chronicle;" and he is also so called in the "First Part of the Contention." Shakespeare, thinking that name harsh or ridiculous, as Malone supposes, softened it to Hume. But in Holinshed this clerical conjuror is named Hun; "and so, undoubtedly, or perhaps for softness, Hune he would have been called in the original play, if Shakespeare had been the author of it; for Holinshed, and not Hall, was his guide." We have already stated that Malone's only proof that Shakespeare consulted no historian but Holinshed in the composition of all his English historical dramas, is, that he followed that writer in a single passage in "King Henry V.," and we have, at the same time, endeavoured to show the utter unreasonableness of that argument. The employment here made of it will certainly not add to its authority. It is clear that Shakespeare must have read either Hall or Holinshed before he wrote this scene, for he introduces as one of its characters, Southwell, who does not appear in any way in the "First Part of the Contention," but of whom special mention is made by both the chroniclers:

"At the same season were arrested, as aiders and councillors to the said Duchess, Thomas Southwell, priest, and canon of St. Stephen's, in Westminster; John Hum, priest; Roger Bolingbroke," &c. And again, "John Hum had his pardon, and Southwell died in the Tower before execution." (Hall, fol. 146). Holinshed (p. 623) alludes to Southwell in almost identically the same terms. But if Shakespeare consulted either Hall or Holinshed in this instance, there is obviously an end of Malone's whole argument, which is founded on these two assumptions—first, that Shakespeare could not have referred to Hall, whom he never used as his guide in his historical dramas; and secondly, that if he had been following Holinshed, he would have called this priest Hun or Hune. This last statement, however, we may observe, cannot by any means be considered absolutely certain; for, although Holinshed gives the name of "John Hun" in his text, he places these words very conspicuously in the margin, "alias John Hum." But whatever opinion we may form upon this latter point, it is manifest that Malone's whole position is utterly untenable.

It is, perhaps, hardly necessary to dwell any further upon this subject. But Malone goes on to remark, that "by the alteration of this priest's name Shakespeare has destroyed a rhyme intended by the author of the original play, where Sir John begins a soliloquy with this jingling line:—

> Now, Sir John Hum, no word but mum:
> Seal up your lips, for you must silent be.

which Shakespeare has altered thus:—

> But how now, Sir John Hume?
> Seal up your lips, and give no words but mum.

We must observe, in reference to these two passages, that we do not place any absolute reliance on the spelling of names in Shakespeare's time as a means of ascertaining their pronunciation; and we are very much inclined to believe that he must have intended a rhyme in his lines, for their general construction seems to imply such a jingle, and they are introduced into an address which ends with a rhyme, and which is throughout thrown into a ludicrous form. It seems even still more likely that the actor at the theatre gave to them this particular sound; and if that were so, we should at once be able to account for a copyist calling the name "Hum," without having recourse to the supposition that he had used Hall as his guide in the construction of his work.

We now turn to the larger question, whether the original writer of these two dramas confined his reading, as Malone assumes, to only one historian. It is as clear as anything in criticism can be that we must answer this question in the negative, and that the author of the "First part of the Contention," as well as the author of the "True Tragedie," found his incidents and allusions sometimes in Hall and sometimes in Holinshed.

In pp. 46, 47 of the "First Part of the Contention," the dying Cardinal Beaufort exclaims:—

> Oh death, if thou will let me live but one whole year,
> I'll give thee as much gold as will purchase such another island.

The corresponding lines in the "Second Part of King Henry VI." (Act III., Scene III.,) run thus:—

> If thou be'st death, I'll give thee England's treasure,
> Enough to purchase such another island,
> So thou wilt let me live, and feel no pain.

There can be no reason to doubt that this address was copied from the following passage in Hall's "Chronicle" (fol. 152), of which there is not a trace in Holinshed:—"Dr. John Baker, his privy councillor, and his chaplain, wrote that he, lying on his death-bed, said these words: 'Why should I die, having so much riches? If the whole realm would save my life, I am able either by policy to get it, or by riches to buy it. Fie! will not death be hired, nor will money do nothing?'" In the representation of the battle of Towton a son has killed his father, and a father has killed his son, in p. 147 of the

"True Tragedie," and in Act II., Scene V., of the "Third Part of King Henry VI." These incidents seem clearly to have been suggested by the following reflection made by Hall (fol. 187) on that scene of slaughter:—"This conflict was in manner unnatural, for in it the son fought against the father, the brother against the brother, the nephew against the uncle, and the tenant against his lord." In the corresponding passage in Holinshed it is merely stated that the slain were "all Englishmen, and of one nation."

The evidence which goes to show that the original author or authors of these two plays consulted Holinshed is, perhaps, still more striking, and, if possible, still more unmistakable. The representation given in the "First Part of the Contention" (pp. 50 and following), and in the "Second Part of King Henry VI." (Act IV., Scenes II., III., &c.), of the insurrection of Jack Cade and his followers, is manifestly taken, in a great measure, from the account of the rising of Wat Tyler, Jack Straw, and others, in the reign of Richard II., which is described at length by Holinshed, and to which there is naturally no allusion whatever in Hall, for the reign of Richard is not included in the work of this latter writer. We shall hereafter quote, in detail, the passages in Holinshed which the dramatist has clearly imitated in this portion of his work; and we need not, therefore, here allude any further to that subject. In the "True Tragedie" (pp. 130, 131), and in the "Third Part of King Henry VI." (Act I., Scene IV.), York, after he has been made prisoner at the battle of Wakefield, is put standing on a "molehill," and has a mock crown there placed upon his head. All that Hall (fol. 183) states in reference to this incident is, that York was first slain, and that Clifford afterwards "came to the place where the dead corpse of the Duke of York lay, and caused his head to be stricken off, and set on it a crown of paper, and so fixed it on a pole, and presented it to the Queen, not lying far from the field, in great despite and much derision." Holinshed (p. 659) gives this passage almost literally, and he then adds :—" Some write that the Duke was taken alive, and in derision caused to stand upon a molehill; on whose head they put a garland instead of a crown, which they had fashioned and made of sedges or bulrushes; and, having so crowned him with that garland, they kneeled down afore him," &c. Malone appears to have been the very first of the commentators who pointed out the manifest connection between the above passage and the scene in the " Third Part of King Henry VI. ;" and yet, strange to say, throughout the whole of his subsequent dissertation, he has persisted in the statement that the original author of these three plays never looked into the pages of Holinshed.

In another part of his essay Malone, following the course he had before adopted in discussing the authorship of the " First Part of King Henry VI.," endeavours to show that, while there are many coincidences of thought and language between passages in Shakespeare's First and Second Parts of " King Henry VI.," and passages in his other works, those coincidences are almost exclusively confined to those portions of these two dramas which are entirely new, and which could not have been suggested to him by the " First Part of the Contention " or by the " True Tragedie." Malone admits that there are in the latter works three of those resemblances; but he adds, somewhat questionably, as we cannot help thinking, that those three exceptions to his general statement do not much diminish the force of his argument. Here again, however, his memory was manifestly at fault, and he affords another striking example of the proverbial danger of laying down large and unqualified negative propositions. We can certainly add to his parallelisms. In drawing up the following list, we have placed first the three resemblances which were pointed out by Malone himself :—

> You have no children, devils; if you had,
> The thought of them would then have stop't your rage.
> THE TRUE TRAGEDIE, *p.* 183.

He has no children.*
MACBETH, *Act IV., Scene III.*

Why died he not in his bed?
What would you have me do then?
Can I make men live whether they will or no?
THE FIRST PART OF THE CONTENTION, *p.* 47.

Think you I bear the shears of destiny?
Have I commandment on the pulse of life?
KING JOHN, *Act IV., Scene II.*

To whom do lions cast their gentle looks? &c.
The smallest worm will turn, being trodden on,
And doves will peck in rescue of their brood, &c.
Unreasonable creatures feed their young;
And though man's face be fearful to their eyes,
Yet in protection of their tender ones,
Who hath not seen them even with those same wings
Which they have sometime used in fearful flight,
Make war with him that climbs unto their nest,
Offering their own lives in their youngs' defence?
THE TRUE TRAGEDIE, *pp.* 139, 140.

---

* The same cry of nature escapes from the heart of Constance, in reply to the consolations addressed to her by Pandulph, the Papal Legate, on the occasion of the loss of her son, Prince Arthur:—

"He talks to me, that never had a son."
KING JOHN, *Act III., Scene IV.*

† In Hall (fol. 199, and in Holinshed, p. 671) we find the following passage in the "persuasion of the Earl of Warwick unto his two brethren [the Archbishop of York and the Marquis of Montacute] against King Edward the Fourth":—"What worm is touched, and will not once turn again? What beast is stricken that will not roar or sound? What innocent child is hurt that will not cry? If the poor and unreasonable beasts, if the silly babes that lacketh discretion, groan against harm to them profferred, how ought an honest man to be angry when things that touch his honesty be daily against him attempted?" The original author of the "True Tragodie" must, no doubt, have read this passage, and it may be that it was from it he formed the lines we have quoted in the text. But there is another work with which Shakespeare, we may feel assured, was specially

> The poor wren,
> The most diminutive of birds, will fight,
> Her young ones in her nest, against the owl.
> MACBETH, Act IV., Scene II.

So far Malone; we now proceed to add to his quotations :—

> Sometimes he calls upon Duke Humphrey's ghost,
> And whispers to his pillow as to him.
> THE FIRST PART OF THE CONTENTION, p. 45.

> Infected minds
> To their deaf pillows will discharge their secrets.
> MACBETH, Act V., Scene I.

> Wouldst have me weep? why, so thou hast thy wish,
> For raging winds blow up a storm of tears;
> And when the rage allays, the rain begins.
> THE TRUE TRAGEDIE, p. 132.

> This windy tempest, till it blow up rain,
> Held back his sorrow's tide, to make it more;
> At last it rains, and busy winds give o'er.
> LUCRECE.

acquainted—"The Hystorie of Hamblet," on which the play of "Hamlet" was manifestly founded—which might also have suggested to him the whole or the principal portion of those images. Hamlet is addressing his mother, and reproaching her with having delivered him up to the treachery of his uncle:—"It is not the part a woman," &c., "thus to leave her dear child to fortune in the bloody and murderous hands of a villain and traitor. Brute beasts do not so, for lions, tigers, ounces, and leopards, fight for the safety and defence of their whelps; and birds that have beaks, claws, and wings, resist such as would ravish them of their young ones."—*Mr. Collier's Shakespeare's Library*, Vol. I., pp. 144, 145. We cannot determine how far either of these passages might have been present to the mind of Shakespeare in composing his drama. But the coincidences which they furnish are undoubtedly somewhat singular; and the surprise with which we read the extract from the "History of Hamlet," in particular, is increased when we find, as we shall do in a subsequent page, that another very remarkable passage in the "True Tragedie," and in the "Third Part of King Henry VI.," very nearly resembles one in the same story.

This shower blown up by tempest of the soul.
KING JOHN, *Act V., Scene II.*

For self-same wind, that I should speak withal,
Is kindling coals, that fire all my breast,
And burn me up with flames, that tears would quench.*
KING HENRY VI., *Part III., Act II., Scene I.*

See, see, what showers arise,
Blown with the windy tempest of my heart.*
Ibidem, Scene V.

Where are my tears? rain, to lay this wind.
TROILUS AND CRESSIDA, *Act IV., Scene IV.*

And if thou tell the heavy story well,
Upon my soul the hearers will shed tears.
THE TRUE TRAGEDIE, *p.* 133.

Tell thou the lamentable tale of me,
And send the hearers weeping to their beds.
KING RICHARD II., *Act V., Scene I.*

Bring forth that fatal screech-owl to our house,
That nothing sung to us but blood and death.
THE TRUE TRAGEDIE, *p.* 151.

Out on ye, owls! nothing but songs of death?
KING RICHARD III., *Act IV., Scene IV.*

Tut, I can smile, and murder when I smile.
THE TRUE TRAGEDIE, *p.* 158.

There's daggers in men's smiles: the near in blood,
The nearer bloody.
MACBETH, *Act II., Scene III.*

O villain, villain, smiling, damned villain!
My tables,—meet it is, I set it down,
That one may smile, and smile, and be a villain.
HAMLET, *Act I., Scene V.*

---

* There is no trace of either of those passages in the "True Tragedie." They must, therefore, have been written by Shakespeare, and we have a perfect right to quote them upon this occasion.

Here we have eight, and not three merely, of those repetitions of the same thought or form of expression; and some of them are as remarkable and as characteristic as any which the whole drama of Shakespeare supplies. We are not prepared to attach so much importance as Malone has done to such coincidences, as a proof of the authorship of any particular work; but they may create a strong presumption in a question of this description; and they are in this instance so numerous and so striking, that we think it not improbable that, if we could appeal to that candid critic himself, they might lead him again to modify his views on the subject of Shakespeare's connection with these two early dramas.

We shall take this opportunity of noticing another very remarkable form of this spirit of imitation. Both versions of these works contain many repetitions; and this circumstance will, we believe, afford us another most important aid in our attempt to determine the question of their original authorship. We have just seen that Shakespeare reproduced more than once, in these Three Parts of "King Henry VI.," his representation of the effect of sorrow, in calling forth sighs and tears; and we have found that the author of the "True Tragedie" employed twice nearly the same lines, in describing the death of Warwick's father and that of Warwick's brother. There are other instances in which sometimes one, and sometimes both, of those writers repeat the same idea in the same, or nearly the same, language.

We take, first, a number of passages which are given twice in Shakespeare's works, and are found only once in either part of the " Contention : "—

> Inferring arguments of mighty force.
> KING HENRY VI., Part III., *Act II., Scene II.*
> Inferreth arguments of mighty strength.
> *Ibidem, Act III., Scene I.*

> Thou setter up and plucker down of kings.
> *Ibidem, Act II., Scene III.*

> Proud setter-up and puller-down of kings.
>> *Ibidem, Act III., Scene III.*
>
> And, if thou fail us, all our hope is done.
>> *Ibidem, Act III., Scene III.*
>
> If that go forward, Henry's hope is done.
>> *Ibidem.*

Each of the above three passages occurs only once in the corresponding scenes of the older volume:—

> Inferring arguments of mighty force.
>> THE TRUE TRAGEDIE, *p.* 140.
>
> Thou setter up and puller down of kings.
>> *Ibidem, p.* 145.
>
> And, if this go forward, all our hope is done.
>> *Ibidem, p.* 159.

The line, "Thou setter up," &c., in the "Third Part of King Henry VI.," and the corresponding one in the "True Tragedie," are both addressed by Edward to the Deity; but the other form of the same thought, "Proud setter up," &c., is addressed by Queen Margaret to Warwick; and this repetition, under such a change of circumstances, must naturally be supposed to be the result of some special forgetfulness or inadvertence.

In the "Two Parts of the Contention"—and the fact is, we think, in its way, of some importance—we find no repetition which is not also to be met in Shakespeare's dramas, with the exception of the feeble employment three times (pp. 52 and 57) of the trivial phrase, "the score and the tally," and the resemblances in the descriptions of the fate of Warwick's father and brother, which appear to be the result of an exceptional and a careful effort on the part of the writer.

There are several instances in which the same thought is rendered more than once in both editions, and in nearly the same language:—

> And therefore, Peter, have at thee with a downright blow.
>> KING HENRY VI., Part II., *Act II., Scene III.*

And so have at you, Peter, with downright blows.
                    THE FIRST PART OF THE CONTENTION, *p.* 29.

I cleft his beaver with a downright blow.
                    KING HENRY VI., Part III., *Act I., Scene I.*

I cleft his beaver with a downright blow.
                    THE TRUE TRAGEDIE, *p.* 117.

  Such mercy, as his ruthless arm,
With downright payment, show'd unto my father.
                    KING HENRY VI., Part III., *Act I., Scene IV.*

  Such mercy as his ruthful arm,
With downright payment, lent unto my father.
                    THE TRUE TRAGEDIE, *p.* 129.

See, how the pangs of death do make him grin.
                    KING HENRY VI., Part II., *Act III., Scene III.*

See, how the pangs of death doth gripe his heart.
                    THE FIRST PART OF THE CONTENTION, *p.* 47.

I should not for my life but weep with him,
To see how inly sorrow gripes his soul.
                    KING HENRY VI., Part III., *Act I., Scene IV.*

I could not choose but weep with him to see,
How inly anger gripes his heart.
                    THE TRUE TRAGEDIE, *p.* 133.

We have this last image introduced into the "First Part of the Contention" in an earlier page than any of the preceding extracts, and without any corresponding line in the same portion of Shakespeare's work :—

For sorrow's tears hath gripp'd my aged heart.
                    THE FIRST PART OF THE CONTENTION, *p.* 28.

There is one passage in which a line of Shakespeare's is found, in a not greatly altered form, not only in an earlier scene, but in an earlier play :—

    O Clifford, boist'rous Clifford, thou hast slain
    The flower of Europe for his chivalry.
                    KING HENRY VI., Part III., *Act II., Scene I.*

In the corresponding scene in the "True Tragedie" (p. 135), there is nothing in any way like these lines; but we are somewhat surprised at finding Jack Cade, immediately after having been vanquished by Iden, use an exclamation so similar, that it seems hardly possible one of the two writers should not have been copying the other :—

<blockquote>
Oh, villain, thou has slain the flower of Kent for chivalry.
THE FIRST PART OF THE CONTENTION, <i>p.</i> 63.
</blockquote>

The nearest resemblance in the "Second Part of King Henry VI." to this exclamation of Cade's, is to be found in the following words :—

<blockquote>
Tell Kent from me, she hath lost her best man.
KING HENRY VI., Part II., <i>Act IV., Scene X.</i>
</blockquote>

We now come to two repetitions or resemblances to which Malone (pp. 587-88) refers, for the purpose of showing that Shakespeare transposed the language of the author whom he was generally following. We do not think, however, that the passages themselves will at all bear out this conclusion. In the "Third Part of King Henry VI." (Act. II., Scene I.,) a messenger thus commences his account of the final fate of the Duke of York :—

<blockquote>
Environed he was with many foes;
And stood against them, as the hope of Troy
Against the Greeks, that would have enter'd Troy,
But Hercules himself must yield to odds.
</blockquote>

In the corresponding passage in the "True Tragedie" (p. 184), there is no allusion whatever to this "hope of Troy," or to the "Greeks," or to "Hercules;" but further on in that work (p. 174) we have the following line :—

<blockquote>
Farewell, my Hector, my Troy's true hope.
</blockquote>

And this line is also to be found in the corresponding scene in the "Third Part King Henry VI. (Act IV., Scene VIII.) :—

<blockquote>
Farewell, my Hector, and my Troy's true hope.
</blockquote>

There is here another singular coincidence between the

two versions of this play. The line in Shakespeare containing the allusion to Hercules, and which he nowhere repeats, is omitted from the corresponding address in the "True Tragedie," but is introduced, without the smallest change, into another portion (p. 178) of this latter work :—

But Hercules himself must yield to odds.

Malone takes it for granted that Shakespeare imitated this line, as well as the one in which he refers to the "hope of Troy," from the subsequent addresses in the "True Tragedie," and that he again employed the latter illustration in the scene in which alone it occurs in his model. But there is no reason whatever why we should suppose that he might not have been the original author of the two passages. On the contrary, we have good grounds for believing that it was he who supplied both those images to his imitator. They are written in perfect harmony with many other of his unquestioned contributions to these dramas. Those portions of the two plays which appeared for the first time in the Folio of 1623 actually abound in classical quotations and references, and, above all, perhaps, in references to the Trojan war; while there is observable throughout both parts of the "Contention" a general absence of any such allusions, of so marked a character, considering the period at which these works were produced, that it naturally gives rise to a strong suspicion that the writer or writers could not have been classical scholars. We are further led to think that the author of the "True Tragedie" was in this case the copyist, from the whole context of one of the two passages in his work. The line, "But Hercules himself must yield to odds," is introduced for the first time in the "True Tragedie" in an address of the dying Warwick, immediately preceding that announcement made to him by Somerset of the death of his brother Montague, which we have already quoted, and which is manifestly itself partly made up from the same writer's own account of the death of Salisbury, Warwick's father. We believe, too, that it is impossible to read the dialogue between

Warwick and Somerset in the "True Tragedie" without suspecting that it is throughout laboriously manufactured; for the intelligence communicated by Somerset of the end of Montague seems to have no kind of connection with the preceding language of Warwick; while in the "Third Part of King Henry VI." the corresponding passage forms a natural reply to the anxious inquiries of the dying king-maker.

The second case in which, as Malone believed, Shakespeare transposed the language of the writer whom he was imitating does not seem entitled to any very serious notice. In the "First Part of the Contention" (not in the "True Tragedie" as it is stated in p. 588 of Malone's "Dissertation)," the Duke of York, after having slain the elder Clifford, exclaims (p. 70) :—

Now, Lancaster, sit sure; thy sinews shrink.

There is no such line in the corresponding portion of the "Second Part of King Henry VI.;" but in the Third Part (Act V., Scene II.) Edward cries out, as he brings in the wounded Warwick :—

Now, Montague, sit fast; I seek for thee.

It is manifest, we think, that from so slight a resemblance as this, and in the case of an expression which may be considered a mere proverb, no conclusion on the subject of the imitation of one author by the other can be drawn with the smallest approach to certainty. But even if it were otherwise, there is nothing whatever to prevent us from believing that it was the writer of the old copy who, in this as in other instances of the same kind, remembered the later passage in his model.

We shall produce two other passages, which will afford a remarkable proof of the cautious, pains-taking mode in which the writer or writers of the "Contention" executed their task. In the "Second Part of King Henry VI." (Act II., Scene II.,) York says :—

> We thank you, lords. But I am not your king
> Till I be crown'd, and that my sword be stain'd
> With heart-blood of the house of Lancaster.

In the "First Part of the Contention" (p. 26), the corresponding words are printed as prose:—

I thank you both. But, lords, I am not your king until this sword be sheathed even in the heart-blood of the house of Lancaster.

The latter portion of this passage is repeated literarily in the "True Tragedie" (p. 135):—

> I cannot joy till this white rose be dyed
> Even in the heart-blood of the house of Lancaster.

There is nothing in any way like these two lines in the corresponding address in the "Third Part of King Henry VI." Act II., Scene I.; but in a preceding scene of that drama (Act I., Scene II.) we find the following passage:—

> I cannot rest,
> Until the white rose that I wear, be dyed
> Even in the lukewarm blood of Henry's heart.*

These extracts present another singular instance of transposition and of most elaborate imitation on the part of one or other of the two writers; and we think that the evidence leaves us no reasonable room to doubt which of them was the copyist. The passage in the "First Part of the Contention" forms portion of the scene in which the Duke of York explains to Salisbury and to Warwick his title to the crown, and which, as we shall hereafter have occasion to notice, is filled with a mass of stupid errors and inconsistencies that at once and unmistakably proclaims that it could not have come directly from the hand of the original author of these dramas. The perfect exactness, too, with which a portion of the words in the "First Part of the Contention" are reproduced in the "True

---

* Malone (p. 384) has erroneously marked these lines as if they did not resemble any portion of the "Contention."

Tragedie" creates a presumption that the writer must, in his turn, have taken them deliberately from the preceding publication; and we think we are even justified in regarding it as probable that both works were made up by one and the same copyist.

There is in these curiously-constructed dramas another repetition to which we have to call the attention of our readers. In the "Second Part of King Henry VI.," Act I., Scene I., York thus expresses his regret at the surrender made by Henry of Anjou and Maine :—

> Cold news for me; for I had hope of France,
> Even as I have of fertile England's soil.

And again, in Act III., Scene I., of the same play, on learning that all France is lost to the English, he exclaims :—

> Cold news for me; for I had hope of France,
> As firmly as I hope for fertile England.

In the "True Tragedie" the same thought is expressed in the same words, and without the change of a single letter, in each of the two corresponding scenes (pp. 8 and 34) :—

> Cold news for me; for I had hope of France,
> Even as I have of fertile England.

All those passages constitute, we believe, one of the strangest instances of imitation in the whole history of letters. There are two things which they must be held to prove directly and beyond the possibility of controversy: first, that the earlier of the two writers, whoever he may have been, must have had a singular habit of self-repetition; and, secondly, that his copyist must have had his memory absolutely saturated with the language of his model, and must afterwards have followed him with the most watchful and patient servility. We do not see how it is possible to doubt which of these characters we are to assign to Shakespeare. This self-imitative temper is a most unusual, and must therefore be regarded as a most distinguishing quality in any original writer. But we know, upon the most direct evidence, that it has been displayed by Shakespeare throughout the composition of his whole drama; while, on the other hand, that drama, with all its power, is written with a negligence which forms another of its extraordinary characteristics, and which seems utterly incompatible with the anxious labour that alone could have enabled him to construct his Second and Third Parts of "King Henry VI." out of the Two Parts of the "Contention." We cannot possibly believe that he was immediately preceded by a writer —and a writer of whose existence we can find no other trace —who most closely resembled him, not only in his genius, but in those minute peculiarities of manner which afford the most decisive indications of any man's special individuality.

The very form of these imitations, even if it stood alone, would justify a strong suspicion that Shakespeare was the original author of the two works. In the passages in which he has repeated himself there is always some variation in the language, which shows that he was expressing, with a certain amount of freedom, the favourite conceptions of his own fancy. In the "Contention" the same words are repeated in two instances, at all events, with a literal accuracy for which we can only account upon the supposition that the writer returned to the passages as they were at first written, and deliberately transferred them to other portions of his copy. These are facts which seem to lead to only one conclusion, and which we feel persuaded will weigh most with those who are most accustomed to trace the characteristics of individual minds through the searching process of minute comparative criticism.

We have no further answer to make to the special arguments which Malone has advanced in support of his theory. But before we finally leave them we have one general observation to offer upon their singular inconclusiveness. The numerous errors into which he has been betrayed, creates, in our opinion, no slight presumption of the falsehood of the cause he has been maintaining. The advocate of truth can seldom or never be so uniformly unlucky and mistaken in his facts and his reasoning.

We shall now proceed to state a number of additional reasons which induce us to adhere to the opinion that Shakespeare was substantially the author of the "First Part of the Contention" and of the "True Tragedie," however imperfectly his work may have been copied in those two publications.

It is evident that the smaller details of the controversy are strangely involved, and some persons may think that they are still inconclusive. We shall, therefore, pass at once to a consideration of those more obvious characteristics of the two works by which this question will perhaps be best decided. We believe that those characteristics distinctly reveal the hand of Shakespeare. On any large review of these two dramas, we are at once struck by the close connection which exists, not only between them and the "First Part of King Henry VI.," but also between them and "King Richard III." The unity of design which seems to connect the four works naturally leads us to think that they must all have proceeded from one and the same mind; and this impression is considerably strengthened by the completeness with which the identity of character is preserved in the dramatic personages, and more especially in Margaret and Richard, the two most striking figures in the whole scene. The very vigour with which these most distinguishing personages are presented, even in single passages, seems decidedly Shakespearian, and we are strongly disposed to believe that no such characterisation was within the reach of any other dramatist of that generation.

But arguments drawn from the general spirit or form of a work are peculiarly open to dispute, and they must necessarily, perhaps, appear to lose in their diffusion something of the force which they intrinsically possess. It is very possible that we may be able, by less general references, to place this question in a clearer light. There are in the "Second Part of King Henry VI." two passages which have frequently been cited as striking manifestations of the dramatic power of Shakespeare. These are Warwick's description of the suspicious appearance presented by the corpse of the murdered Gloster, and the death scene of Beaufort. We shall give each of them from the "First Part of the Contention," as well as from the "Second Part of King Henry VI.;" so that our readers may have an opportunity of at once seeing what is the amount of genius and originality displayed by each author, if more than one author was really engaged in their composition :—

> Oft have I seen a timely-parted ghost,
> Of ashy semblance, pale, and bloodless:
> But lo! the blood is settled in his face,
> More better coloured than when he lived;
> His well-proportioned beard made rough and stern;
> His fingers spread abroad as one that grasp'd for life,
> Yet was by strength surpris'd: the least of these are probable.
> It cannot choose but he was murder'd.
>
> THE FIRST PART OF THE CONTENTION, p. 41.

> *Warwick.* See, how the blood is settled in his face!
> Oft have I seen a timely-parted ghost,
> Of ashy semblance, meagre, pale, and bloodless,
> Being all descended to the labouring heart;
> Who, in the conflict that it holds with death,
> Attracts the same for aidance 'gainst the enemy;
> Which with the heart there cools, and ne'er returneth
> To blush, and beautify the cheek again.
> But see, his face is black, and full of blood;
> His eyeballs farther out than when he liv'd,
> Staring full ghastly, like a strangled man:
> His hair uprear'd, his nostrils stretch'd with struggling,
> His hands abroad display'd, as one that grasp'd
> And tugg'd for life, and was by strength subdu'd.
> Look on the sheets, his hair, you see, is sticking;
> His well-proportioned beard made rough and rugged,
> Like to the summer's corn by tempest lodg'd.
> It cannot be, but he was murder'd here;
> The least of all these signs were probable.
>
> KING HENRY VI., Part II., *Act III., Scene II.*

> *Cardinal.* Oh death! If thou wilt let me live but one whole year, I'll give thee as much gold as will purchase such another island.

King. Oh, see, my lord of Salisbury, how he is troubled.
Lord Cardinal, remember Christ must save thy soul.
  Cardinal. Why, died he not in his bed?
What would you have me to do then?
Can I make men live whether they will or no?
Sirrah, go fetch me the strong poison which the 'pothecary sent me.
Oh, see, where Duke Humphrey's ghost doth stand,
And stares me in the face. Look, look, comb down his hair.
So now, he's gone again; Oh, oh, oh.
  Salisbury. See how the pangs of death doth gripe his heart.
  King. Lord Cardinal, if thou diest assured of heavenly bliss,
Hold up thy hand, and make some sign to us.
                              [*The Cardinal dies.*
Oh, see, he dies, and makes no sign at all.
Oh, God, forgive his soul!
  Salisbury. So bad an end did never none behold:
But as his death, so was his life in all.
  King. Forbear to judge, good Salisbury, forbear!
For God will judge us all.
Go, take him hence, and see his funerals be perform'd.
          THE FIRST PART OF THE CONTENTION, *pp.* 46, 47.

  King Henry. How fares my lord? Speak, Beaufort, to thy
    sovereign.
  Cardinal. If thou be'st death, I'll give thee England's treasure,
Enough to purchase such another island,
So thou wilt let me live, and feel no pain.
  King Henry. Ah, what a sign it is of evil life,
When death's approach is seen so terrible!
  Warwick. Beaufort, it is thy sovereign speaks to thee!
  Cardinal. Bring me unto my trial when you will.
Died he not in his bed? Where should he die?
Can I make men live, whe'r they will or no?—
Oh, torture me no more, I will confess.—
Alive again? Then show me where he is:
I'll give a thousand pound to look upon him.—
He hath no eyes, the dust hath blinded them.—
Comb down his hair: look! look! it stands upright,
Like lime-twigs set to catch my winged soul!—
Give me some drink; and bid the apothecary
Bring the strong poison that I bought of him.
  King Henry. Oh, thou Eternal Mover of the heavens,
Look with a gentle eye upon this wretch!

Oh, beat away the busy meddling fiend,
That lays strong siege unto this wretch's soul,
And from his bosom purge this black despair!
   Warwick. See, how the pangs of death do make him grin.
   Salisbury. Disturb him not, let him pass peaceably.
   King Henry. Peace to his soul, if't God's good pleasure be!
Lord Cardinal, if thou think'st on heaven's bliss,
Hold up thy hand, make signal of thy hope.—
He dies, and makes no sign: O God, forgive him!
   Warwick. So bad a death argues a monstrous life.
   King Henry. Forbear to judge, for we are sinners all.—
Close up his eyes, and draw the curtain close;
And let us all to meditation.
           KING HENRY VI., Part II., *Act III., Scene III.*

All the essential truth and power of the above passages are, we think, to be found in the earlier publication; and the imperfect form in which those qualities are there displayed only goes to show that the writer was producing a mere mutilated copy of some more perfect work. There is, in our opinion, a clipped curtness, or baldness, in his language, and there is certainly an inability to conform to the commonest requirements of versified composition, that seem utterly incompatible with the dramatic vitality which the original conception of such scenes naturally implies.

From the extraordinary celebrity which those two passages have acquired, we have thought it desirable to give them as they are printed, both in the old play and in the "Second Part of King Henry VI." In the other extracts we are about to make from the former work, or from the "True Tragedie," we shall abstain from this double labour, and allow them to stand by themselves. It will be easy for any one that may please to consult the corresponding scenes in Shakespeare; and in any case the lines in the older volumes will of themselves enable our readers to judge how far they are likely to have been inspired by the matchless genius of our great dramatist.

We take, first, the parting of Margaret and Suffolk,

which corresponds with a passage in Act III., Scene II., of the "Second Part of King Henry VI.:—"

> *Suffolk.*. And if I go I cannot live; but here to die,
> What were it else, but like a pleasant slumber
> In thy lap?
> Here could I breathe my soul into the air,
> As mild and gentle as the new-born babe,
> That dies with mother's dug between his lips.
> Where from thy sight I should be raging mad,
> And call for thee to close mine eyes,
> Or with thy lips to stop my dying soul,
> That I might breathe it so into thy body,
> And then it liv'd in sweet Elysium.
> By thee to die, were but to die in jest;
> From thee to die, were torment more than death:
> Oh, let me stay, befal what may befal.
>   *Queen.* Oh, might'st thou stay with safety of thy life,
> Then should'st thou stay; but heavens deny it,
> And therefore go, but hope ere long to be repeal'd.
>   *Suffolk.* I go.
>   *Queen.*. And take my heart with thee.
>   [*She kisses him.*
>   *Suffolk.* A jewel lock'd into the woful'st cask,
> That ever yet contain'd a thing of worth.
> Thus, like a splitted bark, so sunder we;
> This way fall I to death.   [*Exit* SUFFOLK.
>   *Queen.* This way for me.   [*Exit* QUEEN.
>   FIRST PART OF THE CONTENTION, *p.* 46.

We know of no other writer of that age, but Shakespeare himself, that ever rivalled the ease, grace, pathos, and imaginativeness of the above dialogue. We may justly object to the deep charm, unaccompanied by any distinct warning or qualification, which the poet has thrown over this guilty passion. It is, no doubt, untrue to the highest purposes, and even to the strongest effect of creative art. But Shakespeare in his dramas was never a very earnest moralist; and we can easily conceive that, in his earliest works, he was specially unconscious of his own powers, and specially thoughtless of the uses to which they were to be applied.

We now pass to the comedy of Jack Cade and his Followers; and we are much deceived or we shall be able to discover in it the hand of our great dramatist, at least as unmistakably as in any of these more serious scenes. We shall be guilty of no unfairness if we select the most striking passages in the dialogue, premising that we make that selection, and leaving our readers to determine for themselves how far they are thus reminded of the airy humour of Shakespeare. We make our quotations from pp. 50—58 of the "First Part of the Contention." The corresponding scenes in the "Second Part of King Henry VI." will be found in the fourth act of that play:—

Nick. 'Twas never merry world with us since these gentlemen came up.

George. I warrant thee, thou shalt never see a lord wear a leather apron now-a-days.

* * * * *

Cade. Therefore, be brave, for your captain is brave, and vows reformation: you shall have seven half-penny loaves for a penny, and the three-hooped pot shall have ten hoops; and it shall be felony to drink small beer, and if I be king, as king I will be.

All. God save your majesty!

Cade. I thank you, good people; you shall all eat and drink of my score, and go in my livery, and we'll have no writing but the score and the tally, and there shall be no laws but such as comes from my mouth.*

* * * * *

Cade. And what do you use to write your name?
Or do you, as ancient forefathers have done,
Use the score and the tally?

---

* Malone was evidently mistaken when he marked, as he has done in pp. 311 and 312 of his "Second Part of King Henry VI.," the two following passages, as if there was nothing resembling them in the "First Part of the Contention:"—"Only that the laws of England may come out of your mouth."—"My mouth shall be the Parliament of England." The whole of these particular scenes, however, are differently arranged in the two versions of the play; and that was, no doubt, the source of his error.

Clerk. Nay, true, sir, I praise God I have been so well brought up, that I can write mine own name.

Cade. Oh, he has confessed; go hang him with his penny inkhorn about his neck.

* * * * * *

Cade. But dost thou hear, Stafford, tell the king that for his father's sake, in whose time boys played at span-counter with French crowns, I am content that he shall be king as long as he lives. Marry, always provided I'll be protector over him.

Stafford. Oh, monstrous simplicity!

* * * * * *

Cade. Sir Dick Butcher, thou has fought to-day most valiantly, and knocked them down as if thou hadst been in thy slaughter-house. And thus I will reward thee. The Lent shall be as long again as it was: thou shalt have license to kill for four-score and one a week.

* * * * * *

    Cade. Now is Mortimer lord of this city.;
And now, sitting upon London Stone, we command
That the first year of our reign,
The * * * conduit run nothing but red wine.
And now henceforward, it shall be treason
For any that calls me any otherwise than
Lord Mortimer.

* * * * * *

    Cade. So, sirs, now go some and pull down the Savoy,
Others to the Inns of Court: down with them all.

    Dick. I have a suit unto your lordship?

    Cade. Be it a lordship, Dick, and thou shalt have it
For that word.

    Dick. That we may go burn all the records,
And that all writing may be put down,
And nothing used but the score and the tally.

Cade. Dick, it shall be so, and henceforward all things shall be in common, and in Cheapside shall my palfry go to grass.

Why is't not a miserable thing, that of the skin of an innocent lamb should parchment be made, and then with a little blotting over with ink, a man should undo himself?

* * * * * *

Cade. And more than so, thou hast most traitorously erected a grammar-school, to infect the youth of the realm; and against the king's crown and dignity thou hast built up a paper-mill; nay, it will be said to thy face, that thou keep'st men in thy house that daily read of books with red letters, and talk of a noun and a verb, and such abominable words as no Christian ear is able to endure it.

Englishmen have gone on for generations quoting these, or very similar passages, as unquestionable emanations of the comic genius of Shakespeare; and it would be passing strange if they were in reality the production of some other writer who has left behind him no further trace in any way of his original and admirable humour.

We have already stated that many portions of these comic scenes appear to have been imitated from Holinshed's account of the insurrectionary movements of Wat Tyler, Jack Straw, &c., in the reign of Richard II., and the following extracts from his work will leave no room for a doubt upon that point:—

> The number of those unruly people marvellously increased, in such wise as now they feared no resistance, and therefore began to show proof of those things which they had before conceived in their minds, beheading all such men of law, justices, and jurors, as they might catch and lay hands upon, without respect of pity or remorse of conscience, alleging that the land could never enjoy her native and true liberty, till all those sorts of people were dispatched out of the way. This talk liked well the ears of the common uplandish people, and by the less conveying the more, they purposed to burn and destroy all records, evidences, court-rolls, and other monuments, that the remembrance of ancient matters being removed out of mind, their landlords might not have whereby to challenge any right at their hands. . . . In furious wise they ran to the city, and at the first approach, they spoiled the borough of Southwark, broke up the prisons of the Marshalsea, and the King's Bench, set the prisoners at liberty, and admitted them into their company.* . . . . They ran the same day to the said Duke's house of the Savoy, to the which in beauty and stateliness of building, with all manner of princely furniture, there was not any other in the realm comparable, which in despite of the Duke, whom they called traitor, they set on fire, and by all ways and means endeavoured utterly to destroy it. . . . Now after that these wicked people had thus destroyed the Duke of Lancaster's house, and done what they could devise to his reproach, they went to the Temple, and

---

* P. 430.

burnt the men of laws' lodgings, with their books, writings, and all that they might lay hand upon.* ... At length the King sent to him [Wat Tyler] one of his knights, called Sir John Newton, to request him to come to him, that they might talk of the articles which he stood upon to have inserted in the charter; of the which one was to have had a commission to put to death all lawyers, escheaters, and other which by any office had anything to do with the law. ... It was reported, indeed, that he should say with great pride, the day before these things chanced, putting his hands to his lips, that within four days all the laws of England should come forth of his mouth.† ... What wickedness was it, to compel teachers of children in grammar schools to swear never to instruct any in their art. Again, could they have a more mischievous meaning than to burn and destroy all old and ancient monuments, and to murder and dispatch out of the way all such as were able to commit to memory either any new or old records. For it was dangerous among them to be known for one that was learned; and more dangerous if any men were found with a penner and ink-horn at his side; for such seldom or never escaped from them with life.‡

These are, manifestly, the very scenes, and even the very expressions, to which the poet has given the magic illusion of the stage. In the more purely comic portions of his work he does not appear to have made by any means so large a use of either Hall's or Holinshed's account of the proceedings of Cade himself. The following is, we believe, the only striking passage which he has there imitated from either of those historians; we give it from Hall (fol. 159, 160) because he is the older writer; but it is to be found, in almost exactly the same words, in Holinshed:—" The captain being advertised of the King's absence, came first into Southwark," &c. " But after that he entered into London, and cut the ropes of the drawbridge, striking his sword on London Stone, saying, 'Now is Mortimer lord of this city,' and rode in every street like a lordly captain."

We shall now proceed to make two extracts from the "True Tragedie." They are both of special importance in this

---

* P. 431.   † P. 432.   ‡ P. 436.

controversy, inasmuch as they seem clearly to disclose to us the character of Gloster, or Richard, which Shakespeare afterwards only further developed in his " King Richard III." The first of them is a soliloquy of Richard's, corresponding with that which he delivers in the " Third Part of King Henry VI." (Act III., Scene II.) :—

> *Glo.* Ay, Edward will use women honorably.
> Would he were wasted, marrow, bones, and all,
> That from his loins no issue might succeed,
> To hinder me from the golden time I look for:
> For I am not yet look'd on in the world.
> First is there Edward, Clarence, and Henry,
> And his son, and all the look'd-for* issue
> Of their loins, ere I can plant myself:
> A cold premeditation for my purpose!
> What other pleasure is there in the world beside?
> I will go clad my body in gay ornaments,
> And lull myself within a lady's lap,
> And witch sweet ladies with my words and looks.
> Oh, monstrous man, to harbour such a thought!
> Why, love did scorn me in my mother's womb;
> And, for I should not deal in her affairs,
> She did corrupt frail nature in the flesh,
> And plac'd an envious mountain on my back,
> Where sits deformity to mock my body,
> To dry mine arm up like a withered shrimp,
> To make my legs of an unequal size:
> And am I then a man to be belov'd?
> Easier for me to compass twenty crowns.
> Tut, I can smile, and murder when I smile;
> I cry content to that which grieves me most;
> I can add colours to the chameleon,
> And for a need change shapes with Proteus,
> And set the aspiring Cataline to school.
> Can I do this, and cannot get the crown?
> Tush, were it ten times higher, I'll pull it down.
> THE TRUE TRAGEDIE, *pp.* 157-8.

---

* " They lookt for " in the edition of 1595; " they look for " in the editions of 1600 and 1619.

The second great soliloquy of Richard is preceded by his murder of King Henry. The corresponding passage in the "Third Part of King Henry VI." will be found in Act V., Scene VI. :—

> *Glo.* Die, prophet, in thy speech, I'll hear no more ;
> [*Stabs him.*
> For this amongst the rest was I ordain'd.
> *Henry.* Ay, and for much more slaughter after this.
> O God! forgive my sins, and pardon thee !   [*He dies.*
> *Glo.* What! will the aspiring blood of Lancaster
> Sink into the ground? I thought it would have mounted.
> See how my sword weeps for the poor king's death.
> Now may such purple tears be always shed,
> For such as seek the downfal of our house.
> If any spark of life remain in thee,   [*Stabs him again.*
> Down, down to hell, and say I sent thee thither;
> I, that have neither pity, love, nor fear.
> Indeed, 'twas true that Henry told me of,
> For I have often heard my mother say,
> That I came into the world with my legs forward.
> And had I not reason, think you, to make haste,
> And seek their ruins that usurp'd our rights ?
> The women wept, and the midwife cried,
> "O, Jesus bless us, he is born with teeth ! "
> And so I was, indeed, which plainly signified,
> That I should snarl and bite, and play the dog.
> Then, since heaven hath made my body so,
> Let hell make crook'd my mind to answer it.
> I had no father, I am like no father ;
> I have no brothers, I am like no brothers ;
> And this word love, which greybeards term divine,
> Be resident in men like one another,
> And not in me ; I am myself alone.
> Clarence, beware ! thou keep'st me from the light,
> But I will sort a pitchy day for thee :
> For I will buz abroad such prophecies,
> As Edward shall be fearful of his life,
> And then to purge his fear, I'll be thy death.
> Henry and his son are gone ; thou, Clarence, next,
> And one by one I will dispatch the rest,
> Counting myself but bad, till I be best.

> I'll drag thy body in another room,
> And triumph, Henry, in thy day of doom.
>   THE TRUE TRAGEDIE, *pp.* 185—6.

The large and negligent energy of this passage at once reminds us of the hand of Shakespeare; and if we had to believe that it was the work of any other writer, we should feel utterly perplexed by the presence of so wholly unappreciated and unknown a portent in the world of letters. There are three lines in the above address which, in their splendid audacity, might almost of themselves be sufficient to decide this controversy :—

> And this word love, which greybeards term divine,
> Be resident in men like one another,
> And not in me; I am myself alone.

We find other brief passages in these dramas which seem distinctly to reveal the same origin. The agony of Margaret on witnessing the murder of her son, Prince Edward (Act V., Scene V.), is rendered with striking power. We have already quoted the piercing exclamation of the bereaved mother—"You have no children, devils." Towards the close of the scene she gives us another of those flashes of character and passion which, in the electric shock of nature and imagination, so often light up the pages of Shakespeare. After having in vain implored of Clarence to kill her, too, she turns and asks :—

> Where's the devil's butcher, hard-favour'd Richard?
> Richard, where art thou? He is not here:
> Murder is his alms-deed; petitioners
> For blood he ne'er put back.
>   THE TRUE TRAGEDIE, *p.* 183.

"Murder is his alms-deed; petitioners for blood he ne'er put back." It is only in the drama of Shakespeare that the world has as yet found these vivid and pregnant images.

Malone admits, in the very first sentence of his essay,

that "several passages in the Second and Third Parts of 'King Henry VI.' appear evidently to be of the hand of Shakespeare." But he is compelled, by the whole tenour of his argument, to suppose that those passages are only to be found in the folio edition of the two works; and in his "preliminary remarks" (p. 164), he speaks of "the embroidery with which Shakespeare ornamented the coarse stuff that had been awkwardly made up for the stage by some of his contemporaries." Such language does not call for any serious discussion. Its extravagance will at once be obvious to every reader of the few extracts we have made from the older volumes. If Shakespeare's hand is not apparent in them, we shall look in vain for any trace of it in the later versions of these dramas.

We not only do not coincide in the opinion that Shakespeare's peculiar dramatic power is only distinguishable in the later editions of those plays, but we believe that the passages which we find there for the first time are, for the most part, specially uninformed with the finer qualities of his genius; and that, if the older copies were the work of a mere compiler writing from more or less incomplete and hurried notes, he made his selections with considerable skill, however imperfectly his hand may afterwards have seconded his judgment. We have already inserted in our notice of the "First Part of King Henry VI." (pp. 253, 254), two passages from Shakespeare's undisputed contributions to the Third Part, which seem to us to be written after the heavy and pedantic manner of his immediate dramatic predecessors; and we shall now proceed to make two quotations from the Second Part, which will show that the additions which it contains to his supposed original are very far from being uniformly unquestionable improvements.

In the "First Part of the Contention" (p. 49), the sea-captain, who has made Suffolk prisoner, and who is about to order his immediate execution, concludes an address to him as follows:—

> And thou, that
> Smil'dst at good Duke Humphrey's death,
> Shalt live no longer to infect the earth.

Instead of these lines we have the following passage in the "Second Part of King Henry VI." (Act IV., Scene I.):—

> And thou, that smil'dst at good Duke Humphrey's death,
> Against the senseless winds shall grin in vain,
> Who, in contempt, shall hiss at thee again:
> And wedded be thou to the hags of hell,
> For daring to affy a mighty lord
> Unto the daughter of a worthless king,
> Having neither subject, wealth, nor diadem.
> By devilish policy art thou grown great,
> And, like ambitious Sylla, overgorg'd
> With gobbets of thy mother's bleeding heart.
> By thee, Anjou and Maine were sold to France;
> The false revolting Normans, thorough thee,
> Disdain to call us lord; and Picardy
> Hath slain their governors, surpris'd our forts,
> And sent the ragged soldiers wounded home.
> The princely Warwick, and the Nevils all,—
> Whose dreadful swords were never drawn in vain,—
> As hating thee, are rising up in arms:
> And now the house of York,—thrust from the crown
> By shameful murder of a guiltless king,
> And lofty, proud encroaching tyranny,—
> Burns with revenging fire; whose hopeful colours
> Advance our half-fac'd sun, striving to shine,
> Under the which is writ—*Invitis nubibus.*
> The commons here in Kent are up in arms;
> And, to conclude, reproach and beggary
> Is crept into the palace of our king,
> And all by thee.—Away! convey him hence.

In Act V., Scene I. of the same play, the King addresses Warwick and Salisbury in a passage of which there is no trace in the older volume:—

> Why, Warwick, hath thy knee forgot to bow?—
> Old Salisbury,—shame to thy silver hair,
> Thou mad misleader of thy brain-sick son!—
> What, wilt thou on thy death-bed play the ruffian,

> And seek for sorrow with thy spectacles?—
> O, where is faith? O, where is loyalty?
> If it be banish'd from the frosty head,
> Where shall it find a harbour in the earth?—
> Wilt thou go dig a grave to find out war,
> And shame thine honourable age with blood?
> Why art thou old, and want'st experience?'
> Or wherefore dost abuse it, if thou hast it?
> For shame! in duty bend thy knee to me,
> That bows unto the grave with mickle age.

There is nothing specially Shakespearian in those lines, and we believe we could quote from the editions in the Folio many others written in a tone of much the same crude or languid extravagance. The only addition of any considerable length in either of the two last parts of "King Henry VI." in which we can at all clearly recognise the hand of our great poet is the conclusion of Henry's soliloquy (Act II., Scene V., of the Third Part) during the progress of the tremendous battle, on the issue of which his crown was at stake. The thirty-four last lines, beginning, "O God! methinks it were a happy life," appear for the first time in the Folio. We are aware that they have received the marked commendation of some of the poet's critics; but we must confess that, although we think we can at once trace them to Shakespeare, we only find his genius displayed in them in its tamer and more prolix mood. There is a shorter passage, introduced for the first time in the Second Part, in which, as it seems to us, his special imaginative vitality is much more distinctly visible. In Act III., Scene II., King Henry exclaims:—

> What stronger breast-plate than a heart untainted?
> Thrice is he arm'd, that hath his quarrel just;
> And he but naked, though lock'd up in steel,
> Whose conscience with injustice is corrupted.*

---

* Malone thought this passage was imitated from the following lines in a play entitled "Lust's Dominion," which was published in 1657, as one of the works of Marlowe:—

We should have felt the strongest confidence, upon the internal evidence alone, that those lines must have been written by Shakespeare; but there are detached passages in the older editions which seem to bear not less unmistakably the impress of his genius; and those passages are so numerous that they at once create a suspicion with respect to the true authorship of those works which we feel to be wholly irresistible.

There are other additions in the folio which seem to us to deserve a detailed notice. We allude to the Latin and French quotations, which form a very remarkable characteristic of the two dramas. In the Second Part we find:—*Aio te, Æacida, Romanos vincere posse*, Act I., Scene IV.; *Tantæne animis cœlestibus iræ*, Act II., Scene I.; *Medice teipsum*, Act II., Scene I.; *invitis nubibus*, Act IV. Scene I.; *gelidus timor occupat artus*, Act IV., Scene I.; *bona terra, mala gens*, Act IV., Scene VII.; *sancta majestas*, Act V., Scene I.; *La fin couronne les œuvres*,* Act V. Scene II.; and in the Third Part we have, *Dii faciant, laudis summa sit ista tuœ,*† Act I. Scene III.

Of all these, for the most part, unnecessary, and sometimes very incorrect or inappropriate, quotations, there is not a trace in the early plays, with the exception of the words *bona, terra*, and *sancta majesta*, and those publications contain no other Latin words, except the very familiar exclamation—" *Et tu, Brute* (p. 176); and at this we can feel no surprise, for it is pretty clear that to the writer or compiler Latin was

---

"Come, Moor; I'm arm'd with more than complete steel,
    The justice of my quarrel."

But Mr. Collier has shown (in a note in "Dodsley's Old Plays," vol. ii., p. 311, ed. 1825) that, as "Lust's Dominion" contains unmistakable references to the death of Philip II. of Spain, which occurred in 1598, it could not have been written by Marlowe, who died in 1593.

* Malone (p. 350) gives this French phrase as an imitation, but there is nothing in any way like it in the "First Part of the Contention."

† Malone (p. 390) marks this line as if it was taken literally from the "True Tragedie," but not a word of it is to be found there.

an unknown tongue.* There are several classical allusions scattered over what Malone supposes to be Shakespeare's additions to these dramas; but we shall quote only three out of the number. In Act. I., Scene I., of the Second Part, York thus compares his own fate to that of Meleager :—

> Methinks, the realms of England, France, and Ireland,
> Bear that proportion to my flesh and blood,
> As did the fatal brand Althea burn'd
> Unto the prince's heart of Calydon."

In Act V., Scene II., of the same play, the younger Clifford, who has just discovered the dead body of his father, says :—

> Henceforth, I will not have to do with pity;
> Meet I an infant of the house of York,
> Into as many gobbets will I cut it,
> As wild Medea young Absyrtus did.

In Act III., Scene II., of the Third Part the following lines are introduced into Richard's first soliloquy, and do not certainly appear to add in any way to its originality and vigour :—

> I'll drown more sailors than the mermaid shall;
> I'll slay more gazers than the basilisk;
> I'll play the orator as well as Nestor;
> Deceive more slily than Ulysses could;
> And, like a Sinon, take another Troy.

---

* The usual announcement at the close of the scenes in the "First Part of the Contention" is—"*Exet omnes.*" In the last interview between Margaret and Suffolk, she states ("Second Part of King Henry VI.," Act III., Scene II.,) that wherever he goes she will have an "Iris," that shall find him out. The name of this celestial messenger is given in the "First Part of the Contention" (p. 45) as an "Irish." The "tigers of Hyrcania" in Act I., Scene IV., of the "Third Part of King Henry VI." are mentioned as "the tigers of Arcadia" in the "True Tragedie" (p. 133). It is just possible that these may all be errors of the press; but the almost total absence of any classical allusion or quotation from these dramas, when we remember the period at which they were written, seems to afford a sufficient proof that the author was no Latin scholar.

This parade of classical illustrations was, no doubt, made in conformity with the fashion of Shakespeare's age, and, to some extent, in the indulgence of his own immature taste; but we should find it very difficult to believe that he would, at any period of his career, have been prepared to overlay with these idle embellishments the works of Marlowe, or of any other of his more distinguished dramatic contemporaries. Indeed, the attempt, under almost any circumstances, to amend the productions of living writers would seem to be necessarily invidious and presumptuous, and would in no way harmonise with our notions of the inoffensive temper of Shakespeare.

We may go further, and state that Malone's theory is directly at variance with all that we know of the whole form of our great poet's workmanship. It is true that he constructed a large portion of his dramas on plays, tales, and histories, which are still extant; but we find that he very rarely, in any one of them, copies, in a single line, the language of his originals. The popular notion—a notion which seems to have had its origin mainly, if not exclusively, in the supposed history of these two last parts of "King Henry VI."—that he began his connection with the stage as an amender of the writings of more inventive or more ambitious minds, is opposed to all the direct and unquestionable evidence by which its truth or its falsehood can now be determined. It is a notion, too, which is almost wholly incompatible with all our conceptions of the characteristics of his genius. We can hardly imagine this large, negligent workman engaged in the literary drudgery of omitting, enlarging, transposing, and amending the thoughts of another writer, and proceeding, at each step of his progress, with a constant and minute reference to his model. We believe that his rapid and airy fancy would have wholly failed him in such a task; and this, surely, was not the kind of work by which he was to astonish and to overshadow all the dramatists of his age.

There is another and a very remarkable question which we must try to answer, before we are to come to the conclusion that this was the labour in which he was here engaged. It is clear enough that the publisher must have experienced some difficulty in procuring what every one will admit to be his more or less imperfect versions of the two old plays. But where did Shakespeare himself get the copies on which his works were founded? He could not have had recourse to Millington's editions of 1594 and 1595, unless Greene's allusion to him in 1592—the source of so many elaborate conjectures—had no connection whatever with the authorship of those dramas. On the other hand, we cannot possibly suspect him of having obtained them surreptitiously; and neither can we suppose that he trusted to memory, or to imperfect notes; for the closeness of the imitation, independently of any other consideration, must have been beyond the reach of any one but a most laborious and practised copyist. It seems as if he could have had but one other available resource, and that was, that he should have got the manuscripts from the theatrical company into whose possession they had passed. But that was, upon the theory we are now considering, a rival company; and it is very unlikely that he would have asked, or that they would have granted, such a favour. We are aware that there can never be anything absolutely conclusive in conjectures of this description, dealing with merely possible contingencies, which we can never feel sure that we have wholly exhausted. But this is essentially a question of probabilities; and, in endeavouring to find for it the most reasonable solution, the difficulty of Shakespeare's having got possession of the materials which he is supposed to have employed cannot in fairness be altogether overlooked.

We do not wonder that Malone displayed some inconsistency in the difficult attempt to fix on the probable author of the two old plays. But we cannot help thinking that the successive judgments at which he arrived upon this point were founded upon very insufficient evidence, and were much too confidently maintained. At first, he thought that the principal writer of the two pieces was Robert Greene. He drew this conclusion from the passage in the "Groat's Worth of Wit," in which Greene seemed to him to put forward a claim to that distinction. There are a few other circumstances which may be supposed to afford some ground for the conjecture. In Act IV., Scene I., of the "Second Part of King Henry VI.," Suffolk says that the captain by whom he has been arrested—

> Threatens more
> Than Bargulus the strong Illyrian pirate.

In the corresponding address in the "First Part of the Contention" (p. 49), instead of Bargulus, we have—"Abradas, the great Macedonian pirate;" and it is a somewhat curious fact that the only other mention of this strange personage which the research of the commentators has been able to discover consists of the following passage in a work by Greene entitled "Penelope's Web," which was published in 1588:—"Abradas, the great Macedonian pirate, thought every one had a letter of mart that bare sails in the ocean." Again, in the "True Tragedie," Richard, as he stabs the dead King Henry, exclaims:—

> If any spark of life remain in thee,
> Down, down to hell, and say I sent thee thither.

In the opening address of the Second Act of Greene's "Alphonsus" a similar thought is expressed:—

> Go pack thou hence unto the Stygian lake,
> And make report unto thy traitorous sire
> How well thou hast enjoy'd the diadem
> Which he by treason set upon thy head;
> And if he ask thee who did send thee down,
> Alphonsus say, who now must wear thy crown.*

---

* In the "Third Part of King Henry VI." (Act V., Scene VI.) the lines are thus given:—

> "If any spark of life be yet remaining,
> Down, down to hell; and say I sent thee thither."

In the "Hystorie of Hamblet," on which the play of "Hamlet"

We fear we should never know where to stop in our attempts to trace the authorship of our old and disputed dramas if resemblances of this description were to be held to constitute a title on behalf of any particular writer. We take it for granted that Greene was not the author either of the "First Part of the Contention" or of the "True Tragedie," on the plain ground that any such work was wholly placed beyond the reach of his capacity.

Malone also believed that there were good reasons for supposing that these two plays were written by the author of the old "King John," which was printed in 1591. In the "First Part of the Contention" (p. 47) King Henry asks the dying Cardinal Beaufort to hold up his hand in proof of his trust in the Divine mercy; and a similar entreaty is addressed to King John towards the close of the old play which bears his name. Again, in the "True Tragedie" (p. 164), we have the following line:—

Let England be true within itself; *

---

was either directly or indirectly founded, Hamlet, immediately after murdering his uncle, exclaims:—

"Now go thy ways, and when thou comest in hell, see thou forget not to tell thy brother (whom thou traitorously slewest) that it was his son that sent thee thither."—*Collier's Shakespeare Library*, vol. i., p. 161.

These words recall, even more distinctly than the lines in Greene, the passage in the "Third Part of King Henry VI.," and we have already seen (p. 313) that this is not the only resemblance between the drama and the story. These coincidences naturally give rise to an impression, which other evidence strongly confirms, that some of the smaller elements of the great Shakespearian drama were drawn from a strange variety of sources; and they ought, at the same time, to teach us how uncertain would be the result of any attempt to decide on the authorship of the poet's supposed works from any such real or apparent imitations.

* The corresponding passage in the "Third Part of King Henry VI." (Act IV., Scene I.) runs as follows:—

"Why, knows not Montague, that of itself
England is safe, if true within itself?"

and at the end of the old "King John" we find the same thought expressed in very nearly the same words :—

> Let England live but true within itself.

With respect to the first of these parallel passages, we cannot help remembering that it refers to a not uncommon practice in the Roman Catholic Church; and even if the idea were one of the most striking originality, we should not therefore be justified in concluding that it might not have been imitated by one writer from another. A still more decisive answer may be given to the argument founded on the second of these coincidences. The expression appears to have become a proverbial one at the time when it was used in the two dramas; and it has been traced back as far as Dr. Andrew Borde's "Fyrst Boke of the Introduction of Knowledge," published in 1542, where it is said of the English that "yf they were true within themselfes, thei nede not to feare, although al nacions wer set against them."

We must further observe that Malone's conjecture only affords us a specimen of that worst of all illustrations—*ignotum per ignotius*. We have not the smallest trace of any independent information to enable us to ascertain who was the author of the old "King John;" while, on the other hand, we find some means of guessing—even if we cannot do more than guess—who was the writer of the "Whole Contention;" and we should therefore, in any case, have to reverse the order of Malone's inquiries, and then to infer from his quotations that that writer, whoever he may have been, whether Shakespeare, or Greene, or Marlowe, also produced, very probably, another drama, whose origin had for a time been involved in much more complete obscurity.

But the opinion to which Malone finally adhered upon this question, and the one which is also adopted by the great majority of the more recent commentators, is, that Marlowe was the principal, if not the sole writer of the "True Tragedie," and that he had also, perhaps, a large share in the composition of the "First Part of the Contention." In coming to this conclusion, this honest and laborious, but hasty critic seems to have again displayed some rashness of judgment, and a want of a perfect knowledge of his subject. He found that one of the most striking passages in the "True Tragedie" closely resembles certain lines in Marlowe's "Edward the Second;" and he therefore thought it probable that both works proceeded from the same author:—

> What! will the aspiring blood of Lancaster
> Sink into the ground? I had thought it would have mounted!
> THE TRUE TRAGEDIE, *p.* 185.

> Frown'st thou thereat, aspiring Lancaster?
> EDWARD THE SECOND, *p.* 184, *Dyce's ed.*, 1859.

> And, highly scorning that the lowly earth
> Should drink his blood, mounts up to the air.
> *Ibidem, p.* 212.

These were the only parallelisms which Malone, aided by his friend Dr. Farmer, discovered between the Two Parts of the "Contention" and Marlowe's "Edward the Second." But more attentive eyes have since been fixed upon those works, and the number of those resemblances that are now known to us form one of the many curious incidents in the history of Shakespeare's dramas. In Mr. Dyce's "Some Account of Marlowe and his Writings," prefixed to his edition of Marlowe's works, we find the following quotations (pp. 49, 50, ed. 1859):—

> I tell thee, Poole, when thou didst run at tilt,
> And stol'st away our ladies' hearts in France.
> FIRST PART OF THE CONTENTION, *p.* 13.

> Tell Isabel, the Queen, I look'd not thus,
> When for her sake I ran at tilt in France.
> EDWARD THE SECOND, *p.* 220.

> Madam, I bring you news from Ireland;
> The wild O'Neil, my lords, is up in arms,
> With troops of Irish Kerns, that, uncontroll'd,
> Doth plant themselves within the English pale.
> FIRST PART OF THE CONTENTION, p. 37.

> The wild O'Neil, with swarms of Irish Kerns,
> Lives uncontroll'd within the English pale.
> EDWARD THE SECOND, p. 197.

> Stern Faulconbridge
> Commands the narrow seas.
> THE TRUE TRAGEDIE, p. 124.

> The haughty Dane commands the narrow seas.
> EDWARD THE SECOND, p. 197.

> Thus yields the cedar to the axe's edge,
> Whose arms gave shelter to the princely eagle.
> THE TRUE TRAGEDIE, p. 177.

> A lofty cedar tree, fair flourishing,
> On whose top branches kingly eagles perch.
> EDWARD THE SECOND, p. 195.

Of the above four passages from the "First Part of the Contention" and the "True Tragedie," the first very closely resembles one in the "Second Part of King Henry VI.," Act I., Scene III.;[*] the third and fourth are reproduced in exactly the same words in the "Third Part of King Henry VI.," Act I., Scene I., and Act V., Scene II.; but the announcement in the second is given in Act III., Scene I., of the Second Part in an entirely different form, and one which cannot be supposed to bear any immediate relation to the lines in Marlowe—

> Great lords, from Ireland am I come amain,
> To signify that rebels there are up,
> And put the Englishmen unto the sword.

Marlowe died in the month of May, 1593. We can ad-

---

[*] It is there given as follows:—
> "I tell thee, Poole, when in the city Tours
> Thou ran'st a tilt in honour of my love,
> And stol'st away the ladies' hearts of France."

vance no decisive proof that his "Edward the Second" was produced before either part of the "Contention." But we have fair presumptive evidence in support of that conclusion.* And besides, the whole character of Marlowe's writings leads us to believe that his genius was essentially self-reliant, and that most probably it was his work that suggested the above passages to the author or authors of the two dramas with which Shakespeare's name is so singularly connected. If we are not mistaken in that supposition, the writer of the "First Part of the Contention" must have directly copied "Edward the Second" in one passage in which his example was not followed by Shakespeare. But, on the other hand, Shakespeare, too, must, upon that hypothesis, have derived from the same source one of his images. In "Edward the Second" (p. 193) we find the following line:—

> He wears a lord's revenue on his back.

---

* Warton, in his "History of English Poetry" (vol. iii., p. 438, ed. 4to), mentions incidentally that "Edward the Second" was "written in the year 1590;" but he has given no authority for the statement. The earliest date we now find affixed to any edition of this drama is 1598. It was entered, however, at Stationers' Hall on the 6th of July, 1593; and Mr. Dyce, in his Addenda to his "Some Account of Marlowe," &c., states that he has an imperfect copy of the work, in which the title-page, which is supplied in very old hand-writing, ends with the date "1593." We have reason to believe, too, from an entry in Henslowe's Diary (p. 30, ed. Shak. Soc.), that Marlowe's "Massacre of Paris" was brought out as a new play on the 30th of January, 1593; while there is a still further probability that from that period until his death he was engaged in the composition of his "Tragedy of Dido, Queen of Carthage" (see Dyce's "Some Account," &c., p. 35), and of his poem of "Hero and Leander," both of which he left unfinished. From all these circumstances we naturally conclude that his "Edward the Second" must have been written before the summer of 1592, which, from Greene's allusion to Shakespeare, is the date we can most reasonably assign to the production of the "True Tragedie." It may be worth while further to observe that the writer of this latter play could very probably have imitated "Edward the Second" from a printed copy.

This is clearly another version of a line in the "Second Part of King Henry VI.," Act I., Scene III.:—

> She bears a duke's revenues on her back.

There is nothing in any way analogous to this latter picture of ostentatious extravagance in the editions of the "First Part of the Contention" published in 1594 and 1600; but in the edition of 1619 we find the following words introduced for the first time:—

> She bears a duke's whole revenues on her back.

Shakespeare, in one of these plays, has also, perhaps, copied a passage in another work of Marlowe's:—

> What sight is this! my Lodovico slain!
> These arms of mine shall be thy sepulchre.
> THE JEW OF MALTA, p. 161.

> These arms of mine shall be thy winding-sheet:
> My heart, sweet boy, shall be thy sepulchre.
> KING HENRY VI., Part III., *Act II., Scene V.*

These two last lines must have been written by Shakespeare, for they do not appear in any way in the "True Tragedie;" but as they express what may be regarded as one of the familiar images of poetry, we can entertain no very decided conviction that he borrowed them directly from another writer.

The principal point, however, which we have here to examine is whether the many resemblances which exist between passages in the Two Parts of the "Contention" and Marlowe's "Edward the Second" would justify us in believing that those dramas are the productions of one and the same author. We most certainly think that they do not fairly lead to such a conclusion, and that Malone must have been labouring under a very strange delusion when he relied upon such an argument. It may be that the repetition of certain thoughts and expressions forms a characteristic of a particular writer; and we believe that an examination of the dramas of

Shakespeare will show that he was habitually led to the adoption of this free or negligent species of workmanship. But whenever we are left without any proof of the existence of such a special habit—and there is not a trace of it in the writings of Marlowe—we naturally conclude that we can discover in an imitative work the hand of a new author. We have, at the same time, much stronger reasons than this presumption for believing that Marlowe was not the writer either of the "First Part of the Contention" or of the "True Tragedie." We believe that every one who has read his works must feel convinced that Nature had wholly denied him the gift of dramatic humour, and that it is impossible he could have written the scenes in which the follies of Jack Cade and his "rabblement" are so vividly delineated. The very negligences which distinguish these old dramas—their frequent disregard of consistency in the details, and the irregular form of their versification—seem alien to the whole character of his undoubted compositions; for he is, within his own limits, a remarkably careful and finished writer. In the higher and finer qualities which they often display amidst all their imperfections, and more especially in their flexibility and variety, they seem to be at least as distinctly removed beyond the sphere of his powers. His acknowledged dramas are uniformly and even singularly monotonous; and this circumstance alone ought, in any intelligent and impartial criticism, to have excluded him from all claim to be regarded as the author of the whole, or of any considerable portion, of the two divisions of the "Contention." We can find in all his writings no such largely and vigorously drawn characters as Clifford, and Warwick, and Margaret, and Richard: we can find nothing even in any way resembling them. We may further observe that he never, like the author of these two disputed plays, carries the ease and the truth of Nature into the more ambitious efforts of his fancy. In those supposed "raptures" which won for him the special admiration of his contemporaries, he is strangely tumid and extravagant, and he only approaches to any real imitation of life in that lower and more subdued mood in which his "Edward the Second"—his most readable drama—is throughout conceived and executed. It is hardly too much to say, on the other hand, of his great contemporary, that it is in his very highest creations he is most observant of the conditions of the world of truth and reality. Shakespeare alone is at once supremely imaginative and supremely natural; and this combination seems clearly to distinguish his works from those of all the other dramatic poets of the world.

The whole tenour of Malone's argument would lead us to the conclusion that there was substantially a distinct author for each of the Three Parts of "King Henry VI.," and, of course, for "King Richard III." But we cannot believe in the existence of four such dramatists. We find, in all the literature of the age in which they are supposed to have laboured, no trace of such a prodigality of original genius, dealing, too, with the same incidents and characters in essentially the same spirit; and upon this ground alone Malone's theory seems wholly inadmissible.

We now come to what is, in our opinion, one of the most decisive questions in this controversy. Are the "First Part of the Contention" and the "True Tragedie" printed as they were originally written, or are they mere mutilated copies of more complete works? If it can be shown that they are more or less imperfect, and that it is impossible they should contain the dramas as they were at first written, no one, we are persuaded, will be prepared to dispute that we must look to Shakespeare's Second and Third Parts of "King Henry VI." for their originals; and unless we are much mistaken, we can establish the hypothesis from which that conclusion would naturally follow.

In reading over those early volumes, and more especially the "First Part of the Contention," we are perpetually struck by the baldness and the crudeness of form which they exhibit, amidst frequent manifestations of a power of expression, as well as of conception, which, considering the age in which they were written, may be pronounced wholly unparalleled. Many portions of the dialogue seem to have been left unfinished; the versification is sometimes strangely irregular and defective; and passages are introduced as prose which must, we feel assured, have found a musical utterance in the mind of the original writer. We are not aware that there is any example in literature of so strange a contrast as that which they afford of rapid intellectual energy and helpless intellectual feebleness, if we are to accept them as a complete and final creation. But we need not trust to mere general impressions upon this subject. We believe that we can select from these works a single passage which is sufficiently long, and sufficiently characteristic, to enable us clearly to distinguish in it the hand of an ignorant and an impotent copyist. In Act II., Scene II., of the "Second Part of King Henry VI.," the Duke of York thus explains to Salisbury and to Warwick the pedigree of his house and his own title to the crown :—

> Then thus :—
> Edward the Third, my lords, had seven sons:
> The first, Edward the Black Prince, Prince of Wales;
> The second, William of Hatfield; and the third,
> Lionel, Duke of Clarence; next to whom
> Was John of Gaunt, the Duke of Lancaster;
> The fifth was Edmund Langley, Duke of York;
> The sixth was Thomas of Woodstock, Duke of Gloster;
> William of Windsor was the seventh, and last.
> Edward, the Black Prince, died before his father;
> And left behind him Richard, his only son,
> Who, after Edward the Third's death, reigned as king,
> Till Henry Bolingbroke, Duke of Lancaster,
> The eldest son and heir of John of Gaunt,
> Crown'd by the name of Henry the Fourth,
> Seized on the realm; depos'd the rightful king;
> Sent his poor queen to France, from whence she came,
> And him to Pomfret; where, as all you know,
> Harmless Richard was murder'd traitorously.
> * * * * * *
> *Salisbury.* But William of Hatfield died without an heir.
> *York.* The third son, Duke of Clarence (from whose line

I claim the crown), had issue—Philippe, a daughter,
Who married Edmund Mortimer, Earl of March :
Edmund had issue—Roger, Earl of March ;
Roger had issue—Edmund, Anne, and Eleanor.
  Salisbury. This Edmund, in the reign of Bolingbroke,
As I have read, laid claim unto the crown ;
And, but for Owen Glendower, had been king,
Who kept him in captivity till he died.
But, to the rest.
  York. His eldest sister, Anne,
My mother, being heir unto the crown,
Married Richard, Earl of Cambridge, who was son
To Edmund Langley, Edward the Third's fifth son.
By her I claim the kingdom : she was heir
To Roger, Earl of March ; who was the son
Of Edmund Mortimer ; who married Philippe,
Sole daughter unto Lionel, Duke of Clarence :
So, if the issue of the elder son
Succeed before the younger, I am king.

Instead of this passage, we have, in the " First Part of the Contention " (pp. 25, 26), the following one, which we print exactly as it stands in the original, with the single exception that we adopt the modern spelling and punctuation, as we do for all the works of Shakespeare :—

York. Then thus, my lords—
Edward the Third had seven sons:
The first was Edward, the Black Prince,
Prince of Wales ;
The second was Edmund of Langley,
Duke of York ;
The third was Lionel, Duke of Clarence ;
The fourth was John of Gaunt,
The Duke of Lancaster ;
The fifth was Roger Mortimer, Earl of March ;
The sixth was Sir Thomas of Woodstock ;
William of Windsor was the seventh and last.

Now, Edward, the Black Prince, he died before his father, and left behind him Richard, that afterwards was king ; crown'd by the name of Richard the Second, and he died without an heir. Edmund of Langley, Duke of York, died and left behind him two daughters, Anne and Eleanor. Lionel, Duke of Clarence, died and left behind

Alice, Anne, and Eleanor, that was after married to my father, and by her I claim the crown as the true heir to Lionel, Duke of Clarence, the third son to Edward the Third. Now, sir, in the time of Richard's reign, Henry of Bolingbroke, son and heir to John of Gaunt, the Duke of Lancaster, fourth son to Edward the Third, he claimed the crown, deposed the mirthful king, and, as both you know, in Pomfret Castle harmless Richard was shamefully murdered; and so, by Richard's death, came the house of Lancaster unto the crown.

Salisbury. Saving your tale, my lord, as I have heard, in the reign of Bolingbroke, the Duke of York did claim the crown, and, but for Owen Glendower, had been king.

York. True; but so it fortuned then, by means of the monstrous rebel Glendower, the noble Duke of York was done to death; and so, ever since the heirs of John of Gaunt have possessed the crown. But, if the issue of the older should succeed before the issue of the younger, then am I lawful heir unto the kingdom.

Before we attempt to offer any comment on the above extracts, we will endeavour to point out the source to which Shakespeare was in this case indebted for his information. We believe there can be no doubt that he was copying either a passage in Hall's " Introduction into the History of King Henry IV." (fols. 1, 2), or a portion of Holinshed's recital of the articles of agreement between King Henry VI. and the Duke of York (pp. 657, 658). The two passages contain precisely the same statement, and in very nearly the same words, with this exception, that there are in Holinshed's copy of the names a few manifest errors of transcription. We quote the more correct account of the pedigree from Hall:—

King Edward [the Third] had issue—Edward, his first-begotten son, Prince of Wales; William of Hatfield, the second-begotten son; Lionel, Duke of Clarence, the third-begotten son; John of Gaunt, Duke of Lancaster, the fourth-begotten son; Edmond of Langley, Duke of York, the fifth-begotten son; Thomas of Woodstock, Duke of Gloucester, the sixth-begotten son; and William of Windsor, the seventh-begotten son. The said Prince Edward died in the life of his father, King Edward the Third, and had issue—Richard, born at Bordeaux, which, after the death of King Edward the Third, as cousin and heir to him, that is to say, son to the said Edward, Prince of Wales, son to the said King Edward the Third, succeeded him in royal estate and dignity, lawfully entitled and called King Richard the Second, and died without issue. Lionel, Duke of Clarence, the third-begotten son of the said King Edward the Third, had issue—Philippe, his only daughter, which was married to Edmond Mortimer, Earl of March, and had issue—Roger Mortimer, Earl of March: which Roger had issue—Edmond Mortimer, Earl of March, Anne and Eleanor, which Edmond and Eleanor died without issue. And the said Anne was married to Richard, Earl of Cambridge, son to Edmond of Langley, Duke of York, the fifth-begotten son of the said King Edward the Third, which Richard had issue the famous prince, Richard Plantagenet, Duke of York, &c.

We find, moreover, in the "Duke of York's Oration made to all the Lords of the Parliament" (Hall, fols. 177, 178, and Holinshed, pp. 655—7), besides a less detailed allusion to York's descent from Edward III., special mention of the deposition and murder of Richard II., and of a claim made to the crown during the reign of Henry IV., by the Earl of Northumberland and the Lord Percy, on behalf of Edmund Mortimer, Earl of March, who was himself at the time "in captivity with Owen Glendower, the rebel, in Wales;" * and we have thus

---

* We may, we think, take it for granted that it was this passage in the chroniclers that suggested to Shakespeare the statement that Mortimer would have become king but for Owen Glendower.

"Who kept him in captivity till he died."

Malone, in his text (p. 217), marks this last line as an imitation of some portion of the "First Part of the Contention." But there is in the latter work no allusion whatever to the "captivity" of Mortimer, or of the Duke of York, as he is there erroneously called, although it is no doubt stated that by means of Glendower he was "done to death." Under these circumstances Malone's annotation can hardly be considered perfectly correct, and it would certainly be apt to mislead a reader who had no opportunity of comparing the two copies of the drama. The misapprehension, too, which might thus be created, would be one of some importance. Shakespeare, upon this, as upon every other occasion in which he differs from the author of "The Contention" in his mode of treating any historical incident, shows that he

no difficulty in ascertaining the sources from which all the principal portions of the statement in Shakespeare were derived.

But we have not yet completed our quotations. The passage we have given from the edition of the "First Part of the Contention," published in 1594, remained unaltered in the two editions of 1600. But Pavier, or his copyist, endeavoured to amend it in the quarto containing the "Whole Contention," issued in 1619; and there it stands as follows:—

Edward the Third had seven sons:
The first was Edward, the Black Prince,
Prince of Wales;
The second was William of Hatfield,
Who died young;
The third was Lionel, Duke of Clarence;
The fourth was John of Gaunt,
The Duke of Lancaster;
The fifth was Edmund of Langley,
Duke of York;
The sixth was William of Windsor,
Who died young;
The seventh and last was Sir Thomas of Woodstock, Duke of York.

Now, Edward, the Black Prince, died before his father, leaving behind him two sons—Edward, born at Angouleme, who died young, and Richard, that was after crowned king by the name of Richard the Second, who died without an heir.

---

had consulted the chronicles; while the writer whom he is supposed to be imitating does not, as far as we are aware, in any single instance, seem to have had any such authority to follow. This circumstance would of itself be sufficient to outweigh all the reasoning in Malone's "Dissertation." We can hardly have any better means of determining who was the original author of these plays than by ascertaining which of the two writers learned his facts from the narratives on which the whole work must unquestionably have been founded; and, in every case in which we can institute the necessary comparison, it will be found, unless we are much mistaken, that it was Shakespeare who possessed this independent information.

Lionel, Duke of Clarence, died, and left him one only daughter, named Philippe, who was married to Edmund Mortimer, Earl of March and Ulster; and so, by her I claim the crown as the true heir, &c.

The rest of the passage is then continued as in the original edition. The principal amendments introduced into it were taken, perhaps, from the following account given by Holinshed (p. 412), of the issue of King Edward III., towards the close of his history of that monarch's reign :—

He [King Edward III.] had issue by his wife, Queen Philippe, seven sons—Edward, Prince of Wales; William of Hatfield, that died young; Lionel, Duke of Clarence; John of Gaunt, Duke of Lancaster; Edmund of Langley, Earl of Cambridge, and after created Duke of York; Thomas of Woodstock, Earl of Buckingham, after made Duke of Gloucester; and another William, which died likewise young.

A little before (p. 397) Holinshed had stated that "in the city of Angouleme was born the first son of Prince Edward, and was named after his father, but he departed this life the seventh year of his age;" and we also find him mentioning, in the same page, the birth of the future Richard II. There is, however, in Stow's "Chronicle" (p. 277, ed. 1615), a statement of the issue of Edward III., which very much resembles the passage we have just quoted from Holinshed; and it is, of course, quite conceivable that Stow was the authority whom the editor of 1619 was following. The manifest errors, however, in what the copyist must have meant for an improvement of the preceding editions form one of those vagaries of ancient writing, or printing, of which it is impossible for us to give any reasonable account.

All the above extracts will, we believe, help us to come to a clearer conclusion with respect to the authorship of the "First Part of the Contention," and of the closely related "True Tragedie." They seem absolutely decisive upon many of the points involved in this controversy. They dispose, even more completely than the passages which describe the fate of Warwick's brothers, of the assumption that the author of the "Contention" founded his work upon Hall's narrative, while

Shakespeare followed that author, and not one or both of the chroniclers. They do much more; they prove that the writer who prepared the "First Part of the Contention" for publication was, in this instance, at all events, an ignorant and a bewildered copyist, vainly attempting to recall the language of some imperfectly known model; for it is utterly impossible that the man of rare genius who planned the whole of these dramas, and who was the original author of the many fine scenes which they contain, could voluntarily have written the illiterate and stupid trash of this supposed genealogy. Nothing could have induced any man of sense to enter into these very unnecessary details, save a desire to repeat some information which must have been distinctly brought under his immediate notice; and, indeed, there are very few writers who would have indulged such a taste under any circumstances. But we know that this minute copying of historical narrations is one of the characteristics of the manner of Shakespeare; and its adoption in any disputed drama of that epoch would of itself create a fair presumption that the work proceeded from his hand. No one doubts that he was the original author of the long passage in "King Henry V." in which, following Holinshed, he makes the Archbishop of Canterbury describe the line of the French monarchy; and it seems to us to be equally certain that it is he that must first have conceived the design of copying from one or both of the chroniclers, as he alone has actually copied, the names of the children of King Edward III., and the order of the rightful succession to the English crown. We believe, also, and upon precisely the same description of evidence, that the writer of this first edition of the "Second Part of King Henry VI.," like the writer of the first edition of "King Henry V.," must have produced his volume from imperfect notes. It is manifest that, in the one case, as in the other, the copyist could not have had before him either Shakespeare's work, or the chronicle on which that work was founded. We may add, that it is just as inconceivable that Greene or Marlowe, as it is that Shakespeare himself, should have been the original writer of such a passage.

We know of only one mode by which the adherents of Malone's theory can attempt to evade the force of this evidence; and that is, by supposing that the "First Part of the Contention" was made up from any accidental sources which offered themselves to the writer, and that in this particular instance he most probably endeavoured to imitate Shakespeare. But there will be very little gained by this evasion of the difficulty. If the compiler of the old play copied Shakespeare even in a single line, Shakespeare's drama must have previously been in existence. We have not the smallest objection to urge against the supposition that the copyist in this case exercised a certain amount of freedom in the arrangement, and even in the selection of his materials. We even think that the internal evidence fairly warrants that conclusion; and it is manifestly one which would afford us an important aid in any attempt to account for those occasional alterations, and even enlargements, of Shakespeare's works which we find in both parts of the "Contention." But if we are to adopt this hypothesis, we must adopt it with its legitimate consequences, and we must believe that Shakespeare was the author from whom were copied all those passages in the earlier editions in which his hand seems fairly distinguishable, and, indeed, all those passages which are to be found in his two undisputed dramas.

Thomas Pavier published the "Whole Contention" in 1619, as "newly corrected and enlarged;" and there was some truth in this announcement. We have already seen that the account of the genealogy of the House of York was partially amended, the changes being, as it appears, made from the pages either of Stow or of Holinshed, but from a portion of those pages which did not supply the whole of the information which was required. This circumstance naturally gives rise to a suspicion that the publisher had no copy of a distinct and complete play, which he could employ for the purpose of collation;

and this suspicion is strongly supported by the mode in which some of his other corrections appear to have been effected. There are a few of them which we cannot trace to any origin; but there are others, and among them some of the most important of the whole series, which we have no hesitation in concluding must have been made from the two still unpublished plays of Shakespeare. In the very opening address of the "First Part of the Contention," as it was printed in 1594 and in 1600, Suffolk enumerates, among the great personages who were present at the espousals of Margaret,

> The Dukes of Orleans, Calaber, Bretaigne, and Alençon,
> Seven earls, twelve barons, and then the reverend bishops.

In the edition of 1619, instead of the words "then the" in the second of these lines, we have the word "twenty" as it is found in Shakespeare, who no doubt copied it, as he did all the rest of the passage, from either Hall or Holinshed.*

In the earlier copies of the same play (p. 9), Humphrey, Duke of Gloster, had a dream, which he thus relates:—

---

* The passage in Hall (fol. 148) is literally copied by Holinshed (p. 625), and is as follows:—"There were also the Dukes of Orleans, of Calaber, of Alençon, and of Bretaigne, seven earls, twelve barons, twenty bishops, beside knights and gentlemen." The lines in the drama are manifestly very deficient in metrical harmony. But we have no right, on that account, to suppose that they were not written by Shakespeare. It is clear, from his enumeration of the "twenty" bishops, that he must here have consulted one or other of the chroniclers, and we have reason to believe that in following them in passages of this description, he would not have hesitated to allow himself this licence. In King Richard II. (Act II., Scene I.) we find the following lines:—

> Sir Thomas Erpingham, Sir John Ramston,
> Sir John Norbery, Sir Robert Waterton, and Francis Quoint.

These and other names in the same address are evidently taken from a passage in Holinshed (p. 498):—" Sir Thomas Erpingham and Sir Thomas Ramston, knights, John Norburie, Robert Waterton, and Francis Coint, esquires."

> This night, when I was laid in bed, I dreamt that
> This, my staff, mine office-badge in court,
> Was broke in two, and on the ends were plac'd
> The heads of the cardinal of Winchester,
> And William de la Poole, first Duke of Suffolk.

This address is thus altered in the edition of 1619 :—

> This night when I was laid in bed, I dreamt that
> This my staff, mine office-badge in court,
> Was broke in twain; by whom I cannot guess:
> But, as I think, by the cardinal. What it bodes
> God knows ; and on the ends were plac'd
> The heads of Edmund Duke of Somerset,
> And William de la Poole, first Duke of Suffolk.

In Act I., Scene II., of the "Second Part of King Henry VI.," the corresponding passage runs as follows :—

> Methought, this staff, mine office-badge in court,
> Was broke in twain ; by whom, I have forgot,
> But, as I think, it was by the cardinal ;
> And on the pieces of the broken wand
> Were plac'd the heads of Edmond Duke of Somerset,
> And William de la Poole, first Duke of Suffolk.
> This was my dream ; what it doth bode, God knows.

We shall give another of these alterations. The Duchess of Gloster thus unfolds her ambitious designs in the different editions of the "First Part of the Contention," and in the "Second Part of King Henry VI." :—

> I'll come after you, for I cannot go before :
> But ere it be long, I'll go before them all,
> Despite of all that seek to cross me thus.
> THE CONTENTION, 1594 and 1600, *p.* 10.

> I'll come after you, for I cannot go before,
> As long as Gloster bears this base and humble mind:
> Were I a man, and protector as he is,
> I'd reach to th' crown, or make some hop headless :
> And being but a woman, I'll not behind
> For playing of my part, in spite of all that seek to cross me thus.
> *Ibidem*, 1619, *p.* 77.

> Follow I must, I cannot go before,
> While Gloster bears this base and humble mind.
> Were I a man, a duke, and next of blood,
> I would remove these tedious stumbling-blocks,
> And smooth my way upon their headless necks:
> And, being a woman, I will not be slack
> To play my part in fortune's pageant.
>
> KING HENRY VI., Part II., *Act I., Scene II.*

No one, we believe, on reading these extracts, will much hesitate in coming to the conclusion that the amendments in the edition of 1619 were founded upon the corresponding passages in Shakespeare's undisputed drama, and that they were taken from it by means of imperfect notes, or from memory. If that be so, they give rise to a reasonable suspicion that it was in the same manner other portions of the copy of the old publication were originally obtained. They are marked by precisely the same apparent defects of imitation as the greater part of the rest of the volume into which they are introduced, and they seem to show that the publisher must in each case have had the same model to follow. They do not, perhaps, entitle us to decide with any certainty upon this whole problem, but they may fairly be regarded as minor links in that complex and firm chain of probabilities which seems directly to connect the Two Parts of the "Contention" with the early genius of Shakespeare.

We are not yet, however, free from the curious perplexities which seem more or less inseparable from any theory that may be adopted with respect to the formation of these two plays. No one can compare the versions of them in the older volumes with those in the Folio of 1623 without being struck by the complete, or almost complete, identity of the copies in a number of long addresses, and occasionally throughout entire scenes. The whole dialogue, for instance, between York and Margaret, which precedes York's death, in Act I., Scene IV., of the "Third Part of King Henry VI." is inserted in the "True Tragedie" with almost literal exactness; and our first impression on reading it undoubtedly is, that it is only by referring to a perfect copy the later of the two writers could have produced so close an imitation of the work of his predecessor. But, on careful consideration, we doubt whether we should be justified in drawing this conclusion. We are, perhaps, apt to forget in this case the circumstances under which the labours of the copyist were conducted. It is by no means necessary we should suppose that he wrote after a single hearing of the original dramas. On the contrary, we believe that he must have had an opportunity of seeing them frequently performed upon the stage, for they appear to have been produced two or three years before they were printed; and we can hardly fix any limits to the accuracy with which a man of trained memory might under such circumstances have repeated those passages with which his fancy must have been specially impressed. It is only, we think, in such passages that the imitation is here remarkably complete; the copyist would naturally have been led to bestow special pains on the perfect reproduction of the very incident which gives its title to his work; and we find that large portions of the three last and least striking acts of the "Third Part of King Henry VI." are omitted altogether from the "True Tragedie." We do not of course consider it at all impossible that some of the actors in the original dramas may have been tempted to aid in furnishing more complete versions of the parts they had sustained, or even that more or less imperfect playhouse copies may have been used in the construction of these singular volumes. We offer these observations, however, as mere conjectures: They may serve to show that the accuracy of imitation which is observable in many parts of the earlier editions may have been owing to a number of causes which we cannot now clearly define. We must further observe that the objection which we are now considering does not affect what is, after all, the main point involved in this discussion. Even if it were true that the old publications could not have been the work of a mere copyist, it is quite as open to us to assume that they came from Shakespeare himself as from any other hand, for we believe we have shown that no reliance can be placed on the arguments by which Malone sought to controvert that position. If the Two Parts of the "Contention" were original compositions, we should feel compelled, in spite of the many objections which may be urged against such a conclusion, to trace them to the only writer to whom they can with the smallest show of probability be assigned. We regard them as more or less mutilated copies, solely because we believe that they carry on the face of them the marks of such an origin; because they exhibit at once a literary power and a literary incapacity which could not, as it seems to us, co-exist in one and the same mind; because we think it was absolutely impossible that the writer of such a passage as that which describes the pedigree of the house of York in the "First Part of the Contention" could have been the original author of what are essentially the two most varied and most vital dramas which all the genius of his age had yet produced. The "Whole Contention" is manifestly a piece of literary patchwork, and as such we must accept it, whatever difficulty we may experience in attempting to account for the inequalities of imitation or of reproduction which it displays.

We believe that the earlier publications are substantially creations of Shakespeare's genius; and we do not see how it is possible to entertain any very serious doubt upon that subject. But, if we are not mistaken in that conclusion, we find in the internal evidence, furnished by a comparison of the two copies, further reasons for thinking that the first editions are more or less incomplete. The most remarkable additions made to them in the Folio consist of misplaced Latin quotations, and far-fetched and very unnecessary classical allusions. But such a change of workmanship in Shakespeare would be to no small extent inconsistent with all our conceptions of his growing taste, and even with all our knowledge of the actual history of his dramas. Those pedantic displays are manifestly vices of style which he inherited from his immediate predecessors, and we know that he more and more renounced them as his genius, in the natural course of its development, gradually found freer play for the exercise of its inherent energy and originality. We have already stated that we cannot suppose he would, even at the commencement of his career, have encumbered with those ostentatious and ambitious illustrations a work of Marlowe's, or of any other of his contemporaries; and we think it quite as unlikely that he would in his rapidly growing maturity have added them to one of his own earlier compositions.

But if these two old plays are, as we believe them to be, mere mutilated copies of Shakespeare's dramas, they are undoubtedly in their way very remarkable productions.* Malone was specially struck by the differences between the two versions; we confess that we feel much more embarrassed by their resemblances. But some of the differences, too, present themselves in a rather unexpected form. We would suggest that they may to some extent have had their origin in the existence of some older drama which Shakespeare's imitator, as well as

---

* The early editions have been used with advantage for the purpose of correcting manifest errors or supplying manifest omissions in the two dramas as they appeared in the Folio. The "First Part of the Contention" (p. 48) has thus furnished a line in one of the last addresses of Suffolk ("Second Part of King Henry VI.," Act IV., Scene I.):—

"Jove sometime went disguised, and why not I?"

And, a little farther on, the following passage in the dialogue between Suffolk and the sea-captain has been taken from the same source:—

"*Captain.* Yes, Poole,
Suffolk.   Poole!"

In the same way the eighth line of the address of the dying Clifford in Act II., Scene VI., of the "Third Part of King Henry VI."—

"The common people swarm like summer flies,"

has been supplied by the "True Tragedie" (p. 149). All these additions are clearly necessary to the completion of the dialogue, and have very properly been adopted by the modern editors; but it is evident that they can in no way prove that the early plays were not themselves more or less imperfect copies.

Shakespeare himself, occasionally followed. There is certainly nothing extremely improbable in such a supposition. We may even go further and say that it is unlikely the Wars of the Roses had not down to the time of Shakespeare been made the subject of dramatic treatment; and we know that an immense mass of the plays of that period must have perished. We need not, however, insist upon this topic. It may be that in this petty inquiry we are placed in a position somewhat analogous to that of the astronomers searching through space for the unseen disturber of the planetary system; but, unlike them, we can never hope actually to discover the source of our perplexity; and there could be no use in our indulging, in reference to this obscure subject, in mere vague, and perhaps worthless, conjectures.

We have now done with this controversy. We do not think it necessary that we should here attempt to recapitulate the arguments we have advanced in support of our position. Many people will perhaps be disposed to think that we have already prolonged this inquiry to an extravagant length. But this is essentially a question of small details; and, if it is at all to be made a subject of discussion, an examination of those details cannot by any possibility be avoided. We believe, too, that its full and complete consideration must serve to throw an incidental light on many of the difficulties which arise in the largest and most general criticism of the genius and the writings of our great dramatist.

We cannot now undertake to say how far our arguments may affect the convictions of our readers, and it is of course possible that we have no right to place in them any absolute confidence ourselves. In all matters of doubt and controversy the comprehensive and impartial scepticism of the nineteenth century has consigned mere "facts" to special discredit; and there is some reason why we should, upon this occasion, look upon them with more than usual suspicion. Malone supported his theory by a mass of evidence which has found a general acceptance among the succeeding commentators, and which attracted the marked approbation of one of the greatest scholars and critics whom modern times have produced.* And yet Malone's whole essay now seems to us a singular and an almost unparalleled series of mis-statements and misapprehensions. It may be, however, that we have not done justice to his reasoning, or that we have overrated the force of the arguments which have led us to the adoption of a different conclusion. The whole truth, perhaps, was never told by any one who was specially engaged in combating either real or supposed error. We are, at all events, now ready to admit that, in complicated literary problems of this description, we can never trust to the decision of any one individual mind, and that the value of any solution of them which may be offered can only ultimately be determined by the general mass of competent scholars, representing and interpreting the common sense of mankind at large.

HAMLET.

"Hamlet" is the most universally interesting of all the dramas of Shakespeare. It is the most abrupt and the most perplexing; it unites the greatest diversity of thought and feeling in its central figure; and this figure seems to have impressed the form of its own astonishing personality on the whole vivid, agitated, rapid, and original composition.

The mere external history of this great work is involved in more or less of that petty obscurity which seems inevitably to meet us in all our attempts to follow the labours of our

---

* Boswell, in p. 64 of his "Biographical Memoir of Malone," prefixed to vol. i. of his edition of Malone's "Shakespeare," makes the following statement:—"Professor Porson, who, as every one who knew him can testify, was by no means in the habit of bestowing hasty or thoughtless praise, declared to the writer of this account that he considered the 'Essay on the Three Parts of Henry VI.' as one of the most convincing pieces of criticism that he had ever read."

wonderful dramatist. But we are not, at all events, left in absolute ignorance of its probable origin. We learn from a variety of contemporary allusions that a play of "Hamlet" must have been in existence about the very earliest period to which Shakespeare's connection with the stage can with any probability be assigned. The first of these curious passages is contained in an "Epistle" by Thomas Nash, prefixed to Robert Greene's "Menaphon," which appears to have been first published either in the year 1587 or the year 1589 :*—

I'll turn back to my first text of studies of delight, and talk a little in friendship with a few of our trivial translators. It is a common practice now-a-days, amongst a sort of shifting companions, that run through every art and thrive by none, to leave the trade of *Noverint* whereto they were born, and busy themselves with the endeavours of art, that could scarcely latinize their neck-verse if they should need; yet English Seneca read by candle-light yields many good sentences, as *Blood is a beggar*, and so forth: and if you entreat him fair in a frosty morning, he will afford you whole *Hamlets*, I should say handfuls of tragical speeches."

In Henslowe's Diary (p. 35, ed. Shak. Soc.) we find the following entry :—

9 of June, 1594. Rd at Hamlet 8s.

Thomas Lodge, in his "Wits' Misery," &c., published in 1596, thus describes a certain fiend :—

He walks for the most part in black under colour of gravity, and

---

* Mr. Dyce mentioned in his earliest list of Greene's prose works. that "Menaphon" was first printed in 1587. But he has since been unable to find the authority on which he made that statement. Mr. Collier, in his "Sketch of the English Stage" which precedes his "Life of Shakespeare," (vol. i., p. 26, of "Shakespeare's Works,' ed. 1858), seems to have no doubt that "Menaphon" was in print in 1587. He says that Nash alludes to that fact in an introduction to another of Greene's tracts, dated the same year. No earlier edition, however, than one of 1589 appears to be now extant. "Menaphon" was at a later period published under the name of "Greene's Arcadia."

looks as pale as the vizard of the ghost who cried so miserably at the theatre, like an oyster-wife, *Hamlet, revenge!*

We have already quoted (p. 75) the following note, written by Gabriel Harvey in his copy of "Chaucer's Works:"—

The younger sort take much delight in Shakespeare's "Venus and Adonis;" but his "Lucrece" and his tragedy of "Hamlet, Prince of Denmark," have it in them to please the wiser sort.

We shall at once observe in reference to this last extract that there seems to be no sufficient reason for assigning to it, as Steevens has done, the date of 1598. Harvey entered that year at the beginning, and again at the end, of the volume, but he probably only meant by those figures to indicate the period when it came into his possession. In another note he alludes to "translated Tasso," meaning, no doubt, Fairfax's translation of "Tasso," which was not published until the year 1600.

The passage in Nash's "Epistle" will naturally attract more attention. It curiously coincides with the tradition—if indeed it did not contribute to its creation—that Shakespeare was in early life an apprentice, or an assistant, in a lawyer's office, as well as with the much more generally adopted and better authenticated opinion respecting the small amount of his classical acquirements. But, on the other hand, he does not seem to have been at any time a translator, or to have been in any way indebted to Seneca; and the fact that Meres does not attribute to him any play upon so remarkable a subject as the fate of Hamlet, leads us to suppose that he had not written such a work previously to the year 1598. It is, however, impossible for us to come to any absolute conclusion upon this point. The commentators think it likely that Thomas Kyd was the author of this old and lost play of "Hamlet." The grounds for that conjecture are that this writer was one of the popular dramatists of the period which immediately preceded the advent of Shakespeare, that he published a tragedy called "Cornelia," which is a translation from the French, and that there is in his most celebrated work, the "Spanish Tragedy,"

Y

a sort of play within the play, as there is in the only version of "Hamlet" which is now known to us, or which appears to have ever been published.

The entry in Henslowe's Diary refers most probably to the same work. It appears that at the period at which that entry was written some sort of connection existed between the Lord Admiral's and the Lord Chamberlain's theatrical companies; but we do not find in that circumstance any good ground for believing that the "Hamlet" in the Diary was one of the works of Shakespeare.

The passage, again, in Lodge's tract relates, we may assume, to the original "Hamlet." It is only important inasmuch as it proves that the ghost scene formed a portion of that early drama.

The date of Shakespeare's undoubted "Hamlet" may, we think, be fixed with considerable probability. The Stationers' Registers contain the following entry:—

26 July, 1602.
James Roberts.] A book, "The Revenge of Hamlet Prince of Denmark," as it was lately acted by the Lord Chamberlain his servants.

The words in this announcement—"as it was lately acted"—which are very seldom found in the notices of our early dramas, seem to indicate that this "Hamlet" must have been a new work in the month of July, 1602; and there is some evidence furnished by the play itself which appears to strengthen that supposition. In Act II., Scene II., Hamlet having asked how it happens that the tragedians of the city—Shakespeare's company—are travelling through the country, Rosencrantz replies that "their inhibition comes by the means of the late innovation." These words are not wholly free from obscurity. But we need not hesitate to conclude that they refer to an attempt made towards the close of the sixteenth, and the beginning of the seventeenth centuries, to limit the performance of plays in the metropolis.

On the 19th of February, 1597-8, an order was issued

by the Privy Council to the effect that only two companies of public players—the Lord Admiral's and the Lord Chamberlain's—should be permitted to act in London or its neighbourhood;* and by another order, dated the 22nd of June, 1600, the Council commanded that only two public theatres—the Fortune, in Golding Lane, and the Globe, on the Bankside—should be opened for stage performances.† This latter injunction does not seem to have been at once rigorously enforced. The consequence was, that on the 31st of December, 1601, letters were addressed by the Council to the Lord Mayor of London, and to the justices of Middlesex and Surrey, censuring them for their negligence, and directing them, in the most imperative language, to carry out the instructions they had previously received.‡ We are persuaded, however, that the order of the month of June, 1600, must have been so far carried into execution that Shakespeare's company had at once been compelled to surrender their house in the Blackfriars. The evidence seems absolutely conclusive upon that point. The Globe was built by the company for their use during the summer; and yet we find that on the 7th of February, 1601, they performed in it, at the request of the partisans of the Earl of Essex, a play founded on certain events in the reign of King Richard II. In the patent of the month of May, 1603, by which they were constituted the King's players, the Globe alone is mentioned as their theatre; and we hear no more of their connection with the Blackfriars house until after the burning of the Globe in 1613, from which period, until the closing of the theatres in 1641, the Blackfriars establishment appears to have been the great centre of all the dramatic life of the metropolis. It seems to have been occupied, during the earlier years of the seventeenth century, by the youths

---

* This order is inserted in Mr. Collier's "Annals of the Stage" (p. 309).

† *Ibidem* (p. 312).   ‡ *Ibidem* (p. 316).

known as the "Children of the Queen's Chapel," as they were called in the time of Queen Elizabeth, or as the "Children of Her Majesty's Revels," which was the name given to them after the accession of James I. to the throne.* These juvenile actors were, in the language of that day, regarded as a private company, and did not, therefore, come under the interdict of the Privy Council, which was directed exclusively against "common stage plays" and players.

The inhibition, it is said, "came by the means of the late innovation." It has been generally supposed that this "late innovation" was the practice of making theatrical performances a vehicle for attacks on private individuals. But there is not the slightest reason to suppose that any such practice prevailed in any special manner at that particular period; and the Privy Council make no allusion whatever to it in their detailed enumeration of those "manifold abuses and disorders" arising out of the multiplication of theatres and theatrical performances, which had induced them to issue their injunction of the month of June, 1600. It may be that this "innovation" was some circumstance with which we are now unacquainted; but we think it much more likely that it was the order itself of the Council, and that the meaning of the passage is, that it was in consequence of that measure the players were prevented from performing at one of their theatres in London.

The allusion which immediately follows to the "eyry of children, little eyases, that cry out on the top of question" will perhaps help us to throw some further light on the date of the composition of this drama. It involves, however, another of the many small perplexities which beset the Shakespearian critic. A doubt has been raised whether it relates to the "Children of Paul's," that is to say, the singing boys of St. Paul's Cathedral, or to the "Children of Her Majesty's Chapel." There exists distinct evidence that the former of

---

* Mr. Collier's "Annals of the Stage" (p. 352).

these juvenile societies, after having been for some years interdicted from engaging in theatrical performances, were again acting, and with considerable success, at the commencement of the seventeenth century. In a piece entitled " Jack Drum's Entertainment," first published in 1601, we find the following dialogue :—

<blockquote>
Sir Edw. Fortune. I saw the Children of Paul's last night,
And, troth, they pleas'd me pretty, pretty well :
The apes in time will do it handsomely.
Planet. I' faith, I like the audience that frequenteth there,
With much applause, &c.
Brabant, jun. 'Tis a good, gentle audience,* &c.
</blockquote>

Many of the commentators have taken it for granted that the passage in "Hamlet" was pointed at those choir-boys of St. Paul's; but we are very strongly disposed to adopt a different opinion, and to believe that the poet meant his rebuke or remonstrance for the " Children of the Queen's Chapel." The boys of St. Paul's seem to have performed at this period in their own singing-school. With the limited accommodation which was all we must suppose that such a building afforded, they could hardly have become the successful rivals of the proprietors of a great public theatre ; and, in all probability, their " good, gentle audiences" were not the rushing multitudes which carried away "Hercules and his load too." † The young singers of the Queen's Chapel, on the other hand, were in possession of a regular theatrical establishment. We know that they performed Ben Jonson's "Cynthia's Revels" in the year 1600, and his "Poetaster" in the year 1601. Both these plays contain a number of caustic allusions to the dramatists and actors of the day, including the members of the Globe company; they involved their author in a bitter literary warfare ; and Shakespeare seems to us very distinctly to refer to this contest, and to complain temperately, but firmly, of the "wrong" which was done to the youths them-

---

* Mr. Collier's "Annals of the Stage " (p. 282).

† "Hercules carrying the Globe " was the sign of the Globe Theatre.

selves by making them the vehicles of an attack on the members of a profession to which they might themselves one day belong.*

The conclusion which we draw from all these passages is that "Hamlet" was most probably written towards the end of 1601, or the commencement of 1602, and that it was first acted in the spring or early in the summer of the latter year. The whole tenour of its composition confirms us in this judgment. It does not seem at all likely that it was one of the fruits of the poet's earlier genius and immaturer experience of the world.†

James Roberts appears to have met with some unexpected obstacle in the accomplishment of the intention with which he made his entry in the Stationers' Registers in the month of July, 1602. The first edition of "Hamlet" was issued in the year 1603, under the following title:—

The Tragical History of Hamlet, Prince of Denmark. By William Shakespeare. As it hath been divers times acted by His Highness' Servants in the City of London: as also in the two Universities of Cambridge and Oxford, and elsewhere. At London, printed for N. L. and John Trundell, 1603.

This edition was unknown to the commentators of the last century. There are but two copies of it now extant: one of them is in the library of the British Museum, and the other is the property of the Duke of Devonshire. The former wants the

---

* For some further remarks upon this subject, see Appendix, Note 7.

† We find, from Henslowe's Diary (p. 224, ed. Shak. Soc.), that on the 7th of July, 1602, twenty shillings were advanced by Henslowe to Henry Chettle, as earnest money for the production of "a Danish Tragedy." This was, perhaps, a play to be written upon the same subject which Shakespeare's "Hamlet" had just rendered popular. There is no notice of such a work in any other portion of the Diary, and it would be no wonder if, on further reflection, Chettle shrank from the attempt to fulfil his engagement. But it is also quite possible that he was to some extent connected with the production of the mutilated edition of "Hamlet" which appeared in the year 1603.

title-page, and the latter the last leaf. A small number of reprints of the Devonshire volume was issued in the year 1825.

This edition of 1603 is, we feel assured, an imperfect copy made up from notes taken at the theatre, or from other casual sources. That is, we believe the opinion of every one who has examined the volume. But Mr. Knight thinks that it is, at the same time, a mutilated version of the poet's own first and incomplete sketch of his drama. We do not see the slightest ground for adopting that conjecture. The work has, no doubt, its peculiarities; but they are never greater than we might reasonably have expected from a copyist who had no perfect materials before him, and whose own ingenuity or fancy must have been perpetually called into requisition for the purpose of supplying this deficiency.

The first correct edition of the play was issued in the year 1604. It is stated in the title-page to be "newly imprinted and enlarged to almost as much again as it was, according to the true and perfect copy." Three other early quartos followed, and the work was next inserted in the Folio of 1623.

There are some curious differences between all these copies. The edition of 1603 re-produces some passages of the play with considerable accuracy; but it presents many deviations from the later versions, in the shape of transpositions, omissions, and alterations. It places the famous soliloquy, "To be, or not to be," &c., before a large portion of the scenes which it ought to follow. It contains nearly all the snatches of song sung by Ophelia during her distraction; but it reverses their order, and runs them strangely into one another. After the return of Hamlet from his intended journey to England, it gives an interview between the Queen and Horatio, of which there is no trace in the later copies. Among its slighter, but still singular, peculiarities, it calls Polonius and Reynaldo Corambis and Montano. It has been suggested, as the most probable explanation of this latter change, that the copyist may have taken his names from the older play of "Hamlet."

The edition of 1604 was, no doubt, an authentic copy of the work. It is even the longest, and, so far, the most complete version of it which we have received. It contains a number of passages which are not inserted in the Folio of 1623; and among them the fine address of Horatio in Act I., Scene I., beginning with "A mote it is to trouble the mind's eye," and then proceeding with the splendid image of the re-appearance of the "sheeted dead," "in the most high and palmy state of Rome, a little ere the mightiest Julius fell."

Another sketch, which is only to be found in the quartos, is that portion of the fourth scene of the fourth act which extends from the entrance of Hamlet, Rosencrantz, and Guildenstern, down to its close, which thus includes one of Hamlet's remarkable soliloquies. But there are, also, some important passages in the folios omitted from the quartos, as, for instance, a number of the earlier addresses of Hamlet, Rosencrantz, and Guildenstern, in Act II., Scene II., with the exclamations, "Denmark's a prison," and "O God! I could be bounded in a nut-shell," &c.;* and again, the whole of the dialogue relating to the "eyry of children, little eyases," &c.,† in the same scene. We can hardly entertain a doubt that this latter passage was inserted in the work as it was originally written, for the address of Hamlet, which immediately follows, seems distinctly to imply that he has just heard of the success which some new popular fashion had obtained. The only conclusion, we believe, which we can draw from these variations is, that the play was more or less abridged in the stage copies from which the different editions were printed; and it is only natural that this should have been done;

---

* The omission here commences with "Let me question more in particular," in the middle of one of the addresses of Hamlet, and ends with "I am most dreadfully attended," towards the close of another.

† This omission begins with Hamlet's question, "How comes it?" &c.? and ends with Rosencrantz's statement, "Ay, that they do, my lord; Hercules and his load too."

for the work in its complete shape is one of very exceptional, and even inconvenient, length.*

This drama is, no doubt, founded, either directly or indirectly, on The "Hystorie of Hamblet," which is a translation of a tale in the "Histoires Tragiques" of Belleforest, who seems himself to have derived his version of the story from the Danish historian, Saxo Grammaticus. The earliest known edition of the work in its English dress is dated 1608, but there can be no doubt, from the general character of its style, that it must have been written at an earlier period. Capell thought it first appeared about the year 1570, and Mr. Collier assigns to it the conjectural date of 1585.†

It is a singularly crude and spiritless production. It differs in some important particulars from the story set forth in the drama, and more especially towards its close, where Hamlet is made to succeed to the throne after he has slain his uncle. But it contains, at the same time, all the principal incidents in the great work of the poet. In the history, as in the play, Hamlet, for the purpose of ensuring his own safety, feigns madness after the death of his father. A young woman is thrown in his way, with the object of ascertaining the real state of his mind. A "counsellor" hides himself behind the arras previously to an interview between him and his mother; he discovers this intruder, and slays him, while he exclaims, "A rat, a rat!" He is sent to England, and on his way defeats—by altering the king's letter—the scheme laid for his destruction on his arrival at his destination. There are some minor details, too, in the story, which must have been present to the

---

* If the passage relating to the "children" formed an episode in the quarrel with Jonson, which must have terminated in the year 1603, when his "Sejanus" was performed by Shakespeare's company, it would almost necessarily have then been struck out of the acting copies of the play; and its omission would thus perfectly coincide with our conjecture respecting its origin and its meaning.

† It is inserted by Mr. Collier in the first volume of his "Shakespeare's Library."

mind of the dramatist, as, for instance, the allusion to the "over great drinking" at the Court, "a vice common and familiar among the Almains, and other nations inhabiting the north parts of the world."* The feigned madness of Hamlet is made to assume, in the "History," the most grotesque and degrading form, but there is a sentence in the general account given of it which perfectly harmonises with the poet's conception of the same subject:—" Hamlet, in this sort counterfeiting the madman, many times did divers actions of great and deep consideration, and often made such and so fit answers, that a wise man would soon have judged from what spirit so fine an invention might proceed."† It may be, however, that it is a passing allusion to Hamlet's "over great melancholy"‡ that principally contributed to supply Shakespeare with the key-note of his whole composition. There is in the "History" no mention of the appearance of the ghost of Hamlet's father, and we must suppose that this incident was first introduced into the older play of "Hamlet," to which Lodge was, no doubt, referring in his tract published in the year 1596.

"Hamlet" is the great enigma among the productions of Shakespeare's genius. For the first century and a half after its appearance no one seems to have suspected that this work occupied any exceptional position in the poet's dramas; but its strange and dark complexity has become an object of the most special fascination to the anxious, agitated, inquiring intellect of more recent generations. Goethe, in his "Wilhelm Meister," has devoted a separate study to the elucidation of its construction, its purpose, and its ultimate meaning. Schlegel and Coleridge have also sought to penetrate its supposed mystery. We doubt, however, whether much has been added, or, perhaps, ever can be added, by the labours of the critic to the obvious impression which the work leaves on every

---

* "Shakespeare's Library," vol. i., p. 160.
† *Ibidem*, p. 138.   ‡ *Ibidem*, p. 154.

mind of ordinary sensibility and intelligence. We are all aware that Hamlet becomes startled, amazed, saddened, and overwhelmed by the discovery of a crime which has involved all that is nearest to him in its guilt or its ruin; and that, when he is called upon to take vengeance upon its author, he dallies and procrastinates with the uncongenial mission. But we still read this stupendous tragedy with a large amount of wonder and bewilderment. We are unable perfectly to reconcile Hamlet's anomalous history with Hamlet's fine intellect and elevated character; we are lost in the "strange labyrinth of his many moods and singularities."

We cannot help thinking that the perplexity to which we are thus exposed is founded on conditions which, from their very nature, are more or less irremovable. It has its origin, as it seems to us, in two sources. It is owing, in the first place, to the essential character of the work itself; and, in the second place, it arises, in no small degree, from the large licence which the poet has allowed himself in dealing with his intrinsically obscure and disordered materials.

All Nature has its impenetrable secrets, and there seems to be no reason why the poet should not restore to us any of the accidental forms of this universal mysteriousness. The world of art, like the world of real life, may have its obscure recesses, its vague instincts, its undeveloped passions, its unknown motives, its half-formed judgments, its wild aberrations, its momentary caprices. The mood of Hamlet is necessarily an extraordinary and an unaccountable mood. In him exceptional influences agitate an exceptional temperament. He is wayward, fitful, excited, horror-stricken. The foundations of his being are unseated. His intellect and his will are ajar and unbalanced. He has become an exception to the common forms of humanity. The poet, in his turn, struck with this strange figure, seems to have resolved on bringing its special peculiarities into special prominence; and the story which he dramatised afforded him the most ample opportunity of accomplishing this design. Hamlet is not only, in reality, agitated and bewildered, but he is led to adopt the disguise of a feigned madness, and he is thus perpetually intensifying and distorting the peculiarities of an already over-excited imagination. It was, we think, inevitable that a composition which attempted to follow the workings of so unusual an individuality should itself seem abrupt and capricious; and this natural effect of the scene is still further deepened, not only by the exceptionally large genius, but by the exceptionally negligent workmanship of the poet.

Shakespeare not only used the details of his wonderful story with the most unconfined freedom, but he sometimes exaggerated its contrasts, and violated its natural proportions. He was driven, too, perhaps, in some measure, to this exaggeration, by the consciousness that he had to develop a history of thought rather than a history of action, and that it was only by the most rapid variety of moods and scenes he could give to his work the highest dramatic vitality.

There was, we think, in the original conception of the work another element of almost inevitable confusion. On the story of a semi-barbarous age the poet has engrafted a most curious psychological study; and there is naturally a certain want of probability and harmony between the refined and sensitive spirit of Hamlet and the rude scenes amidst which he is thrown, and the rude work of vengeance which he is commissioned to perform.

We believe we can discover in the history of the drama a further reason why its details were not always perfectly harmonised. It was written under two different and somewhat conflicting influences. The poet throughout many portions of its composition had, no doubt, the old story which formed its groundwork directly present to his mind; but he did not apparently always clearly distinguish between the impressions in his memory and the creations of his imagination; and the result is, that some of his incidents now seem to his readers more or less inexplicable or discordant. In the novel it is distinctly stated that the woman who answers to the Ophelia of the drama was used by the King as a means of discovering whether Hamlet's apparent madness was only pretended, and that he was carefully warned of the danger to which he was thus exposed. This circumstance was, perhaps, remembered by the poet, and may have contributed to give much of its strange form to the language which Hamlet addresses to Ophelia; but this portion of the dialogue, as it stands in the play, looks unnecessarily extravagant and offensive, from the absence of any such preliminary explanation. Again, in the story, the officious intruder who conceals himself behind the arras is an unmistakable enemy of Hamlet's, and we are not surprised at the fate by which he is overtaken; but in the drama Polonius cannot be supposed to occupy the same position, and the wild levity with which the death of the alleged "foolish, prating knave" is treated by the Prince seems more or less inexplicable, as it is manifest that he does not act from any distrust of his mother, and as he addresses her with the utmost unreserve during the remainder of their interview. It is true that she afterwards says—"He weeps for what is done;" but we hardly know how to credit the statement.

The fact is, we believe, that the dramatist, using another licence, has sometimes run closely and even inextricably together the feigned madness and the real mental perturbation of Hamlet. We should have had no difficulty in accepting this representation of the character if it were only consistently maintained: it would even, under the circumstances, have been perfectly natural; but we find that, in his real mood, he retains throughout the drama, as throughout the story, the perfect possession of his faculties; his only confidant, Horatio, must evidently feel quite assured upon that point; and we are compelled, in spite of a few equivocal passages, entirely to share his conviction.

There are a few instances in which we can give but a qualified belief to the incidents which the poet himself seems to have wholly invented. We are not quite sure that Hamlet abstained from killing the King because he found him at his prayers; and this passage looks too much like a device got up for the particular occasion. We are still more perplexed by the part which he plays at the funeral of Ophelia; and here again he seems under the influence both of some real and of some pretended distraction. He afterwards expresses to Horatio his regret at having forgotten himself to Laertes, and states that he was actually moved to a "towering passion." But we cannot feel absolutely certain that the whole scene was perfectly free from all constraint and affectation; and we doubt, in particular, his assurance of the extremity of his love for Ophelia. That is one of the points which the poet himself seems to have left in convenient shadow. We can now only conjecture that Hamlet's attachment, though real, had but little enduringness or intensity. A man can have but one absorbing passion at a time; and love was clearly not the absorbing passion of the Danish Prince from the commencement to the close of this drama.

The mode in which the poet has treated the age of his chief personage affords another instance of his readiness to look on the minor accidents of his story with the large freedom of his imagination. In the earlier scenes Hamlet appears as a mere youth, who intends "going back to school in Wittenberg," and who is struck with a fatal blight at the very threshold of active life, and in the most picturesque of all positions; but in a later act, with an intellect rapidly ripened, and while curiously moralising on the skull of Yorick and the dust of Alexander, he is made a mature man of thirty, although we can find no room for any large lapse of time during all the intermediate action. We have here again to make a choice for ourselves between two conflicting representations of the character; and our pervading and final impression is, that Hamlet struggled and perished in the bloom of early manhood.

Some of the minor figures in the scene bring with them their own perplexities. The King does not form one of the distinguishing creations of Shakespeare. The general moderation, and even insipidity, of character which he exhibits seems hardly compatible with the tremendous and remorseless career of crime he has pursued. The fact is, that the vigorous, and even the clear, presentment of every other agent in the scene is made subordinate to the manifestation of the wonderful personality of Hamlet himself; and hence it is, perhaps, that the Queen, too, meets us in indistinct and shadowy outline. It would, perhaps, be idle to attempt to determine whether or not she was privy to the murder of her first husband. It did not suit the immediate purpose of the poet to afford us any means of forming an absolute judgment upon that subject. Her guilt, in the early scenes, hardly admits of any extenuation; but, as we proceed, her character is naturally depicted in less repulsive colours; and we should otherwise be unable to sympathise with her attachment to her son and her resolution to save his life at all hazards. The portraiture of Polonius has also received a double treatment. The explanation of the contrasts in the character is in the main, no doubt, to be found in the circumstance that he has begun to sink into senility or dotage. But he seems to have but scanty justice dealt out to him by the dramatist; and we do not willingly witness the contempt and ridicule of which he is finally made the object. The part assigned to Laertes presents a far more reckless contrast. The impetuous, vindictive, but frank and fearless youth could not possibly have consented, on the first light offer, to become the principal agent in a scene of dark and hideous treachery, in which the presence of the King himself is barely credible.

There is one, however, of the secondary characters in "Hamlet" which must be considered decidedly Shakespearian. The poet, it is true, has still touched but lightly the passion and the sorrow of Ophelia; but it is impossible to mistake the beauty and the grace of her nature, or the immediate form of the inevitable and inexplicable destiny to which she falls a helpless victim.

There is one episode in this play which has given rise to a large amount of conjecture. The critics are divided in opinion as to the origin and purport of the lines on ". Priam's slaughter," recited by the player in Act II., Scene II. Dryden and Pope thought they were introduced as a burlesque of the extravagant style which commonly distinguished the dramas of the age of Shakespeare. The modern commentators in general believe, on the contrary, that the poet was in earnest in the praises of them which he puts into the mouth of Hamlet; and some of them go so far as to suppose that they formed a portion of some early work which he himself had written. It seems to us that it would be a mistake to adopt either of these opinions without any reservation. We think that the passage was produced by Shakespeare himself for the occasion, and that it was written by him in that large, disengaged, mimetic mood, which was the favourite mood—which was even the natural mood—of his dramatic genius. He seems throughout the whole scene, and, indeed, throughout the whole play, to yield to the ardour of his own imaginative inspiration; but he does not, we take it for granted, appear in it in any way in his own personal character. He composed those verses in the spirit of the dramas of his time, and he praised or blamed them in imitation of the common taste of his contemporaries; but in doing so he naturally gave a certain amount of exaggeration to their distinguishing peculiarities, for the purpose of affording the requisite contrast between their artificial emphasis and the supposed directness of his own more immediate revival of the actual world.

"Hamlet" is, perhaps, of all the plays of Shakespeare, the one which a great actor would find it most difficult to embody in an ideally complete form. It would, we think, be a mistake to attempt to elaborate its multiform details into any distinctly harmonious unity. Its whole action is devious, violent, spasmodic. Its distempered, inconstant irritability is its very essence. Its only order is the manifestation of a wholly disordered energy. It is a type of the endless perplexity with which man, stripped of the hopes and illusions of this life, harassed and oppressed by the immediate sense of his own helplessness and isolation, stands face to face with the silent and immovable world of destiny. In it the agony of an individual mind grows to the dimensions of the universe; and the genius of the poet himself, regardless of the passing and somewhat incongruous incidents with which it deals, rises before our astonished vision, apparently as illimitable and as inexhaustible as the mystery which it unfolds.

It is manifest that "Hamlet" does not solve, or even attempt to solve, the riddle of life. It only serves to present the problem in its most vivid and most dramatic intensity. The poet reproduces Nature; he is in no way admitted into the secret of the mystery beyond Nature; he could not penetrate it; he only knew of the infinite longings and the infinite misgivings with which its presence fills the human heart.

"Hamlet" is, in some sense, Shakespeare's most typical work. In no other of his dramas does his highest personality seem to blend so closely with his highest genius. It is throughout informed with his scepticism, his melancholy, his ever-present sense of the shadowiness and the fleetingness of life. He has given us more artistically complete and harmonious creations. His absolute imagination is perhaps more distinctly displayed in the real madness of King Lear than in the feigned madness, or the fitful and disordered impulses, of the Danish Prince. But the very rapidity and extravagance of those moods help to produce their own peculiar dramatic effect. Wonder and mystery are the strongest and the most abiding elements in all human interest; and, under this universal condition of our nature, "Hamlet," with its unexplained and inexplicable singularities, and even inconsistencies, will most probably for ever remain the most remarkable and the most enthralling of all the works of mortal hands.

MACBETH.

"Macbeth" offers a most striking contrast to the complexity of "Hamlet," in the simplicity of its general design, and in its direct, rapid, vigorous action. It is a drama of gigantic crime and terror, relieved by the most magnificent imaginative expression.

The very history of this play is free from any perplexing obscurity. The earliest mention of it which has reached us consists of an account given of its plot in the Diary of Dr. Simon Forman, who saw it acted "at the Globe, 1610, the 20th of April, Saturday." We have no reason for believing that it was then a new work, for Forman notices, in the same year, a number of dramas which must have succeeded each other at more or less distant intervals. But we may take it for granted that it was written after the accession of James I. to the throne in the month of March, 1603. In the vision which it presents of the long line of Banquo's issue (Act IV., Scene I.) we meet with an evident allusion to that monarch, carrying "two-fold balls and treble sceptres;" and it seems probable, as Mr. Collier observes, that this compliment was paid before James had been long in the enjoyment of his English inheritance.

Malone discovered some passages in the work itself which led him to believe that it was written towards the close of the year 1606. In the singular address of the porter (Act II., Scene III.), among the supposed arrivals in the lower regions is that of "a farmer that hanged himself in the expectation of plenty." Malone learned, from the audit book of Eton College, that corn was unusually cheap during the summer and the autumn of 1606, and he supposed that the fate of this farmer contained an allusion to that circumstance. That, however, may be a mere imaginary inference. He seems to have found a better argument in support of his conjecture in the introduction into the same address of the "equivocator, that could swear in both the scales against either scale; who committed treason enough for God's sake, yet could not equivocate to heaven." Malone was of opinion that this passage referred to the conduct of Garnet, the Superior of the Jesuits in England, on the occasion of his trial for his connection with the Gunpowder Plot. Garnet appears to have met the charge with a striking absence of candour and consistency. The trial took place on the 20th of March, 1606, and he was executed on the 3rd of May in the same year. The language of the dramatist so completely fits this remarkable and exceptional incident in the history of the time, that it does not seem likely the coincidence between them is merely accidental.

It is impossible to entertain a doubt with respect to the source from which the materials of this play were derived. Dr. Farmer thought that the original idea of the work might have been suggested to Shakespeare by an address which is said to have been delivered by three students of St. John's College to James I. when he visited Oxford in the year 1605. But this address itself seems to have been since discovered, and, as it presents no resemblance whatever to the drama, beyond an allusion to the tradition that three witches, or sybils, once accosted Banquo, it is manifest that, even if it had become known to Shakespeare—which is, in itself, very unlikely—it is impossible that he could have been indebted to it for any portion of his scenes.

Mr. Collier states that there are some grounds for thinking it probable that, before "Macbeth" was written, there was in existence another drama founded upon the same historical incidents. The Stationers' Registers, under the date of 1596, contain an entry in which mention is made of a ballad called the "Taming of a Shrew," and of a ballad called "Macdobeth." But we have no reason to conclude that either the one or the other of those works was a play. Mr. Collier also tells us that, in Kemp's "Nine Days' Wonder," printed in 1600, there is a passage which speaks of "A penny poet, whose first making was the miserable stolen story of Macdoel, or Macdobeth, or Macsomewhat, for I am sure Mac it was, though I never had the maw to see it." Every one, we believe, will at once admit that it is impossible to found any safe conclusion upon vague and unconnected allusions of this description.

Shakespeare, it is clear, drew the materials of "Macbeth"

from Holinshed's " History or Description of Scotland," which is itself a compilation from the Latin of Hector Boetius, or Boece. We are even astonished, as we read the rude pages of the chronicler, to find in them nearly every one of the incidents, and a number, too, of the minor illustrations, to which the genius of the poet has lent such unparalleled splendour. The story of Duncan and of Macbeth is told in pp. 168—176 of Holinshed.* We shall now proceed to select all those portions of it on which the dramatist raised his magnificent structure; and we shall, perhaps, by this means enable our readers to obtain a nearer view of the form of his workmanship.

Duncan and Macbeth, we learn from the Chronicle, were the children of daughters of the late king. They are described as follows:—

Macbeth was a valiant gentleman, and one that, if he had not been somewhat cruel of nature, might have been thought most worthy the government of a realm. On the other part, Duncan was so soft and gentle of nature, that the people wished the inclinations and manners of these two cousins to have been so tempered and interchangeably bestowed betwixt them, that where the one had too much of clemency, and the other of cruelty, the mean virtue betwixt these two extremities might have reigned by indifferent partition in them both; so should Duncan have proved a worthy king, and Macbeth an excellent captain.

The reign of the gentle Duncan was soon disturbed by an insurrection among his turbulent subjects. In this movement the chief agent was Macdowald, a man of great energy and powers of persuasion, who,

In a small time, had gotten together a mighty power of men; for out of the Western Isles there came unto him a great multitude of people, offering themselves to assist him in that rebellious quarrel; and out of Ireland, in hope of the spoil, came no small number of Kernes and Gallowglasses, offering gladly to serve under him, whither it should please him to lead them.

The rebels are overcome by the valiant Macbeth, aided by

---

* This story is inserted by Mr. Collier in his "Shakespeare's Library."

Banquo. Immediately afterwards appears upon the scene Sueno, King of Denmark and Norway, who "arrived in Fife with a puissant army to subdue the whole realm of Scotland." These invaders were ultimately all but annihilated; and the remains of those among them who had fallen were "buried in Saint Colme's Inch." But peace was still denied to Scotland:—

> Shortly after happened a strange and uncouth wonder, which afterward was the cause of much trouble in the realm of Scotland, as ye shall after hear. It fortuned, as Macbeth and Banquo journied towards Fores, where the King then lay, they went sporting by the way together without other company, save only themselves, passing through the woods and fields, when suddenly, in the midst of a laund, there met them three women in strange and wild apparel, resembling creatures of elder world, whom, when they attentively beheld, wondering much at the sight, the first of them spake and said, "All hail, Macbeth, Thane of Glammis!" (for he had lately entered into that dignity and office by the death of his father Sinell). The second of them said, "Hail, Macbeth, Thane of Cawdor!" But the third said, "All hail, Macbeth, that hereafter shalt be King of Scotland!".
>
> Then Banquo: "What manner of women (saith he) are you, that seem so little favourable unto me, whereas to my fellow here, besides high offices, ye assign also the kingdom, appointing forth nothing for me at all?" "Yes (saith the first of them), we promise greater benefits unto thee than unto him; for he shall reign in deed, but with an unlucky end: neither shall he leave any issue behind him to succeed in his place; where contrarily thou in deed shalt not reign at all, but of thee those shall be borne which shall govern the Scottish kingdom by long order of continual descent." Herewith the foresaid women vanished immediately out of their sight. This was reputed at the first but some vain fantastical illusion by Macbeth and Banquo, insomuch that Banquo would call Macbeth, in jest, King of Scotland; and Macbeth, again, would call him, in sport likewise, the father of many kings. But afterwards the common opinion was, that these women were either the weird sisters, that is (as ye would say), the goddesses of destiny, or else some nymphs or fairies, indued with knowledge of prophecy by their necromantical science, because everything came to pass as they had spoken. For shortly after, the Thane of Cawdor being condemned at Fores of treason against the King committed, his lands, livings, and offices were given of the King's liberality to Macbeth.

Macbeth now began to be agitated by a desire to obtain possession of the crown, but seemed at first disposed to wait until Providence should, in the common order of events, enable him to gratify his ambition.

But shortly after it chanced that King Duncan having two sons by his wife, which was the daughter of Siward, Earl of Northumberland, he made the elder of them, called Malcolm, Prince of Cumberland, as it were thereby to appoint him his successor in the kingdom immediately after his decease.

Macbeth witnessed with dissatisfaction the creation of this obstacle to his succession to the throne. By it he seemed to suffer a positive wrong; for, by an ancient law of the realm, "if he that should succeed were not of able age to take the charge upon himself, he that was next of blood unto him should be admitted." With this grievance, he soon proceeded to consider how he might usurp the kingdom:—

The words of the three weird sisters also (of whom before ye have heard) greatly encouraged him hereunto, but specially his wife lay sore upon him to attempt the thing, as she, that was very ambitious, burning in unquenchable desire to bear the name of a queen.

At length, after having communicated his purpose to "his trusty friends, amongst whom Banquo was the chiefest," he slew Duncan, "caused himself to be proclaimed King, and forthwith went unto Scone, where (by common consent) he received the investure of the kingdom according to the accustomed manner."

Malcolm Cammore, and Donald Bane, the sons of Duncan, then fled, the one into Cumberland, from which he afterwards passed to the court of King Edward the Confessor in England; and the other to Ireland, "where he was tenderly cherished by the King of that land."

Macbeth displayed for some time the qualities of a great ruler; but his apparent zeal in the promotion of the welfare of his subjects was merely counterfeited. He lived in constant fear "lest he should be served of the same cup as he had ministered to his predecessor." *

The words, also, of the three weird sisters would not out of his mind, which, as they promised him the kingdom, so likewise did they promise it at the same time unto the posterity of Banquo. He willed, therefore, the same Banquo, with his son named Fleance, to come to a supper that he had prepared for them, which was indeed, as he had devised, present death at the hands of certain murderers, whom he hired to execute that deed, appointing them to meet with the same Banquo and his son without the palace, as they returned to their lodgings, and there to slay them. * * * It chanced yet, by the benefit of the dark night, that though the father were slain, the son yet, by the help of Almighty God, reserving him to better fortune, escaped that danger, and afterwards, &c., to avoid further peril, fled into Wales.

After the murder of Banquo nothing prospered with Macbeth. Distrust sprung up between him and his followers. His thirst for blood grew insatiable. In order that he might with impunity continue his iniquitous rule, he resolved to build a strong castle on the top of a high hill called Dunsinane. He summoned his nobles, and among them Macduff, Thane of Fife, to aid him in accomplishing this undertaking. Macduff disobeyed the order:—

And surely hereupon had he put Macduff to death, but that a certain witch, whom he had in great trust, had told that he should never be slain with man born of any woman, nor vanquished till the wood of Birnane came to the castle of Dunsinane. By this prophecy Macbeth put all fear out of his heart, supposing he might do what he would, without any fear to be punished for the same; for by the one prophecy he believed it was impossible for any man to vanquish him, and by the other impossible to slay him.

Macduff, in order to avoid the danger to which his life was exposed in Scotland, resolved on seeking refuge in England.

---

*   This even-handed justice
    Commends the ingredients of our poison'd chalice
    To our own lips.
           MACBETH, *Act I., Scene VII.*

Macbeth—who "had in every nobleman's house one sly fellow or other in fee with him, to reveal all that was said or done within the same"—became aware of his intention, marched into his territory, seized upon his castle without any resistance, and then "most cruelly caused his wife and children, with all other whom he found in that castle, to be slain."

But Macduff was already escaped out of danger, and gotten into England unto Malcolm Cammore, to try what purchase he might make, by means of his support, to revenge the slaughter so cruelly executed on his wife, his children, and other friends. At his coming unto Malcolm, he declared unto what great misery the estate of Scotland was brought by the detestable cruelties exercised by the tyrant Macbeth. * * *

Though Malcolm was very sorrowful for the oppression of his countrymen, the Scots, in manner as Macduff had declared, yet, doubting whether he was come as one that meant unfeignedly as he spake, or else as sent from Macbeth to betray him, he thought to have some further trial, and thereupon dissembling his mind at the first, he answered as followeth:—

"I am truly very sorry for the misery chanced to my country of Scotland, but though I have never so great affection to relieve the same, yet, by reason of certain incurable vices which reign in me, I am nothing meet thereto. First, such immoderate lust and voluptuous sensuality (the abominable fountain of all vices) followeth me, that if I were made King of Scots . . . mine intemperancy should be more importable unto you than the bloody tyranny of Macbeth now is." Hereunto Macduff answered: "This surely is a very evil fault, for many noble princes and kings have lost both lives and kingdoms for the same; nevertheless there are women enough in Scotland, and therefore follow my counsel. Make thyself king, and I shall convey the matter so wisely, that thou shalt be so satisfied at thy pleasure in such secret wise, that no man shall be aware thereof."

Then said Malcolm: "I am also the most avaricious creature on the earth, so that if I were king, I should seek so many ways to get lands and goods, that I should slay the most part of all the nobles of Scotland by surmised accusations, to the end I might enjoy their lands, goods, and possessions. . . . Therefore," saith Malcolm, "suffer me to remain where I am, lest if I attain to the regiment of your realm, mine unquenchable avarice may prove such that ye would think the displeasures which now grieve you, should seem easy in respect of the unmeasurable outrage which might ensue through my coming amongst you."

Macduff to this made answer, "how it was a far worse fault than the other: for avarice is the root of all mischief, and for that crime the most part of our kings have been slain and brought to their final end. Yet, notwithstanding, follow my counsel, and take upon thee the crown. There is gold and riches enough in Scotland to satisfy thy greedy desire." "Then," said Malcolm again, "I am furthermore inclined to dissimulation, telling of leasings, and all other kinds of deceit, so that I naturally rejoice in nothing so much as to betray and deceive such as put any trust or confidence in my words. Then sith [since] there is nothing that more becometh a prince than constancy, verity, truth, and justice, with the other laudable fellowship of those fair and noble virtues which are comprehended only in soothfastness, and that lying utterly overthroweth the same; you see how unable I am to govern any province or region: and, therefore, sith you have remedies to cloak and hide all the rest of my other vices, I pray you find shift to cloak this vice amongst the residue."

Then said Macduff: "This yet is the worst of all, and there I leave thee, and therefore say, Oh, ye unhappy and miserable Scottishmen which are thus scourged with so many and sundry calamities, each one above other! Ye have one cursed and wicked tyrant that now reigneth over you, without any right or title, oppressing you with his most bloody cruelty. This other, that hath the right to the crown, is so replete with the inconstant behaviour and manifest vices of Englishmen, that he is nothing worthy to enjoy it: for by his own confession he is not only avaricious, and given to unsatiable lust, but so false a traitor withal, that no trust is to be had unto any word he speaketh. Adieu, Scotland! for now I account myself a banished man for ever, without comfort or consolation." And with those words the brackish tears trickled down his cheeks very abundantly.

At the last, when he was ready to depart, Malcolm took him by the sleeve, and said, "Be of good comfort, Macduff, for I have none of these vices before remembered, but have jested with thee in this manner, only to prove thy mind: for divers times heretofore hath Macbeth sought by this manner of means to bring me into his hands, but, the more slow I have showed myself to condescend to thy motion and request, the more diligence shall I use in accomplishing the same." Incontinently hereupon they embraced each other, and promising to be faithful the one to the other, they fell in consultation how they might best provide for all their business, to bring the same to good effect.

Malcolm invades Scotland with a force of 10,000 Englishmen, commanded by Siward, Earl of Northumberland. Macbeth is advised by his few remaining followers to retreat before the overwhelming power of his enemies. "But he had such confidence in his prophecies, that he believed he should never be vanquished, till Birnane Wood were brought to Dunsinane; nor yet to be slain with any man that should be, or was, born of woman."

Malcolm, following hastily after Macbeth, came the night before the battle unto Birnane Wood; and when his army had rested awhile there to refresh them, he commanded every man to get a bough of some tree or other of that wood in his hand, as big as he might bear, and to march forth therewith in such wise that on the next morrow they might come closely and without sight in this manner within view of his enemies. On the morrow when Macbeth beheld them coming in this sort, he first marvelled what the matter meant, but in the end remembered himself that the prophecy which he had heard long before that time, of the coming of Birnane Wood to Dunsinane Castle, was likewise to be now fulfilled. Nevertheless, he brought his men in order of battle, and exhorted them to do valiantly; howbeit his enemies had scarcely cast from them their boughs, when Macbeth perceiving their numbers, betook him straight to flight; whom Macduff pursued with great hatred, even until he came to Lunfannaine, where Macbeth perceiving that Macduff was hard at his back, leapt beside his horse, saying:—"Thou traitor, what meaneth it that thou shouldst thus in vain follow me that am not appointed to be slain by any creature that is born of a woman? Come on therefore, and receive thy reward which thou hast deserved for thy pains;" and thereinthat he lifted up his sword, thinking to have slain him.

But Macduff, quickly avoiding from his horse, yer [ere] he came at him, answered (with his naked sword in his hand), saying: "It is true Macbeth, and now shall thine insatiable cruelty have an end, for I am even he that thy wizards have told thee of, who was never born of my mother, but ripped out of her womb: therewithal he stept unto him, and slew him in that place. Then cutting his head from his shoulders, he set it upon a pole, and brought it unto Malcolm.

Shakespeare not only largely used this history of Duncan and of Macbeth, but he also borrowed one of the most picturesque of his incidents from another portion of the pages of the same chronicler. In p. 150 of Holinshed, and under a date some seventy or eighty years earlier, an account is given of the end of King Duffe, which evidently suggested to the poet the principal circumstances in the murder of Duncan. Duffe, having succeeded in suppressing an insurrection among his subjects, captured a number of the leaders of the movement. Among those captives were some relatives of Donwald, one of his own most trusted officers. Donwald begged that their lives might be spared; this request was refused him; and upon this disappointment his first feeling of shame, or sorrow, soon gave way to a brooding passion for revenge.

Which his wife perceiving, ceased not to travell [travail] with him till she understood what the cause was of his displeasure. Which at length when she had learnt by his own relation, she as one that bore no less malice in her heart towards the King, for the like cause on her behalf that her husband did for his friends, counselled him (sith the King oftentimes used to lodge in his house without any guard about him other than the garrison of the castle, which was wholly at his commandment), to make him away, and showed him the means whereby he might soonest accomplish it. Donwald thus being the more kindled in wrath by the words of his wife, determined to follow her advice in the execution of so heinous an act. Whereupon devising with himself for a while which way he might best accomplish his cursed intent, at length got opportunity, and sped his purpose as followeth. It chanced that the King, upon the day before he purposed to depart forth of the castle, was long in his oratory at his prayers, and there continued till it was late in the night. At the last, coming forth, he called such afore him as had faithfully served him in pursuit and apprehension of the rebels, and giving them hearty thanks, he bestowed sundry honourable gifts amongst them, of the which number Donwald was one, as he that had been ever accounted a most faithful servant to the King. At length, having talked with them a long time, he got him into his privy chamber, only with two of his chamberlains, who, having brought him to bed, came forth again, and then fell to banqueting with Donwald and his wife, who had prepared divers delicate dishes and sundry sorts of drinks for their rare supper or collation, whereat they sat up so long till they had charged their stomachs with such full gorges, that their heads were no sooner put to the pillow, but asleep they were so fast that a man might have removed the chamber over them sooner than to have awaked them out of their drunken sleep. Then Donwald, though he abhorred the act greatly in heart, yet through instigation of his wife, he called four of his servants unto him (whom he had made privy to his wicked intent before, and framed to his purpose with large gifts), and now declaring unto them after what sort they should work the feat, they gladly obeyed his instructions, and speedily going about the murder, they enter the chamber (in which the King lay), a little before cocks crow, where they secretly cut his throat as he lay sleeping. . . . Donwald, about the time that the murder was in doing, got him amongst them that kept the watch, and so continued in company with them all the rest of the night. But in the morning, when the noise was raised in the King's chamber how the King was slain, his body conveyed away, and the bed all beraied with blood, he with the watch ran thither, as though he had known nothing of the matter, and breaking into the chamber, and finding cakes of blood in the bed and on the floor about the sides of it, he forthwith slew the chamberlains as guilty of that heinous murder.

The imagination of the dramatist must evidently have been coloured not only by the general outlines, but even by the minute details of these narratives. The only great incident in the play which we miss in the uninspired pages of the chronicler is the appearance of Banquo's ghost at the festival, and even this fine image of tragic terror looks as if it might have arisen without an effort out of the gloomy and supernatural element which pervades the whole story. The "weird sisters" of the simple and credulous historian are manifestly the shadowy, wandering visitants from some unknown world on whom the genius of the poet has bestowed so intensely vivid a reality. Macbeth himself, as we see him in his first obscure origin, seems to reveal, through his ambition and his restlessness, nearly every one of the familiar features of the most famous and the most imaginative of all murderers. But it is, perhaps, in the character of Lady Macbeth that the influence of the story-teller over the dramatist is most distinctly visible. Every reader of the play must have looked with some surprise, and even with some distrust, at the prominent and unrelenting part which a woman—and a woman apparently unimpelled by any specially vindictive or ungovernable passion—fills in this tremendous scene of guilt and slaughter. But, on examining the old fabulous record, it is impossible to mistake the source from which this conception of the character was derived, and it becomes at once manifest that the chronicler furnished the original outline of the figure. In each of the two episodes from which the poet has drawn the materials of his plot, the wife of the murderer acts as a domestic fury; she looks upon the commission of the crime without misgiving and without pity, and it is she that appears ultimately to fix his wavering resolution. There can be no doubt that Shakespeare, with his usual readiness to conform to the events or the traditions of the actual world, took up unhesitatingly this view of the character, and afterwards harmonised it, as far as he found desirable or convenient, with the freer and larger play of his own imagination.

There is, however, one element in the drama which it was impossible the history or legend could have supplied. The imaginative form of its language not only stands alone amidst all the other literature of that age, but it even fills a peculiar place in the writings of the great poet himself. The rude times and the bloody deeds of Macbeth were, in their naked ferocity, unsusceptible of any large poetical treatment. They would, at the most, have furnished the materials for a few strong, but repulsive, dramatic episodes. The poet gives grandeur and elevation to the narrow scene by raising it, through the force of mere expression, into the wide region of imaginative passion. He idealises the whole form of his characters and his incidents, and this bold and brilliant colouring is evidently the distinguishing characteristic of the entire composition. It is visible in all its details, and it affords the only reasonable solution of the difficulties which the development of its story presents.

The dramatist seems, from the very commencement, to have made up his mind to the special form which his work was to receive. The witches, first of all, finely foreshadow the wild and stormy grandeur of the scenes which are to follow. The wounded soldier who then enters announces his intelligence from the battle-field in language of an imaginative emphasis, which bears no immediate relation to the humble part which he fills; and Rosse, immediately afterwards, completes the history of the contest in the same exaggerated strain :—

> *Soldier.* Doubtfully it stood;
> As two spent swimmers, that do cling together,
> And choke their art. The merciless Macdonwald
> (Worthy to be a rebel—for to that,
> The multiplying villanies of nature
> Do swarm upon him), from the western isles
> Of Kernes and Gallowglasses is supplied;
> And fortune, on his damned quarrel smiling, &c.
>
> * * * * *
>
> *Duncan.* Whence cam'st thou, worthy thane?
> *Rosse.* From Fife, great king,
> Where the Norweyan banners flout the sky,
> And fan our people cold.
> Norway himself, with terrible numbers,
> Assisted by that most disloyal traitor,
> The thane of Cawdor, began a dismal conflict;
> Till that Bellona's bridegroom, lapp'd in proof,
> Confronted him with self-comparisons,
> Point against point rebellious, arm 'gainst arm,
> Curbing his lavish spirit; and, to conclude,
> The victory fell on us.

These addresses, however, serve but as preludes to the dramatic amplitude in which the character of Macbeth himself is arrayed. The poet, it is clear, has endeavoured to give interest and elevation to the gloomy monotony of the usurper's career by attributing to him meditations and distresses beyond his own narrow, uninspired sphere, and lending to his language a form of the most original and imposing splendour. He has accomplished this object with his usual large licence, and it is perfectly open to any one to assert that in this instance he has occasionally overstepped the limits of truth and nature. Dryden states that "Ben Jonson, in reading some bombastic speeches in 'Macbeth' which are not to be understood, used to say that it was 'horror.'" The modern critics, in general, are not prepared to assign any limitation to the enthusiasm with which they regard this great creation of the poet's genius. But it seems impossible to deny that he has treated his subject with an exceptional freedom, and that in doing so he sometimes gives to his language a magnificent inflation which we cannot follow without an effort, and that he indulges in a rapid and perplexed involution of thought and imagery which we find it impossible perfectly to unravel:—

> If it were done when 'tis done, then 'twere well
> It were done quickly. If the assassination
> Could trammel up the consequence, and catch,
> With his surcease, success; that but this blow
> Might be the be-all and the end-all here,
> But here, upon this bank and shoal of time,—
> We'd jump the life to come. But, in these cases,
> We still have judgment here; that we but teach
> Bloody instructions, which, being taught, return
> To plague the inventor.
> *Act I., Scene VII.*

No one can be insensible to the manifest Shakespearian flashes which light us through this passage; but they light us, as from a cloud, fitfully and capriciously, revealing at the same time the surrounding darkness. The mere scenic splendour in which the poet has sometimes clothed the passion of his dialogue will, we think, be again readily distinguishable in the extravagance which accompanies the last and most agitated adjuration which Macbeth addresses to the weird sisters:—

> I conjure you, by that which you profess,
> (Howe'er you come to know it), answer me:
> Though you untie the winds, and let them fight
> Against the churches; though the yesty waves
> Confound and swallow navigation up;
> Though bladed corn be lodg'd, and trees blown down;
> Though castles topple on their warders' heads;
> Though palaces, and pyramids, do slope
> Their heads to their foundations; though the treasure
> Of nature's germins tumble all together,
> Even till destruction sicken,—answer me
> To what I ask you.
> *Act IV., Scene I.*

The poet, it must, we think, be admitted, has in these lines exaggerated the imaginative representation of life. In his development of the personal history of Macbeth we feel that we can again discover the free, negligent drawing of the pencil of Shakespeare. The character is ultimately invested with a large, deep reverie or melancholy which seems hardly consistent with its original rude elements, but which is introduced so insensibly, and is in itself so magnificent and so impressive, that we find it impossible to wish that its tone should be lowered or in any way materially altered.

The language, as well as the character, of Lady Macbeth is less melo-dramatic; she is more reserved and more inflexible than her companion. But there are touches in this portrait, too, which reveal the rapid freedom of the dramatist:—

> I have given suck, and know
> How tender 'tis to love the babe that milks me.
> *Act I., Scene VII.*

We do not know, and we do not even believe, that she had ever been a mother; but we still have no desire to object to this large use of the imaginative life of the drama. When, however, later on, in the scene in which Duncan is murdered, she says:—

> Had he not resembled
> My father as he slept, I had done 't,

we feel compelled more strongly to doubt whether she was, at that time at all events, open to the influence of any such humanising remembrance. The final treatment of the character is left unexplained by the poet. She sinks into an overpowering moodiness and despair, for reasons which are not stated to us, which may be merely accidental, and on which we feel that we have no right to arrive at any positive conclusion. Her prostration and her agony are just within the remote and undefined possibilities of nature, and that is, rightly or wrongly, all that the poet cared for in the production of the new scene of tragic grandeur in which she perishes. We do not see how it is possible to accept the interpretation of the character given by some critics, that she possessed from the commencement the tender and devoted nature of woman, and that she fell a victim to her readiness to gratify what she knew to be the fixed ambition of her husband. If Shakespeare's representation of his grandest female figure stands in need of any such sophistry as this, it must, indeed, be hopelessly indefensible.

The poet has, at all events, afforded us the most ample compensation for the startling licence in which he has throughout these scenes frequently indulged. The play, however forced it may seem in some of its conditions, conforms in its essence to the highest requirements of dramatic art. There is in the literature of all ages no scene of pure natural terror so true, so vivid, so startling, as the murder of Duncan, with all its wonderful accompaniments. Through the magic art of the poet we lose our detestation of the guilty authors of the deed in the absorbing sympathy with which we share their breathless disquietude. In another and a still more directly natural scene, the laceration of the heart with which Macduff learns the destruction of his whole household—of all his "pretty chickens and their dam at one fell swoop"—is rendered with that imaginative vitality which forms the supreme privilege of Shakespeare's genius.

Some critics claim for "Macbeth" the distinction of being the poet's greatest work. We believe that judgments of this description can only be adopted with many qualifications. "Macbeth" wants the subtle life which distinguishes some of the other dramatic conceptions of Shakespeare. Its action is plain, rapid, downright; and its largest forms of expression seem now and then somewhat constrained and artificial. But it was evidently written in the very plenitude of the poet's powers, and in its wonderful scenic grandeur it must for ever occupy a foremost place among the creations of his majestic imagination.

UNIV.
CALIF.

N° 1

N° 2

N° 3

N° 4

APPENDIX.

Note 1 (*p.* vii., *Preface*).

THE SPELLING OF SHAKESPEARE'S NAME.

IN the books or the records of the sixteenth and seventeenth centuries, not less than twenty-five different ways of spelling the name of Shakespeare have been counted; and it is quite possible that even that list does not in this case exhaust the licence of ancient orthography. Three of those forms of the name still hold a place in our literature— "Shakespeare," "Shakspeare," and "Shakspere." The first of these was almost universally adopted in the printed works of the poet's own age; it is the spelling of the four early Folios; and what is, perhaps, still more important, it is the spelling of the dedications of the "Venus" and the "Lucrece" to Lord Southampton, in 1593 and 1594. "Shakspere," on the other hand, was the name under which were entered, in the Stratford registers, his baptism in 1564; the baptisms of his daughter Susanna in 1583, and of his son Hammet and his daughter Judith in 1585; and his own burial in 1616. It is also, we may take it for granted, the form of the three signatures to his will, as well as of the signatures to the two deeds of the year 1613, and of the less unquestionable entry in the Florio edition of Montaigne published in 1603.* The writing in some of these cases, and more particularly in one of the signatures to the will, is somewhat indistinct; but those six signatures taken together leave no room for a doubt that the poet usually, and very probably even uniformly, as far as can now be ascertained, wrote his name "Shakspere." Malone and Steevens misread the spelling in the will, and, chiefly through their authority, "Shakspeare" became the general orthography of the

---

* We give in the accompanying plate four of these six signatures.

name throughout the latter portion of the last, and the earlier years of the present centuries. Malone himself subsequently acknowledged his mistake (see *note* in p. 1, vol. ii., of Malone's "Shakespeare, by Boswell"); but he still adhered to his spelling, upon the ground that the word " spear " is usually written with an *a*, although it is clear that he ought, upon the same evidence, to have omitted his final vowel. General usage, besides, no longer lends any countenance to his innovation, and it is very unlikely that it will henceforward be at all extensively retained. Our choice is thus limited to "Shakespeare" or " Shakspere." The latter spelling is that which has been adopted by Mr. Charles Knight, and by the framers of the catalogues at the British Museum. But there is opposed to them what we must regard as an overwhelming array of authority. Under the name of " Shakespeare " have been published all the works of the "Shakespeare Society," of Mr. Collier, of Mr. Dyce, of Mr. Halliwell, of Messrs. Singer and Lloyd, of Mr. Howard Staunton, and of the editors of the "Cambridge Shakespeare;" and these names comprise the great mass of the best known Shakespearian scholars of our time. Neither are we at all surprised at the selection which they have made. A rigorous adherence to ancient forms, in defiance of established usage, in so very unimportant and so very arbitrarily determined a matter as orthography, must always appear pedantic and misplaced. We doubt, too, whether the innovators in this case can claim for themselves the weight of mere traditional testimony. Our great dramatist took his place in English literature under the name of "Shakespeare." It was as "William Shakespeare" that he published the only two volumes which he himself passed through the press, and in a book treating of him we can hardly go wrong if we follow the example which has thus been set us by himself.

Note 2 (*p.* 41).

NEW PLACE.

NEW PLACE, as we are informed by Dugdale, was originally built by Sir Hugh Clopton, in the time of Henry VII., and was "a fair house built of brick and timber." In Sir Hugh's will it is called "the Great House." It continued in the possession of the Clopton family until 1563, when it was bought by William Bott. Some time previously to the year 1570 it was sold to William Underhill, of whom it was purchased by Shakespeare in 1597. On Shakespeare's death it came into the possession of his daughter, Mrs. Hall, and passed from her to her daughter, Elizabeth Nash, afterwards Lady Barnard. In 1643 Mr. and Mrs. Nash enjoyed the remarkable distinction of entertaining Henrietta Maria, the wife of Charles I., at New Place, where she kept her court for a period of three weeks. After Lady Barnard's death, in 1670, by a variety of changes, it reverted to the possession of the Clopton family; and Sir Hugh Clopton, at a subsequent period, so completely altered it as to confer upon it the character of an entirely new building. In 1753 it was sold to the Rev. Francis Gastrell, Vicar of Frodsham, in Cheshire. In the garden attached to it was a mulberry tree, which, according to tradition, had been planted by Shakespeare. This tree soon became an object of dislike to Mr. Gastrell, because it subjected him to the importunities of travellers, whose veneration for Shakespeare prompted them to make to it frequent visits. In an evil hour he cut it down and hewed it to pieces for firewood. The greater part of it, however, was purchased by Thomas Sharp, a watchmaker, in Stratford, who turned it to considerable advantage by converting every fragment into trifling articles of utility or ornament. New Place itself did not long escape the destructive hand of its new owner. A disagreement between him and the overseers of the parish, respecting an assessment for the maintenance of the poor, fixed its fate. In the heat of his anger he declared that *that* house should never be assessed again; and accordingly, in 1759, he razed the building to the ground, disposed of the materials, and left Stratford amidst the rage and execration of the inhabitants.

It had long been supposed that it was Shakespeare himself who first gave to "the Great House" the name of "New Place." But Mr. Halliwell, in his "Life of William Shakespeare" (pp. 165, 166), has produced an extract from a survey taken in 1590, and preserved in the Carlton Ride Record Office, which mentions—"quandam domum vocatam the newe place."

Note 3 (*p.* 18).

AUBREY'S ACCOUNT OF SHAKESPEARE.

AUBREY's manuscripts are preserved in the Ashmolean Museum. He was so credulous an antiquarian or gossip, that we can place but very little reliance on any traditions which he has collected. The following is his account of Shakespeare :—

"Mr. William Shakespear was born at Stratford-upon-Avon in the county of Warwick; his father was a butcher, and I have been told heretofore by some of the neighbours that when he was a boy he exercised his father's trade, but when he killed a calf he would do it in a high style and make a speech. There was at that time another butcher's son in this town that was held not at all inferior to him for a natural wit, his acquaintance and cœtanean, but died young. This Wm., being inclined naturally to poetry and acting, came to London, I guess about 18, and was an actor at one of the play-houses, and did act exceedingly well. Now B. Jonson was never a good actor, but an excellent instructor. He began early to make essays at dramatic poetry, which at that time was very low and his plays took well. He was a handsome well-shaped man, very good company, and of a very ready and pleasant smooth wit. The humour of . . . . the constable in 'Midsummer Night's Dream,' he happened to take at Grendon in Bucks, which is the road from London to Stratford, and there was living that constable about 1642, when I first came to Oxon. I think it was Midsummer night that he happened to lie there. Mr. Jos. Howe is of that parish and knew him. Ben Jonson and he did gather humours of men daily wherever they came. One time as he was at the tavern at Stratford-super-Avon, one Combes, an old rich usurer, was to be buried, he makes there this extemporary epitaph :—

> Ten in the hundred the Devil allows,
> But Combes will have twelve he swears and vows ;
> If any one asks who lies in this tomb,
> Hoh! quoth the Devil, ''Tis my John o' Combe.'

He was wont to go to his native country once a year. I think I have been told that he left 2 or 300 *lib* per annum there and thereabout to a sister. I have heard Sir Wm. Davenant and Mr. Thomas Shadwell (who is counted the best comedian we have now) say that he had a most prodigious wit (*v.* his Epitaph in Dugdale's 'Warw.'), and did admire his natural parts beyond all other dramatical writers. He (Ben Jonson's Underwoods) was wont to say that he never blotted out a line in his life; said Ben Jonson, 'I wish he had blotted out a thousand.' His comedies will remain wit as long as the English tongue is understood, for that he handles *mores hominum:* now our present writers reflect so much upon particular persons and coxcombities, that twenty years hence they will not be understood. Though, as Ben Jonson says of him that he had but little Latin and less Greek, he understood Latin pretty well, for he had been in his younger years a schoolmaster in the county.

"From Mr. . . . . Beeston."

This "Mr. Beeston" is no doubt introduced into Aubrey's manuscript as the name of the person from whom he derived the latter portion of his information.

Note 4 (*p.* 24).

DOWDALL'S ACCOUNT OF SHAKESPEARE.

ON the 10th of April, 1693, a person of the name of Dowdall addressed a small treatise in the form of a letter to Mr. Edward Southwell, endorsed by the latter, "Description of Several Places in Warwickshire," in which we find the following account of Shakespeare:—

"The first remarkable place in this county that I visited was Stratford-super-Avon, where I saw the effigies of our English tragedian Mr. Shakspeare; part of his epitaph I sent Mr. Lowther, and desired he would impart it to you, which I find by his letter he has done: but here I send you the whole inscription.

"Just under his effigies in the wall of the chancel is this written—

>   Judicio Pylum, genio Socratem, arte Maronem,
>   Terra tegit, populus mœrett, Olympus habet.
>
>   Stay, passenger, why goest thou by soe fast?
>   Read, if thou canst, whom envious death hath plac't

> Within this monument : Shakspeare, with whome
> Quick nature dyed ; whose name doth deck the tombe
> Far more then cost, sith all that he hath writt
> Leaves liveing art but page to serve his witt.
>   Obii. A. Dni. 1616.
>   Ætat. 53, Die 23 Apr.

Near the wall where this monument is erected, lieth a plain free stone, underneath which his body is buried with this epitaph, made by himself a little before his death—

> Good friend, for Jesus' sake forbeare
> To digg the dust inclosed here !
> Blest be the man that spares these stones,
> And curs't be he that moves my bones !

The clerk that shewed me this church is above eighty years old ; he says that this Shakespeare was formerly in this town bound apprentice to a butcher, but that he ran from his master to London, and there was received into the playhouse as a serviture, and by this means had an opportunity to be what he afterwards proved. He was the best of his family, but the male line is extinguished : not one for fear of the curse above-said dare touch his gravestone, though his wife and daughters did earnestly desire to be laid in the same grave with him."

Note 5 (p. 27).

DAVIES' ACCOUNT OF SHAKESPEARE.

THE Rev. William Fulman, who died in 1688, bequeathed his biographical collections to his friend the Rev. Richard Davies, Rector of Sapperton in Gloucestershire, who made several additions to them. Davies died in 1708, and those manuscripts were afterwards presented to the Library of Corpus Christi College, Oxford, where they are still preserved. Under the article *Shakespeare,* Fulman wrote but a few notes, which are of no kind of importance ; but Davies made to them the following curious additions as they are marked by italics :—

" William Shakespeare was born at Stratford-upon-Avon in Warwickshire, about 1563-4. *Much given to all unluckiness in stealing venison and rabbits, particularly from Sr.* . . . *Lucy, who had him oft whipt and sometimes imprisoned, and at last made him fly his native country to his great advancement, but his revenge was so great that he is his Justice Clodpate, and calls him a great man, and that in allusion to his name bore three louses rampant for his arms.* From an actor of plays he became a composer. He died April 23rd, 1616, *ætat.* fifty-three, probably at Stratford, for there he is buried, and hath a monument (Dugd. p. 520), *on which he lays a heavy curse upon any one who shall remove his bones. He died a papist.*"

Note 6 (*p.* 63).

WARD'S ACCOUNT OF SHAKESPEARE.

THE Rev. John Ward, Vicar of Stratford, wrote in that town, between the month of February, 1662, and the month of April, 1663, a manuscript miscellany, which is now preserved in the Library of the Medical Society of London. We naturally feel surprised and disappointed, considering the time and place at which he engaged in his work, that the following meagre paragraphs are all the references of any importance that he has made to Shakespeare:—

"Shakespeare had but two daughters, one whereof Mr. Hall, the physician, married, and by her had one daughter—to wit, the Lady Barnard of Abingdon.

"I have heard that Mr. Shakespeare was a natural wit, without any art at all; he frequented the plays all his younger time, but in his elder days lived at Stratford, and supplied the stage with two plays every year, and for that he had an allowance so large that he spent at the rate of £1,000 a-year, as I have heard.

"Shakespeare, Drayton, and Ben Jonson, had a merry meeting, and, it seems, drank too hard, for Shakespeare died of a fever there contracted.

"Remember to peruse Shakespeare's plays, and be versed in them, that I may not be ignorant in that matter."

Note 7 (pp. 55 and 374).

SHAKESPEARE AND BEN JONSON.

THE relations which may be supposed to have subsisted between Shakespeare and Ben Jonson have been made the subject of some angry controversy, and have given rise to some manifest errors. Rowe was, we believe, the first writer who attempted to enter into any details with respect to the nature of the connection between the two dramatists. According to his account, Shakespeare's "acquaintance with Ben Jonson began with a remarkable piece of humanity and good-nature. Mr. Jonson, who was at that time altogether unknown to the world, had offered one of his plays to the players, in order to have it acted; and the persons into whose hands it was put, after having turned it carelessly and superciliously over, were just upon returning it to him with an ill-natured answer, that it would be of no service to their company, when Shakespeare luckily cast his eye upon it, and found something so well in it, as to engage him first to read it through, and afterwards to recommend Mr. Jonson and his writings to the public." Jonson was born in 1574, and was, therefore, Shakespeare's junior by ten years; and it is, of course, possible that there is some truth in Rowe's statement; but that statement is not supported by any kind of collateral evidence, and we can place on it little or no reliance. Malone, Steevens, and other critics thought they could discover several invidious references to Shakespeare in the writings of Jonson, and more particularly in a passage in the prologue to his "Every Man in his Humour," and again in a passage in the "Induction" to his "Bartholomew Fair":—

> Though need make many poets, and some such
> As art and nature have not better'd much ;
> Yet ours for want hath not so loved the stage,
> As he dare serve the ill customs of the age,
> Or purchase your delight at such a rate,
> As, for it, he himself must justly hate :
> To make a child now swaddled, to proceed
> Man, and then shoot up, in one beard and weed,
> Past threescore years ; or, with three rusty swords,
> And help of some few foot and half-foot words,

Fight over York and Lancaster's long jars,
And in the tyring-house bring wounds to scars.
He rather prays you will be pleased to see
One such to-day, as other plays should be ;
Where neither chorus wafts you o'er the seas,
Nor creaking throne comes down the boys to please.

If there be never a servant-monster in the fair, who can help it, he says, nor a nest of antiques? He is loth to make Nature afraid in his plays, like those that beget tales, tempests, and such-like drolleries.

The first of these two extracts has not unnaturally been supposed to contain a satirical allusion to some of Shakespeare's plays, and more especially to his Second and Third Parts of "King Henry VI.," "King Henry V.," and "Cymbeline." It is true that the version of "Every Man in his Humour" to which this prologue is attached was first acted in 1598 by Shakespeare's own company, and with Shakespeare himself sustaining one of the characters; and it is not at all likely that any attempt would have been made under those circumstances to throw discredit upon his own compositions. We are, besides, convinced that neither "King Henry V." nor "Cymbeline" was in existence in 1598. But Jonson might at a later period have added this prologue to his play, and we think it very probable that that was the course which he actually adopted.

The passage in the "Induction" to "Bartholomew Fair" seems to refer still more distinctly to Shakespeare's "Tempest" and "Winter's Tale," and more particularly to the part of Caliban in the first of these dramas; and, as "Bartholomew Fair" was produced in 1614, there is no kind of inherent improbability in the supposition that they were the objects of Jonson's satire. The frank and generous tribute which he afterwards offered to the memory of Shakespeare cannot afford any proof that he did not at one time indulge in those depreciatory allusions; for he seems to have been a man of an essentially warm and forgiving, although an arrogant and a self-sufficient, temper; and we know that his celebrated quarrel with Marston was followed, for some time, at all events, by a perfect reconciliation. It would now be unfair to judge him by the infirmities of his nature; and our final impression of his relations with his greatest contemporary must be mainly shaped by our remembrance of the generous admiration which in his later and calmer years he expressed for Shakespeare's genius and character.

Gifford, in discussing this question, has fallen into at least one mistake, which has contributed to mislead many of the later critics. He believed that "Every Man in his Humour" was acted by Henslowe's company on the 25th of November, 1596. But we suppose that he must here have misread the authority which he quotes, namely, Malone's extracts from Henslowe's Diary. In that Diary, as printed for the Shakespeare Society, under the editorship of Mr. Collier, "The Comodey of Umers" is entered (p. 87) as a new play, under the date of the 11th of May, 1597;* and the same play is entered on the same day in Malone's "Shakespeare by Boswell," vol. iii., p. 307. This was no doubt Jonson's first version of his comedy, and the one which was published in a small quarto in 1601; while the play which Jonson himself inserted in the first volume of his works in 1616, as it was performed by the Lord Chamberlain's company, was clearly the wholly remodelled one in which he removed his scene from Italy to England. We are reminded by this change of another error into which the modern Shakespearian commentators have fallen. They have almost all taken it for granted that Shakespeare learnt the pronunciation of Stephano as it is correctly given in the "Tempest," while it is incorrectly introduced in the "Merchant of Venice," from Jonson's "Every Man in his Humour," in which he himself performed a part in 1598. But the version of Jonson's play acted by the Lord Chamberlain's company was, as we learn upon the testimony of Jonson himself, the amended or the English one, in which no such name as Stephano is to be found.

The most interesting question, however, which arises out of the relations of Shakespeare and Jonson is the possibility of our discovering what was the nature of some rebuke which we find upon contemporary evidence was addressed by the former to the latter dramatist. We have little doubt ourselves that it was the allusion in "Hamlet" (Act II., Scene II.) to the company of young players, and the

---

* Henslowe's entry (p. 82) for the 25th of November, 1596, is as follows:—
"Rd at long meage 11ˢ."

"wrong" that was done to them by their "writers" in "making them exclaim against their own succession." In the "Return from Parnassus," which was first printed in 1606, but which must have been written about the year 1602, Kemp and Burbadge are introduced, and the former is made to say:—" Few of the University pen plays well; they smell too much of that writer, Ovid, and that writer *Metamorphosis*, and talk too much of Proserpine and Jupiter. Why, here's our fellow Shakespeare puts them all down: ay, and Ben Jonson too. O, that Ben Jonson is a pestilent fellow, he brought up Horace giving the poets a pill; but our fellow Shakespeare hath given him a purge that made him bewray his credit." The commentators have been wholly at a loss to conjecture what this "purge" may have been; but we do not see why we need hesitate to suppose that it was the passage in "Hamlet" to which we have just referred. There is, we believe, no other portion of the writings of Shakespeare to which this allusion can be held to bear any relation; and here it seems perfectly applicable with all its accompaniments. The candour, too, and the moderation of the language which the great poet employs in defence of himself or his associates, perfectly harmonise with all our conceptions of his fine sense and unobtrusive temper. We are aware, at the same time, that we can never apply with perfect certainty so slight an allusion as that which we find in the "Return from Parnassus." But we still see no ground for entertaining any serious doubt that Shakespeare in the whole passage in "Hamlet" was referring to the children of the Queen's Chapel, and to the performance upon their stage of Jonson's "Cynthia's Revels" in 1600, and of his "Poetaster" in 1601. The production of those plays formed so remarkable an episode in the dramatic annals of that period, that we do not believe Shakespeare's audiences could have hesitated in their interpretation of his language. The disagreement, however, in this case was clearly not pushed to an extremity upon either side; and from our whole knowledge both of Shakespeare's and of Jonson's characters, we are not surprised to find that the "Sejanus" of the latter writer was acted in 1603 by "his Majesty's servants," as the former Lord Chamberlain's company were now called, and that it was they again who first brought upon the stage his "Volpone, or the Fox," in 1605. Mr. Collier, in vol. v., p. 520, of his Shakespeare's Works, ed. 1858, after stating that the passage in

"Hamlet" relating to the children was not inserted in the edition of that play published in 1604, proceeds as follows:—"In the Quarto of 1603 there are sufficient traces of this part of the scene to enable us to be certain that it was acted when the play was originally produced: it was omitted, therefore, for some unexplained reason in 1604, and restored entire in 1623." The termination, which we may feel certain took place in 1603, of the misunderstanding with Jonson, would at once afford us this unexplained reason; and its partial renewal before the "Induction" to "Bartholomew Fair" was written in 1613, would enable us further to account for the re-insertion of that portion of the scene in Shakespeare's drama.

THE END.

www.ingramcontent.com/pod-product-compliance
Lightning Source LLC
Chambersburg PA
CBHW020543300426
44111CB00008B/782